Luxury in Global Perspective

Global history is predicated on connections and exchange: how connections between far-flung people, places, and objects are forged through a variety of exchanges. As world history has matured as a field, its practitioners have found the movement of commodities between peoples, places, and time a fruitful vehicle for research and teaching. Studies of "bulk" items like salt, spices, coffee, and other globally traded commodities abound, but few scholars have examined the role of luxury goods in global perspective.

This book charts the many different contexts in which luxury objects have been used across the globe, ranging from the social practices linked to these objects to their production, exchange, and consumption, as well as how these practices varied over time and space and how different societies attributed diverse meanings to the same objects. Using luxury goods as a conduit, *Luxury in Global Perspective* enriches our understanding of global history.

Bernd-Stefan Grewe is professor of Modern History and Didactics of History at the University of Education in Freiburg, Germany.

Karin Hofmeester is senior researcher at the International Institute of Social History in Amsterdam and professor of Jewish Culture at Antwerp University.

Studies in Comparative World History

Editors

Michael Adas, *Rutgers University*
Patrick Manning, *University of Pittsburgh*
Philip D. Curtin, *The Johns Hopkins University*

Luxury in Global Perspective

Objects and Practices, 1600–2000

BERND-STEFAN GREWE

University of Education, Freiburg

KARIN HOFMEESTER

International Institute of Social History, Amsterdam

CAMBRIDGE
UNIVERSITY PRESS

32 Avenue of the Americas, New York NY 10013

Cambridge University Press is part of the University of Cambridge.

It furthers the University's mission by disseminating knowledge in the pursuit of education, learning and research at the highest international levels of excellence.

www.cambridge.org
Information on this title: www.cambridge.org/9781107108325

© Cambridge University Press 2016

This publication is in copyright. Subject to statutory exception and to the provisions of relevant collective licensing agreements, no reproduction of any part may take place without the written permission of Cambridge University Press.

First published 2016

Printed in the United Kingdom by Clays, St Ives plc

A catalog record for this publication is available from the British Library.

Library of Congress Cataloging in Publication Data
Names: Hofmeester, Karin, 1964– editor. | Grewe, Bernd-Stefan, editor.
Title: Luxury in global perspective: objects and practices, 1600–2000 /
edited by Karin Hofmeester, Bernd-Stefan Grewe.
Description: New York : Cambridge University Press, 2016. |
Series: Studies in comparative world history |
Includes bibliographical references and index.
Identifiers: LCCN 2016009407 | ISBN 9781107108325 (hardback)
Subjects: LCSH: Luxury – History. | Wealth – History. | Economic history.
Classification: LCC HC52 .L89 2016 | DDC 338.4/7–dc23
LC record available at http://lccn.loc.gov/2016009407

ISBN 978-1-107-10832-5 Hardback

Cambridge University Press has no responsibility for the persistence or accuracy of URLS for external or third-party Internet Web sites referred to in this publication and does not guarantee that any content on such Web sites is, or will remain, accurate or appropriate.

Contents

Figures

Maps

Tables

Notes on contributors

Martha Chaiklin teaches at Zayed University. She has a broad experience in studying the history of material culture. She has worked on ivory, the trade of the Dutch East India Company in Asia, the culture of gift giving, and international exhibitions.

Anne Gerritsen (PhD Harvard) is professor of Chinese History at the University of Warwick, and since 2013 combines this with a Chair at the Leiden University Institute for Area Studies. In 2013–14, she was fellow-in-residence at the Netherlands Institute of Advanced Study in Wassenaar, Netherlands.

Bernard Gissibl is a postdoctoral researcher at the Leibniz-Institute of European History in Mainz, Germany. His research interests focus on the history of conservation, imperial history, and human-animal relations in transnational and global perspective.

Bernd-Stefan Grewe is professor of Modern History and Didactics of History at the University of Education in Freiburg, Germany. His research interests include environmental history and rural history; he studies the global history of gold in the twentieth century with a special focus on South Africa, India, and Great Britain and became fascinated by the field of material culture.

Karin Hofmeester is senior researcher at the International Institute of Social History (IISH) in Amsterdam and professor of Jewish Culture at Antwerp University. She is project leader of the Global Collaboratory on the History of Labour Relations 1500–2000 and studies the global commodity chain of diamonds from the sixteenth to the twentieth century.

Jonas Kranzer is a PhD student at the University of Konstanz and works on a dissertation about the global commodity chain of ivory in the nineteenth and twentieth century.

Karin Pallaver is associate professor at the Department of History and Cultures, University of Bologna. She completed her doctorate at the University of Cagliari and has worked as researcher in the "Money in Africa Project" at the British Museum. Her research focuses on nineteenth-century East African economy and trade, with a special focus on monetary history.

Giorgio Riello is professor in Global History and Culture at the Department of History at the University of Warwick. He has widely published on fashion, product innovation and design in eighteenth- and nineteenth-century Europe, and the global trade and the manufacturing of textiles.

Silvia Ruschak holds a PhD in history from the University of Vienna. She currently teaches in the Master Programme for Global History at the Department of Economic and Social History at the University of Vienna. Her major research interests lie in the field of global textile and gender history with a special focus on West Africa.

Kim Siebenhüner holds a research professorship of the Swiss National Fonds in early modern history at the History Department of the University of Bern. Her research interests include the history of material culture and consumption, early modern Indian history, autobiographical writing, and the history of religion. Currently, she works on a research project focusing on cotton textiles in early modern Switzerland and Germany.

Acknowledgments

Every book has its own history. The history of this book started when we met for the first time at a workshop at the University of Konstanz in February 2009. Some of our authors and their forthcoming articles had been recruited on this occasion: Anne Gerritsen, Giorgio Riello, Jonas Kranzer, Silvia Ruschak and Kim Siebenhüner. Then we decided to ask some other authors studying other related and fascinating topics to join our project and we were happy to get the contributions of Martha Chaiklin, Bernhard Gissibl and Karin Pallaver. It is a pleasure to acknowledge our authors for their rich expertise they brought into our book and for the amount of work they have put into it, and also for their patience during the period from their first draft version of their articles to the final copy reading.

We would like to thank three grand academics in the field of global history who were of great significance for the making of this book, each of them in a particular phase of the project. First of all Prof. Dr. Jürgen Osterhammel who raised funds for a Junior Research Group (Nachwuchsgruppe) "Dynamics of Transnational Agency" at the University of Konstanz. All PhD students and the coordinator of the group studied global history and worked on the spot in different countries such as Tanzania, South Africa, India or China, to name just a few. Bernd-Stefan Grewe, then leader of the research group, had the idea to organize a first workshop on "History of Commodities and Commodity Chains," which was then followed up by two other workshops in 2010 and 2011. Second, we thank Prof. Dr. Marcel van der Linden, of the International Institute of Social History (IISH) in Amsterdam, who inspired us during these workshops with his interpretation of the Commodity Chain Approach and stimulated us to make a book on luxury commodities. Third, Prof. Dr. Patrick Manning of the World History Center of the University of Pittsburgh read the first version of the manuscript and encouraged us to submit it to the Cambridge Studies in Comparative World History Series. We are grateful for his helpful comments as well as of those of the anonymous reviewers of the manuscript.

Karin Hofmeester would like to express her gratitude to the Fritz Thyssen Stiftung for their generous grant that enabled her to spend two years almost full-time on research. The work on this book and a number of articles on diamonds would not have been possible without it. She also wants to thank the members of the IISH research staff that replaced during her absence and that commented upon her work during various presentations.

We learned a lot about many other global commodities from the participants at the workshops "History of Commodities and Commodity Chains" (2009), "Parallel Commodity Chains: Substitutes and Informal Economy" (2010), and "Fragility and Disconnections of Global Commodity Chains" (2011). Some of the other papers presented here have been published in Jonathan Curry –Machado (ed.), *Global Histories, Imperial Commodities, Local Interactions,* Basingstoke: Palgrave Macmillan 2013.

The workshops at Konstanz would not have been realized without the generous support of the Center of Excellence "Cultural Foundations of Social Integration." Thanks to its speaker Prof. Dr. Rudolf Schlögl and his team (especially Fred Giroud and Jan Kröger) who made it possible to use its nice facilities at the Bischofsvilla on the banks of the Rhine. The Center also financed the costs for the translation and for the editing work by James Fearns, thank you again.

Comments we received during presentations we gave at other conferences also inspired us, we would like to thank Beverly Lemire commentator and chair as well as the participants of our session "Global Luxury Commodities: Production, Exchange, Consumption and Valuation" organized at the European Social Science History Conference held in Vienna (2014) as well as the participants of the workshops of the Indian Association of Labour Historians in Delhi held in 2010 and 2014.

Many thanks to Joel Golb for his excellent work of translating the German versions of the introduction and of the articles by Jonas Kranzer, Silvia Ruschak, Kim Siebenhüner, and Bernd-Stefan Grewe. A big thank you to Markus Himmelsbach for his support with indexing this volume.

Finally, we thank the team of Cambridge University Press – especially Deborah Gershenowitz, Dana Bricken, and David Morris – for their guidance in realizing this project, for meticulous help we thank Nishanthini Vetrivel, and for careful copy-editing Christine Dunn. We apologize for any remaining errors or omissions and would be grateful if notified of any corrections that should be incorporated in future reprints or editions of this book.

Abbreviations

ADATIG	*Anglo Dutch African Textile Investigation Group*
BCE	*Before Common Era*
B.E.A.	*British East Africa*
CE	*Common Era*
CITES	*Convention on International Trade in Endangered Species of Wild Fauna and Flora*
EAPHA	*East African Professional Hunters' Association*
EIC	*East India Company*
GCA	*Game Controlled Areas*
GTP	*Ghana Textile Printing Company*
NGO	*Nongovernmental organization*
VOC	*Dutch East India Company (Vereenigde Oostindische Compagnie)*
WWF	*World Wildlife Fund*

Introduction

Luxury and global history

Bernd-Stefan Grewe and Karin Hofmeester

Luxury is a global phenomenon. (European) books and calligraphy in China; jewels and diamonds in South Asia and Europe; and glass beads and Indian textiles in Africa are or were luxury goods. Nearly all societies know objects whose value is not measured by usefulness and whose possession means more than the usual possession of objects by its members. But luxury does not only exist in the form of objects; just as important are luxurious practices fulfilling similar social and cultural functions. Such practices include attending concerts and the opera, traveling with special forms of transportation, certain acts of consumption, certain types of hunting, and generous gift giving. Luxury commodities are often global commodities, produced in one part of the world and consumed in another, its "exoticness" being one of its luxurious qualities. If we perceive global history as the history of connections, then commodities can be seen as traveling "things" that connect people in different regions of the world. Doing global history by way of commodities, following their production, exchange, and consumption along the global commodity chain is not new. However, up until now, global historians preferred to follow bulk commodities and perhaps even more luxury commodities that later became mass consumption products like coffee, tea, and sugar. An important reason for this omission is probably the influence of Immanuel Wallerstein's *A modern world system*, who determined the paradigm of commodity research for quite some time. In his view luxury goods are per definition socially low-valued items in areas outside a capitalist world system and high-valued, high-priced goods in internal areas. The trade in luxury goods was therefore not essential to the functioning of either party and therefore of no importance to his theory.[1] An important critic of Wallerstein's distinction between luxury and bulk and its consequences is Jane Schneider, who states that it is difficult to distinguish between luxuries and necessities because, for example, in precapitalist society the tribute system was maintained through the distribution of luxuries and imperialism necessitated "winning distant people with kindness." Also, Schneider rightfully claims that Wallerstein has no good explanation for precapitalist social change because he has no eye for the importance of the urge for luxury: this made people start traveling, going overseas, and so forth: "the luxury trade could induce massive alterations in technology, leadership, class structure, and ideology within trading populations and in 'relay' populations on the transit routes."[2] Her suggestion is to focus on the relationship between luxuries and essentials rather than on the distinction. We would like to take this argument one step further and show how luxury in various settings functioned and how local variations in taste could influence (global) economic interactions. This is linked up with the ideas of Christopher Bayly who states that "certain products such as basic grains and basic cloths were more or less universally required and universally produced in all pre-modern agrarian economies. Economic activities based on production and consumption at this level were predictable ... by contrast there were other products and patterns of consumption which were both geographically specific and heavily determined by cultural preference: Arab horses, otter skins, certain types of medical spices and diamonds for instance."[3]

This volume explicitly focuses on luxury commodities and practices for two important reasons. The first is to enrich global history by looking at the global production, exchange, and consumption of luxury goods and services. Following world-system theory and dependency theory, much critical research has been done to reveal the asymmetric economic relations in global economy in the past and present. But economic and most global historians, too, tended to overlook the specific meaning that all those who were involved in the production, trade, and consumption associated with these things and practices. Some others, such as the economic historian Jan de Vries have examined the Western European

[1] Immanuel Wallerstein, *The Modern World-System III: The Second Era of Great Expansion of the Capitalist World-Economy, 1730s–1840s* (Berkeley: University of California Press, 2011), xv, 131–2.

[2] Jane Schneider, "Was There a Pre-Capitalist World-System?," *Peasant Studies* 6 (1977): 20–9.

[3] Christopher A. Bayly, "'Archaic' and 'Modern' Globalization in the Eurasian and African Arena, c. 1750–1850" in A.G. Hopkins (ed.) *Globalisation in World History* (London: Pimlico, 2002), 55.

consumption of luxury goods over the course of the "Long Eighteenth Century," developing the interesting thesis of an "industrious revolution." De Vries views the increasing consumption of coffee, tea, and sugar as a central factor in the emerging orientation of the private household away from a subsistence economy and toward wage labor.[4] Christopher Bayly and Anne McCants have taken this approach further, seeing the development as not limited to the North Atlantic region but also at work in China and Japan, parts of India, and the Middle East.[5] Until the present, such distant effects of luxury consumption have been studied principally for wares such as coffee, tea, cocoa, sugar, and tobacco, whose exclusive character eventually waned so that they became daily consumer goods with exotic origins. The work of Kenneth Pomeranz represents one exception to this tendency, focusing on several types of luxury goods, underscoring the importance for the global economy of wares such as silk and certain furniture that would only be accessible for an elite.[6] The present collection is intended to contribute to a debate oriented along the same lines, while freeing itself from a perspective centered on North Atlantic consumers. Unlike earlier historiography, we will not only study the pre-modern period and the eighteenth century, but also the nineteenth and twentieth centuries.

We believe that following luxury commodities will help us to better understand the specific functioning of global connections. Different societies and within these different social groups developed own material cultures and possessed a specific social logic attached to objects, practices, and ideas. Through economic interaction, not only on a global level, but on regional and local levels too, these different material cultures got in contact with each other and stimulated economic exchange that was also shaped by differences in economic power. The relevance of these cultural issues has often been underestimated by global (economic) historians, and studying luxuries and luxurious practices could thus provide useful new insights for the relevance of cultural differences for the functioning of global connections. The fundamental assumption is that the social and cultural context of the participants in a global chain of luxury

---

[4] Most recently in Jan de Vries, *The Industrious Revolution: Consumer Behavior and the Household Economy, 1650 to the Present* (Cambridge: Cambridge University Press, 2008).

[5] Bayly, *Birth of the Modern World*, 49–50; Anne E. C. McCants, "Exotic Goods, Popular Consumption, and the Standard of Living: Thinking about Globalization in the Early Modern World," *Journal of World History* 18 (2007): 433–62.

[6] Kenneth Pomeranz, *The Great Divergence: China, Europe and the Making of the Modern World Economy* (Princeton, NJ: Princeton University Press, 2000), 114–66.

commodities or luxurious practices was crucial not only for the way it was produced, traded, transported, or marketed, but also for how it was consumed. Through the analysis of specific social and cultural contexts, we try to better understand the functioning of global connections. The focus of our studies will often be local, but the perspective is transcultural and global.

The second goal of same importance is to enrich the historical conception of luxury by looking at it from a global perspective. By and large, earlier research on the history of luxury focused initially on court culture and later on emerging bourgeois culture, with more recent work concentrating on the development of European consumer society starting in the late eighteenth century. In contrast, the chapters in this volume break sharply with the traditional focus on northwestern Europe and the neo-European societies in the North Atlantic. This volume puts a thematic emphasis on those objects and practices whose most important customers were located in Asia and Africa. Furthermore, the phenomenon of luxury is here no longer reduced to its consumption; rather, those objects are examined as products of work and interpreted as part of a global division of labor. Until now, research on the critique of luxury within a cultural-studies framework has tended to elide the darker aspects of the European luxury-goods consumption – aspects often emerging outside Europe. For that reason alone, there is really no alternative to a global, transnational historical approach to the theme. The negative effects accompanying the production of luxury goods – oppression and exploitation of workers; long-term damage to health and the environment – have often been neglected because the emphasis has tended to be on highly qualified and specialized craftsmen and the goods' manufacturers.[7] Our aim is not a criticism of the capitalistic connections around the luxury trade and its unfair socioeconomic consequences, but we would like to understand the social logic of the different people involved in these specific productions of luxury.

---

[7] Typical in this respect are the otherwise excellent essays in Robert Fox and Anthony Turner, eds., *Luxury Trades and Consumerism in Ancien Régime Paris: Studies in the History of the Skilled Workforce* (Aldershot, UK: Ashgate, 1998). See Ulrich-Christian Pallach, *Materielle Kultur und Mentalitäten im 18. Jahrhundert: Wirtschaftliche Entwicklung und politisch-sozialer Funktionswandel des Luxus in Frankreich und im Alten Reich am Ende des Ancien Régime* (Munich: Oldenbourg, 1987); Natacha Coquery, *L'hôtel aristocratique: Le marché du luxe à Paris au XVIIIe siècle* (Paris: Publ. de la Sorbonne, 1998); Jean-Claude Daumas and Marc de Ferrière le Vayer, "Les métamorphoses du luxe vues d'Europe," *Entreprises et Histoire* 46 (2007): 6–16.

METHODOLOGY

Most chapters in this volume use (either implicitly or explicitly) the global commodity chain approach to follow the commodities from their origin to the consumer to reconstruct the linkages and interconnectivity of societies around the world. Many earlier works have reconstructed and criticized the connections that are manifest in commodity chains, especially the negative impact on the "periphery."[8] In their basic conception, these works are often oriented toward the "dependency theory" of André Gunder Frank[9] and Immanuel Wallerstein's "world system."[10] This allows a description of the imbalance of economic power between countries located in that "periphery" and European and North American "metropolises." Nevertheless, those supply chains not aimed at North Atlantic consumers have been broadly overlooked in such research. Although here assigned to the production side, "peripheral" countries have thus frequently not been perceived as consumers of goods and as value producers.[11] As valuable as these debates were, when the asymmetry of global political and economic connections has been substantiated, the assumed asymmetry of these power relations is already part of the research design. This volume wants to avoid this by bringing together those luxury researchers who take the agency of people outside Europe and North America more seriously and study their patterns of consumption and production, seeking to understand the meaning they attribute to their participation in these global linkages. We looked for luxury practices in regions like Africa and India that are rarely studied as a consuming part of global economy just like China and to a lesser extent Japan.[12]

[8] See Gary Gereffi and Miguel Korzeniewicz, eds., *Commodity Chains and Global Capitalism* (Westport, CT: Greenwood Press, 1994). An earlier form of the concept in Terence K. Hopkins and Immanuel Wallerstein, "Commodity Chains in the World-Economy Prior to 1800," *Review: A Journal of the Fernand Braudel Center for the Study of Economics, Historical Systems, and Civilizations* 10, no. 1 (1986): 157–70.

[9] Andre Gunder Frank, *Capitalism and Underdevelopment in Latin America: Historical Studies of Chile and Brazil* (New York: Monthly Review Press, 1967).

[10] Wallerstein, *The Modern World-System I: Capitalist Agriculture and the Origins of European World-Economy in the Sixteenth Century; Modern World-System II: Mercantilism and the Consolidation of the European World-Economy, 1600–1750; Modern World-System III: The Second Era of Great Expansion* (Berkeley: University of California Press, 2011).

[11] For a critical assessment Steven Topik, Carlos Marichal, and Zephyr Frank, eds., *From Silver to Cocaine: Latin American Commodity Chains and the Building of the World Economy, 1500–2000* (Durham, NC and London: Duke University Press, 2006).

[12] An exception to the rule is Frank Trentmann, ed., *Oxford Handbook of the History of Consumption* (Oxford: Oxford University Press, 2012) with articles by Craig Clunas on

As the global commodity chain approach helps us to see the connections between the different segments in the chain, the "social biography" approach shows us how people in different societies, or even within one society in different social contexts, attributed different meanings to the same objects. Since Arjun Appadurai's pathbreaking work *The Social Life of Things: Commodities in Cultural Perspective*[13] biographies of objects have become quite widespread; but they have hardly found a place in approaches tied to global history. This is all the more remarkable as many such biographies, to the extent the objects are not locally produced, are the products of cross-border, global networks.[14] Our intent is not simply to tie luxury as a social phenomenon to the group of those enjoying it, but to reconstruct the "social biographies" of luxurious objects, which is to say the history of their origin, production, transport, marketing, and consumption in various social and cultural contexts. The more seriously we consider the specific material and qualitative properties of these luxury commodities and the values people attributed to them exactly because of their specific properties, the more inviting such an approach appears. The hardness of diamonds, the glint of glass beads, or the purity and the seemingly everlasting lure of gold were important features to make them attractive.[15]

The concepts of global commodity chains and of biographies of objects can serve as lenses through which to view the global entanglement without neglecting the diversity of sociocultural contexts through which the objects passed. Something we see in the following chapters on the history of jewels, diamonds, and gold, but also of Chinese porcelain, Indian cotton, Dutch wax print cloths, glass beads, and ivory. In addition,

China and Jeremy Prestholdt on Africa; Douglas Haynes, Abigail McGowan, Tirthankar Roy, and Haruka Yanagisawa, eds., *Towards a History of Consumption in South Asia* (New Delhi: Oxford University Press, 2010) is useful though focusing very much on the late nineteenth and twentieth centuries.

[13] Arjun Appadurai, ed., *The Social Life of Things: Commodities in Cultural Perspective* (Cambridge: Cambridge University Press, 1986).

[14] See Patrick Manning, *Navigating World History: Historians Create a Global Past* (New York and Basingstoke, UK: Palgrave Macmillan, 2003).

[15] One might suggest to use the Actor-Network-Theory (ANT) as an analytical approach, too. But ANT, and especially Bruno Latour, is very tacit about the cultural dimension of assemblages of things. ANT research usually does not study the representations that actors link with objects and they often ignore the important notion of intentionality. The intention of an actor to consume or practice one form of luxury or another and thus to express his or her social rank or aspiration is something that can't be studied within an ANT framework. See Bruno Latour, *Reassembling the Social: An Introduction to Actor-Network-Theory* (Oxford: Oxford University Press, 2005); John Law and John Hassard, eds., *Actor Network Theory and After* (Oxford and Keele: Blackwell, 1999).

the examples of glass beads and ivory make clear how objects are evaluated differently in various sociocultural contexts. In Africa, ivory was no luxury; in Europe or the United States, it was part of luxurious leisure "instruments" such as piano keys and billiard balls. Inversely, where in Europe glass beads had a relatively profane function; in an East African society they gained entirely different meaning as a luxury good and highly valued means of exchange.[16] Such examples point to an important second question this volume wants to answer – as a follow up on Appadurai's thesis – that of the extent to which these "regimes of value," that is, the varying valuation of things and practices in different societies, were constitutive for transcultural, global economic relations – whether they in fact were responsible for global economic exchange in the first place.

In contrast to many studies on luxury that either ignore the cultural and social implications of luxury or that turn a blind eye to its economic dimension, we try to connect the two. We intend not to neglect questions of prices, costs, and profits. Though this is not a collection on the global economic history of luxury, this does not necessarily mean that the analyses presented here are not interesting for economic historians. The previously mentioned recognition by some historians for the economic importance of premodern luxury commodity production, exchange, and consumptions should be broadened as their importance for later period global economic connections are also large. Here, our integrated cultural and economic approach, combining the global commodity chain with the social life of things approach, can not only help to enrich luxury studies but also deepen our understanding of global economic connections. When economists study the balance of trade, and in the course of this the flow of luxury commodities, they often use categories that were developed and defined on what North Atlantic customers considered luxurious, but there is little reflection on whether these concepts could also be applied to study balances in other regions of the globe. We need to keep in mind that a considerable portion of the Southern Hemisphere's trade has not been quantitatively grasped, and that the evaluation of objects in different societies can vary markedly – both factors calling into question the usefulness of the categories in play here. In short, the unquestioned classification upon which the quantification of these commodity flows is based is only accurate from the standpoint of European

---

[16] See Akinwumi Ogundiran, "Of Small Things Remembered: Beads, Cowries, and Cultural Translations of the Atlantic Experience in Yorubaland," *The International Journal of African Historical Studies* 35, no. 2–3 (2002): 427–57.

and North American culture. In other sociocultural contexts, the same objects could have a completely different meaning: cowries seemed to be worthless for Europeans, but were of high importance for African trades because they had a very high exchange value in the hinterland; in other regions, copper was of higher value than other metals; and jade, too, was much more important in Pre-Columbian America, in ancient China, or for the Maori, than for Europeans. These examples illustrate why we study the sociocultural context and analyze which meanings the (economic) actors attach to the different objects and practices. But first, we will need to define what *luxury* is.

DEFINING LUXURY

Different societies and different groups within them have always had their own ideas about what is to be considered luxurious. Objects and practices thought to be so in one sociocultural context are deemed profane and everyday in another such context. On the level of cognitive theory, this definitional problem is inherently present in the polysemy of both the objects and the trade in them[17] – what seems self-evident and standard to some seems a luxury to others, and this understanding could even differ within a single social group what is especially the case when individuals are confronted with a new, not yet precisely classifiable form of object or practice. Luxury is thus a socially defined and multivalent material phenomenon.

Consistently, luxury is experienced *sensorially*, with certain luxury goods and practices tied to each of the senses: perfume and other scents for smell; champagne and truffles for taste; fine art and architecture for the eye; silk and other fine textiles for touch; opera and concerts for the ears. Although this sensuality shows that luxury is tied to pleasure, the question remains open of how luxury goods are to be distinguished from other goods. In this respect, several features come to mind tentatively defining such goods beyond any cultural differences.[18] In the

---

[17] On the polysemy and subversive power of objects, see Henri Lefebvre, *Critique of Everyday Life II: Foundations for a Sociology of the Everyday*, trans. John Moore (London and New York: Verso, 1991).

[18] A pioneering distinction between different types of luxury is found in Werner Sombart, *Der moderne Kapitalismus*, 5th ed. (Munich and Leipzig: Duncker and Humblot, 1922), 719–20. Sombart defines *luxury* as a relational concept determined in face of what is "necessary"; he here distinguishes between "physiology need" and "cultural need." The additional distinction he draws from this between objective and subjective luxury no longer seems sustainable.

first place, within the social context where they are considered luxurious, luxury goods are as a rule *not mass goods* but special, unusual objects. A brilliant-cut diamond, an ermine fur, and a Mouton Rothschild vintage 1945 are, for example, all relatively rare objects that cannot be reproduced on a mass scale.[19] Second, in cases in which they are indeed traded, such goods are usually very expensive, excluding much of the populace from their ownership *a priori*.[20] But their exclusive quality need not stem from purchasing price. In the period preceding the intensified interconnectiveness of the world that began in the 1860s, for example, exclusivity often lay in the exotic character of an object hard to procure because of its *special origins* – like Colombian emeralds in India; or mummies and shrunken heads being especially macabre examples. Many objects were exclusive because they were new and strange for other members of a group or society; and once everyday and accessible to many, the objects' exclusivity vanished. In contrast to novel objects, used luxury objects had exclusive character only on rare occasions – for instance when antiques came into fashion in eighteenth-century Paris.[21]

In the third place, the purchase and use of luxury objects moves *beyond the realm of everyday practicality*. Rather, they often are meant to make one or another practice or action more discriminating, cultivated, refined, or sophisticated. Typical examples for objects that have served such functions are a golden snuffbox, a gem-studded water pipe, a crystal wine carafe, or a tortoiseshell dildo. Such luxury goods serve to orchestrate the function of other consumer goods and endow their enjoyment with an aura of luxury.

In the fourth place (and this dimension of luxury is often not taken seriously enough in research on material culture), the objects involved here possess special *material qualities* distinguishing them from other objects: in the case of gold, diamonds, and jewels, there is, for example, sheer, nigh-eternal material durability, which on a more practical level

---

[19] Even Haute Couture who creates exclusive custom-fitted clothing, but also offer some expensive ready-to-wear lines, is presented in fashion houses in the cities around the globe as if it was very exclusive – although it is not rare but in fact it is a mass product of high quality and high priced.

[20] This does not mean that luxury can only exist in societies resting on a money economy. The exchange value expressed in a money economy merely has another referential factor. On conspicuous consumption see Thorstein Veblen, *The Theory of the Leisure Class* (1899; repr., Oxford and New York: Oxford University Press, 2007), 49–69.

[21] See Ulrich-Christian Pallach, "Auktionen und Auktionskataloge des 18. Jahrhunderts: Bemerkungen zum Luxusmarkt des französischen Ancien Régime," *Francia* 8 (1980): 648–66.

produces ideal objects of enduring value for storage and hoarding. But other objects have been considered luxurious precisely on account of their *transience* – perfume, for example, with its evanescent scent, cut flowers in vases, selected exotic fruit, tiger hunting in Mughal India, roast game, or luxurious holidays such as safaris. Often, the *finesse* with which a piece of work is crafted has played a decisive role – the case for both furniture made of precious fine-grained wood and watches or jewelry.[22] By the same token, the very *fragility* of crystal glass products is what distinguished them from other glass products. These examples strongly suggest that material qualities and their refinement play as strong a role in determining which goods are to be considered luxurious as their social construction by contemporaries.

In the fifth place, luxury objects almost always have a *special aesthetically pleasing quality* for their owners. In this respect, let us simply note that the close connection aesthetic sensation and judgment have with habit, hence with the social origins of those doing the judging, needs no explicit justification. Finally, a sixth, especially important quality of luxury objects is their function as *symbols of social status*, as a marker of class. Often, their owners wish to communicate a specific message through them – a specific picture of person and social rank. Where hierarchical societies mark elevated position in this manner, in those of the modernized West upwardly striving individuals use such symbols to signal their ambition to break the class divide, an aspirational practice. Inversely, luxury is also used as compensation for loss of footing – to accentuate the "actual" value of a group or person.

Luxury is a special material language. This language is understood and shared by everyone, but only an exclusive number of people can express themselves at free will without material and financial constraints. Most classes were condemned to share the language of luxury in a more passive way. Luxury must be considered to be a mode of social distinction.[23]

THE PRACTICE OF LUXURY

Recent historical research has clearly mapped out luxury's semiotic and communicative functions in Europe's court society, its nobility, and

---

[22] See Michael Stürmer, *Handwerk und höfische Kultur: Europäische Möbelkunst im 18. Jahrhundert* (Munich: Beck, 1982).

[23] See Pierre Bourdieu, *La Distinction: Critique Sociale du Jugement* (Paris: Les Éditions de Minuit, 1979).

bourgeoisie.[24] At present we can observe, outside the discursive dimension, a stronger focus on performative aspects of the theme – on practices of luxury and its social construction. Important in this respect are sensory practices tied to luxury objects. Considered chronologically, such practices have their starting point in customs of purchase and receipt, of the sale and marketing of an object as a luxury good, together with exchange and gift giving.[25] In India, a piece of clothing first worn by the Mughal emperor then handed over to a courtier served to symbolically acknowledge the hierarchical relationship while being interpreted by the man receiving the gift as an exclusive attestation of favor. The clothing given out by the emperor was passed down over generations and worn on special ceremonious occasions.[26]

Ownership of a luxury object takes in an entire spectrum of practices ranging from corporal presentation with the help of clothing, jewelry, and scent to the presentation of objects in display cases, on walls, and either as fixtures in household realms frequented by guests and visitors or as demonstratively used items. Here the emblematic message related to a specific, present social environment has special significance because luxury objects emerge as an indispensable attribute of a person's self-staging. We find this function strongly foregrounded in Renaissance pictorial sources, with portraits presenting individuals in their richest garb or against a background of special, luxurious objects.

In Figure 1, a successful German merchant in London, does not only wear some expensive red clothes with a fur, but there are many objects that refer to his social rank and his international relations. On the table we can identify a precious carpet from Anatolia with Arabic ornaments, a golden pocket watch (a so-called Nuremberg Egg), and a Venetian vase with flowers on it. In the background there is also a balance to weigh gold and silver coins.

In the allegorical watercolor painting of an imagined meeting between Mughal emperor Jahangir and his Persian rival Shah Abbas (c. 1620) we see the same function of luxury (Figure 2). Jahangir is depicted with a

---

[24] See Michael Sikora, *Der Adel in der Frühen Neuzeit* (Darmstadt: Wissenschaftliche Buchgesellschaft, 2009), 68–105; Gudrun Gersmann, ed., *Adelige Lebenswelten im Rheinland: Kommentierte Quellen der Frühen Neuzeit* (Cologne: Böhlau, 2009).

[25] See Ulf Christian Ewert, "Sozialer Tausch bei Hofe: Eine Skizze des Erklärungspotentials der Neuen Institutionenökonomik," in *Hof und Theorie: Annäherungen an ein historisches Phänomen*, ed. R. Butz, J. Hirschbiegel, and D. Willoweit (Cologne: Böhlau, 2004), 55–75.

[26] Annemarie Schimmel, *Im Reich der Großmoguln: Geschichte, Kunst, Kultur* (Munich: Beck, 2000), 68–70.

FIGURE 1. Hans Holbein, "Georg Gisze, a German merchant in London" (1532). *Source*: Hans Holbein. Courtesy of The Yorck Project: *10.000 Meisterwerke der Malerei* http://commons.wikimedia.org/wiki/File:Hans_Holbein_d._J._051.jpg.

halo, his status as a universal patron is symbolized by various luxury objects from all over the world: an Italian table and ewer, a small porcelain Chinese cup, a Venetian glass bottle shaped like a pilgrim flask, and (in the hands of Khan Alam the Mughal ambassador to the Persian court on the right) a clockwork statuette of Diana on a stag from Augsburg.[27]

There are ninety years between these two paintings, but a striking parallel: in both paintings the objects attest to the portrayed person's

[27] Ebba Koch, "How the Mughal Padshas Referenced Iran in Their Visual Construction of Universal Rule," in *Universal Empire: A Comparative Approach to Imperial Culture and Representation in Eurasian History*, ed. P. F. Bang and D. Kolodziejczyk (Cambridge: Cambridge University Press 2012), 194–209, see p. 201. Also see Robert Finlay, *The Pilgrim Art: Cultures of Porcelain in World History* (Berkeley and Los Angeles: California University Press, 2010), 247, and Nuno Vassallo e Silva, "Precious Stones, Jewels and Cameos: Jacques de Coutre's Journey to Goa and Agra," *Goa and the*

FIGURE 2. "Jahangir Entertains Shah Abbas from the *St. Petersburg Album*" (India c. 1620).
Source: St. Petersburg Album Opaque water color, gold, and ink on paper, H: 25.0 W: 18.3 centimeters. Courtesy of © Freer Gallery of Art, Smithsonian Institution, Washington, DC, F1942.16a.

status and concomitant qualities. In England and India, for German merchants or Mughal emperor, luxury objects here function as a code meant to be deciphered by the observer (Table 1).

Great Mughal, ed. Nuno Vassallo e Silva and Silva and Jorge Flores (Lisbon: Calouste Gulbenkian Museum, 2004), 128–30.

TABLE 1. *Typologies of luxury*

Differentiation according to the selected categories, each row representing one possible typology.

Material dimension: luxury objects

Material qualities	Durability (diamonds, gold)	Transiency (flowers, scent)	Finesse and craftsmanship (snuff box, water pipe with jewels)	Fragility (crystal glass, porcelain)	Efficiency, speed (private jet, Arab horse)	Other material qualities (weight, size, comfort, color, brilliance etc.)
Sensory stimulation	Taste (Fugu fish, Black Ivory coffee, caviar, champagne)	Smell (perfume, roses)	touch (silk, fur, ivory)	Sight (paintings, architecture)	Hearing (chants, concert, opera)	Perception drugs altering mood or consciousness (cocaine, cigar, water pipe)

Performative dimension

Exclusivity and accessibility	Unique and not accessible for anybody else (gift exchange with the Mughal emperor, painting)	Rare and difficult to access, often expensive or restricted by law (snorting or smoking cocaine, buying elephant tusk)	Exotic and difficult to access (photographing the Big Five)	Expensive and accessible for the financially powerful (membership in yachting club, luxury brand)	Democratized, accessible for everybody – no more luxury (flying, sugar, coffee)

Social dimension

	Public			Private		
Social space	Public, profane, and informal (using elephants or sedans for transport)	Public, profane, and formal (smoking/evening gown, court clothing)	Public, ritual, and ceremonial (priest garb, golden vessels, wedding dress)	Semi-public (visiting hall, entry, courtyard, garden)	Private sphere (luxurious bedroom, satin sheets)	Private (discrete body jewelry, silk underwear, tortoiseshell dildo)
Forms of display	Permanent (palace, monuments, garden, display case)	Situational, occasional, functional (jewelry, playing golf, luxurious means of transport)	Documentary (evidence of luxury practices in the past, hunting trophies)	Prospective, luxury register (hoarding of luxury objects like precious stones, expensive high heels)		

Communicative dimension

	Other directed					Self-directed	
Motivation	Ambition, social elevation and aspiration (expensive cars or clothing)	Social distinction, marking social distance (clothing reserved for a caste or social group)	Membership, receiving affection (court clothing, fashion brands)	External reward, prestige, glamour (wearing a medal, diamonds)	Relaxation, pleasure (massage, delicious food)	Competence, mastery, masculinity/femininity (playing polo, hunting, cosmetics, cosmetic surgery)	Fulfill a dream, inner peace, escapism, hedonism ("I am worth it") (climbing on Mt. Everest, sailing around the world, enjoying alone a water pipe)

In this way, the message luxury communicates is read by recipients and usually understood. This can be seen most clearly in the repeated striving for luxury and imitation of it. If the striving is absent, this can be interpreted as a sign that luxury has failed to fulfill its communicative function; and both the striving and imitation have an entire series of effects. For one thing, the luxury function of a practice or object is here confirmed in a clear-cut manner – although at the same time imitation is capable of eviscerating luxury's exclusive quality. This is above all the case when precious objects are imitated or falsified with such skill that they can hardly be distinguished from the original exclusive object, or when imitations are in fact of better quality or durability such as plastic instead of ivory billiard balls, or hairpins made of plastic instead of tortoiseshell. Entire markets with imitation luxuries – from gold-plated instead of gold watches to silver-plated instead of silver cutlery and onward to silkily glistening cloth made of calico – eventually emerged to satisfy a strong need for these imitation goods.[28]

In much of the work written in a material culture framework, another approach to luxury objects is overlooked: an approach not outwardly oriented toward demonstration, presentation, and representation but sufficient in itself.[29] "Because I'm worth it" is not only a well-known advertising slogan but corresponds to an individual-centered form of luxury – a form taking in fine lingerie and jewelry worn in concealed fashion, or with a concealed part like the beautiful Indian reverse-side enameled (*pichhari ko mina*) jewelry that could only be noticed and enjoyed by the wearer.[30] Other luxury objects are owned secretly because their open possession might spark disapproval. In such cases possession serves a private need for self-confirmation. Nevertheless, just like the collections of unworn women's shoes that have become

[28] In Paris on the eve of the French Revolution, we find a strong secondhand market in both luxury goods and their imitations. Laurence Fontaine, "The Circulation of Luxury Goods in Eighteenth Century Paris: Social Redistribution and an Alternative Currency," in *Luxury in the Eighteenth Century: Debates, Desires and Delectable Goods*, ed. M. Berg and E. Eger (Basingstoke, UK: Palgrave Macmillan, 2003), 89–102. Fontaine here points to the function of luxury goods as a credit source, e.g., as a lendable deposit.

[29] A corresponding interiorization of a luxurious way of life in Jan de Vries, "Luxury in the Dutch Golden Age in Theory and Practice," in ibid., 41–56. For a very different interpretation of luxury in the same time and place see Simon Schama, *An Embarrassment of Riches: An Interpretation of Dutch Culture in the Golden Age* (London: Collins, 1987).

[30] One of the explanations for this tradition is the appreciation of the skill by the purchaser. "She is the sole person who, when the object of such a necklace is worn, has sure knowledge of the presence of this decoration." Oppi Untracht, *Traditional Jewelry of India* (New York: Thames and Hudson, 2008), 361.

a misogynist cliché, such objects have a certain potential for eventual open display as luxury goods. The anticipatory pleasure at such staging is often just as or even more satisfying than an actual realization that perhaps will never take place. In contrast, theft of a famous painting makes no social sense as its incapacity to be shown to third parties renders it communicatively worthless. In the case of such stolen good, the motivational structure may be even more strongly hedonistic, just as with the isolated enjoyment of fine whisky or cigars, an opium pipe, or pralines. There has been little historical research on the secret hoarding of precious things.

In any event, luxurious practices are not limited to the possession of objects. They also involve, for example, the use of things belonging to others. Among the English and French nobility, lending out jewelry for celebrations has been a custom, with close observation of who wears what jewelry on what occasion. Guy de Maupassant's famous short story *The Necklace* (*La Parure*, 1884) tells about a borrowed diamond necklace that is lost at a party and thus puts a young couple into deepest troubles in order to replace it. The irony of the story is that the lost necklace turns out to have been just an imitation. Much more secret was the lending of jewelry in rural India, when families lent their jewelry to unmarried daughters or the bride. Another practice is the use of unusually expensive and thus exclusive body-care services such as manicuring and hairdressing. But the service realm where both social distinctions and exclusivity are most noticeable is that of mobility. Traditionally, when it comes to urban transportation, those having themselves borne along in sedans, or who can peer down on pedestrians from horses, camels, and elephants, have not only moved from one to another locus but also at the same time demonstrated their superior social position. In long-distance travel the social differences are even greater, with most forms of transport continuing to distinguish different passenger classes. (This not only applies to ships, planes, and trains, but even to cars, with the clear distinction between ordinary and luxury-class vehicles.[31])

---

[31] See Marie-Françoise Berneron-Couvenhes, "La Croisière: Du Luxe au Demi-Luxe: Le Cas des Messageries Maritimes, 1850–1960," *Entreprises et Histoire* 46 (2007): 34–55; Annette von Pelzer, ed., *Faszination Auto: Autowerbung von der Kaiserzeit bis heute* (Berlin: Westermann Kommunikation, 1994); Kristina Vaillant, *Vom "Ervolkswagen" zum Designer-Schmuckstück: Automobilwerbung in Publikumszeitschriften, 1954–1994* (Berlin: Wissenschaftszentrum Berlin für Sozialforschung, 1995).

Other luxurious practices include participation in expensive, exclusive events such as operas and concerts,[32] dining in luxury restaurants, belonging to exclusive clubs of one sort or another, and being active in certain forms of sport such as polo or yachting. In the past, the European big-game hunt in the colonies, continued after the end of colonialism, was one such practice that was comparable with tiger hunting in Mughal India and camel racing in the Emirates.[33] That these and similar practices were traditionally the reserve of men is a reflection of the subordinate and domestic role women had in European bourgeois society.[34]

To summarize: luxury goods and practices have had to possess a set of qualities located within social, cultural, and material domains. The importance and indispensability of each domain, the need to treat them all equally, becomes clear with close historical scrutiny of these goods and practices. The growing fragility of the category of luxury could have both social and material origins.

THE FRAGILITY OF LUXURY

Status as a luxury good can be lost through a shift in a society's values, a typical example of this being the change in the attitude toward precious fur that became apparent in the 1970s and 1980s. Until then, a mink or leopard-skin coat was a prized status symbol for bourgeois women, to be worn mainly on special occasions. When the animal rights movement decisively stamped public discourse by condemning the wearing of furs as a source of cruelty to animals and a threat to the survival of endangered species, many furriers had to close shop; what emerged as one characteristic of the animal rights campaign was a relatively radical attack on the luxury-message conveyed by fur – paint attacks on opera-goers, attention-grabbing adhesive labels condemning fur wearers without even raising the animal-protection theme, and so forth.[35] One much earlier

---

[32] When it comes to opera, Italy has been the great exception because it traditionally has been popular among all social groupings.

[33] See William K. Storey, "Big Cats and Imperialism: Lion and Tiger Hunting in Kenya and Northern India, 1898–1930," *Journal of World History* 2 (1991): 135–73; Peter Boomgaard, "Death to the Tiger! The Development of Tiger and Leopard Rituals in Java, 1605–1906," *South East Asia Research* 2 (1994): 141–75.

[34] India offers different examples, as Nur Jahan, favorite wife of Mughal Emperor Jahangir, was a famous tiger hunter.

[35] It is highly likely that social envy here played an at least subliminal role. An entire series of labels also underscored intergenerational differences, defining the wearing of fur as an age-linked phenomenon and suggesting a causal connection between the bodily changes accompanying aging and fur wearing. The main focus was on instilling a bad conscience among purchasers of fur.

example of a campaign directed against consumer behavior was organized by the eighteenth-century British antislavery movement, in the form
of antisugar propaganda.[36] Another example is the Swadeshi movement
in India: after 1905 Bengali nationalist leaders and later Gandhi stimulated the Indian population to boycott all British-made manufactures
and use home-produced commodities instead.[37] In the 1990s, the campaign against African "blood diamonds" (i.e., diamonds mined in areas
of civil war) offers a second example of an effort to deflate the valuation
of previously prized objects. But in fact, similar campaigns accompanied
the decolonization movement, in that case aimed to destroy the acceptance of Western status symbols.

By contrast, those contemporary and critical discourses on luxury that
have frequently been studied by cultural historians, have been markedly
less effective than those formulating the discourse would have intended.
The effects of these criticism is rarely analyzed by historians but is simply
taken for granted. The constant resuscitation of the critique of luxury
actually reflects not merely an inability to undermine its effect of exclusivity but indeed the critique's paradoxical intensification of that effect
through the emphasis placed upon it. The privileged groups and classes
able to enjoy luxurious products interpret the critique as a form of envy
and only rarely are moved to a change of habit. (To this extent, campaigns directed at certain luxury goods or practices in the hope of changing public opinion tend to show they have in a sense been democratized
and are very widespread.[38])

---

[36] See David Turley, *The Culture of the English Anti-Slavery, 1780–1860* (London:
Routledge, 1991). An example from the Ottoman Empire: Ariel Salzmann, "The Age
of Tulips: Confluence and Conflict in Early Modern Consumer Culture, 1550–1730,"
in *Consumption Studies and the History of the Ottoman Empire, 1550–1922: An
Introduction*, ed. D. Quaetaert (Albany: State University of New York Press, 2000),
83–106. Japan: Sheldon Garon, "Japan's Post-war 'Consumer Revolution', or Striking
a 'Balance' between Consumption and Saving," in *Consuming Cultures, Global
Perspectives: Historical Trajectories, Transnational Exchanges*, ed. J. Brewer and
F. Trentman (Oxford and New York: Berg, 2006), 189–217, see p. 191.

[37] Christopher A. Bayly, "The Origins of Swadeshi (Home Industry): Cloth and Indian
Society, 1700–1930," in Appadurai, *Social Life of Things*, 285–321.

[38] On the critique of luxury see, among other writing, Rémy G. Saisselin, *The
Enlightenment against the Baroque: Economics and Aesthetics in the Eighteenth
Century* (Berkeley: University of California Press, 1992); Rainer Wirtz, "Kontroversen
über den Luxus im ausgehenden 18. Jahrhundert," *Jahrbuch für Wirtschaftsgeschichte*
1996, no. 1: 165–75; Sulevi Riukulehto, *The Concepts of Luxury and Waste in American
Radicalism, 1880–1929* (Helsinki: Finish Academy of Science and Letters, 1998); Astrid
Ackermann, "Die Sittlichkeit des Luxus," in *"Der Teutsche Merkur": Die erste deutsche Kulturzeitschrift?*, ed. A. Heinz (Heidelberg: Winter, 2003), 276–93; E. J. Clery, *The*

When states and rulers have moved to limit or suppress such enjoyment through laws and decrees, the main motivation was usually their own material – for the most part fiscal – interests, not a change of attitude by the citizens or subjects or concern for their welfare. For the most part the motive has been concern that the money spent on luxuries could deplete the taxpayers' means.[39]

A new valuation of objects or practices does not have to be grounded in a shift of social values, as we see in the shift of the symbolic meaning of having a servant or coachman/chauffeur. Where in the eighteenth and nineteenth century, this was a self-evident attribute of the nobility and of aspiring bourgeoisie, a normal element of a standard way of life, at the latest since the end of the Great War, with rising average wages it became a symbol of luxury.[40] In this case rising costs endowed possession of permanently employed domestic servants with that status, discourse thus here simply following socioeconomic development. In countries of the Global South from Latin America to East Asia, it is still normal for middle classes to have house personnel like drivers, cooks, and maids.

In general, then, when a good lost its luxury status, this was less often discursively grounded than a result of material changes. New manufacturing techniques and the accompanying loss of exclusivity profaned many luxury goods and democratized their ownership. This is especially evident with some dyes – carmine from lice and crimson from snails – whose use in clothing had been a sign of exclusivity and distinction for centuries – something changed by the German chemical industry's development of synthetic

Feminization Debate in Eighteenth-Century England: Literature, Commerce and Luxury (Basingstoke, UK: Palgrave Macmillan, 2004); Till Wahnbaeck, *Luxury and Public Happiness: Political Economy in the Italian Enlightenment* (Oxford: Clarendon Press, 2004); Matthew Hilton, "The Legacy of Luxury: Moralities of Consumption since the 18th Century," *Journal of Consumer Culture* 4 (2004): 101–23; Jeremy Jennings, "The Debate about Luxury in Eighteenth- and Nineteenth-Century French Political Thought," *Journal of the History of Ideas* 68 (2007): 79–105.

[39] See Benno König, *Luxusverbote im Fürstbistum Münster* (Frankfurt: Klostermann, 1999), 225–9. In China and Japan, rich people did their best not to draw the attention of those in power through an ostentatious way of living. Wealth was usually kept hidden. See Jürgen Osterhammel, *Die Verwandlung der Welt: Eine Geschichte des 19. Jahrhunderts* (Munich: Beck, 2009), 328–30.

[40] Having dark-skinned personnel had long been considered an especially exotic symbol of luxury and status as had been the possession of domestic slaves. See Heather J. Sharkey, "Luxury, Status, and the Importance of Slavery in the Nineteenth- and Early-Twentieth-Century Northern Sudan," *Northeast African Studies* 1 (1994): 187–206. Werner Sombart's distinction between quantitative and qualitative luxury should be noted here. His example for the former type is having a hundred menials where one

colors that could be cheaply produced on a mass scale.[41] Other goods experienced the same process: soap in the 1860s and glass after the invention of artificial soda. Here the sinking prices could result from either technological progress or increasing competition, especially with cash crops like coffee, cocoa, and cane sugar.[42] But in the latter case of cane sugar, the lower prices for European and American consumers were usually purchased by exploitation of workers in other regions of the world.[43] The artificially low production costs tied to slavery and other forms of unfree labor, together with policies of massively beating down daily wages, have been the shadow side of the democratization of consumption – and of the cheapening of former luxury goods in colonial and postcolonial societies.[44] This dimension of the development of European and North American material culture and consumer history has often been omitted or marginalized in discussion of luxury.[45] When considered from the perspective of global history, the connections at work here become apparent.

The question of who displays luxury and in what situations is central to our theme. For to a great degree, whether or not a good could stand out positively as a luxury within a given social circle depended on each individual situation. The borderline between material and stylistic attributes of clothing and jewelry considered socially necessary, on the one hand, and a movement from such attributes to an exclusive realm, on the other hand, was often fluctuating. For many individuals, at court or

would do; the latter type involves refinement and the use of better goods. (See Sombart, *Der moderne Kapitalismus*, 719.)

[41] See Alexander Engel, *Farben der Globalisierung: Die Entstehung moderner Märkte für Farbstoffe 1500–1800* (Frankfurt: Campus, 2009).

[42] On coffee: John Talbot, "The Struggle for Control of a Commodity Chain: Instant Coffee from Latin America," *Latin American Research Review* 32, no. 2 (1997): 117–35; Mark Pendergrast, *Uncommon Grounds: The History of Coffee and How It Changed Our World* (New York: Basic Books, 1999); William Clarence-Smith and Steven Topik, eds., *The Global Coffee Economy in Africa, Asia and Latin America, 1500–1989* (Cambridge and New York: Cambridge University Press, 2003); John Griffith, *Tea: The Drink That Changed the World* (London: Andre Deutsch, 2007). On cocoa: Andrea Franc, *Wie die Schweiz zur Schokolade kam: Der Kakaohandel der Basler Handelsgesellschaft mit der Kolonie Goldküste, 1893–1960* (Basel: Schwabe, 2008). On sugar: Sidney Mintz, *Sweetness and Power: The Place of Sugar in Modern History* (New York: Viking, 1985); Ulbe Bosma, Juan Gusti, and Roger Knight, eds., *Sugarlandia Revisited: Sugar and Colonialism in Asia and in the Americas, 1800–1940* (New York: Berghahn, 2007).

[43] See James Walvin, *Fruits of Empire: Exotic Produce and British Taste, 1660–1800* (New York: New York University Press, 1997).

[44] See Topik et al., *From Silver to Cocaine.*

[45] See the critique of an Austrian exhibition on luxury goods (organized by Roman Sandgruber): Werner Zips, "Reise ins Schlaraffenland: Eine Ausstellungskritik," *Österreichische Zeitschrift für Geschichtswissenschaften* 5 (1994), 433–40.

on social occasions a stylistically self-assured presentation was meant to express affiliation with a specific hierarchal group rather than to stand out from it. Many members of the social strata involved lost a sense that luxury goods and practices counted among the firm elements of elite convention. The memoirs of Saint Simon and the (often invented) anecdotes of Marie Antoinette offer drastic examples of this, but the history of glass beads in East Africa does as well.[46]

The impact of a luxury object as a status symbol is situatively endangered when, for example, two women at court or two film divas in Hollywood or Bollywood encounter each other in the same dress. In such episodes, the symbolic effect of a piece of clothing, however exquisite, is destroyed. For this reason, colonial rulers were usually not very enthusiastic about colonized Indians or Africans appropriating certain items of clothing and using them as status symbols. A similar effect was brought about when certain status symbols and practices were read in a completely different way than intended – a misunderstanding especially manifest in initial transcultural encounters. The more the actors knew of each other, the less probable the chances of such mistaken readings. Many customs and habitual styles can have a downright ridiculous effect when transferred into a very different cultural context.

What can especially and enduringly ruin the pleasure socially privileged people take at luxury goods is their purchase and demonstrative display by those who are hierarchically subordinate. When Fouquet, the French finance minister, met still youthful Louis XIV in the minister's own castle of Vaux le Vicomte, in the process demonstrating a luxury going far beyond that of the Louvre, he incurred the permanent anger of the young monarch, thus sealing his eventual downfall. Such breaches with hierarchal expectations were by no means rare in the early modern period. They emerged not only at court, but also in the cities. In their colonies neither the Spaniards nor the English liked it when their colonial subjects started to wear European dress because they felt that this

---

[46] Louis Rouvroy de Saint-Simon, *Mémoires*, 43 vols. (written appr. 1739–50), (Paris: Hachette, 1879–1930); Emmanuel Le Roy Ladurie, *Saint-Simon ou le Système de la Cour* (Paris: Fayard, 1997); Vivian R. Gruder, "The Question of Marie-Antoinette: The Queen and the Public Opinion before the Revolution," *French History* 16 (2002): 269–98; Caroline Weber, *Queen of Fashion: What Marie Antoinette Wore to the Revolution* (New York: H. Holt, 2006); Jeremy Prestholdt, "On the Global Repercussion of East African Consumerism," *American History Review* 109, no. 3 (2004): 755–81.

would endanger their authority.[47] The exactly regulated dress code of estate-centered society was meant to both prevent excesses of luxury and fix the status quo. In the face of this basically conservative intent, almost everywhere transgressions were on the agenda.[48]

CONSTRUCTION OF THE VOLUME

Global history is the history of interconnection and divergence. This volume shows how people from different regions of the world developed their own ways of handling and dealing with luxury. The theme of luxury thus offers new insights regarding how the divergence of material cultures contributed to bring the world together. Without the different regimes of value that societies from around the world attached to things and practices the global connections could not have functioned. This topic is more suited than others to illustrate this fundamental assumption, firstly, because the attribute of things and practices to be a luxury most obviously depended on its social context and could vary a great deal from one context to another. Secondly, the status of these practices was more debated than the production, trade, and consumption of any other group of commodities. There are few themes in economic history where the relevance of divergent cultures becomes more visible.

The organizational structure of this book reaffirms our commitment to write a decentered, global history of luxury. This book has an exploratory character, staking no claim to offering a comprehensive survey. But in considering foundational questions with the help of case studies, it intends to mark out a space for more intensive scrutiny of luxury as a historical phenomenon. The cases have been carefully chosen from different parts of the globe and different cultural backgrounds, rather than further collecting studies on European luxury consumption or revisiting contemporary luxury debates.

[47] Bernard Cohn, "Cloth, Clothes, and Colonialism: India in the Nineteenth Century," in *Consumption: Critical Concepts in the Social Sciences*, ed. D. Miller (London and New York: Routledge, 2001), 405–30.

[48] See, e.g., Michael Frank, "Verbotener Luxus oder Was hat der Kaffee in der Mühle zu suchen? Aufwandsordnungen und deren Umsetzung in der Grafschaft Lippe, 1680–1800," in *Kontinuität und Umbruch in Lippe: Sozialpolitische Verhältnisse zwischen Aufklärung u. Restauration 1750–1820*, ed. Johannes Arndt and Peter Nitschke (Detmold: Landesverband Lippe, 1994), 145–64. A non-European example: Erhard Rosner, "Luxusgesetze in China unter der Mandschu Dynastie, 1644–1911," *Saeculum* 25 (1974): 325–37.

The first principle was to choose luxury commodities with very different material characteristics, in order to illustrate how and to which extent the material features shaped their history. The chapter by Kim Siebenhüner on jewelry, by Karin Hofmeester on the history of diamonds, and by Bernd-Stefan Grewe on the role of gold in India focus on very durable luxury commodities. Here the durability enables us to follow their social life (their biography) and to better understand the relevance of the social context, stones or jewelry passing from one to another sometimes without being transformed physically.

Manufactured commodities like Chinese porcelain in Anne Gerritsen's contribution, cotton textiles studied by Giorgio Riello and Sylvia Ruschak, and Venetian glass beads to trade in East Africa in Karin Pallaver's chapter stimulated very different reaction. The cases of porcelain and glass beads illustrate how essential the material attributes of these commodities were. Although the raw materials were available in other places too, the skills of the producers made them unique and limited the output, thus making them rare enough to be exclusive – first in Imperial China and later around the globe. Many European mercantile projects tried to produce porcelain, but few were able to compete with the Chinese who asserted their share of the market. But it also illustrates how intense the network of porcelain trade worked, if European tastes influenced the decoration patterns in Jingdezhen. The lack of technical skills made glass beads a luxury and a marketable means of exchange for East Africans, especially for the caravan traders to buy slaves and ivory and to pay for supplies and porters. Surprisingly enough, this technological disadvantage did not work exclusively for the benefit of the Europeans. Cotton textiles show a different development: they were sold in a broad variety of qualities and colors with different prints and patterns. Both chapters on textiles show how in very different social contexts some of these fabrics became luxuries and conserved this status for long periods of time while others, often similar products, were no longer recognized to be luxurious. They lost their status as luxury and became some of the first global commodities. At some point in both developments, the material qualities became less important than fashion – which highlights again the relevance of local cultures for the transformation of global economic relations. These cultural forces often made luxury fragile.

The third group of luxuries is materially different because these were linked to animals. The chapters of Martha Chaiklin on tortoiseshell in Japan and of Jonas Kranzer on the commodity chain of ivory illustrate how these animal materials could be used for different purposes; but because they could not be reproduced in unlimited quantities they remained a luxury. Interestingly both cases enforce the thesis of fragility of luxury, once plastics became available that substituted the formerly rare animal materials. Thus the objects that had been made of tortoise-shell and ivory became consumer goods. Both stories illustrate that these developments were not exclusively due to material changes, but merely to changes in value systems. The protection of elephants and other char-ismatic animals also played a major role in the restrictions that were put on safari hunting in Africa, as shows the chapter by Bernhard Gissibl. Conservation movements did not only preserve the surviving of rare mammals, but also the exclusive character of big-game hunting. From colonialism to the postcolonial period, big-game hunting persisted as a highly ritualized hunting of wild animals for the rich.

Unlike most traditional studies on luxury consumption, this book has a broad geographical and chronological scope. Ours is not a history centered on the Atlantic and on European dominance. Although we do not deny the strong European influence in many regions of the world and the existing power arrangements, especially from the late nineteenth century onward. We deal with people outside Europe and from non-European societies and try to see the global history from their perspective. We prefer to study diamond workers and rural marriages in India, Chinese manu-facturers, East African chiefs and hunters, female Japanese, or African consumers in order to understand how their participation in producing, trading, and enjoying luxuries shaped the connections between different cultural spheres.

Furthermore, we do not limit our analyses to the early modern period, as most other books on luxury do, but we put a stronger emphasis on the nineteenth and twentieth century. The extensive neglect of luxury in the late nineteenth and twentieth century by historians is due to the fact that this trade lost much of its former importance during the rev-olution in transportation. In early modern times, transportation costs were often much too high to make far-distance trade with other goods than luxuries profitable. Railways, steamships, the Suez Canal, and the Panama Canal revolutionized transportation and had a major impact on global trade. The lower costs now fostered mass production and trade with other commodities all around the globe. Other goods became economically more interesting and changed the relative importance of luxuries. While losing some of their former relevance, the global net-works around luxury commodities did not vanish, but rather expanded.

Trade with luxuries lost importance not in absolute numbers; but what had changed was its economic importance in comparison to other commodities.

The geographic and thematic choice of our case studies is not arbitrary; there are many links and interconnections between the chapters that should make comparisons possible and parallels visible. The three chapters on India complete each other with their focus; Siebenhüner's and Grewe's studies of gift exchanges in the Mughal and the postcolonial period both question whether objects can be essential luxury goods or whether this status depends less on the material character, but more on the social situation in which they played a role. The theme of jewelry is then completed with Hofmeester's closer look on the history of production and marketing. Again in Riello's, Ruschak's, and Gerritsen's analyses of cottons and porcelain and in Pallaver's analysis of the glass beads, the global interconnections already become obvious in the production process. It is surprising to which extent the tastes of remote consumers from Africa or Europe influenced the manufacturing in Venice, Jingdezhen, and Bombay, respectively. The trade with ivory from East Africa (Kranzer) was not only linked to the history of big-game hunting (Gissibl) and to the history of glass beads (Pallaver) – the most important means of exchange to get ivory for bangles in India and piano keyboards in Europe and the United States – but it also showed significant parallels with the history of tortoiseshell in Japan (Chaiklin).

In this book, we do not want to give the usual story of luxuries from exotic places in Africa or Asia that eventually were consumed by Europeans or Americans, but we like to offer a different perspective. Taking the agency of people in other areas of the world more seriously, we asked how these people shaped the global history of luxury in their own way, how they acted not only as producers of luxury commodities, but also how they contributed to the trade and how they developed their own, often completely independent, tastes and practices of luxury. We assume that the divergence of the material cultures was of vital importance to the functioning of global economic interaction. The global history of luxury was never a one-way street, but the global connections have to be studied in two directions.

1

Precious things in motion: Luxury and the circulation of jewels in Mughal India

Kim Siebenhüner

In May 1739, one of the largest Indian diamonds, the Koh-i-Noor or Mountain of Light, changed hands.[1] A few months before, the Persian ruler Nādir S͟hāh (ruled 1736–47) had invaded northern India.[2] His march into the country took place at a time when the empire was disintegrating politically, marked by the Mughal ruler's diminished power and by financial crisis.[3] Following a decisive battle at Karnal in February 1739, Muḥammad S͟hāh (ruled 1719–48) was neither politically nor militarily in a position to defy the Persian shah and his troops. He was forced to accept payment of an astronomically high tribute and watch Nādir S͟hāh enter Delhi, declare himself supreme ruler, and take over the palace and treasury keys.[4] In leaving

[1] This chapter was translated from the German by Joel Golb. On the history of the Koh-i-Noor see Ian Balfour, *Famous Diamonds* (London: Christie's, 2000); Abdul Aziz, *The Imperial Treasury of the Indian Mughuls* (Lahore: Aziz, 1942), 182–250; Valentine Ball, Appendix I, "The Great Mogul's Diamond and the True History of the Koh-i-Nūr," in Jean-Baptiste Tavernier, *Travels in India by Jean-Baptiste Tavernier, Baron of Aubonne*, ed., trans., and annot. William Crooke and Valentine Ball, 2 vols. (1925; New Delhi: Oriental Books Reprint Corp, 1977), 2: 331–48. The best account until now has been offered by Arndt Mersmann, "'Diamonds Are Forever' – Appropriations of the Koh-i-Noor," *Journal for the Study of British Cultures* 8, no. 2 (2001): 175–91.

[2] The orthography of all Persian names and expressions follows the system of the *Encyclopaedia of Islam*, 2nd ed. Exceptions are proper names that are commonplace in their simplified form in the English-speaking world, e.g., "Mughal" and the rulers' names Bābur, Humayun, Akbar, Jahangir, Shah Jahan, and Aurangzeb. In these cases, I follow the orthography used in the *Encyclopedia Britannica Online*. I would here like to extend special thanks to Andreas Bolleter, who carefully reviewed and unified my spelling of Persian names and expressions; I am responsible for any remaining errors.

[3] Muzaffar Alam, *The Crisis of the Empire in Mughal North India: Awadh and the Punjab, 1707–1748* (Delhi: Oxford University Press, 1986).

[4] William Irvine, *Later Mughals: Edited and Augmented with the History of Nadir Shah's Invasion by Jadunath Sarkar*, 2 vols. (bound together) (1921–2; repr., Delhi: Oriental

Delhi, Nādir Shāh granted Muḥammad Shāh his life and let him keep his ruler's title.[5] But alongside hundreds of millions of rupees; precious chattels; and elephants, horses, and camels, the Persian conqueror took away a large portion of the Mughal's magnificent collection of jewels, accumulated over eight generations – one of these pieces was the Koh-i-Noor.[6]

The diamond's transfer marked the continuation of a long history that would reach its end in the Tower of London. When Nādir Shāh died in 1747 as the result of an attack, his treasures were plundered. The Koh-i-Noor fell to Nādir Shāh's grandson, who in 1751 gave it as a gift to Aḥmad Shāh Durrānī, ruler of Kabul, as thanks for his support in the struggle over succession to the throne. In 1813, the stone thus ended up in the hands of one of Aḥmad Shāh Durrānī's successors, the Sikh ruler of Punjab, Ranjit Singh (ruled 1801–39).[7]

When, in March 1849, Great Britain's East India Company annexed the Punjab, which had been the last obstacle to British colonial rule over India,[8] the diamond was owned by Dalīp Singh, Punjab's last ruler. The British annexation of the Sikh state was sealed by the Treaty of Lahore, which contained a passage demanding the handing over of the Koh-i-Noor to the British. In a seemingly legal manner that covered an act of pillage, shortly afterward, in July 1850, the stone was duly transferred to the possession of Queen Victoria.[9] This physical transfer was accompanied by a sweeping process of appropriation and fresh interpretation. Already a few months after its arrival in England, the diamond was presented at the Great Exhibition in London in 1851.[10] The Koh-i-Noor was incorporated into the emerging urbane, industrialized, Western consumer world, while in fact

---

Books Reprint Corp, 1971), 330–64. Muḥammad Shāh was obliged to pay a tribute of two hundred million rupees. See ibid., 357.

[5] On the events see Irvine, *Later Mughals*, 2: 330–79.

[6] James Fraser, *The History of Nadir Shah, Formerly Called Thamas Kuli Khan, the Present Emperor of Persia: To Which Is Prefix'd a Short History of the Moghol Emperors* (London: A. Millar, 1742), 220–1; Irvine, *Later Mughals*, 371; Balfour, *Diamonds*, 158.

[7] Balfour, *Diamonds*, 165-7.

[8] On the history of the events see Henry H. Dodwell, ed., *British India, 1497–1858* (Cambridge: Cambridge University Press, 1929), 539–57; Christopher Alan Bayly, *Indian Society and the Making of the British Empire* (Cambridge: Cambridge University Press, 1988), 126–8.

[9] Balfour, *Diamonds*, 25; Susan Stronge, "The Myth of the Timur Ruby," *Jewellery Studies* 7 (1996): 8; Mersmann, "Appropriations of the Koh-i-Noor," 178.

[10] Mersmann, "Appropriations of the Koh-i-Noor," 184; on the Great Exhibition, see id., *"A True Test and a Living Picture": Repräsentationen der Londoner Weltausstellung von 1851* (Trier: WVT Wissenschaftlicher Verlag, 2001); Thomas Richards, *The Commodity Culture of Victorian England: Advertising and Spectacle, 1851–1914* (Stanford, CA: Stanford University Press, 1990), 3–5, 17–72.

being anything but a commodity: for centuries it had been in the possession of Indian and Central Asian rulers and represented their power. Through the diamond's placement in the exposition's Indian Court, new meanings were now being inscribed onto its body. This venue was meant, in fact, to represent British colonial rule over India, and to convey an Orientalist vision of the subcontinent as a subjected yet profitable, and in any case radically different, culture.[11] In this context, the Koh-i-Noor was to be perceived above all as a symbol of Oriental despotism and the Oriental economy – a glorious but largely illegitimate form of rule and a premodern economy located outside the realm of democratic mass consumption.[12]

This interpretation did not last long; following the exposition the diamond wandered back to the royal house. Newly cut, in 1853 it was set in one of the queen's tiaras.[13] As a crown jewel, the Koh-i-Noor now once again stood for rule over an empire. But for the first time, this involved a Western colonial power.[14]

The history of the Koh-i-Noor makes clear that precious stones were global goods. For a long time diamonds were found exclusively on the Indian subcontinent, with deposits being discovered in Brazil in 1725 and in South Africa in the 1860s.[15] Other valuable stones were also mainly

---

[11] Lara Kriegel, "Narrating the Subcontinent in 1851: India at the Crystal Palace," in *The Great Exhibition of 1851 – New Interdisciplinary Essays*, ed. Louise Purbrick (Manchester, UK: Manchester University Press, 2001), 146–78; on the Koh-i-Noor in the Indian court see the commentary on the paintings in the court by Joseph Nash in the Victoria and Albert Museum (henceforth VAM): "The Indian Court," VAM, http://collections.vam.ac.uk/item/O25439/the-indian-court-print-nash-joseph   (accessed November 7, 2014), as well as Mersmann, "Appropriations of the Koh-i-Noor," 180–1; on the "imperial display" at the Great Exhibition and following exhibitions see Paul Greenhalgh, *Ephemeral Vistas: The "Expositions Universelles," Great Exhibitions and World's Fairs, 1851–1939* (Manchester, UK: Manchester University Press, 1988), 52–64.

[12] Mersmann, "Appropriations of the Koh-i-Noor," 180–2.

[13] Ibid., 186; Herbert Tillander, *Diamond Cuts in Historic Jewellery 1381–1910* (London: Art Books International, 1995), 149–50.

[14] The stone would be reset a number of times; at present it is in a platinum crown made in 1937 for Queen Elizabeth, the mother of the present British queen, and is on display in the Tower of London. See Balfour, *Diamonds*, 171–2. Since the independence of India and Pakistan in 1947, the Koh-i-Noor has been an object of diplomatic controversy. See Mersmann, "Appropriations of the Koh-i-Noor," 188–9; Seema Alavi, "The Koh-i-Noor reflects Our Multifaceted Past," *Indian Express*, June 30, 2000, www.indianexpress.com/Storyold/154905 (accessed December 12, 2012).

[15] On the Brazilian-European diamond trade see Harry Bernstein, *The Brazilian Diamond in Contracts, Contraband and Capital* (Lanham, MD: University Press of America, 1986); on the discovery of the South African deposits see Godehard Lenzen, *Produktions- und Handelsgeschichte des Diamanten: Zeitlich geordnete Beiträge unter besonderer Berücksichtigung der Preisbildung und der Konzentrationsbestrebungen der Urproduktion* (Berlin: Duncker and Humblot, 1966), 171–2.

stored outside Europe in the early modern period, including emeralds on the African coast of the Red Sea and in Colombia;[16] rubies in Arakan and Pegu (present-day Myanmar);[17] and sapphires in Sri Lanka, on the Malabar Coast, and in the vicinity of Vijayanagara.[18] For the Europeans, trade with these goods was an important spur to opening new Indian Ocean markets.[19] Starting around 1500, through a network of Jewish and Armenian traders, European East India societies, smaller firms, and private customers, a growing number of diamonds and other precious stones reached Europe. The itinerary of these stones from the mines to European consumers reveals the complexity of the commercial paths involved; what was required to purchase, ship, smuggle, and then sell, for instance, a diamond; and how global relationships grew denser through commercial exchange in the early modern period.[20]

[16] Duarte Barbosa, *The Book of Duarte Barbosa, an Account of the Countries Bordering on the Indian Ocean*, trans., ed., and annot. Mansel Longworth Dames, Vol. 2 (1918; Nendeln: Kraus, 1967), 225–6n2; Garcia da Orta, *Colloquies on the Simples and Drugs of India*, trans. with an introduction and index by Sir Clements Markham, ed. and annot. the Conde de Ficalho (London: Henry Sotheran and Co, 1979), 359; Tavernier, *Travels*, 2: 81–2; John Huyghen van Linschoten, *The Voyage of John Huyghen van Linschoten to the East Indies*, ed. Arthur Coke Burnell and Pieter Anton Tiele, 2 vols. (1885; repr., New Delhi: Asian Educational Services, 1988), 2: 140; E. Allan Jobbins, "Sources of Gemstones in the Renaissance," in *Princely Magnificence: Court Jewels of the Renaissance, 1500–1630: 15th October–1st February 1981* (London: Debrett's Peerage, 1980), 16.

[17] Ludovico de Varthema, *Reisen im Orient*, ed. Folker Reichert (Sigmaringen: Thorbecke, 1996), 211; Barbosa, *Book of Duarte Barbosa*, vol. 2: 160, 217–19; Cesare Federici and Gasparo Balbi, *Viaggi di Cesare Federici e Gasparo Balbi alle Indie orientali*, ed. Olga Pinto (Rome: Istituto poligrafico dello stato, 1962), 54–5, 227.

[18] Barbosa, *Book of Duarte Barbosa*, 2: 116, 222–3; Varthema, *Reisen im Orient*, 192–4; da Orta, *Colloquies*, 354; Linschoten, *Voyages*, 1: 80.

[19] Alvaro Velho, *A Journal of the First Voyage of Vasco da Gama, 1497–1499*, trans. and ed. with notes, an introduction and appendices by Ernst Georg Ravenstein (1898; repr., New Delhi: Asian Educational Services, 1998), 48–9, 69–70, 76.

[20] On the Indian-European diamond and jewelry trade see Tapan Raychaudhuri, *Jan Company in Coromandel 1605–1690: A Study in the Interrelations of European Commerce and Traditional Economies* (Gravenhage: Nijhoff, 1962); James C. Boyajian, *Portuguese Trade in Asia under the Habsburgs, 1580–1640* (Baltimore: Johns Hopkins University Press, 1993); João Teles e Cunha, "Hunting the Riches: Goa's Gem Trade in the Early Modern Age," in *The Portuguese, Indian Ocean and European Bridgeheads 1500–1800: Festschrift in Honour of Prof. K. S. Mathew*, ed. Pius Malekandathil and Jamal Mohammed (Tellicherry: Institute for Research in Social Sciences and Humanities of MESHAR, 2001), 269–304; Soren Mentz, *The English Gentleman Merchant at Work: Madras and the City of London 1660–1740* (Copenhagen: Museum Tusculanum Press, University of Copenhagen, 2005); Francesca Trivellato, *The Familiarity of Strangers: The Sephardic Diaspora, Livorno, and Cross-cultural Trade in the Early Modern Period* (New Haven, CT: Yale University Press, 2009), esp. ch. 9 and 10; Kim Siebenhüner,

At the same time, the history of the Koh-i-Noor shows that the growing global relationships were not only – indeed were perhaps not primarily – of a commercial nature. The jewel did not arrive in Europe at the behest of merchants but rather of politicians and colonial masters. In the course of its history it was neither purchased nor sold; no negotiations were held concerning a price. Instead it changed owners through gift exchange and plunder. Aside from the intermezzo at the London exposition, the diamond did not circulate as a commodity but as a gift, heirloom, trophy, or insignia of rule.

In other words, a "commodity chain" approach to the diamond's history could hardly do it justice. Such an approach is aimed at examining the complex commercial itineraries of goods and the political-social conditions in which these itineraries are situated, thus making visible their framework of transnational and cross-cultural interrelationships.[21] But it tends to reduce things to commodities and to discover a linearity in commodity chains that obscures the confused, convoluted paths marked out by the history of objects.

Many precious stones wandered, not through the hand of early modern trading agents, but through those of diplomats, travelers, and missionaries.[22] And many did not end up in Europe, but circulated on the subcontinent in cycles of commerce, an economy of pillage, gift exchange, and dynastic transfer. The history of the Koh-i-Noor until 1849 is an example of this.

This chapter considers the circulation of jewels in Mughal India.[23] A look at the peregrinations of these objects makes clear how closely

"Kostbare Güter globaler Herkunft: Der Juwelenhandel zwischen Indien und Europa," in *Kultureller Austausch: Bilanz und Perspektiven der Frühneuzeitforschung*, ed. Michael North (Cologne: Böhlau, 2009), 327–42; id., *Die Spur der Diamanten: Eine Sozial- und Kulturgeschichte der Juwelen in der Frühen Neuzeit* (Forthcoming: Cologne: Böhlau, 2016), ch. 4; and Chapter 2 by Karin Hofmeester in this volume.

[21] Steven Topik, Carlos Marichal, and Zephyr Frank, eds., *From Silver to Cocaine: Latin American Commodity Chains and the Building of the World Economy, 1500–2000* (Durham, NC: Duke University Press, 2006); Frank Taussig, *Principles of Economics*, Vol. 1 (New York: MacMillan, 1921), 15; Terence K. Hopkins and Immanuel Wallerstein, "Commodity Chains in the World-Economy Prior to 1800," *Review: A Journal of the Fernand Braudel Center for the Study of Economics, Historical Systems, and Civilizations* 10, no. 1 (1986): 157–70; Marcel van der Linden, "Commodity Chains: Some Introductory Thoughts," Keynote address for the workshop on "The History of Commodities and Commodity Chains," Konstanz, February 26–8, 2009, 1–15, esp. 2–3.

[22] Siebenhüner, *Spur der Diamanten*, ch. 4.

[23] For a conceptual approach to the circulation of objects see Hans Peter Hahn and Hadas Weiss, "Introduction: Biographies, Travels and Itineraries of Things," in *Mobility, Meaning and the Transformations of Things: Shifting Contexts of Material Culture through Time and Space*, ed. Hans Peter Hahn and Hadas Weiss (Oxford: Oxbow

the various utility values and interpretations of things were tied to their mobility. Moving from one to another context, changing geographical locus and owner, meant accepting different functions and ascriptions. Almost always, an exchange of precious things was connected to displacements or the new creation of symbolic and imaginative values.

A great deal of museological and historiographical work has focused on identifying and describing precious stones and jewelry from Mughal India and placing the objects in various contexts.[24] But social historians and art historians have, for the most part, not adequately inquired into the extent the objects were part of social practices. I would here like to argue that jewels played a central role in Mughal India's political, economic, and cultural spheres of activity. This is best shown in the court context for two reasons. First, jewelry circulation is better documented on this level than on the level of ordinary people. Otherwise than is the case for Europe, we have scanty documentation for India offering insight into either urban or rural daily life. Second, demand for jewelry was especially strong among the Mughal elite. Especially because jewels played an important role in the exercise of rule, they were frequently exchanged.

Books, 2013), 1–14. Among the classics see Arjun Appadurai, ed., *The Social Life of Things: Commodities in Cultural Perspective* (Cambridge: Cambridge University Press, 1986); Krzysztof Pomian, "Für eine Geschichte der Semiophoren: Anmerkungen zu den Vasen aus den Medici-Sammlungen," in *Der Ursprung des Museums: Vom Sammeln* (Berlin: Wagenbach, 1993), 73–90; Nicholas Thomas, *Entangled Objects: Exchange, Material Culture and Colonialism in the Pacific* (Cambridge, MA: Harvard University Press, 1991). On the biographical approach see Igor Kopytoff, "The Cultural Biography of Things," in *The Social Life of Things: Commodities in Cultural Perspective*, ed. Arjun Appadurai (Cambridge: Cambridge University Press, 1986), 64–91; Chris Gosden and Yvonne Marshal, "The Cultural Biography of Objects," *World Archaeology* 31, no. 2 (1999): 169–78.

[24] See Anna Jackson, Amin Jaffer, and Christiane Lange, eds., *Maharaja: Pracht der indischen Fürstenhöfe*, catalog to the exhibition of the same name in the Victoria and Albert Museum, London and the Kunsthalle der Hypo-Kulturstiftung, Munich, October 10, 2009–May 24, 2010 (Munich: Hirmer, 2010); Manuel Keene, *Treasury of the World: Jewelled Arts of India in the Age of the Mughals*, catalog to the exhibition of the same name in the British Museum 2001 (2001; repr., London: Thames and Hudson, 2004); Oppi Untracht, *Traditional Jewelry of India* (1997; London: Thames and Hudson 2008); Momin Latif, *A Kaleidoscope of Colours: Indian Mughal Jewels from the 18th and 19th Centuries*, catalog to the exhibition of the same name in the Provinciaal Diamantmuseum, May 8–August 17, 1997 (Antwerp: Provinciaal Diamantmuseum, 1997); Susan Stronge, ed., *The Jewels of India* (Bombay: Marg Publications, 1995); Victoria and Albert Museum, *The Indian Heritage: Court Life and Arts under Mughal Rule*, Exhibit in VAM, April 21–August 22, 1982 (London: Victoria and Albert Museum, 1982); Aziz, *The Imperial Treasury of the Indian Mughuls*. A series of important essays were published in Vol. 10 of *Jewellery Studies*; see esp. Assadullah Souren Melikian-Chirvani, "The Jewelled Objects of Hindustan," *Jewellery Studies* 10 (2004): 9–32.

Consequently, the Mughal court is the locus where we can best study the circulation of jewels.

But before considering this empirical topic, we need to look at the concept of luxury. Jewels seem to possess all the characteristics of a luxury good. Nevertheless, in the Mughal Empire context the concept of luxury is less self-evident than might initially seem the case. In the end it makes sense to problematize the concept because a discussion of "luxury" in a global perspective cannot avoid the question of the concept's range of applicability and the presence of different semantic frameworks in different cultural contexts.

LUXURY IN THE MUGHAL CONTEXT

In many respects the contemporary concept of luxury is a result of European debates. Whether we like it or not, the controversies and semantic displacements of centuries resonate in the concept and are part of its problematics.[25]

Before the eighteenth century, in the European context the concept of luxury, whether expressed as English *luxury*, French *luxe*, German *Luxus*, and so forth, was above all associated, accurately from an etymological perspective, with Latin *luxus* and *luxuria*, both denoting not only luxury but excess and dissipation. In whatever Romance or Germanic language, the Latin-derived term thus had principally negative connotations.[26] This is apparent in, for example, the French-Latin dictionary of the Jesuit Philibert Monet (published 1636), which defines *luxe* as "excessive sumptuousness in clothes, furnishings, way of living, viands, and similar things," singling out *luxuria* as the word's etymological basis.[27] The term thus entered early modern discourses as morally loaded, in a matter applying, essentially, to all life's pleasures.[28] Not least of all countless

---

[25] The problematic nature of the European genealogies of research concepts has been closely examined over recent years in postcolonial studies and other disciplines. See, e.g., Talal Asad, *Genealogies of Religion: Discipline and Reasons of Power in Christianity and Islam* (Baltimore, MD: Johns Hopkins University Press, 1997); Almut Höfert, "Europa und der Nahe Osten: Der transkulturelle Vergleich in der Vormoderne und die Meistererzählungen über den Islam," *Historische Zeitschrift* 287 (2008): 561–97, esp. 566–9.

[26] Dorit Grugel-Pannier, *Luxus: Eine begriffs- und ideengeschichtliche Untersuchung unter besonderer Berücksichtigung von Bernard Mandeville* (Frankfurt: Peter Lang, 1996), 64–115; Ulrich Wyrwa, "Luxus und Konsum – begriffsgeschichtliche Aspekte," in *"Luxus und Konsum" – eine historische Annäherung*, ed. Reinhold Reith and Torsten Meyer (Münster: Waxmann, 2003), 47–59, esp. 48.

[27] Philibert Monet, *Invantaire des deus langues, françoise, et latine: Assorti des plus utiles curiositez de l'un, et de l'autre idiome* (Lyon: Obert, 1636), 522.

[28] Grugel-Pannier, *Luxus*, 64–115; Wyrwa, *Luxus und Konsum*, 48–9.

European sumptuary laws attempted – sometimes well into the eighteenth century – to limit and control a luxury perceived as sinful.[29] This did not, however, exclude an acceptance of luxury on a practical level: on the one hand, the outfitting of a bourgeois private citizen with clothing, jewelry, furnishings, and precious objects, corresponding to his estate, was not considered luxury but as honorable expenditure; on the other hand, display of splendor and sumptuousness was part of the self-understanding of early modern nobility.[30]

In the eighteenth century, this conception of luxury began to change. In the course of an intensification of global trade, new habits of consumption, and the spread of goods such as porcelain, Indian silk and cotton, coffee, and tea, a polyphonic debate now unfolded about luxury and its definition.[31] As Maxine Berg and others have shown, the concept was now tied to the positive effects of growing trade, the refinement of craftsmanship, and the cultivation of taste. For the first time, luxury was associated less with excess than with convenience and commerce promoting the common good.[32]

The history of the luxury concept raises immediate questions about its scope within a global perspective. Its range of meanings emerged from European debates taking place above all since the eighteenth century. But these limitations are not sufficiently mirrored in the research literature,

---

[29] Neithard Bulst, "Zum Problem städtischer und territorialer Kleider-, Aufwands- und Luxusgesetzgebung in Deutschland (13. – Mitte 16. Jahrhundert)," in *Renaissance du pouvoir legislatif et genese de l'etat,* ed. André Gouron and Albert Rigaudiere (Montpellier: Société d'Histoire du Droit et des Institutions des Anciens Pays de Droit Écrit, 1988), 29–57; Neithard Bulst, "Vom Luxusverbot zur Luxussteuer: Wirtschafts- und sozialgeschichtliche Aspekte von Luxus und Konsum in der Vormoderne," in *Der lange Weg in den Überfluss: Anfänge und Entwicklung der Konsumgesellschaft seit der Vormoderne,* ed. Michael Prinz (Paderborn: Schöningh, 2003), 47–60.

[30] Renata Ago, "Luxus," in *Enzyklopädie der Neuzeit,* Vol. 7 (Stuttgart: Metzler, 2008), cols. 1047–8.

[31] Maxine Berg and Elizabeth Eger, "The Rise and Fall of the Luxury Debates," in *Luxury in the 18th Century: Debates, Desires and Delectable Goods,* ed. Maxine Berg and Elizabeth Eger (Basingstoke, UK: Palgrave, 2003), 7–27; on the eighteenth-century debates see esp. the articles by Edward Hundert, Jan de Vries, and Michael McKeon in the same volume. On the expansion of the consumption of luxury goods see Maxine Berg, *Luxury and Pleasure in Eighteenth-Century Britain* (Oxford: Oxford University Press, 2005); id., "In Pursuit of Luxury: Global History and British Consumer Goods in the Eighteenth Century," *Past and Present* 182 (2004): 85–142; Linda Levy Peck, *Consuming Splendour: Society and Culture in Seventeenth-Century England* (Cambridge: Cambridge University Press, 2005).

[32] Berg and Eger, "The Rise and Fall," 7; Mark Häberlein and Christof Jeggle, eds., *Luxusgegenstände und Kunstwerke vom Mittelalter bis zur Gegenwart: Produktion – Handel – Formen der Aneignung* (Konstanz: UVK Verlagsgesellschaft, 2014).

luxury being used there as a general term. In this way a historically demarcated concept has become an analytic concept whose universal validity is, however, highly questionable. That the implicit meanings present in a concept of luxury stamped by the West are valid in societies adhering to different religious systems seems more a tacit assumption than the result of concrete research. The question thus needs to be posed of the extent to which different cultures actually perceived, defined, and practiced luxury.

In respect to Ming period China, Craig Clunas has discussed a literary genre that comments in great detail on the possession and treatment of exquisite things. Works such as the seventeenth century's "Treatise on Superfluous Things" offered the elite instruction on how to display taste in – and gain distinction through – the selection of calligraphy, vases, clothing, scent, and other expensive things.[33] A discussion of luxury can draw on such sources. In the Chinese context the acquisition of costly things thus seems aimed at connoisseurship and social distinction (an understanding of luxury relatively close to that of eighteenth-century Europe).[34]

Comparable research has not yet emerged for the Mughal Empire. We know next to nothing about whether the production and consumption of exquisite goods was perceived as "luxurious"; the extent to which the outlay for clothing, jewelry, room decoration, and architecture in the court and urban milieus was regulated; and whether there was a debate about luxury. Concerning court culture in early medieval India, Daud Ali has shown that tractates circulated prescribing in detail the outfitting of rulers and courtiers, for example what jewelry they were to wear and their use of insignias of rule (e.g., parasols, banners, crowns, and fans).[35] It is known that the Mughal rulers laid claim to a group of practices and objects as exclusive signs of rule, these emblems including thrones, standards and musical instruments,[36] and the prerogatives including hunting

---

[33] Craig Clunas, *Superfluous Things: Material Culture and Social Status in Early Modern China* (Cambridge: Polity Press, 1991).

[34] For a comparative discussion of conspicuous consumption in China, Japan, and Europe, see Peter Burke, "Res et verba: Conspicuous Consumption in the Early Modern World," in *Consumption and the World of Goods*, ed. John Brewer and Roy Porter (London and New York: Routledge, 1993), 148–61; Craig Clunas, "Things in between: Splendour and Excess in Ming China," in *The Oxford Handbook of the History of Consumption*, ed. Frank Trentmann (Oxford: Oxford University Press, 2012), 47–63.

[35] Daud Ali, *Courtly Culture and Political Life in Early Medieval India* (Cambridge: Cambridge University Press, 2004).

[36] See Abū 'l-Faẓl 'Allāmi, *The Ā'īn-i Akbarī*, trans. Henry Blochmann (Vol. 1), H. S. Jarrett (Vols. 2 and 3), ed. Douglas C. Philott, 3 vols. (Calcutta: Asiatic Society of Bengal, 1927–49), 1: 52–4 (Ā'īn 19).

tigers and lions;[37] and that texts such as the *Mīrzānāmas* described the seventeenth-century nobleman's ideal way of life, including his ownership and use of clothing, jewelry, and scent.[38] While it seems clear that explicit norms and values centered on the proper possession and use of precious things were accepted in the Mughal courtly society, we do not know whether the idea of luxury was part of the normative system. Already on the linguistic level, there are no simple correspondences to the word denoting luxury in the various European languages. In the Indo-Persian vocabulary, several terms cover some of its aspects, the plural of Persian *tajammul, tajammulāt* thus being translatable as "dressing, adorning one's person, dignity, retinue, pomp, parade, splendour, magnificence, furniture and conveniences," "movables, household furniture," and "articles of luxury."[39] The word *'aish*, by contrast, signifies "living, food, bread, pleasure, delight, luxury, gratification of the appetites, sensuality, sexual intercourse."[40] In the first case, luxury is connoted as corporeal decoration and accoutrement and the decoration and furnishing of one's house, and the effects these processes have; in the second case as satisfaction of physical needs. It is telling that neither term is associated with what we think of as luxury in the *Farhang-i Jahāngīrī*, one of the most important Persian dictionaries, written in the Mughal court at the start of the seventeenth century.[41] This underscores the need for close consideration of what terms were actually available at the time to denote luxury-linked phenomena and what terms can be productive for a debate over luxury in the Indo-Islamic context.[42]

[37] See Muhammad Azhar Ansari, *Social Life of the Mughal Emperors, 1526–1707* (Allahabad: Shanti Prakashan, 1974), 157; see also Mubarak Ali Khan, "The Court of the Great Mughuls: Based on Persian Sources" (PhD diss., Bochum, 1976), 26–8.

[38] Rosalind O'Hanlon, "Manliness and Imperial Service in Mughal North India," *Journal of the Economic and Social History of the Orient* 42, no. 1 (1999): 47–93; Jennifer Scarce, "A Splendid Harmony: Mughal Jewellery and Dress," *Jewellery Studies* 10 (2004): 33; Annemarie Schimmel, *Im Reich der Großmoguln: Geschichte, Kunst, Kultur* (Munich: Beck, 2000), 271–4.

[39] Francis Joseph Steingass, *A Comprehensive Persian-English Dictionary* (1892; repr., Beirut: Librairie du Liban, 1998), 283.

[40] Ibid., 876.

[41] Husayn Ibn Hasan Injū Shirāzī, *Farhang-i Jahāngīrī, 1608/1609*, 3 vols. (Mashhad: Dānishgāh-i Mashhad, 1972–5). On the author see Linda York Leach, *Mughal and Other Indian Paintings from the Chester Beatty Library*, 2 vols. (London: Scorpion Cavendish, 1995), 1: 321–4.

[42] The discussion has benefited from exchange and advice from colleagues. I especially thank Thomas Hayoz, who generously undertook research in the Farhang-i Jahāngīrī and in the dictionary of F. J. Steingass, without which I could not have begun to reflect on the terminological problem of luxury in Persian discourse of the time.

Given this research challenge, gaining an understanding of the phenomenon of luxury in the Mughal period by way of what we would consider luxury goods – goods marked by material value, rarity, foreign origin, skilled craftsmanship, and limited accessibility due to high acquisition costs and exclusive distribution networks – seems an inviting option. Such goods abounded in the Mughal court. For a start, the rulers' residences – both the mobile field camps and palaces – were characterized by the use of expensive materials. Inlays made of precious and semiprecious jewels decorated the white marble of Shah Jahan's private audience halls in Delhi and Agra.[43] Costly wall hangings and carpets decorated tents and palace architecture.[44] Rooms were perfumed with scents mixed from musk, amber, incense, and camphor,[45] and the court workshops were devoted to the steady production of costly clothing and bejeweled implements.[46] In addition, the Mughals possessed extensive collections of jewels that furnished European visitors with an impression of excessive plenitude. When Jahangir (ruled between 1605 and 1627) showed himself at the jharūka window on his departure from Ajmer to Mandu in 1616, the English ambassador Sir Thomas Roe observed that the wives standing next to him would have been visible in total darkness due to their being densely covered with sparkling diamonds.[47] Rulers such as Jahangir and Shah Jahan (ruled 1628–58) also collected large quantities of European rarities such as paintings, exquisite mirrors, and work in crystal.[48]

The Mughal court was thus undoubtedly a place in which luxury goods, in our sense, were produced, consumed, and exchanged in large quantities. But in acknowledging that fact, we have not solved

---

[43] On the iconography of the inlays, see Ebba Koch, *Mughal Art and Imperial Ideology: Collected Essays* (New Delhi: Oxford University Press, 2001).

[44] Many miniatures of the Padshāhnāma make this clear; see Milo Cleveland Beach, Ebba Koch, and Wheeler Thackston, ed., *King of the World: The Padshahnama: An Imperial Mughal Manuscript from the Royal Library, Windsor Castle* (London: Thames and Hudson, 1997).

[45] Abū 'l-Fazl, *The Ā'īn-i Akbarī*, 1: 78–93 (Ā'īn 30), here 78–9; Schimmel, *Im Reich der Großmoguln*, 250–1.

[46] François Bernier, *Travels in the Mogul Empire: A. D. 1656–1668: A Revised and Improved Edn. Based upon Irving Brock's Transl. by Archibald Constable, 1891* (Delhi: Chand, 1968), 258–9.

[47] Sir Thomas Roe, *The Embassy of Sir Thomas Roe to India, 1615–1619: As Narrated in His Journal and Correspondence*, ed. Sir William Foster (1926; repr., Jalandhar: Asian Publishers 1993), 283.

[48] Pedro Moura Carvalho, "'Rarities from Goa' at the Courts of Humayun, Akbar and Jahangir, 1530–1627," in *Goa and the Great Mughal*, ed. Jorge Flores and Nuno Vassallo e Silva (London: Scala, 2004), 98–115.

our conceptual Eurocentrism. A future debate about luxury will need to address this problem, inquiring more closely into both the semantic range of the luxury concept and practices of luxury on various regions of the world. Whether or not we can develop a notion of luxury from the Mughal sources remains an open question. An idea of luxury that while abstract is not *a priori* universalistic and takes account of global variations might be fruitfully applied in the context of the Mughal court. Research on European court culture has shown that conspicuous consumption at many courts (as it happens, not only in Europe) was closely connected to the use and exchange of costly goods.[49] This connection is also evident at the Mughal court, where the consumption of valuable things had many functions, from marking status to the regulation of domestic social relationships. While not telling us much about the perceptions of luxury, research on the consumer habits of Mughal court society might offer insight into the use of "luxurious" goods. But to speak of "luxury" in the Mughal context will remain problematic until the necessary research process has gotten underway. For this reason, I prefer to speak not of luxury but of precious things – a more neutral notion circumventing the previously described definitional problem while offering an accurate description of the objects concerned.

THE CIRCULATION OF GEMS AND JEWELS
IN MUGHAL INDIA

In the residencies of the Mughal rulers, extensive collections of gemstones, pieces of jewelry, and bejeweled objects were stored and collected, exchanged and transferred elsewhere. Many trajectories thus led to and intersected with the Mughal court, rendering it a shipping point for jewels (Map 1).

Some of the jewels reached the hands of the Mughal rulers along commercial routes. For example, during his India voyages of the 1650s and 1660s, the French jewelry dealer Jean-Baptiste Tavernier (1605–89) sold pearls, emeralds, and other gems that he had imported from Europe to

---

[49] Ulf Christian Ewert and Jan Hirschbiegel, "Nur Verschwendung? Zur sozialen Funktion der demonstrativen Zurschaustellung höfischen Güterverbrauchs," in *Luxus und Integration: Materielle Hofkultur Westeuropas vom 12. bis zum 18. Jahrhundert*, ed. Werner Paravicini (Munich: R. Oldenbourg Verlag, 2010), 104–21. See also Burke, *Res et verba*. On the concept of conspicuous consumption see Thorstein Veblen, *The Theory of the Leisure Class: An Economic Study of Institutions* (New York: The Macmillan Company, 1899).

Map of India with the outside borders
of the Mughal Empire and the borders
of independent kingdoms around 1600

MAP 1. India.
Source: Map drawn by Cambridge University Press.

Aurangzeb (ruled 1658–1707) and his uncle Shāyista Khān (died 1694).[50] But such sales by European traders very likely remained an exception, the trade in gems and jewels being dominated by native merchants. All sorts of precious things could be purchased at the bazaar of the palaces of Agra and Delhi. In August 1618, Jahangir thus recounted that "I walked through all the shops and bought gems, jeweled items, and every sort of thing I liked. I gave Mulla Asiri something from every shop. He got so much stuff he was unable to keep track of it all."[51] In addition, a "fancy bazaar" was set up regularly, with traders from all over the world offering their best wares.[52] Occasionally Jahangir also sent out agents to arrange planned purchases – in April 1613, for instance, he commissioned Muḥammad Ḥusayn Khān Čelebi, a court expert, to purchase turquoise in Persia and rarities in Istanbul.[53] Diamonds were also delivered to the Mughal rulers from mines located in their territories. In February 1616 Jahangir thus noted, in respect to a mine in the Bihar Province supervised by imperial agents, that "Day by day diamonds are found and brought to court. Recently a large diamond worth fifty thousand rupees was found. With a little labor it is probable that fine diamonds will enter the royal gem department."[54] A differentiated infrastructure was available for storing the treasures: diamonds, pearls, and gems entered a special treasury. A professional treasurer with a team of accountants and jewelers was responsible for classifying and storing the gems. In Akbar's period a dozen additional, specialized treasurers were responsible for gold, jewelry pieces, cash payments, gifts, and tributes.[55]

In fact, many jewels arrived at the court as gifts rather than commercially. It is a well-known fact in the historiography of the Mughal Empire that daily political life was stamped by gifts and countergifts.[56]

[50] Tavernier, *Travels*, 1: 245–6, 15–16. On Shāyista Khān see M. Athar Ali, *The Apparatus of Empire: Awards of Ranks, Offices and Titles to the Mughal Nobility, 1574–1658* (Delhi: Oxford University Press, 1985), here S104–S7343 (Mirzā Abū Ṭālib, Shāyista Khān); Beach et al., *The Padshahnama*, 234.

[51] Wheeler M. Thackston, ed., trans., and annot., *The Jahangirnama: Memoirs of Jahangir, Emperor of India* (New York: Oxford University Press, 1999), 273.

[52] Abū 'l-Faẓl, *Ā'īn-i Akbarī*, 2: 286–7 (Ā'īn 23); Peter Mundy, *The Travels of Peter Mundy in Europe and Asia, 1608–1667*, ed. Richard Carnac Temple, Vol. 2: Travels in Asia, 1628–1634 (1914; repr., Nendeln, Liechtenstein: Kraus Reprint, 1967), 238; Mubarak Ali Khan, *The Court of the Great Mughuls*, 84–5.

[53] Thackston, *Jahangirnama*, 143.

[54] Ibid., 188.

[55] See Abū 'l-Faẓl, *Ā'īn-i Akbarī*, 1: 14–16 (Ā'īn 2 and 3).

[56] Harbans Mukhia, *The Mughals of India* (Oxford: Blackwell, 2004), 100–6; Stewart Gordon, ed., *Robes of Honour: Khil'at in Pre-Colonial and Colonial India*

Every nobleman visiting the court was obliged to bring a gift for the ruler, who in turn rarely parted from an official or officer without bestowing a bejeweled dagger, sword, or costly robe of honor (Figure 3).

For example, when Khān-i Khānān, royal tutor of Jahangir and a high-ranking officer in the Deccan Campaign, arrived from Burhanpur in January 1608, he offered "two strings of pearl prayer beads and several rubies and emeralds" together with other precious things.[57] Shortly before – in December 1607 – Murtazā Khān, governor of the Gujarat Province, bestowed a ring with a single thirty-carat ruby; the gift greatly pleased Jahangir.[58]

Such gifts of jewelry were grounded in a complex economy of gift giving. At the time both Khān-i Khānān and Murtazā Khān were high-ranking Mughal Empire officials. But in an empire that since Akbar's days stretched from Bengal to Gujarat and from Kashmir to Deccan, they found themselves far away from the court, even if the court was mobile. Their visits and the accompanying reciprocal gift giving were thus important moments in consolidating rule. The gifts were a materialization of the social bonds between the ruler and the political elite. Where the ruler could display favor and delegate power through the gift of, say, a jewel-inlaid dagger, gifts from the political elite could demonstrate loyalty.

Although at first view it might not appear the case, these mechanisms of gift exchange were distinctly different from those at work in European courts. Because a jāgīr – a piece of land that ensured the holders' revenues – was neither hereditary nor permanent, nobles depended on the emperor's allocation of land throughout their lives. The assignment of a manṣab, too, was in the hands of the Pādishāh.[59] With this organization of land

---

(Oxford: Oxford University Press, 2003); Linda Komaroff, ed., *Gifts of the Sultan: The Arts of Giving at the Islamic Courts* (Los Angeles: County Museum of Art, 2011); Anthony Cutler, "Significant Gifts: Patterns of Exchange in Late Antique, Byzantine, and Early Islamic Diplomacy," *The Journal of Medieval and Early Modern Studies* 38, no. 1 (2008): 79–101; Siebenhüner, *Spur der Diamanten*, ch. 3; id., "Approaching Diplomatic and Courtly Gift-Giving in Europe and Mughal India: Shared Practices and Cultural Diversity," *The Medieval History Journal* 16, no. 2 (2013): 525–46.

57 Thackston, *Jahangirnama*, 96.
58 Ibid., 89.
59 On the Mughal rang system see W. H. Moreland, "Rank (manṣab) in the Mogul State Service, 1936," in *The Mughal State: 1526–1750*, ed. Muzaffar Alam and Sanjay Subrahmanyam (Delhi: Oxford University Press, 1998), 213–33; Percival Spear, "The Mughal 'Mansabdari' System," in *Elites in South Asia*, ed. Emund Leach and Soumyendra Nath Mukherjee (London: Cambridge University Press, 1970), 1–15; Shireen Moosvi, "Evolution of the Mansab System under Akbar until 1596–97," *Journal of the Royal*

FIGURE 3. A young man offers a jewel on a tray. The fine clothing and the long pearl necklace – usually worn only by a high manṣabdār – disclose the man's standing. His gesture points to the importance of gift-giving practices in the courtly context. Dārā S͟hukōh Album (India c. 1635).
Source: Miniature from the Dārā S͟hukōh Album, fol. 35v. Courtesy of the British Library.

and rang the Mughal elite was much more fluid than the European nobility. If nothing is gained by anyone as a matter of right but bestowed upon him as a royal favor, gift giving assumes a crucial role in the political organization of the empire. In order to preserve one's status, it was necessary to gain the emperor's favor.

For this reason, many occasions for gift exchange were ritualized. This was not only the case for court visits but also for birthdays for the ruler, the anniversary to ascension to the throne, the birth of a son or daughter, a military victory, or recovery from an illness.[60] The festival for the New Year, *nawrūz* (celebrated according to the Persian calendar), was one of the most important institutionalized occasions for the empire's political elite to assemble and offer gifts to the ruler: elephants, horses, camels, precious textiles and wood, European furniture, porcelain, hunting birds, and, again and again, precious stones, pearls, and jewelry of all kinds.[61]

Tellingly these gifts from the political elite to the ruler were designated as *pīshkash,* a term designating both a gift to a socially superior person and a payment of tribute. In both cases the reference is to a hierarchical relationship between giver and receiver, and the for us standard distinction between gift and tribute thus being absent. Nevertheless, *pīshkash* stood for different political and legal practices of exchange.[62] As indicated, the empire's amirs were expected to offer regular *pīshkash* in line with their rank; this was usually presented at the festival for the New Year. This was different from the *pīshkash* of subjected local princes, who were obligated, sometimes in writing, to offer annual gifts understood as what Irfan Habib has termed the "hallmark and substance of submission."[63] This form of *pīshkash* resembled a payment of tribute. Finally, a one-time special tribute could also be required at the moment of subjugation. In the following, I will more closely examine these three forms of exchange.

Asiatic Society of Great Britain and Ireland (1981): 173–85; Ali, *The Apparatus of Empire*, xi–xxiv; id., *The Mughal Nobility under Aurangzeb* (Delhi: Oxford University Press, 1997), esp. 38–73 (ch. 2); in general: John F. Richards, *The Mughal Empire* (Cambridge: Cambridge University Press, 1993).

[60] Ali, *Mughal Nobility*, 143.

[61] The New Year festivals between 1610 and 1616 can here serve as an example; see Thackston, *Jahangirnama*, 107, 121, 129, 157, 169.

[62] Ali, *Mughal Nobility*, 143–4; Siebenhüner, "Approaching Diplomatic and Courtly Gift-Giving," 538–41.

[63] Irfan Habib, *The Agrarian System of Mughal India, 1556–1707* (New Delhi: Oxford University Press, 2009), 224–5; Ali, *Mughal Nobility*, 143.

Starting at the end of the sixteenth century, the relation of the Great Mughal to the sultans of the Ahmadnagar, Bijapur, and Golconda became disputed. Under Akbar (ruled 1556–1605) the Mughal Empire had expanded from the Indus to the mouth of the Ganges and from the Himalayas to the northern edge of the Deccan. Although in 1601 portions of Ahmadnagar had been conquered and the Mughal rulers considered themselves as sovereign over the sultans of Bijapur and Golconda, both the titles of the latter and their coinage indicates that they continued to view themselves as independent rulers.[64] Given the victorious Mughal campaigns in Mewar and the southern advances of the Mughal troops, the Sultan of Bijapur, Ibrāhīm ʿĀdil S̲h̲āh II, (ruled 1580–1626), was forced to announce recognition of the Great Mughal's supreme power in 1617. He sent two emissaries to Burhanpur for K̲h̲urram, Jahangir's son and the commander of the Deccan campaign, declaring his loyalty and explaining he was delivering "suitable offerings of gems, jeweled utensils, elephants, and horses"[65] – this a direct payment for being spared military ravages to both land and populace, the jewels thus not being transferred as commodity or a gift but as a form of tribute that Finbarr Flood has aptly referred to as "institutionalized plunder": as the regulated handover of precious things in which "the victim plunders himself while saving his pride by representing such payments as gifts."[66] The sultans' tribute, offered in the context of direct military threat, differed from the annual tributes the Deccan sultans were later obliged to pay by treaty. Although ʿĀdil S̲h̲āh had conceded his dependence on the Mughal Empire in 1617, he did not show himself to be a loyal payer of tribute in the following years. When in 1628 K̲h̲urram succeeded his father as Shah Jahan, the Deccan was still an open project. Finally, following military pressure a formal treaty was arranged in 1635, with the sultans of Bijapur and Golconda again recognizing supreme rule of the Pādis̲h̲āh and agreeing to an annual tribute of, respectively, two million and six hundred thousand rupees.[67] Such a tribute could partially be satisfied in jewels, as we will see.

---

[64] Sanjay Subrahmanyam and Muzaffar Alam, "The Deccan Frontier and Mughal Expansion, ca. 1600: Contemporary Perspectives," *Journal of the Economic and Social History of the Orient* 47, no. 3 (2004): 357–89, esp. pp. 367–8; Sir Richard Burn, ed., *The Cambridge History of India*, Vol. 4: The Mughul Period (Cambridge: Cambridge University Press, 1937), 148, 165; Thackston, *Jahangirnama*, 216, 225–31.

[65] Thackston, *Jahangirnama*, 225.

[66] Finbarr B. Flood, *Objects of Translation: Material Culture and Medieval "Hindu-Muslim" Encounter* (Princeton, NJ: Princeton University Press, 2009), 127.

[67] See Henry Miers Elliot and John Dowson, eds., *The History of India as Told by Its Own Historians: The Muhammadan Period*, 7 vols. (1867–77; repr., Delhi: Low Price Pub.,

With the jewels handed by 'Ādil S͟hāh to K͟hurram in 1617, the story was not yet over, for K͟hurram gave at least a portion of the treasure to Jahangir. After successfully completing the Deccan Campaign, K͟hurram moved to the court in Mandu, where he was lavishly greeted (Figure 4).

Under the eyes of the assembled court society, as a sign of thanks Jahangir called his son over to him on the balustrade and embraced him:[68] an unusual gesture of favor, with even being placed in the throne's vicinity considered an honor.[69] Beyond this, K͟hurram's military services resulted in an extraordinary increase in honor and status. Jahangir elevated his son to the personal rank of 20'000 – a rank reserved for the highest male members of the imperial family – and gave him the title of Shahjahan.[70] In this manner a symbolic triumph supplemented his military success.

Like other of the empire's grandees, K͟hurram offered his father precious gifts in this reunion. In the ceremony, further relaying of the tribute hardly distinguished from K͟hurram's offering to his father. That included "a precious ruby that had been purchased for him [K͟hurram] in the port of Goa for two lacs [1 lac = a unit of 100,000] rupees." But it also included precious objects from 'Ādil S͟hāh's tribute: a sapphire weighing more than 130 carats estimated at one hundred thousand rupees by the court jewelers; a diamond of close to twenty-six carats worth forty thousand rupees; and a large emerald.[71]

The passing on of these jewels from K͟hurram to Jahangir was a symbolically highly loaded act. For alongside the monetary value of the objects, which, we should note, Jahangir documented in scrupulous detail, they were the material expression of the subjugation of a powerful empire. As emerging in the short section treating 1617–18, the history of the stones was propelled forward by military confrontation, new arrangements of power, and asymmetric relationships at the court. Where at the moment of subjugation the jewels stood for promises of loyalty by the ruler of Bijapur, at the moment of the exchange of gifts they embodied K͟hurram's homage to his father. With each such transfer, one layer of meaning after

1990), 7: 51, 57 ('Abd al-Ḥamīd Lāhūrī, Pādshāhnāma); Burns, *Cambridge History of India*, 4: 196–9; Richards, *Mughal Empire*, 138.

68 Thackston, *Jahangirnama*, 228.
69 Ebba Koch, "The Hierarchical Principles of Shah-Jahani Painting," in *Mughal Art*, ed. id., 133; Thackston, *Jahangirnama*, 229.
70 Thackston, *Jahangirnama*, 229.
71 Thackston, *Jahangirnama*, 231–2.

FIGURE 4. Jahangir receives K̲h̲urram after his victorious campaign on the Deccan. Mandu, Diwān-i ʿām, 10 October 1617.
Source: Padshahnama, fol. 48b, painted by Ramdas, ca. 1640. Courtesy of the Royal Library, Windsor Castle.

another became attached to the jewels. Hence one effect of circulation was an accrual of symbolic value.

Following the transfer to Jahangir, we lose the trace of the jewels of 'Ādil Sh̲āh. In any case, we do know from other, comparable episodes that the precious stones were carefully classified by color and weight and brought to the jewel treasury.[72] This marked a turning point in the stones' itinerary because it meant their withdrawal from the exchange cycle for an unspecified time. The *pīsh̲kash̲* now became an object of collection and treasury storage. Many especially important jewels were even supplied with an inscription, as in the case of a cherry-size ruby belonging to the ruler of Mewar, Amar Singh, which only a few years earlier had ended up with Jahangir, under similar circumstances as had the jewels of 'Ādil Sh̲āh. The engraved words indicated that the ruby had been given to Prince K̲hurram on the occasion of homage paid by Amar Singh.[73] Some of these engraved jewels are extant (Figure 5).

One 114-carat ruby, for example, is inscribed "Akbar 971" (= 1563/64), "Jahangir" (undated), and "Shah Jahan 1038" (= 1628/29).[74] Engraved in another precious stone are the names of the Timurid ruler Ulugh Beg, the Persian shah Abbas I, Jahangir, Shah Jahan, Aurangzeb, and the Afghan ruler Aḥmad Sh̲āh (1754/1755).[75] The inscriptions recorded the stone's transfer among the most powerful rulers in Persia, Central Asia, and India between the fifteenth and eighteenth centuries; they rendered the object into a repository of memory and the tradition of rule.[76] What was here being inscribed into the stone in the most literal sense was the transfer of power. Engraved precious stones thus became objects symbolically encapsulating genealogy, history, and power; they emerged as what sociologists have termed "identity goods" – artefacts preserving the history and identity of their owners.[77]

---

[72] See Abū 'l-Faẓl, *Ā'īn-i Akbarī*, 1: 14–16 (Ā'īn 2 and 3).

[73] Thackston, *Jahangirnama*, 174.

[74] Keene, *Treasury of the World*, 135, illus. and no. 12.2.

[75] Ibid., 135, illus. and no. 12.1. Further examples: ibid., 136–41.

[76] On the mnemonic function of precious objects for rulers and their retinue in the European context, see Karl-Heinz Spieß, "Materielle Hofkultur und ihre Erinnerungsfunktion im Mittelalter," in *Mittelalterliche Fürstenhöfe und ihre Erinnerungskulturen*, ed. Carola Fey, Steffen Krieb, and Werner Rösener (Göttingen: Vandenhoeck und Ruprecht, 2007), 167–84, 325–8.

[77] Mihaly Csikszentmihalyi and Eugene Rochberg-Halton, *Der Sinn der Dinge: Das Selbst und die Symbole des Wohnbereichs*, trans. Wilhelm Häberle (Munich: Psychologie Verlags Union, 1989), 48, 69–70; Tilmann Habermas, *Geliebte Objekte: Symbole und Instrumente der Identitätsbildung* (Frankfurt: Suhrkamp, 1996), esp. p. 383.

FIGURE 5. Inscribed royal spinel ("balas ruby"). Cut, drilled, and engraved.
Inscriptions: Ulugh Beg (before 1449); Shah Abbas I (dated 1617); Jahangir
(dated 1621); Shah Jahan (undated); Alamgir (1659–60); Ahmad Shah (dated
1754–5).
Courtesy of © The al-Sabah Collection, Dar al-Athar al-Islamiyyah, Kuwait,
LNS 1660J.

Despite their symbolic valence, that the jewels continued to be viewed
as an economic resource becomes clear in two more examples from 1648,
when the sultan of Golconda, ʿAbdullah Qutb S̲h̲āh (ruled 1626–72),
acquired a large diamond from his empire's mines. When Shah Jahan
learned of the find he ordered a forwarding of "the same to court, where
its estimated value would be taken into account as part of the two lakhs
of huns [200,000 huns = approx. 600,000 rupees], which was the stipu-
lated amount of his annual tribute."[78] Hence in this case the diamond was

---

[78] ʿInāyat Khān, *The Shah Jahan Nama of ʿInayat Khan: An Abridged History of the
Mughal Emperor Shah Jahan, Compiled by His Royal Librarian, The Nineteenth
Century Manuscript Translation of A. R. Fuller*, ed. and compl. Wayne Edison Begley
and Ziyaud-Din A. Desai (Delhi and Oxford: Oxford University Press, 1990), 404.

meant to be transferred as part of a fixed tribute and was treated as an equivalent of money. But this function receded soon after the diamond's arrival in Agra. Shah Jahan first had it cut open. After the processing, the originally 188 ratis (115 carats)[79] heavy raw diamond weighed 100 ratis (61 carats); it was a diamond of extraordinary purity and high quality whose value was estimated by the court jewelers at 150,000 rupees.[80] But unlike other gems of this quality, the diamond was not put into the imperial treasury. Instead, Shah Jahan vowed to bestow a religious gift on the diamond. He thus commissioned the court jewelers to set it alongside countless smaller gems in an amber candelabra. This resulted in a sumptuous object whose worth is estimated by the chroniclers at 250,000 rupees. Two confidants of Shah Jahan were then instructed to bring the object to the prophet's burial place in Medina as a charitable present.[81]

This chapter in the history of diamonds points to the global career of precious objects beyond trade and smuggling. In contrast to the case of the Koh-i-Noor, neither the network of European and Indian merchants nor colonial connections propelled the diamond's movement from one to another continent, but rather geographically overarching religious affiliations. By sending the stone to Medina as a charitable gift, Shah Jahan could draw attention to his self-understanding as a Muslim ruler. Moving along its path the diamond was not only placed into different contexts of usage (from a found object to the equivalent of money and onward to a gift) but was also physically transformed through cutting and setting.

Together with gifts and tributes, pieces of booty played an important role in the flow of jewels. Extensive jewel collections were transferred through military conquest and political upheaval, with courts serving as shipping points. Two episodes marking, respectively, the opening and closing phase of Mughal rule offer good examples of this form of circulation: Bābur's appropriation of the Lūdī treasures and the loss of the Mughal treasure to the Persian ruler Nādir Shāh.

On April 21, 1526, Ẓahīr ud-Dīn Muḥammad Bābur inflicted a decisive defeat on Sultan Ibrāhīm Lūdī (ruled 1517–26) in Panipat, some ninety kilometers north of Delhi – a defeat that led to the collapse of the Delhi sultanate and the foundation of the Mughal Empire. Directly after his victory, Bābur saw to it that the treasures of the Lūdīs were transferred to his

---

[79] Rati = 0.12 grams; 1 carat = 0.2 grams. Conversion according to Untracht, *Traditional Jewelry*, 285.
[80] 'Ināyat Khān, *The Shah Jahan Nama*, 404–5.
[81] Ibid., 405.

possession. He sent his son Humayun, accompanied by a few other people, to Agra to collect treasure being kept in the Lūdī residence there; he
also sent his son-in-law Mahdī Khwāja to the Delhi palace to watch over
additional treasure.[82] Arriving in Delhi a few days later, he had the treasure sealed and the Friday prayer read out, in a confirmation of his claim
to rule. The appropriation of the treasure was symbolically and materially
an important act in Bābur's seizure of power. In Agra, confiscation of the
treasure by Humayun was accompanied by the arrest of the clan of the
Rajput prince Bikramajit, which had its headquarters there. Facing a choice
between either "voluntarily" handing over their jewels or seeing them plundered, they presented Humayun "with many jewels and gems, among which
was a famous diamond Sultan Alauddin had acquired. It is well known that
a gem merchant once assessed its worth at the whole world's expenditure
for half a day. It must weigh eight mithcals."[83]

   Possibly 'Alā' ad-Dīn Khaljī's diamond was in fact the Koh-i-Noor[84] –
that stone's history thus gaining an additional chapter. But the fact that
it only gained its present name in 1739 after falling into the hands of
the Persian ruler Nādir Shāh has caused confusion regarding its identity
before that time. When Bābur arrived in Agra in May, Humayun offered
the diamond to his father, who, however, immediately returned it to his
son. Out of gratitude for guest friendship and asylum, in 1547 Humayun
gave it as a gift to – this is also documented – the Persian shah Tahmasp.[85]
Between that point and the plundering of Delhi in 1739 every trace of
the diamond vanishes; the path along which Bābur's diamond could have
returned to Delhi remains pure speculation, as does the possibility that

---

[82] Wheeler M. Thackston, trans., ed., and annot., *The Baburnama: Memoirs of Babur,
   Prince and Emperor* (Washington, DC: Freer Gallery of Art, 1996), 327; Stephen F. Dale,
   *The Garden of the Eight Paradises: Babur and the Culture of Empire in Central India,
   Afghanistan and India, 1483–1530* (Leiden, The Netherlands: Brill, 2004), 330–5.
[83] Thackston, *Baburnama*, 328. The mentioned Sultan Alauddin is 'Alā' ad-Dīn Khaljī.
       Abū 'l-Fazl indicates that 1 mithcal is approx. 26 surkhs, corresponding to approx.
   23 carats, meaning that the diamond Bābur mentions would have weighed around 184
   carats. See "Appendix A," in Thackston, *Jahangirnama*, 473. 'Alā' ad-Dīn Khaljī (ruled
   1296–1316) was among the great rulers of the Delhi sultanate (1206–1526). The diamond fell into his own hands as a piece of booty. See Catherine Asher and Cynthia
   Talbot, *India before Europe* (Cambridge: Cambridge University Press, 2006), 40.
[84] Balfour, *Diamonds*, 154–64.
[85] Abū 'l-Fazl, *The Akbarnama of Abu-l-Fazl*, trans. Henry Beveridge, 3 vols. (Calcutta:
   Asiatic Society, 1897–1939), 1: ch. 33: "His Majesty Jahānbānī on the day of the great
   festival presented to the Shāh as the gift of a traveller a diamond of great value – worth
   the revenues of countries and climes, together with 250 Badakhshān rubies." The translator and editor notes that the diamond being referred to was without a doubt Bābur's
   diamond and thus presumably the Koh-i-Noor. See also Balfour, *Diamonds*, 158.

the Koh-i-Noor might actually be another diamond, first emerging as a gift to the Mughal ruler Aurangzeb in the seventeenth century.[86]

In any case, the handling of the remaining treasure makes clear that it was regarded as booty. Its distribution to Bābur's troops and entourage corresponded to Islamic tradition.[87] Male family members, high-ranking officers, soldiers, merchants, and students received a total of several hundred thousand coins. Relatives and compatriots in Samarcand, Khorasan, and Persia received gold and silver utensils, jewels, textiles, and slaves. Khwāja Kīlān Beg, an old follower of Bābur, was given the task of delivering precious jewels to female relatives in Kabul, which had long been Bābur's site of rule.[88] In the Kabul residence, tents were to be erected in which every harem woman was to be handed "one special dancing-girl of the dancing-girls of Sultan Ibrahim, with one gold plate full of jewels – ruby and pearl, cornelian and diamond, emerald and turquoise, topaz and cat's eye," together with coin-filled trays studded in mother of pearl.[89] On receipt of the gifts, the women were to genuflect and bow their heads in acknowledgment and thanks: a ritual prostration described as accompanied by prayers and joy over a gift-giving ceremony that lasted three days.[90] Transformed yet again from objects of booty into presents, the jewels seemed to be proof of Bābur's triumphal conquest of Hindustan.

As Richard Davis and Finbarr Flood have shown, the transfer of precious things as war booty in the course of forming empires has a long tradition in medieval India, representing a legitimate practice for both

---

[86] Balfour, *Diamonds*, 158.
[87] F. Løkkegaard, Art. "Ghanīma," in *Encyclopaedia of Islam*, 2nd ed., ed. P. Bearman et al. Brill Online, 2014, http://referenceworks.brillonline.com/entries/encyclopaedia-of-islam-2/g-h-ani-ma-SIM_2459 (accessed November 7, 2014). The practice of distributing booty was based on Sure 48.18–20 and had been formulated by theorists since the eighth century, with the question of which portion belonged to whom not being answered in a unified way. See Richard Davis, "Three Styles in Looting India," *History and Anthropology* 6, no. 4 (1994): 300–1. Thackston, *Baburnama*, 356. In her idealizing description, Bābur's daughter Gulbadan Begam underscored her father's generosity: "The treasures of five kings fell into his hands. He gave everything away. The amīrs of Hind represented that in Hindūstān it was thought disgraceful to expend the treasure of bygone kings, and that people rather added and added to it, while his Majesty, on the contrary, had given all away." Gulbadan Begam, *The History of Humayun (Humayun Nama) by Gulbadan Begam*, ed., trans., with intro., notes, illus., and biographical appendix, and reproduced in the Persian from the only known MS. of the British Museum by Annette S. Beveridge (London: Royal Asiatic Society, 1902), 94.
[88] Gulbadan Begam, *The History of Humayun*, 94–5.
[89] Ibid., 95.
[90] Ibid., 96.

Muslim and Hindu rulers.[91] Richard Davis has argued that the looting practices of Indian rulers were specifically directed to the defeated parties' insignias of rule (e.g., parasols, fans, kettle drums, and thrones) to display their subjugation. But this practice was also known to Islamic rulers,[92] although there are examples of booty expeditions aimed mainly at military and material resources – elephants, horses, and jewels. The campaigns initiated around 1300 by 'Alā' ad-Dīn K͟haljī (ruled 1296–1316) appears to be centered around such resources, which would be offered extensively as tribute by the threatened rulers as a more attractive alternative to being besieged, plundered, and killed. The poet and chronicler Amīr K͟husrow thus describes in detail the huge quantities of diamonds, colored gems, and pearls brought back by K͟haljī's commander Malik Kāfūr in 1311 to his master.[93] In any case, as has been made clear, alongside their material value jewels always also had their own value as symbols of power for both Muslim and Hindu rulers[94] – something manifest both in Bābur's confiscation of the Lūdī treasures so soon after his victory and 'Ādil S͟hāh's acknowledgment of Mughal hegemony through the tribute of jewels.

When in 1739 the Persian ruler Nādir S͟hāh (ruled 1736–47) seized large portions of the Mughal treasure, he was thus following established practice. The British were adapting prevailing custom when they demanded the surrender of the Koh-i-Noor from Dalīp Singh, even if this transfer stood under the sign of colonialism. We here return to this discussion's starting point: with conquest, shifting power relations, and practices tied to gift exchange and an economy of plunder inscribed in the Koh-i-Noor's history, this history was not unique, rather it constituted an especially prominent example of a form of circulation with a long tradition in India. Islamic rulers had undertaken campaigns of plunder on the subcontinent since the eleventh century, seizing the treasures of both rulers and temples.[95]

---

[91] Davis, *Three Styles in Looting India*; Richard H. Davis, "Indian Art Objects as Loot," *The Journal of Asian Studies* 52, no. 1 (1993): 22–48; Flood, *Objects of Translation*, 121–35.

[92] Flood, *Objects of Translation*, 126–35.

[93] See Asher and Talbot, *India before Europe*, 40; Amir Khusrau, *The Campaigns of Alauddin Khalji: Being the English Translation of "The Khaza'inul Futuh" of Amir Khusrau*, trans. Mohammad Habib (Bombay: D. B. Taraporewala, Sons and Co, 1931).

[94] See the example discussed by Davis, *Indian Art Objects as Loot*, 24–6, of the ninth-century rulers of Sri Lanka.

[95] Romila Thapar, *The Penguin History of Early India from the Origins to AD 1300* (New Delhi: Penguin Books, 2003), 428–9; on the plundering of the temple of Somanatha see also Romila Thapar, *Somanatha: The Many Voices of a History* (London: Verso, 2004).

CONCLUSION

In many respects, the life histories of jewels have moved between poles that Igor Kopytoff has described in terms of commoditization and singularization.[96] Kopytoff is here referring, on the one hand, to the transformation of things into saleable wares and their circulation through trade, and, on the other hand, the symbolic charge rendering things unique and leading to their being preserved, locked away, and collected.

As commercial wares, precious stones circulated in the early modern period through a differentiated network of individuals and places. Mine workers, entrepreneurs, traders, and middlemen, goldsmiths and many other artisans all saw to the jewels being mined, sold and resold, cut, polished, and set.[97] As we have seen, they also arrived in the Mughal court as commercial goods. A large portion of them ended up in the imperial treasuries, thus being removed from commercial circulation for some time. This process of singularization left its most distinct mark in the engraving of special precious stones. Through such inscriptions these objects were rendered unique. But their symbolic loading and stylization did not mean a decline of economic potential. To the contrary, running alongside the jewels' symbolic value, their monetary value was constantly registered at the Mughal court.

The speed with which singularized objects could be converted back into money was revealed by European rulers who sold their jewels in financially difficult times. In view of the immense debts of the electorate of Saxony, for example, in 1707 the Saxon elector and Polish king August the Strong pawned a portion of his sapphire collection to the Rotterdam Bank in The Hague.[98] Often, then, singularization and commoditization were narrowly aligned.

At the same time, the circulation of jewels points to the limits of Kopytoff's approach because a large portion of them circulated precisely not as commodities but as tribute, gifts, booty, or inherited objects. Thus very different practices of exchange formed the basis of the stones' mobility. The duration of their itineraries over generations was connected with both their materiality and their perception as precious things. Despite changing owners and locations, as well as functions and significations, the precious nature of jewels was never in doubt. They were always

---

[96] Kopytoff, "The Cultural Biography of Things," 64–91.

[97] Siebenhüner, *Spur der Diamanten*, ch. 4.

[98] Ulli Arnold, *Die Juwelen Augusts des Starken* (Munich: Koehler and Amelang, 2001), 18.

relatively rare goods with high value from the perspective of aesthetics, craftsmanship, and money. This rendered them particularly liable to practices of dynastic transfer, gift exchange, representation of rule, and the economics of plunder. Alongside the proper material preconditions, it was these social practices that gave these jewels their long careers.

2

Diamonds as global luxury commodity

Karin Hofmeester

Diamonds have a large economic value.[1] Seventeenth-century European "Indiamen" sent their profits home in the form of diamonds, rather than in bullion, which is heavier and less easy to hide from thieves and custom officers. Diamonds could be sown into the pockets or seams of clothes, or safely kept in the captain's safe and subsequently be sold profitably in the home country.[2] There are other instances in which diamonds are used for their intrinsic value only; they were and still are used as ransom in kidnap cases and brought to pawnshops in times of need.[3] Even, or perhaps especially, royal families pawned their diamonds, sometimes to pay armies in times of war.[4] In the latter case, the same diamond that was acquired for inclusion in a crown or jewel to illustrate the royal status of its wearer could – temporarily – turn into ordinary currency. Still, for most people diamonds are goods "whose principal use is rhetorical and social" in the terms of Arjun Appadurai, their symbolic value being more

[1] I am grateful to William Clarence-Smith, Bernd Grewe, Marcel van der Linden, Nico Markus, and Kim Siebenhüner for their comments on an earlier version of this chapter.
[2] G. Winius, "Jewel Trading in Portuguese India in the XVI and XVII Centuries," *Indica* 47 (1988): 15–34, esp. p. 23; H. Furber, *Rival Empires of Trade in the Orient, 1600–1800* (Minneapolis: University of Minnesota Press, 1976), 260; S. Mentz, *The English Gentleman Merchant at Work: Madras and the City of London* (Copenhagen: Museum Tusculanum Press, 2005), 73.
[3] J. Evans, *A History of Jewellery 1100–1870* (New York: Dover Publications, 1989), 104; J. Verberckmoes and E. Stols, eds., *Aziatische omzwervingen: Het levensverhaal van Jaques de Coutre, een Brugs diamanthandelaar 1591–1627* (Berchem: EPO, 1988), 154.
[4] Evans, *History of Jewellery*, 104, 130.

important than their intrinsic value.[5] This makes diamonds typical luxury commodities.

Because the attributes of luxury commodities are primarily related to the consumption side, research tends to focus on this specific aspect. If we want to write a truly global history of luxury commodities, we should also look at the production side. By following the diamond commodity chain, this article wants to show how diamond production, trade, and consumption connected a growing number of places, people, and ideas in the world. Over time, the major centers of production, trade, and consumption of diamonds changed. After a short overview of these changes, I will focus on one specific shift: the relocation of the diamond-finishing industry from India to Europe in the course of the sixteenth century. I will also take a quick look at its "return" to India in the twentieth century.

Relocations of production are often explained by economic and political factors; in the case of luxury commodities it is also worthwhile to look at the changing tastes of consumers in different countries and periods. Sometimes a preference for a certain style of cutting could stimulate the relocation of the diamond industry. These varying tastes for diamonds could in their turn be influenced by the varying meanings people attached to these "things" in different geographical areas, time spans, and contexts. Therefore, this article wants to integrate taste and meaning in the analysis of the global commodity chain from the dirt of the mines to the velvet of the jewelry case.

CHANGING TRAJECTORIES

The first diamonds were mined and subsequently finished in India. Already in antiquity, Indians traded the stones with the Romans, whose trading routes brought the stones as far as China, where they were mainly used as tools to drill holes in jade.[6] In the late Middle Ages we see a reemergence of diamond consumption in Europe. The first diamonds that reached Europe from India in the early Renaissance were bought and sold

[5] A. Appadurai, ed., *The Social Life of Things: Commodities in Cultural Perspective* (Cambridge: Cambridge University Press, 2008), 38.

[6] Also no interest in diamonds for jewelry seemed to have developed. C. Clunas's *Superfluous Things: Material Culture and Social Status in Early Modern China* (Cambridge: Cambridge University Press, 1991) mentions mainly jewelry made of jade, pearls, ivory, and silver. See also www.nytimes.com/2005/05/31/business/worldbusiness/31diamonds.html (accessed April 12, 2011), where a young Chinese women states that jade (popular for centuries in China) is outdated and diamonds are more convenient and lightweight to wear. "They make you look sharp."

by individual merchants who transported the stones via caravan routes, using parts of the Silk Route. They sold their merchandise in Venice, where most of the stones were finished. In the sixteenth century, after the Portuguese had discovered short sea routes to India, they became the most important diamond dealers, rerouting the trade from India (often Goa) to Lisbon and from there to Antwerp, where a polishing industry started to flourish. Antwerp already served as the principal market where the Portuguese sold their spices and bought copper, timber, grain, and other essentials for the Asian trade and for the Iberian economies.[7]

The Dutch East India Company (Verenigde Oost-Indische Compagny) entered the diamond trade at the beginning of the seventeenth century, buying stones from local merchants and sending them off from their factory on the Coromandel Coast. Though the VOC for some time made large profits in the diamond trade, by forbidding its employees to engage in the much more profitable private trade it lost its position to the English traders. Amsterdam, however, would become an important diamond trading and finishing center in the sixteenth and seventeenth centuries.

English traders soon surpassed both the Portuguese and the Dutch traders in the seventeenth century. At first the British East India Company (EIC) had a monopoly on the trade of diamonds (and many other commodities). However, after the 1660s it not only allowed company servants to buy small amounts of stones, but also permitted private traders to import Indian diamonds using the EIC officers.[8] The major "export hub" for diamonds in India was now Madras, and the major market for rough diamonds would become London, although an extensive diamond-finishing industry would never develop in England.

When large-scale diamond deposits were found in Brazil in the late 1720s the Portuguese – after a short "free-for-all" period – claimed a monopoly on the exploitation of the mines as well as on the transport and sale of rough diamonds, making Lisbon the city where the rough diamonds first arrived. Because most large merchants were British and a great deal of stones reached the British capital illicitly, London remained the center of the rough trade. This (indirect) line between Rio de Janeiro and London would – in time – end the Indian-European trade in rough diamonds, though it did not stop the mining and finishing of diamonds in India, as we shall see.

---

7 J. A. Boyajian, *Portuguese Trade in Asia under the Habsburgs, 1580–1640* (Baltimore and London: John Hopkins University Press, 1993), 135–6.
8 Mentz, *The English Gentleman Merchant at Work*, 116–17.

Globalization further increased after 1870, when huge diamond deposits were discovered in South Africa. The De Beers Company soon established a mining and rough trade cartel, settling its Central Selling Organization in London. Prices were lowered, the diamond democratized, and a large demand led to a large finishing industry, whose products found their way to the United States. In the course of the twentieth century, new deposits in Africa, Russia, Australia, and Canada were found and new consumer markets were explored. The consequent abundance of relatively cheap rough diamonds was one of the factors that would lead to a shift of the finishing industry back to its cradle in India.

In the rest of this article I will try to analyze these trajectories, pinpoint their effects, and look at the role of the "rhetorical and social" value of diamonds as contexts changed over time and place.

"MINES SUFFICIENT TO FURNISH ALL THE WORLD PLENTIFULLY WITH DIAMONDS"

Diamond mines were located in several regions in India, but the ones in and around the Deccan plateau in South India were the most productive, yielding diamonds "sufficient to furnish all the World" according to a seventeenth-century European traveler.[9] Several European merchants, travelers, and EIC and VOC officials personally visited the Indian diamond mines and wrote eyewitness accounts that give us a good picture of the mining and trading practices and sometimes even of the finishing activities that took place near the mines. The earliest description is by Jaques de Coutre (1591–1627), who was born in Bruges, a center of diamond trade and finishing in the fifteenth century before nearby Antwerp took over. Together with his brother Joseph he left for Lisbon and from there they went to Goa. This city had been ruled by the Portuguese since 1510 and functioned as a truly global trade hub. The De Coutres settled down as merchants in precious stones.[10] In the period from 1611 to 1618 Jaques visited several mines in the Deccan plateau, writing the most detailed report on the mine of Ramallakota (see Map 1 for the locations

---

[9] "A description of the Diamond-Mines, as it was presented by the Right Honourable, the Earl Marshal of England," *Philosophical Transactions of the Royal Society* 7, no. 136 (June 25, 1677): 887–917, esp. p. 908 [i.e., Henry Howard].

[10] De Coutre's son wrote down his father's memoirs in 1640. The original manuscript *Vida de Jacques de Coutre, natural de la ciudad de Brugas, en Madrid, año 1640 por su hijo, Esteban de Couttre, caballero del habito de Santiago* Madrid 1640 is kept in the National Library in Madrid.

of the mines and trading places), situated in the Golconda Sultanate, which was ruled by the Qutb Shahi dynasty. The second description comes from William Methwold, an English merchant in the service of the EIC, who was engaged in buying diamonds.[11] In his ethnographic sketch of several kingdoms along the East Coast he included an account of the Kollur mine that he visited at some time in the 1620s.[12] This mine was situated in the Bijapur sultanate and at the time of Methwold's visit it was ruled by Sultan Ibrahim Adil Shah II. The third and most famous description is by Jean-Baptiste Tavernier, a French jeweler who traveled many times to India in the 1640s, 1650s, and 1660s and bought and sold diamonds and other gemstones, amongst others to Louis XIV.[13] Tavernier's book became a best seller and a guide for later diamond merchants.[14] He gives very detailed descriptions of the Ramallakota mine that he visited in the 1640s. The final sketch is by Pieter de Lange, a Dutch doctor and chief factor (merchant) in the service of the VOC, who would become governor of Masulipatam, one of the factories of the VOC on the Coromandel Coast. In 1663 the VOC sent him to the Kollur mine to buy diamonds. Though he did not succeed in making a good deal and returned without diamonds, he did provide a great deal of information about the exploitation of the mines.[15]

From the descriptions of these merchants and EIC and VOC officials we get a good picture of the activities in and around the mines. Usually the emperor, king, or sultan on whose territory the mines were located also owned the mines. He could choose whether or not he wanted to farm out the mine and if so to whom.[16] He could also decide to close the mine temporarily "to keepe the commoditie in request."[17] The ruler

[11] Mentz, *The English Gentleman Merchant at Work*, 116.

[12] Methwold's Relation was reissued in 1931 as part of the volume of W. H. Moreland, ed., *Relations of Golconda in the Early Seventeenth Century* (London: Hakluyt Society, 1931). On page 33 of this edition Methwold states that the mine was closed in 1622. His *Relation* was first published in 1626.

[13] Tavernier also traveled through the Levant and Persia. His original accounts were published in French: *Le Six Voyages de J. B. Tavernier en Turquie, en Perse et aux Indes* (Paris: 1676).

[14] Mentz, *The English Gentleman Merchant at Work*, 114.

[15] According to Tavernier, Pieter de Lange first worked as a surgeon at the court of the king of Golconda till 1656. Jean Baptiste Tavernier, *Travels in India, Trans. from the Original French Edition of 1676 by Valentine. Ball*, 2 vols. (New Delhi: Oriental Books Reprint Corporation, 1989) (repr.), 1: 240–3. For the report see P. van Dam, *Beschrijvinge van de Oostindische Compagnie*, Book 2, Vol. 2 (The Hague: Nijhoff, 1932), 176–81.

[16] According to Henry Howard, the king of Pegu (Burma, present-day Myanmar) only had the mines dug out privately, "A Description of the Diamond-Mines," 907.

[17] Both T. Raychaudhuri, *Jan Company in Coromandel 1605–1690: A Study in the Interrelations of European Commerce and Traditional Economies* (The Hague: Martinus

leased the mine to the highest bidder. This could be a native entrepreneur, a member of the goldsmith caste, for example, that leased the mine of Kollur, but it could also be a foreigner, such as the Portuguese Albaro Mendez.[18] Governors acted as intermediaries between the king, on the one hand, and the merchants who actually commissioned miners to dig for diamonds, on the other. In the Ramallakota mine, merchants had to pay the king a fee of two pagodas a day per fifty miners, money that the governor of the mine collected.[19] In the mine of Kollur the governor had more responsibilities: here he provided the merchants with workers and made sure they were equipped with tools. The merchants had to pay the governor a fee per worker, part of which went to the king and part to the miners.[20]

Rent was only one part of the king's revenues from the mine; he also received 2 percent of all diamond purchases and sales.[21] If the miners found a diamond weighing more than ten carats they had to hand it over to the governor of the mine, who had to pass it on to the king.[22] Notwithstanding the watchmen guarding the mines, big diamonds were often excavated without reporting them to the governor and directly sold by the miners to "foreigners" for half the price the middleman merchant would ask. If this was discovered, both the miner and the merchant were put to death, though De Coutre escaped this fate because he was a "Frank" (a European).[23] De Lange reported about the Kollur mine that this rule "was not applied too strictly." If the miners found a big stone and reported it, they received a small bonus.[24]

Nijhoff, 1962), 171, as well as Methwold mention the closure of the mine in 1622; see Moreland, *Relations of Golconda in the Early Seventeenth Century*, 33.

[18] For the highest bidder see Mentz, *The English Gentleman Merchant at Work*, 111; for the goldsmith see Methwold in Moreland, *Relations of Golconda in the Early Seventeenth Century*, 31; for the Portuguese see Verberckmoes and Stols, *Aziatische omzwervingen*, 177.

[19] Tavernier, *Travels in India*, 2: 46.

[20] Report by Pieter de Lange as included in van Dam, *Beschrijvinge van de Oostindische Compagnie*, 180.

[21] Tavernier, *Travels in India*, 2: 46.

[22] Verberckmoes and Stols, *Aziatische omzwervingen*, 173; Methwold in Moreland, *Relations of Golconda in the Early Seventeenth Century*, 33; Tavernier, *Travels in India*, 2: 47; Report by Pieter de Lange as included in van Dam, *Beschrijvinge van de Oostindische Compagnie*, 181.

[23] Verberckmoes and Stols, *Aziatische omzwervingen*, 174.

[24] Report by Pieter de Lange as included in van Dam, *Beschrijvinge van de Oostindische Compagnie*, 181. For the bonus see Tavernier, *Travels in India*, 2: 47.

Mining methods differed somewhat from mine to mine – sometimes a tunnel was made (more often a pit) and the type of soil also varied.[25] Basically earth was dug out by men and carried away in baskets by women and children. Methwold counted thirty thousand souls working in the Kollur mine, and some twenty years later Tavernier signaled no less than sixty thousand men, women, and children at work in the same field.[26] Often the soil that was dug out had to be soaked in water and then dried in the sun to "loosen" the diamonds from the surrounding earth. Then the earth would be searched and sieved to discover the diamonds. If the soil was too hard to extract the diamonds, miners would smash the lumps of earth to reveal them.

The miners were often migrants from rural areas. Methwold describes the region of the Kollur mines as a place so barren that before the discovery it was hardly inhabited, whereas now it was "peopled with a hundred thousand souls, consisting of miners, merchants and such others as live by following such concourses."[27] Food and other necessities of life (such a tobacco and betel leaves) had to be brought from other territories, adding import levies to the already expensive commodities. Merchants and miners both lived in the neighborhood of the mines. Miners earned only three pagodas (a pagoda had roughly the value of eight British shillings) a year according to Tavernier, even though the most experienced of them played a very important role in the mining process, as they could indicate the places where diamonds could be found.[28] Other observers recorded monthly wages from 0.5 to 1.5 pagodas. According to Ravi Ahuja, around 1760 a male "general worker" in Madras would have earned a monthly money wage of one pagoda.[29] This would make the monthly earnings of

[25] For an overview of work in the Indian diamond mines see K. Hofmeester, "Working for Diamonds from the 16th to the 20th Century," in *Working on Labor: Essays in Honor of Jan Lucassen*, ed. Marcel van der Linden and Leo Lucassen (Leiden, The Netherlands: Brill 2012), 19–46.

[26] Methwold in Moreland, *Relations of Golconda in the Early Seventeenth Century*, 31; Tavernier, *Travels in India*, 2: 59.

[27] Methwold in Moreland, *Relations of Golconda in the Early Seventeenth Century*, 33.

[28] For the payment see Tavernier, *Travels in India*, 2: 46; the expertise of the experienced miners is also signaled by Methwold in Moreland, *Relations of Golconda in the Early Seventeenth Century*, 31; and in the Report by Pieter de Lange as included in van Dam, *Beschrijvinge van de Oostindische Compagnie*, 180.

[29] For the other observations on mine workers' wages see K. Mukund, "Mining in South India in the 17th and 18th Centuries," *Indica*, 52–3 (1991): 13–52, esp. p. 18. For the wages of a general worker in Madras see R. Ahudja, *Die Erzeugung kolonialer Staatlichkeit und das Problem der Arbeit: eine Studie zur Sozialgeschichte der Stadt Madras und ihres Hinterlandes zwischen 1750 und 1800* (Stuttgart: F. Steiner, 1999), Appendix 8.1.

the mine workers more or less average. However, compared to the other production costs, wages were very low. These low labor costs were also signaled by De Coutre, who stated that they would be much higher in Spain, leading to a higher price per carat. From De Coutre's descriptions we learn that the miners were sometimes "paid" per stone by merchants, who in return supplied them with food. As the miners sometimes would not find a stone for two or three months, they could easily end up in a position of debt bondage.[30] In Kollur, where the governor hired the workers, the miners were worse off if there were no "adventurers" to commission mining, because then they had to work for the king for boarding alone. De Lange described these miners as "slave-like objects."[31]

For the miners and the merchants it was of vital importance to find the diamonds that provided them with subsistence. Believing that divine powers determined whether they would find diamonds or not, they had all kinds of rituals, including prayers and sacrifices of goats to win the favor of the gods.[32] Tavernier describes a feast the night before the mining would start, offered by the merchant employer, where men, women, and children; miners; merchants; and their friends would gather, saying prayers in front of a statue of a god. After that a dinner was offered to the miners to "give them courage and induce them to acquit themselves faithfully."[33]

"THE ARTICLE OF TRADE TO WHICH I AM MOST DEVOTED"

Before we take a closer look at the process that brought the diamonds from the "firsthand" Indian merchants to the European consumers, we should keep an eye on the wider context of this trade. First of all, as the eagerness of the kings for the bigger stones shows us, there was a large internal consumer market for diamonds in India. As we shall see, the Mughal emperors were not the only Indians who owned and cherished diamonds. Second, European traders were not the first and certainly not the only merchants interested in diamonds, but they formed an important part of India's exports to the Indian Ocean region (including South East Asia, the Persian Gulf, and the Southern part of the Arabic

---

[30] Verberckmoes and Stols, *Aziatische omzwervingen*, 172–4.
[31] Report by Pieter de Lange as included in van Dam, *Beschrijvinge van de Oostindische Compagnie*, 179–81.
[32] Verberckmoes and Stols, *Aziatische omzwervingen*, 173; Tavernier, *Travels in India*, 2: 59.
[33] Tavernier, *Travels in India*, 2: 59.

Empire) where, according to Janet Abu-Lughod and André Gunder Frank, a global economy had existed since or even before the fifteenth century.[34] A third issue to be taken into account is that when European traders started to buy diamonds in India and sell them in Europe, their transactions were often part of their intra-Indian trade and of their transnational or transcontinental transactions. We know that the Portuguese bought diamonds through networks of agents in Golconda and Bijapur and also sold them – cut and uncut – to different parts of Asia, including China and the Philippines, from where they sometimes ended up in Mexico and Peru.[35] We can also illustrate the transcontinental element of the trade by looking at some of De Coutre's trading activities.

De Coutre bought luxury commodities made in or transported through Europe and then sold them to the Deccan sultans and even to the envoy of the Mughal emperor Jahangir.[36] Four or five times a year, ships would arrive in Goa, coming from Portugal with Spanish silver coins of eight *reals*, jewelry, rubies from Burma, emeralds and big pearls from "New Spain," coral from Italy, amber from the Baltic Sea region, and chased silverware and trinkets from Germany.[37] As described in the introduction to this volume, these luxuries from all over the world symbolized his status as a universal patron. The green emeralds had an extra symbolic value, representing the color of paradise according to Islam and thus symbolizing the divine origins of Mughal kingship.[38] De Coutre describes how he sold some of his pearls and jewels to Ibrahim Adil Shah II and then went to the mines to buy diamonds he would either sell to the Portuguese king or to individual merchants such as, for example, a dealer from Venice.[39]

---

[34] J. L. Abu-Lughod, *Before European Hegemony: The World System A.D. 1250–1350* (New York: Oxford University Press, 1991); A. Gunder Frank, *ReOrient: Global Economy in the Asian Age* (Berkeley: University of California Press, 1998), 86–96. For the early trade relations in the Indian Ocean region see K. N. Chaudhuri, *Trade and Civilisation in the Indian Ocean: An Economic History from the Rise of Islam to 1750* (Cambridge: Cambridge University Press, 1985), for his remarks on diamonds see pp. 20 and 53.

[35] Boyajian, *Portuguese Trade in Asia under the Habsburgs*, 135.

[36] Verberckmoes and Stols, *Aziatische omzwervingen*, 185, 196, 202.

[37] Ibid., 109, 243. For the coral trade see also: F. Trivellato, *The Familiarity of Strangers: The Sephardic Diapsora, Livorno, and Cross-Cultural Trade in the Early Modern Period* (New Haven, CT and London: Yale University Press 2009); for the emerald trade see K. Lane, *Colour of Paradise: The Emerald in the Age of Gunpowder Empires* (New Haven, CT and London: Yale University Press, 2010).

[38] Lane, *Colour of Paradise*, 151.

[39] Ibrahim Adil Shah II ruled the Bijapur Sultanate from 1580 to 1627. For the transactions see Verberckmoes and Stols, *Aziatische omzwervingen*, 176.

The firsthand Indian merchants were often Banias from Gujarat.[40] Henry Howard, the Earl Marshal of England, who wrote a report about the diamond miners and merchants in 1677, stated that they had a tight grip on the diamond trade and a wide trade network:

The Merchants are the Banians of Guzzarat, who for some Generations have forsaken their own Country to take up the Trade, in which they have had such success, that' tis now solely engros'd by them; who corresponding with their Country-men in Surrat, Goa, Colconda, Visiapore [Bijapur], Agra and Dillee [Delhi], and other places in India, furnish them all with Diamonds.[41]

We know that the early modern European travelers tended to apply the term *Bania* to all Hindu merchants and traders, using it as an occupational category rather than to signal caste affiliation. However, scholars today also explicitly mention the Gujarati Bania diamond traders as playing an important role in the trade, amongst others as middlemen between the mines and the European traders.[42]

The firsthand Indian merchants often sold their diamonds per parcel, entrusting them for several days to the "foreign" merchant, as Tavernier wrote. Payments could be arranged using bills of exchange at Surat, Agra, or Golconda, often through a *sharaf* (a banker or money exchanger). Usually stones were bought and sold in public and weighed by special weighers, employed by the king.[43] However, many stones were not bought and sold in public, as the following account indicates: One night, a Bania trader approached Tavernier and "with a good deal of mystery" took a large diamond (forty-eight-and-a-half carats) from his hair, where he kept it, covered underneath his headdress. Tavernier liked the diamond and bought it the next day to sell it again to a Dutch VOC captain, earning "a fair profit" from the transaction.[44] Unfortunately, Tavernier gives no detailed information on the profit he made by buying rough diamonds near the mines and selling them to his clients. Various remarks give us some idea about the amount of money spent near the mines: this

---

[40] Tavernier, *Travels in India*, 2: 47; report by Pieter de Lange as included in van Dam, *Beschrijvinge van de Oostindische Compagnie*, 179.

[41] "A description of the Diamond-Mines, as it was presented by the Right Honourable, the Earl Marshal of England," 915.

[42] M. Mehta, *Indian Merchants and Entrepreneurs in Historical Perspective* (Delhi: Academic Foundation, 1991), 35. For the present-day observance see R. J. Barendse, *Arabian Seas 1700–1763*, Vol. 2: Kings, Gangsters and Companies (Leiden, The Netherlands: Brill, 2009), 690. See also M. N. Pearson, "Banyas and Brahmins: Their Role in the Portuguese Indian Economy," in *Coastal Western India: Studies from the Portuguese Records*, ed. M. N. Pearson (New Delhi: Concept, 1972), 93–115, esp. p. 104.

[43] Tavernier, *Travels in India*, 2: 47–8, 54.

[44] Ibid., 50–1.

could vary from ten thousand to fifty thousand pagodas: four thousand to twenty thousand pounds. Tavernier's own budget during one of his visits was forty thousand pagodas. The previously mentioned Bania that sold his big diamond illicitly to Tavernier received one hundred pagodas extra (four pounds).[45] The fact that De Coutre and Tavernier bought the diamonds, directly at the mines, is quite exceptional, as most European merchants worked with agents and middlemen merchants. In the trading city Golconda diamonds cost 20 percent more than near the mine.[46] According to one of the traders who bought for his clients in Europe in the late seventeenth century, a commissioner should be able to guarantee his clients 40 to 50 percent profit.[47] However, by the end of the eighteenth century, on some transactions diamond merchant Lyon Prager only made a 6 to 7 percent profit.[48]

The European private merchants needed capital to finance their acquisitions. Often these merchants as well as their financiers were "New Christians," descendants from Iberian Jews who had been forced to convert after 1497. They possessed capital and contacts in Asia, which "forced" the Portuguese kings to do business with them, even though they detested them.[49] In India, especially in Goa and Cochin, these merchants had local agents that could be Portuguese New or Old Christians, openly Jews or Indian Hindus.[50] In turn, they were in close contact with the previously mentioned Gujarati merchants who bought the stones directly at the mines.

In the 1660s English private traders started to take over the trade. They were either EIC officers, who were allowed to trade in diamonds on a small scale, or private traders, who could arrange a growing number of diamond transactions using the "Indiamen."[51] In the English transactions we again meet a great deal of New Christian and Jewish merchants, as Gedalia Yogev and Francesca Trivellato have shown.[52] Some of them

---

[45] Ibid.

[46] Ibid., 50.

[47] From the letter book of John Chomley d.d. December 3, 1669, quoted in Mentz, *The English Gentleman Merchant at Work*, 115.

[48] Elliot v. Willis: *Sale Book of Diamonds and Pearls Purchased by Lyon Prager 1787–1796* f. 73, entrance for December 1793, The National Archives, Kew (hereafter TNA) C111/146.

[49] Boyajian, *Portuguese Trade in Asia under the Habsburgs*, 30, 119.

[50] Ibid., 130.

[51] Trivellato, *The Familiarity of Strangers*, 234–5.

[52] G. Yogev, *Diamonds and Coral: Anglo-Dutch Jews and Eighteenth-Century Trade* (Leicester, UK: Leicester University Press, 1978) and Trivellato, *The Familiarity of Strangers*.

maintained large, transcontinental, cross-cultural networks of traders, as they bought coral from the Sephardic community in Livorno, sent it off to Italians residing in Lisbon, who in turn traded it with Hindu agents in Goa against diamonds.[53] Later on, in the 1740s, these networks connected Livorno, London, and Madras and continued to be characterized by cross-cultural trade relations, as, for example, when Brazilian diamonds entered the trade. The same cross-cultural characteristics can be seen in the network of James Dormer, studied by Tijl Vanneste.[54] Dormer, a British, Catholic merchant who settled in Antwerp, started his own diamond trading house and had very close contacts with members of the well-known Sephardic trading family Salvador from London (who had large-scale contacts in India) as well as with the Protestant banking firms George Clifford & Sons and Hope, both residing in Amsterdam, the latter playing a very important role in the Brazilian diamond trade. Vanneste's thesis shows very well how the trade of a global commodity also depended on personal contacts based on trust, reputation, the exchange of information, and the willingness to provide credit.

What we learn from the correspondence of these merchants is that the EIC liberalized the diamond trade with a reason: diamond retailers, jewelers, and cutters preferred to trade with the private merchants in England because they enjoyed the freedom to have personal contacts with the agents in India, explaining to them exactly what kind of diamonds they preferred. Also, they charged less extra costs than the EIC. The obstinate refusal of the VOC to allow its officers to get involved in the private trade led the Amsterdam jewelers, exactly for the previously mentioned reasons, to prefer doing business with the London-based private merchants.[55] The private merchants also had another important advantage over the EICs: they had more capital at their disposal coming from a wide circle of financiers, and so they were able to invest more in the lucrative but sometimes also quite risky diamond trade.

The merchants of rough diamonds needed expertise to determine the quality of the stones and to settle for a good price. As we have seen, Tavernier's book served later merchants as a guide, and they were also

---

[53] Trivellato, *The Familiarity of Strangers*, esp. ch. 9.
[54] T. Vanneste, "Commercial Culture and Merchant Networks: Eighteenth-Century Diamond Traders in Global History" (PhD diss., European University Institute, Florence, 2009). See also his *Global Trade and Commercial Networks: Eighteenth-Century Diamond Merchants* (London: Pickering and Chatto, 2011).
[55] Mentz, *The English Gentleman Merchant at Work*, 117.

able to consult other handbooks.[56] The expertise needed to assess the quality of diamonds gave the merchants a good position, status, and contacts. Diamonds had a special meaning for these traders, which went beyond the profits they could make. Connoisseur Tavernier called diamonds "the most precious of all stones, and ... the article of trade to which I am most devoted."[57] De Coutre – though he traded in all kinds of luxury commodities – also liked to focus on diamonds "because I know about them."[58]

OF PRINCES, SULTANS, TEMPLE DANCERS, AND BOURGEOIS LADIES: THE CONSUMPTION OF DIAMONDS

Indians were the first and, for a long time, foremost consumers of diamonds. As the hardest natural material known, diamonds had a special meaning everywhere, but in India they were directly related to divine power. Early Sanskrit texts such as the *Ratnapariska* of Buddhabhatta, a manual on gems dating presumably from the beginning of the fourth century, as well as the *Brhat Samhita*, an encyclopedia by Varahamihira from the sixth century, explain the mythic and symbolic values of diamonds and connect these to the different colors diamonds can have. These colors at the same time dictated who could wear which diamond.[59] Regardless of color, diamonds with imperfections (flaws, cracks, and irregular points) could bring bad luck, whereas perfect diamonds brought luck.[60] Women should not wear diamonds, as they were supposed to cause infertility.[61] Of course, the lapidaries inform us about fourth- and sixth-century rules, not about social practices. However, they do indicate that there were rules regarding the consumption of diamonds, restricting the rarest to kings and members of the highest caste.

From the sixteenth- and seventeenth-century European travelogs we know that both men and women wore diamonds in India at that time; even animals could be decorated with them. The gem and jewel treasures

---

[56] E.g., the manuscript Couzas de pedraria, from c. 1600, quoted in Boyajian, *Portuguese Trade in Asia under the Habsburgs*, 49.

[57] Tavernier, *Travels in India*, 2: 41.

[58] Verberckmoes and Stols, *Aziatische omzwervingen*, 54.

[59] Both authors are quoted in L. Finot, *Les lapidaires indiens* (Paris: Bibliothèque de l'École des hautes études, 1896), xxvii. For the dates of both texts see O. Untracht, *Traditional Jewelry of India* (New York: Thames and Hudson, 2008), 313.

[60] Finot, *Les lapidaires indiens*, xxviii.

[61] Ibid.

of the Mughal emperors and the customs linked to them were world famous, as we can learn from Chapter 1 by Kim Siebenhüners in this volume, but there were other "consumers" as well. In the first place there were the kings of the sultanates and their retinues. De Coutre described how each morning a procession of lords went to the court of Ibrahim Adil Shah II, the ruler of the Bijapur sultanate. Mounted elephants, decorated with colored gemstones came in front, followed by horses that wore gold and silver chains with plumes, set off with jewels containing diamonds, rubies, and emeralds.[62] Stressing the difference in wealth between these rich lords and the ordinary population, De Coutre stated that if the members of the latter group possessed any wealth, the men would wear a brooch of gold and filigree and golden earrings with emeralds and rubies. He described the women as "very beautiful in their own way" with ribbons in their hair; a jewel on the forehead set off with diamonds, rubies, or emeralds; a pearl or emerald nose pin; earrings as big as the palm of the hand; and necklaces of heavy pearls, emeralds, and rubies. Everyone was adorned according to his or her means; the poor people avoiding the wrong items as they considered wearing them indecent.[63]

For later periods we know that the possession of diamonds was not restricted to emperors or kings. An inventory of the possessions of the *subahdar* (governor) of Bengal, made in 1728, tells us that he owned (amongst many other things) fifty-two diamond rings.[64] Late-eighteenth-century sources tell us that when the wealthy business man Mohan Das Seth in Bombay died he left his wife a fortune in diamonds.[65] R. J. Barendse, who studied an impressive amount of documents, including wills, concerning the trade and traders on the Arabian seas, concludes that the Indian middling sorts were luxury consumers like the Europeans, spending less of their fortunes on furniture than the latter did, and more on diamonds.[66] He discovered that farmers in eighteenth-century South India possessed golden belts, inlaid with pearls and diamonds. And when the Bombay *devadasi* (temple dancer) Moti died in 1752, she left a considerable fortune in diamonds and jewelry.[67] The possession of these jewels might point in the direction of the tradition of hoarding. However, from De

---

[62] Verberckmoes and Stols, *Aziatische omzwervingen*, 119.

[63] Ibid., 120–1.

[64] Barendse, *Arabian Seas 1700–1763*, 2: 838.

[65] Ibid., 711.

[66] Ibid., 845.

[67] R. J. Barendse, *Arabian Seas 1700–1763*, Vol. 2: Men and Merchandise (Leiden, The Netherlands: Brill, 2009), 919, 922.

Coutre's descriptions we know that the jewels were also actually worn, and seemed to have had at least an equally important social meaning as ornaments that could affirm or enhance the owners' status.

For the emperors and kings, jewels played an even more important role in the positioning of their status. The Mughal emperors' subjects, as well as the local princes like the Deccan sultans who were under his rule, had to give the emperor gifts and tributes. In this context, jewels confirmed power and marked ranks. These transfers, as Siebenhüner rightly argues, can hardly be seen as commodified transactions. However, the lords and sultans that had to pay tribute to the Mughal emperor had to obtain the jewels first, before they could "give them away." De Coutre describes how he sold jewelry to people that only bought them to offer them to the Mughal emperor during the weighing ceremony on the occasion of his birthday, when the emperor received his weight in gems and jewels.[68] Tavernier described how the Mughal emperor could recommodify his gems. Before the festivities he had his jeweler sell quite a number of his stones to several merchants, who sold them to the princes and nobles, who then had to give them to the emperor. In this way the emperor received the money and the gems.[69]

Despite the large Indian consumption and the considerable diamond trade in the Indian Ocean region, diamonds still found their way to Europe in the late Middle Ages. At first they seem to have been used primarily as church jewels and in scepters and crowns of kings and queens, who wore the hardest stone that could be found to show their invincibility. From the second half of the fourteenth century we find diamonds and other gemstone jewelry at the European courts – at first only in France, later also in England.[70] They were worn by the kings and queens and later also by noblemen and women, as markers of their power, wealth, and status, which had to be protected by sumptuary laws. Agnès Sorel, in the mid-fifteenth century the mistress of Charles VII, is believed to be the first nonroyal woman to have worn a diamond. In that same period Emperor Maximilian I is supposed to have given his wife Mary of Burgundy the first diamond engagement ring.[71] In the first half of the sixteenth century

[68] Verberckmoes and Stols, *Aziatische omzwervingen*, 216. For a description of the ceremony see J. Scarce, "A Splendid Harmony: Mughal Jewellery and Dress," *Jewellery Studies* 10 (2004): 33–51.

[69] Tavernier, *Travels in India*, 1: 111.

[70] Evans, *A History of Jewellery*, 53–5.

[71] A. Haas, L. Hödel, and H. Scheider, *Diamant: Zauber und Geschichte eines Wunders der Natur* (Berlin: Springer, 2004), 238–9.

the development of an extended court life in several northern and southern European countries stimulated the trend toward an increasing use of precious stones in jewelry, including diamonds.

In the second half of the sixteenth century, jewelry became more and more women's wear, not least because many European sovereigns were women at that time. As a consequence, jewelry became more abundant, and the *parure*, a set of various items of matching jewelry often mounted with diamonds, became fashionable.[72] Gender was not the only important aspect in consumption patterns. Class, of course, also played a significant part. In the seventeenth century we already find diamonds in the jewel inventories of bourgeois ladies.[73] Glückel von Hameln, a Jewish woman who started a jewelry business with her husband in the 1660s in Hamburg and ran it in a very successful way after he died in 1689, noticed this increasing consumption of jewelry by the bourgeoisie. In 1691 she wrote in her diary that when she and her husband had started their business, non-Jewish burghers and young engaged people wore few or no jewels. After a while, it became fashionable in these circles to wear golden chains, and if gifts were given by young lovers, they would be made of gold. Therefore, their business concentrated on the trade of gold and jewelry made of it. "The trade in jewellery with precious stones is nowadays developing rapidly," she noted at the end of the seventeenth century.[74] Her offspring became very successful diamond dealers; her son-in-law Marcus Moses was an important diamond merchant in India in the eighteenth century and her grandchildren were also active in the business in Madras and London.[75]

Several sources affirm that there was an increase of precious stone jewelry in the late seventeenth century, also in bourgeois circles. This might have been the consequence of a larger supply of gemstones, not only diamonds but also emeralds from Colombia, for example, but it could also be explained by the increasing economic prosperity of the middle classes. Probably it was a combination of both factors.[76] In the eighteenth century we see a specific increase in the use of diamonds in precious stone jewelry. This can be explained by a larger supply and lower prices, but also by a new fashion in diamond cutting: the brilliant.

[72] Evans, *A History of Jewellery*, 105–7.
[73] Ibid., 125.
[74] Bertha Pappenheim, trans. *Die Memoiren der Glückel von Hameln* (Weinheim: Beltz, 2005), 61–2.
[75] Yogev, *Diamonds and Coral*, 89, 131, 157–9.
[76] Ibid.

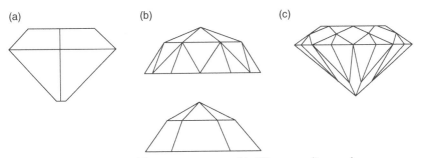

FIGURE 6. Table-cut, rose-cut, and brilliant-cut diamond.
Source: Drawing made by Cambridge University Press.

TASTE IN FINISHING

The diamonds that reached the European courts in the fourteenth century all came from India. Some were finished there, others in Venice. At that time, finishing meant that the surface of the natural octahedron-shaped diamond was polished. In the fifteenth century the so-called table cut was developed, which meant that the top of the octahedron was flattened, giving the diamond a flat "table." as can be seen in drawing a in Figure 6.

The technique of cutting and polishing diamonds was most probably developed in India and spread from there to Venice.[77] A description of a number of gemstones, including a price list, made in 1403 by a Jewish jeweler in Venice, tells us that he knew about the cutting process of diamonds as well as the polishing process.[78]

A century later Bartolomeo di Pasi made a list of all sorts of commodities traded in Venice. He mentions diamonds that were regularly sent from Venice to Lisbon, Antwerp, and Paris. He distinguishes between *diamanti* and *diamanti in punta*. The first were sent to Antwerp, the latter to Lisbon and Paris. Here, a distinction is made between the natural octahedrons with polished surfaces (the *diamanti in punta*), which were sent to Lisbon and Paris, whereas the *diamanti* – that did not have the natural pointed shape and had to be cut and polished to give them the desired shape – were sent to Antwerp, where a diamond finishing industry had developed since the sixteenth century.[79]

---

[77] G. Lenzen, *The History of Diamond Production and the Diamond Trade* (London: Barrie and Jenkins, 1970), 72 and Haas et al., *Diamant*, 231.

[78] C. Sirat, "Les pierres précieuses au XVe siècle," *Annales: Économies Sociétés Civilisations* 23, no. 5 (1968): 1078.

[79] Lenzen, *The History of Diamond Production*, 61.

In the sixteenth century the technique of polishing facets was developed. For this one needs a polishing wheel and bort (diamond dust). In Europe, the first description of this technique was written by Benvenuto Cellini in 1568.[80] Around the same time, the first Indian Mughal emperor Sultan Babur (1463–1530) described how he received a diamond (probably the Koh-i-Noor) from his son. This was covered with triangular facets arranged in a symmetrical radiating pattern, with the bottom of the stone left flat: a so-called rose cut (see drawing b in Figure 6). This simultaneity led several authors to debate the origin of this faceting technique: was it Indian or European?[81] According to Lenzen, the technique developed in both continents independently of each other, which seems unlikely if we take into account all the contacts that existed between India and Europe. To answer the question of the origins of the polishing technique, various authors have looked at documents, but one should also look at people. We know that goldsmiths and jewelers traveled between Europe and India, transferring knowledge, techniques, and tastes along the way. King Manuel of Portugal (1495–1521) employed an Indian goldsmith at his court, and according to some authors Indian jewelry produced in Goa and imported to Portugal highly influenced the design of Portuguese jewelry at that time.[82] We also know of Portuguese goldsmiths and lapidaries who worked in Goa from the sixteenth century onward, producing for the European market while being influenced by local workers. At the same time, European jewelers worked at the Mughal court.[83] William Leeds, an English jeweler who had accompanied a group of British merchants who traveled to India in 1583, ended up in the service of the Mughal emperor Akbar (ruled 1556–1605).[84] Akbar's successor, Jahangir (1605–27), employed the Frenchmen Augustin Hiriart to design a throne for him, whereas his son Shah Jahan (1627–58) employed Abraham de Duyts from Antwerp as a jeweler and diamond polisher.[85]

---

[80] B. Cellini, *Abhandlungen über die Goldschmiedekunst und die Bildhauerei,* trans. R. and M. Fröhlich (Basel: Gewerbemuseum Basel, 1974), 33–6.

[81] Lenzen, History of Diamond Production, 74–81.

[82] N. Vasallo e Silva, "Jewels and Gems in Goa from the Sixteenth to the Eighteenth Century," in *The Jewels of India,* ed. S. Stronge (Mombay: Marg Pubs., 1995), 54–62, esp. pp. 58, 60.

[83] Ibid., 58.

[84] Ralph Fitch, as included in W. F. Foster, *Early Travels in India 1583–1619* (Oxford: Oxford University Press, 1921), 18; and M. Edwardes, *Ralph Fitch: Elizabethan in the Indies* (London: Faber, 1972), 18.

[85] S. Stronge, "The Sublime Thrones of the Mughal Emperors of Hindustan," *Jewellery Studies* 10 (2004): 52–67, esp. p. 57.

We have several descriptions of the work of Indian diamond cutters as performed in India. Jean de Thévenot, a Frenchman who traveled to India in 1666, describes the famous castle of Golconda and how sultan Abdullah Qutb Shah housed his favorite workmen there:

The King will have the good Workmen to live there, and therefore appoints them lodgings, for which they pay nothing: He makes even Jewellers lodge in his Palace, and to these only he trusts Stones of consequence, strictly charging them not to tell any what they work about, least if Aran-Zeb should come to know that his workmen are employed about Stones of great value, he might demand them of him. The Workmen of the Castle are taken up about the Kings common Stones, of which he hath so many that these Men can hardly work for any body else.[86]

The detailed description of the Mughal emperor Akbar's administration as given in the Aín Akbari also mentions "lapidaries, metal casters and other artificers" who were "constantly employed at the Imperial Court where their work is subjected to the test of criticism."[87]

Diamonds were not only cut and polished in the royal workshops; cutters also worked in trading cities and near the mines. Tavernier's description of the Ramallakota mine includes a report on the cutting and polishing activities he saw there. The extraction methods sometimes damaged the diamonds; when the miners smashed the lumps of earth to reveal the diamonds they could cause fractures and flaws in the stones. If the miners noticed a flaw, they immediately cleaved it – "at which they are much more accomplished than we are," according to Tavernier.[88] After the cleaving and cutting, the stone was covered with facets "in order that its defects may not be seen." If the diamonds had no flaws "they do not more than just touch it with the wheel above and below, and do not venture it to give it any form, for fear of reducing weight."[89] In Ramallakota there were numerous diamond cutters according to Tavernier. (It is remarkable that De Coutre, who visited the same mine some twenty to thirty years earlier, did not mention these cutters at all.) Each of them had a steel wheel "about the size of our plate." To find the grain of the diamond the cutters put water on it; to be able to polish the diamond they poured on oil and ample diamond dust, "although it is expensive," in order to make

[86] He is referring to Mughal Emperor Aurangzeb to whom Abdullah Qutb-Shah had to pay tribute. S. Sen, ed., *Indian Travels of Thevenot and Careri* (New Delhi: The National Archives, 1949), 138.

[87] A. Fazl Allámi, *The Aín Akbari*, trans. from the original Persian by H. Blochman and H. S. Jarrett, Vol. 3 (Calcutta: The Asiatic Society, 1873–1907), 312–13.

[88] Tavernier, *Travels in India*, 2: 44.

[89] Ibid.

the stone run faster. "The mill was like ours, the large wheel of which was turned by four blacks" according to Tavernier, but it turned less quickly than the European ones because "the wooden wheel which causes the steel one to revolve is seldom more than 3 feet in diameter."[90] Tavernier felt that "the Indians were unable to give the stones such a lively polish as we give them in Europe": "this I believe, is due to the fact that their wheels do not run as smoothly as ours."[91] There was also another difference. In order to polish the stones, they were pressed against a revolving disk. As these disks would become dull after a while, they had to be ground regularly. As the Indian disks were made of steel (whereas the European disks were made of iron) they had to be taken off the wheel to be ground on emery, whereas the iron disks could stay in place and be ground by a file. As a consequence, the Indian disks were ground less often, and when they were and the disks were put back on the wheel, they could start running less smoothly. Pieter de Lange described – though in less detail – the same process in the Kollur mine; damaged stones would be polished on disks and sold as "lasques."[92]

We may conclude that the technique of facet polishing was well known in the sixteenth and seventeenth century, both in India and Europe, and that more or less the same technique was used. Though no smoking gun has been found as yet, the technique might have been developed in India and spread by traveling artisans to Europe. But the opposite direction is also possible.[93] At this point, in my opinion, the most likely explanation is that the technique developed as a consequence of interactions between Indian and European artisans, rather than the invention having taken place independently at two places, as Lenzen suggests. What we know for sure is that in Europe this facet polishing technique was further developed in the late seventeenth century, when the so-called brilliant cut was invented. It would become the most popular cut in Europe

[90] Ibid., 45.
[91] Ibid.
[92] Report by Pieter de Lange as included in van Dam, *Beschrijvinge van de Oostindische Compagnie*, 177.
[93] Edgar Samuel presents an interesting theory about the development of the diamond polishing wheel. According to him it was an Italian invention based on a Chinese belt-driven silk-twisting machine that was first adapted to polish lenses and later used for diamond polishing. E. Samuel, "The Invention of Diamond Polishing," *Industrial Diamond Review* 40 (January 1980): 5–7. This Chinese invention had reached Italy via the Silk Route, which also passes through India. Though no lenses were made in India at that time, the belt-driven polishing wheel might also have been invented in India.

in the eighteenth century.[94] This brilliant cut required that the diamond not only had a very symmetrically cut and multifaceted top but also a pointed bottom, the so-called pavilion. (See drawing c in Figure 6.) This enhanced the refractory quality of the diamond, increasing its brilliance, but reducing its weight, often up to 50 percent.[95] The latter was anathema to the Indian lapidaries. This is often explained by the fact that one classical Indian text states that the diamond loses its virtues if you cut it.[96] However, the same text also mentions cutting and polishing as normal procedures, so maybe we should not attach too much value to that statement. It is, however, evident that the taste for stones left as big as possible was strongly developed in India. The number of carats was very important in the valuation and therefore the pricing of diamonds in India.[97] In the seventeenth and eighteenth century, the Indian and European tastes for finished diamonds clearly began to diverge.

As early as the 1670s, John Fryer (a scientifically trained employee of the EIC) wrote that the Indian cut and polished diamonds were mostly sold in the country, whereas the rough stones were sent to Europe "they coming short of the Fringies in Fancy." In Europe they were "both set and cut to more advantage."[98] Elsewhere he advised potential buyers in India that "Rough, brute or uncut stones, are in value half the price of cut or polished stones."[99] Rough stones lose weight during cutting and polishing, and this loss is added to the price. Also, customers paid for security: a finished stone reveals its qualities immediately, whereas one cannot always tell how much of a heavy uncut stone is usable after cleaving. Regardless of Fryer's remarks, Tavernier still bought and then sold a number of Indian cut and polished stones to Louis XIV in 1669.[100]

[94] M. H. Gans, *Juwelen en mensen: De geschiedenis van het bijou van 1400 tot 1900, voornamelijk naar Nederlandse bronnen* (Schiedam: Interbook International, 1979), 173.

[95] D. Jeffries, *A Treatise on Diamonds and Pearls* (London: for the author, 1751), 8–9. Jeffries was a famous London jeweler.

[96] Finot, *Les lapidaires indiens*, xxx–xxxi; he quotes the *Agastimata*, a tenth-century manuscript on gemstones with a great deal of later date additions. In an appendix to this manuscript it says that a diamond cut with a blade or worn out by repeated rubbing becomes useless and loses its benevolent virtue. However, in the manuscript cutting and polishing are described as normal, permitted procedures.

[97] Untracht, *Traditional Jewelry of India*, 317–18.

[98] J. Fryer, *A New Account of East-India and Persia in Eight Letters Being Nine Years Travels, Begun 1672 and Finished 1681* (London: Printed by R. R. for R. Chiswell, 1698), 113.

[99] Ibid., 213.

[100] Tavernier, *Travels in India*, introduction by W. Crooke, 1: xxiv and 2: opposite page 100: drawings of diamonds sold to the king, part of which were "white and cleare and were cutt in India."

The conclusion should probably be that there were many different types of diamond cutters and polishers in India. Highly skilled workers finished the most precious stones in the palace of the emperor; lesser skilled cutters and polishers worked in the trading cities; and the least skilled cutters lived near the mines. The latter only tried to hide up flaws and other imperfections with their finishing.

A real shift in taste seems to have occurred in the eighteenth century with the breakthrough of the brilliant cut. In 1751 the London jeweler David Jeffries wrote a very critical review of the Indian cutting and polishing techniques, describing the diamonds finished in Indian as "in general ill shaped"; "none are properly polished; and the chief thing regarded, is that of saving the size and weight of stones: and this is not much be wondered at in them, as they are unacquainted with the beauties of well-wrought diamonds."[101] In short "the wrought stones that come from thence, none of them being fit for use, and therefore are always new wrought when brought to Europe."[102] It is not very likely that there was a lack of knowledge – at least on the part of the highly skilled diamond cutters and polishers who worked for the Indian courts – about the "beauty of a well-wrought diamond," if we take all the beautiful products of Indian artisans into account. The Indian goldsmiths had developed a special technique to set the "left-as-big-as-possible" and therefore irregular stones: they applied the so-called *kundan* setting. This technique involves forcing a twenty-four-carat-gold fillet between the stone and the lower laid parts of the jewel, forming a bezel setting. Also, the stone was often backed with foil, which enhanced the effect of glitter.[103] The application of this specific setting technique, which enhanced the beauty of the irregular stones, made the traditional diamond cut an all-time favorite in India. The "irregular" cut, later dubbed "Mughal cut," of the diamonds can be found in eighteenth-, nineteenth-, and even twentieth-century jewels made in India.[104] It was exactly this irregularity that was disapproved of deeply by Jeffries, who stated that the Indian cut stones were "irregular in their form," "ill-proportioned" with "their tables seldom in the middle or centre of the stone."[105]

[101] Jeffries, *A Treatise on Diamonds and Pearls*, 116–17.
[102] Ibid., 115.
[103] Untracht, *Traditional Jewelry of India*, 317–18.
[104] Ibid., pictures on pp. 322–9. According to Untracht European brilliant-cut stones are a relatively recent innovation, see p. 319.
[105] Jeffries, *A Treatise on Diamonds and Pearls*, 116.

As taste and fashion are important factors in the production and consumption of luxury commodities, one might assume that this European preference for brilliants spurred the relocation of the diamond-finishing industry from India to Europe. We should, however, take into account that the "European taste" was not a homogeneous phenomenon, as Tijl Vanneste has noticed while studying the papers of James Dormer. Nowadays, diamonds are qualified by their cut, color, clarity (amount of flaws), and carat. The same goes for the eighteenth-century consumers. Some preferred the rose cut over the brilliant; the consumers in Lisbon wanted no yellow but only white-colored diamonds; and some consumers in Amsterdam preferred rose cuts "pretty clear but not quite of the first water" whereas the Portuguese preferred smaller stones over bigger stones. As a consequence of these different tastes, parcels of diamonds were sent back and forth between London, Lisbon, Antwerp, and Amsterdam.[106] It is hard to answer the question why the Europeans liked the symmetric and especially the brilliant cut so much. Various suggestions have been made. For Europeans the stones were relatively expensive; if you could own only one then it should have as much brilliance per carat as possible.[107] The same author also has a more essentialist explanation for the first part of the explanation: the Christian feeling that excessive wealth display verged on the pagan.[108] Maybe it was the preference for mathematic symmetry that developed since the Renaissance.[109] If we try to connect taste to the symbolic value of the diamond, we see that in Europe over the centuries it has shifted from a male adornment to a female adornment, from a symbol of power and invincibility to a symbol of wealth, but also of eternal love. The latter symbolic function implied intimacy rather than distance, which might be symbolized in the type of cut. According to Untracht, who wrote a voluminous book on traditional jewelry in India, there "an impression of glitter and brilliance from a distance" was enough.[110] In Europe, a diamond should also have brilliance from a short, more intimate distance.

---

[106] T. Vanneste, "Diamond Trade in the First Half of the Eighteenth Century through the Eyes of an English Merchant: The James Dormer Network" (unpublished paper, European University Institute, 2006), 55–6. Gans, in his *Juwelen en Mensen*, also noticed differences in taste, signaling a long-lasting preference for rose-cut stones in Amsterdam, 166.

[107] Winius, "Jewel Trading in Portuguese India," 18.

[108] Ibid.

[109] Gans, *Juwelen en Mensen*, 162.

[110] Untracht, *Traditional Jewelry of India*, 318.

Of course there were also more prosaic reasons for the relocation of the finishing industry; more value could be added if finishing and cutting could be done in Europe. Cut stones were more expensive, not so much because of the added labor costs for finishing, but, as indicated in the preceding text, because of the part of the diamond that was lost during cutting. From a sale book of diamonds and pearls of Lyon Prager we learn that in 1788 he bought rough diamonds in India at an average price of slightly more than three pounds per carat whereas polished diamonds cost him an average of almost twelve pounds per carat. It should be added that the quality of the polished stone was qualified as super fine.[111] If a merchant had enough skills to value a rough diamond, his profits would be bigger. He could also avoid the recutting that often had to be done in Europe to adapt it to the local taste; however, the labor costs were small compared to the price of the raw material. In 1697, Joseph Cope, a London-based jeweler and diamond finisher charged his clients five shilling per carat for finishing diamonds.[112] In 1771 the jeweler George Robertson "made over" a large India-cut brilliant weighing seven and a half carats for eighteen shillings per carat.[113]

Because more money could be made by buying rough diamonds in India and having them cut in Europe according to the latest brilliant fashion, the discovery of new diamond fields in Brazil seemed to set off a true rearrangement of the diamond commodity chain.

"DIAMONDS AS PLENTY AS TRANSPARENT PEBBLES"

In the late 1720s the discovery of large deposits of alluvial diamonds in the Brazilian Minas Gerais district north of Rio de Janeiro seemed to herald a new era in the diamond trajectory history.[114] No longer was India the sole supplier of rough diamonds (apart from the very small stream

---

[111] Sale book of diamonds and pearls purchased by Lyon Prager 1787 to 1796, Lyon Prager, business papers, TNA C 111/146. Entrance for 1788, f 15. Prices indicated in Calcutta Sicca Ruppees and pounds, currency exchange: 10 Sicca Ruppees is one British pound, see W. Dickinson, *Universal Commerce, Or, The Commerce of All the Mercantile Cities and Towns of the World* (London: Boosey and Sons 1818), 31.

[112] *Cope v. Cope*: Papers relating to the estate and business of Joseph Cope, jeweler, diamond merchant, and banker, receipt dated 1697, TNA C 104/197

[113] Verelst Collection, Accounts with George Robertson for diamonds 1771–6, India Office Records, Mss Eur F 218/56, entrance for April 6, 1771.

[114] Later in the 1740s, diamonds were found in the Mato Grosso district in the East and finally in the 1840s new field were discovered in Bahia.

of diamonds that reached Europe from Borneo since the late seventeenth century), and local kings no longer decided how and by whom the mines would be exploited.[115] The diamond fields in Brazil were exploited by colonial powers in Lisbon, by a Crown that was not in the first place interested in diamonds for its own adornment but in making as much profit out of them as possible. Initially, the new exploiter welcomed all merchants and miners to work the mines, as long as they paid a tax per miner (mostly slaves) to the Portuguese treasury. This caused an enormous flow of rough diamonds, more than five times the value that usually came from India, which led to a price drop of up to a half and, in some cases, even to a third of the usual price.[116] The Indian trade came to a complete standstill.

Startled by the lowered prices and the responses of the European traders – who feared that in Brazil "diamonds were as plenty as transparent pebbles" – the Portuguese crown shut the Minas Gerais mines down in 1734.[117] When the mines reopened in 1739, they established a mining monopoly, with the actual mining entrusted to one single contractor or consortium (in practice usually a Brazilian merchant of Portuguese origin). The contractor had to pay rent per slave and was not allowed to employ more than six hundred slaves in order to avoid overproduction.[118] To stop illegal mining and smuggling, Portuguese soldiers patrolled a strictly defined Diamond District and banned everyone who had no official employment in the mines.[119] A Portuguese *Intendente* was appointed to control the observance of the rules in the district.

The trade in rough diamonds was linked up with this mining monopoly so that representatives of the contractor could only sell their products in Lisbon, where trading procedures were state controlled and officials of the king had the first choice, although – unlike the Indian kings – they paid for the diamonds. Only after this procedure were the representatives

---

[115] Though some publications mention the Borneo mines, no serious attempts have been made to include Borneo in the global diamond commodity chain, which I hope to do in a later stage of research.

[116] For the amounts see Yogev, *Diamonds and Coral*, 116.

[117] Jeffries, *A Treatise on Diamonds and Pearls*, 66.

[118] Vanneste, *Commercial Culture and Merchant Networks*, 231, 281; D. Ramos, "Slavery in Brazil: A Case Study of Diamantina, Minas Gerais," *America: A Quarterly Review of Inter-American Cultural History* 45, no. 1 (1988): 47–59, esp. p. 48.

[119] L. W. Bergad, *Slavery and the Demographic and Economic History of Minas Gerais, Brazil, 1720–1888* (Cambridge: Cambridge University Press, 1999), 48; Vanneste, *Commercial Culture and Merchant Networks*, 282; and C. R. Boxer, *The Golden Age of Brazil, 1695–1750: Growing Pains of a Colonial Society* (Berkeley: University of California Press, 1962), 207–9, 213.

allowed to sell the remaining diamonds to other European merchants.[120] In 1753, the crown – in an attempt to stop the ongoing illegal mining and smuggling – decided to separate the two parts of the diamond commodity chain and established a true trading monopoly alongside the mining monopoly. The Dutch consul in Lisbon, Daniël Gildemeester, obtained this extremely expensive trading monopoly in 1761 and held it for several decades.[121] Concluding that it was impossible to combat the corruption in the mining business, the Portuguese king decided in 1771 that the Crown would be the sole mine exploiter (the Royal Extraction). This situation would last until Brazil's independence in 1822, when the concession system was reintroduced.

What were the consequences of the discovery of this new diamond-mining region for its producers, traders, and consumers? The most striking development was the "import" of slaves from Africa to work in the diamond mines. Slaves were already employed on a large scale in Brazil in sugar cane cultivation and other sectors. Slaves were also already put to work in the Minas Gerais gold mines. The working and living conditions in the diamond fields were harsh and required a constant new supply of slaves.

The colonial context of the diamond mining and trading determined the strict rules in the Diamond District that curtailed the liberties of the mine workers and other inhabitants of the district. At the same time, we have to take into account that Lisbon was far away and controlling the district turned out to be very difficult. In the same period, from 1753 to 1758, more than 30 percent of all slaves ran away. Sometimes they formed coalitions with illegal miners and started to work for themselves.[122] Illegal mining and smuggling occurred on a large scale. The illegal trade in diamonds is estimated to be at least as big as the "legal" trade, also providing free men with an income.[123]

As a consequence of the mining activities, a local economy developed, including agriculture and local trade networks, which made the district self-sufficient for the basic commodities.[124] Later on, it even became an export region for agricultural products. Notwithstanding the heavy import restrictions imposed by the Portuguese Crown, European goods

---

[120] Vanneste, *Commercial Culture and Merchant Networks*, 231, 281.

[121] Ibid., 231–5; and Yogev, *Diamonds and Coral*, 122.

[122] Ramos, "Slavery in Brasil," 51–2; Vanneste, *Commercial Culture and Merchant Networks*, 297.

[123] Yogev, *Diamonds and Coral*, 122.

[124] Bergad, *Slavery and the Demographic and Economic History of Minas Gerais*, 16.

entered Brazil; clothes, textiles, and hats were shipped from Europe to Rio and made their way onto the local market in the Diamond District.[125] When these restrictions were lifted at the beginning of the nineteenth century, English companies such as Samuel, Philips and Co. settled in the area and started to import textiles, iron manufactures, and hardware, and at the same time became exporters of Brazilian diamonds, coffee, hides, and gold.[126]

For Minas Gerais and its ("imported") inhabitants, the discovery of diamonds had a great impact on their daily lives, though the absence of a local "diamond tradition" as existed in India ensured that they did not attach the same meaning to the stones. However, the discovery of a large diamond could pave the way for a slave miner. John Mawe, a British mineralogist who made expeditions to Brazil in the first decade of the nineteenth century, described a slave who found a diamond of more than seventeen carats, who was "crowned with a wreath of flowers and carried in procession to the administrator, who gives him his freedom, by paying his owner for it." Subsequently, the freed slave received permission to work on his own account.[127] Though one might question the veracity of this almost too-good-to-be-true narrative, for the free and unfree miners diamonds meant a combination of hardship and a small chance of finding your way to freedom.

For the traders, Minas Gerais was merely a rough supply region. A local consumer market for diamonds was nonexistent in Minas Gerais; all diamonds were mined to be sold directly in Europe.[128] For the Portuguese Crown, the trade in rough diamonds meant large revenues for the treasury. However, right after their discovery the Brazilian stones had difficulty in conquering the market. When the European market was flooded in the late 1720s and early 1730s, rumor was spread that the Brazilian diamonds were of inferior quality. As a consequence of this

---

125 Vanneste, *Commercial Culture and Merchant Networks*, 293.

126 H. Bernstein, *The Brazilian Diamond in Contracts, Contraband and Capital* (Lanham, MD: University Press of America 1986), 84.

127 J. Mawe, *Travels in the Interior of Brazil, Particularly in the Gold and Diamond Districts of that Country, by Authority of the Prince Regent of Portugal* (London: printed for Longman, Rees, Orme, Brown, 1812), 224.

128 When the Portuguese royal family settled in Rio de Janeiro in 1808, taking refuge from the French troops that had occupied Portugal, they took their (taste for) diamonds with them, as well as the diamond finishers that had served the court. See Bernstein, *The Brazilian Diamond in Contracts, Contraband and Capital*, 57. For more consequences of the move from Lisbon to Rio de Janeiro on diamond production in Minas Gerais see Bergad, *Slavery and the Demographic and Economic History of Minas Gerais*, xviii, 93–4, 128.

rumor and the lowered prices, many Brazilian diamonds were first sent
to Goa and from there sold to Europe, being marketed as "Indian stones."
A small part of these stones were even sent to Venice first, to give them an
irregular cut to imitate the Indian-cut diamonds.[129] In the end, Brazilian
diamonds were accepted as such. To earn as much as possible from their
sale, the Portuguese Crown tried hard to concentrate the trade in rough
diamonds in Lisbon. However, an enormous amount of smuggled diamonds directly found their way from Brazil to London – which kept its
status as an important market in rough diamonds.[130]

The large role of the Dutch trade monopolist Gildemeester as well
as the subsequent role of the Amsterdam based banking firm Hope &
Co. in lending money to the Portuguese Crown in return for diamonds
meant that this city had a constant and direct inflow of rough diamonds
from Brazil.[131] This had two important consequences; London had to
share its position as a rough market with Amsterdam and, more importantly, the position of Amsterdam as *the* finishing center of the world
was consolidated. The governments of England and Portugal – knowing
that a great deal of extra value was added to the diamonds by finishing
them – tried hard to develop the finishing industry in their countries. The
English Parliament abolished the duties on diamonds in 1732, also keeping the position of the London diamond cutters and polishers in mind.[132]
Gedalia Yogev, who wrote a book on the eighteenth-century Jewish
traders in diamonds and coral, signals a "diamond industry of some significance in London" though "its significance should not be overrated.
London's industry could never compare with that of Amsterdam, and its
importance seems to have declined further in the course of the eighteenth
century … its transfer from Amsterdam to London could not have been
accomplished unless a considerable number of experts migrated in the
same direction. There was no cause for such emigration, and it did not
take place."[133] The Portuguese minister Pombal invited "foreign" finishers

[129] Lenzen, *The History of Diamond Production*, 129–30.
[130] Yogev, *Diamonds and Coral*, 122.
[131] In exchange for loans to the King of Portugal, Hope & Co. received an exclusive concession to sell diamonds originating in the Portuguese colony of Brazil. The Hopes would
accept the diamonds and sell them on the Amsterdam market; then they used the proceeds to defray the interest and principal of the loans they had made to Portugal. For
the Diamond Loan see M. G. Buist, *At Spes non fracta: Hope & Co, 1770–1815* (The
Hague: Nijhoff, 1974), ch. 14, for the technical explanation see pp. 386–7.
[132] Yogev, *Diamonds and Coral*, 142.
[133] Ibid. For an estimation of the number of diamond polishers in London see
K. Hofmeester, "Shifting Trajectories of Diamond Processing: From India to Europe and

to settle in Lisbon.[134] He succeeded only partially. In 1790 there were 107 diamond finishers in the Portuguese capital, whereas their numbers rose from six hundred (in 1750) to one thousand (in 1850) in Amsterdam.[135] It was hard to compete with Amsterdam with its availability of capital and trade connections that guaranteed a constant influx of rough diamonds and its large number of finishers offering craftsmanship in the various, specialized branches of the industry for relatively low wages.[136] As a consequence, the trade in finished diamonds also flourished in Amsterdam. The Dutch lawyer, writer, and bookseller Elias Luzac stated in 1780 in his *Hollands Rijkdom* (Holland's Riches):

nergens in Europa is men met het klooven en slijpen van diamanten zoo ver gekomen als te Amsterdam; en nergens wordt er sterker in gehandeld. De pracht en de ontdekking der diamant-mijnen in Brazil hebben dezen tak van nijvere werkzaamheid en koophandel, in "t vervolg nog rijker gemaakt."[137] ['Nowhere else in Europe did the diamond cutting and polishing develop as much as in Amsterdam, and the trade in diamonds is also unsurpassed. Their beauty and the discovery of the diamond mines in Brazil only helped to develop the industry and trade further'.]

For the consumers, finally, the discovery of the mines in Brazil had the effect that diamonds became more abundant and cheaper. This development was further stimulated by the renewed trade with India since the 1740s.[138] As we already noticed, in the eighteenth century a growing circle of bourgeois customers started buying jewelry, and a special taste for diamonds developed as a consequence of the fashionable brilliant cut. Its relative cheapness helped to bring the brilliant within the reach of a wider circle. For those who could not afford a brilliant, an imitation version was developed by Joseph Strass in 1734.[139]

Up until today, London has kept its fame as a center for rough trade. Its position was reinforced when the diamonds that were discovered in South

Back, from the Fifteenth Century to the Twentieth," *Journal of Global History* 8, no. 1 (2013): 25–49, 38–9.

[134] Bernstein, *The Brazilian Diamond in Contracts, Contraband and Capital*, 43–5, 56.

[135] Ibid., 51; H. Heertje, *De Diamantbewerkers van Amsterdam* (Amsterdam: D. B. Centen's Uitgeverij, 1936), 21, 28.

[136] Yogev, *Diamonds and Coral*, 142; Jeffries, *A Treatise on Diamonds and Pearls*, 101.

[137] Quoted in Gans, *Juwelen en mensen*, 178.

[138] Trivellato, *The Familiarity of Strangers*, 244; Lenzen, *The History of Diamond Production*, 130; Yogev, *Diamonds and Coral*, 123.

[139] For the relative cheapness of diamonds in the eighteenth century see Evans, *A History of Jewellery 1100–1870*, 154; for the growing demand see Lenzen, *The History of Diamond Production*, 131; and Gans, *Juwelen en mensen*, 128–9; the latter also mentions the invention of Joseph Strass, see p. 129.

Africa in the 1870s led to the foundation of the De Beers cartel, which monopolized the mining as well as the selling, and the establishment of its Central Selling Organization in the British capital. Amsterdam kept its position as a diamond-finishing city, as its diamond workers started to cut and polish the diamonds from South Africa, catering for an ever-larger group of consumers as the possession of diamonds was "democratized." For Amsterdam, the diamond industry had a special meaning, especially for the large Jewish community that found employment in the industry. For them it was *"the* Trade" where proper wages could be earned and workers (later united in an influential trade union) had a high status.[140] In the end, in the 1920s, the city started losing its position to Antwerp. This city had a steady stream of rough diamonds from the Belgian colony Congo; low (labor) costs, amongst others induced by currency devaluation; and a large group of finishers specialized in smaller and cheaper stones that were very fashionable in the new consumer market of the United States.[141] World War II would bring the real death blow to the Amsterdam diamond industry.

THE FINISHING INDUSTRY "RETURNS" TO ITS CRADLE: INDIA

In the late 1780s, the Indian mines started yielding fewer stones than before and from that point onward Brazilian diamonds truly monopolized the European market until the discovery of the African mines in the 1870s. This is one of the reasons why India disappears from the existing analysis of the late-eighteenth- and nineteenth-century diamond trajectories. However, Indian mines did not stop producing stones completely and Mughal emperors, rajas, and other local princes did not lose their taste for diamonds, so we can assume that the finishing industry did not disappear either.

When Captain Newbold – a geologist in the service of the British army – visited several mines in India in the 1850s he noticed that some of them still yielded diamonds, though not as many as they used to do.[142] The

---

[140] K. Hofmeester, *Jewish Workers and the Labour Movement: A Comparative Study of Amsterdam, London and Paris 1870–1914* (Aldershot, UK: Ashgate, 2004), pt. 1.

[141] E. Laureys, *Meesters van het diamant: De Belgische diamantsector tijdens het nazibewind* (Tielt: Lannoo, 2005), 70; S. Bloemgarten, *Henri Polak sociaal democraat 1868–1943* (The Hague: Sdu, 1993), 355–6; 431–2.

[142] J. T. Newbold was a captain of the Madras Native Infantry from 1836 to 1847, who was subsequently appointed Assistant Resident at Karnuul. He died in 1850, *Centenary*

local population had a very good explanation for this, namely that the tutelary deities of the mines were displeased by the British ascendancy.[143] The mines in Ramallakota were still worked and in Munimudgoo he saw a handful of diamond cutters and polishers, descendants of the artisans who once worked in Golconda.[144] In 1821 the British Captain Buckley described diamonds found, cut, and polished in Panna (also in Madhya Pradesh), where diamonds were still finished in the 1930s and some diamonds are still mined today.[145] We might safely assume that – despite the large-scale relocation of the polishing industry to Europe – some cutting and polishing was still done in India, the knowledge being transferred from one generation to the next, making the "return," which was only a return in scale, in the twentieth century easier.

Paradoxically, the moment that the mines in India started to become too exhausted to have their products reach Europe, the taste for traditionally "Indian cut" gemstones and Indian jewelry in general developed in Europe. The big international exhibitions of the second half of the nineteenth century showed Indian jewelry to a wider audience. There, it found admirers that had developed distaste for the mechanically mass-produced European jewelry. The natural, irregular shapes of the Indian-cut gemstones and the traditional craftsmanship they displayed connected well with the tastes of the Arts and Crafts Movement.[146] At the beginning of the twentieth century, European jewelers like Jacques Cartier developed collections that were highly inspired by Indian designs, colors, and even methods of cutting. Cartier not only left his precious stones in cabochon cut (only having the surface polished, without being faceted), but he also bought a large amount of Indian-cut stones as we can see on Figure 7 where we see Jacques Cartier negotiating with Indian gemstone merchants. At the same time, one of his best Indian customers

---

Review of the Asiatic Society of Bengal: From 1784 to 1883 (Calcutta: Asiatic Society, 1885), 32.

[143] V. Ball, *The Diamonds, Coal and Gold of India: Their Mode of Occurrence and Distribution* (London: Trübner and Co., 1881), 15.

[144] Lieut. Newbold, "Mineral Resources of Southern India, no 8: Diamond Tracts," *The Journal of the Royal Society of Great Britain and Ireland* 7, no. 14 (1843): 226–40, esp. pp. 230–2.

[145] Captain Buckley, "Report of the Diamond Mines at Pannah," Bengal public letter 263–264, January 4, 1821, British Library IOR/F/4/661/18326; and K. P. Sinor, *The Diamond Mines of Panna State in Central India* (Bombay: The Times of India Press, 1930), 79–82.

[146] S. Stronge, "Indian Jewellery and the West; Stylistic Exchanges 1750–1930," *South Asian Studies* 6 (1990): 143–55.

FIGURE 7. Jacques Cartier with Indian gemstone merchants (1911).
Source: Cartier Archives. Courtesy of © Cartier.

was the Maharaja of Patalia, who had some of his pieces reworked by
Cartier in art deco style.[147]

Though some of the Indian mines continued to produce stones, it was
clear that they could not satisfy the appetite of the maharajas and other
princes, so many famous European jewelers came to Delhi to show and sell
their gems.

For the less wealthy and famous customers, Indian merchants started
to import polished stones, mostly from Antwerp traders, who had local
agents in Bombay. To circumvent these middlemen, several jeweler merchants from Palanpur in Gujarat – all Jains – started to travel to Antwerp
to import polished stones.[148] Some twenty Palanpuri dealers traveled up

---

[147] Ibid., 152.
[148] Jainism is a religion that prescribes pacifism and nonviolence toward all living beings.
It is a minority religion whose adherents form quite successful immigrant communities
in North America, Western Europe, and the Far East. For their activities in the diamond
trade see S. Henn, "Transnational Communities and Regional Cluster Dynamics: The
Case of the Palanpuris in the Antwerp Diamond District," *Die Erde* 141 (2010): 127–47,
esp. pp.132–3.

and down to Antwerp in the 1920s.[149] These imports stopped abruptly in 1947. After achieving independence, India's new government established import regulations that forbade the import of polished diamonds. Rather than spending money abroad on "luxury," the government wanted to stimulate investments in the economic developments of India. In 1952 the Indian entrepreneurs were allowed to import diamonds again, on the condition that only 10 percent of their purchases were polished; the rest should be rough stones that had to be polished in India. In this way, the Indian industry would be stimulated. Some Palanpuri merchants invited Antwerp cutters and polishers to India to teach them the modern techniques. These techniques were transferred to the people from the villages in Gujarat.[150] The Indian diamond industry was stimulated by the 1962 Replenishment Scheme. From then on, all import restrictions were repealed as long as the finished goods were exported at a higher price.[151] This led to a growth of the diamond-cutting industry in India. Diamonds were polished as contracted work for European or Israeli firms, though Indian traders also bought stones directly in Antwerp. They even purchased them directly – and sometimes illicitly from the mines in Ghana and Zaire – though these stones were often of very poor quality.[152] Since 1964 Indian merchants have been welcomed as sight holders – authorized purchasers of rough diamonds – at the Central Selling Organization in London.

The discovery of diamond mines in Australia in 1985, which produced mainly small, low-quality gems, really launched the Indian diamond industry, as the Indian entrepreneurs decided to polish very small stones that used to be considered suitable for industrial use only. The price of large, and therefore rare, rough diamonds is very high and labor costs form a relatively small percentage of the total production costs. However, with small stones the value added by the cutting and polishing is greater in proportion to the total price, and this is exactly where the interest of the Indian entrepreneurs lay, as they combined a relatively skilled labor force with the low labor costs that could be achieved by a high input of

---

[149] Ibid., 134.

[150] B. Imhasly, "Schleifen am Familientisch: Über Indiens wichtigste internationale Industrie," *NZZ Folio* 12/93.

[151] Henn, "Transnational Communities and Regional Cluster Dynamics," 136; and M. Sevdermish, A. R. Misiak, and A. A. Levinson, "The Rise to Prominence of the Modern Diamond Cutting Industry in India," *Gems and Gemology* 34 (Spring 1998): 4–23, esp. p. 6.

[152] Henn, "Transnational Communities and Regional Cluster Dynamics," 134–6; and Sevdermish et al., "The Rise to Prominence," 7.

child labor.[153] The tiny stones were very fashionable in the United States, where a fast expanding market developed when the American department store chain Walmart started selling jewelry set with small stones.[154] To illustrate the growth of the industry in India: in 1966, 6 percent of the world's diamonds were polished in India, in 1996, 92 percent.[155]

From a country with a long mining, finishing, and consumption tradition, India is a finishing center for all types of diamonds, from small to large, and it is also developing itself again as a diamond consumption center. A fast-growing Indian middle class is developing a true taste for diamonds, and diamonds are beginning to replace gold as traditional dowry: "Indians have traditionally been one of the largest sources of gold jewelry demand. Now that's changing, both due to high gold prices and a cultural shift away from the heavy gold chains of the past. Increasingly, it appears women now opt for workmanship over weight when choosing their jewelry made from gold – and increasingly diamonds."[156]

CONCLUSION

If we look at the various shifts in the diamond commodity chain that have been discussed in this chapter we see that although nature determines where diamonds are located, power relations often defined how they were mined and by whom. Whether the prime exploiter was a local sultan, a colonial ruler at a distance, or an international cartel, they all tried to monopolize the trade in rough diamonds, keeping them scarce and in demand. However, for the various exploiters, the diamond had different meanings; the Deccan sultans and Mughal emperors were big consumers of their own diamonds, demanding that the large stones be

---

[153] For a very critical review of the diamond sector, including child labor in the Indian sweat shops see J. Roberts, *Glitter and Greed: The Secret World of the Diamond Cartel* (New York: Disinformation, 2003), ch. 2.

[154] T. Zoellner, *The Heartless Stone: A Journey through the World of Diamonds, Deceit and Desire* (New York: St. Martins Press, 2006), 199.

[155] Sevdermish et al., "The Rise to Prominence," 8.

[156] Vincent Fernando, "India's Enormous Gold Market Slammed as Modern Women Discover That Heavy Gold Chains Are Gaudy," www.businessinsider.com/modern-indian-women-ditching-heavy-gold-chains-for-diamonds-2010–1#ixzz13IyH969j (accessed November 7, 2014). It is even stated that in 2008 about 90 percent of the jewelry business was concerned with gold. It now stands at 50 percent. The rest is occupied by diamonds, thanks to an ever-growing domestic consumption fueled – according to a Standard Chartered Bank report – by India's $22 billion wedding industry. See www.tehelka.com/story_main44.asp?filename=Buo80510Cutting_Edge.asp (accessed October 29, 2010).

preserved for them. Likewise, the Portuguese king had first choice when the Brazilian diamonds arrived in Lisbon, though he was supposed to pay for them. For De Beers, diamonds just meant profits.

Mines were often situated in remote, barren areas, where the workers were wage earning migrants or slaves, or something in between. Working conditions and remunerations were bad and rules and regulations severe, though there always was a parallel world, with "shadow" segments of the chain consisting of illicit mining and trading processes. For the miners, diamonds meant hardship and misery but also the hope for that one big stone that could change their life. One needed luck for that or maybe the help of the gods whose favor the miners tried to win by offerings and prayers.

As we have seen, the Europeans had a simple one-way trade neither with India nor with Brazil. We know that the diamond merchant James Dormer, who bought diamonds from Minas Gerais, also sold Flemish fabrics in Rio de Janeiro that ended up in the Diamond District. In the mining area local economies developed; apart from the fact that "mining the miners" gave local people an income, they also developed a consumption pattern for "foreign goods." In India, local consumers appreciated the more luxurious commodities; not only "rough" products such as emeralds from "New Spain" or coral from the Mediterranean were sold on a large scale, but also jewelry made in Europe. These luxury commodities were often part of highly complex, transcontinental trade systems, managed by large, cross-cultural networks that had representatives all over the globe. For most of these merchants, diamonds probably meant merely profit, but for some they had a very special meaning, not least because the knowledge needed to judge rough diamonds enhanced their status.

Not only "things" but also people traveled from one continent to another, and they took their ideas about beauty and how things should be made with them. Indian princes liked German trinkets, and Indian jewelry was highly appreciated at the Portuguese court. Indian jewelers worked at the Portuguese court, just as English and Flemish jewelers worked at the courts of the Deccan sultans and the Mughal emperors. But this "transcontinentalism" had its limits. In the eighteenth century, the Europeans clearly developed a different taste for diamond cuts (though we should not see this taste as too monolithic), which was possibly determined by the different meanings Europeans and Indians had started to attach to diamonds over time. From robust stones worn by sultans and emperors to impress their subjects from a distance, diamonds have turned to smaller, more sparkling stones, worn by women, given to them as tokens of eternal love in intimate settings.

Currently, with help of the De Beers advertising campaigns using Bollywood actresses as role models, the diamond engagement is gaining ground in India. The finishing industry, having "returned" to where it started, bringing large profits to some and subsistence wages to most, is no longer producing for foreign markets only, but also for a growing internal market, though the meaning people attach to the diamond has changed over the centuries.

3

Gold in twentieth-century India: A luxury?

Bernd-Stefan Grewe

The fascination of the Indians with gold is proverbial. For centuries, India has been considered the embodiment of an insatiable hunger for gold. Already in the seventeenth century, the French doctor and traveler to India François Bernier was struck by the way gold and silver, until then circulating in world trade, simply vanished in the Mughal Empire.[1] India seemed a "bottomless sink" for immeasurable quantities of both metals.[2] And in fact, in early modern trade with the East Indies, a great portion of the precious metal mined and looted by the Europeans in America flowed into Asia, for the sake of purchasing valuable goods for the North Atlantic consumer. In the nineteenth century as well, the Indian market could absorb large quantities of gold; an uninterrupted stream of it flowed into that country until the time between the world wars. Aside from the central banks of the countries on the gold standard, Indian consumers were the most important gold customers, actually

---

[1] This is already clear in his book's title: *Voyages de François Bernier, Docteur en Medecine de la Faculté de Montpellier, Contenant la Description des Etats du Grand Mogol ... Et où l'on voit comment l'or et l'argent après avoir circulé dans le monde passent dans l'Hindousthan d'où ils ne reviennent plus* (Amsterdam: Marret, 1699).

[2] *India in 1930–31. A Statement Prepared for Presentation to Parliament in Accordance with the Requirements of the 26th Section of the Government of India Act (5 & 6 Geo. V., Chap. 61)* (Delhi, 1985), 294: "Her [India's] vast imports of bullion are proverbial; and have been at a time so extensive as to cause serious monetary embarrassment to other countries, especially owing to her habit of absorbing and immobilizing a large proportion of what she acquires." On the gold-absorbing role of India in the early modern period, see the chapters by M. N. Pearson and Om Prakash in John McGuire, Patrick Bertola, and Peter Reeves, eds., *Evolution of the World Economy, Precious Metals and India* (New Delhi and New York: Oxford University Press, 2001).

purchasing between 15 percent and 30 percent of worldwide gold production. There were also gold mines in Kolar (Mysore), South India,
but the gold mined there was a long way from satisfying the domestic
demand for the metal.[3]

Most of the gold was not stockpiled in India in bar form but processed
into very skillfully crafted earrings, necklaces, pendants, ear and nose
studs, rings, and bracelets. Until the present, every Indian region, even
individual locations, has its own specific style; in the city street-scene,
few women are present without gold or gold-gleaming jewelry, and men
sometimes also wore gold chains alongside rings. In light of the precious
metal's ubiquity in the country, the question arises of whether it could
indeed serve as a luxury good. In actuality, in India, as elsewhere, gold
has always been expensive and considered very valuable: that initially
this may not seem the case is tied to the frequent wearing of cheap, imitation gold jewelry among lower castes and in poorer social strata. As long
as such jewelry is not examined closely, its nature goes unrecognized. In
Delhi's Karol Bagh or in the Zaveri bazaar in Bombay, there are many
stores selling the imitations – in close proximity to goldsmiths and jewelers. Basically the widespread presence of imitations shows how strong the
myth of gold remains.

The aesthetics of Indian jewelry has a very long tradition behind it.
On the wall paintings in Ajanta, which are more than 1,500 years old,
we find depictions of pendants and earrings whose form is still manufactured and worn in Maharashtra. Whether this marks the revival of a
past tradition or its continued life is hard to tell because older jewelry
has often been reworked or melted down. For instance, parallel to the
start of the monumental 2008 film *Jodhaa Akbar* (as the title indicates,
its theme is the life of Mughal emperor Akbar), Tanishq, a large jewelry firm owned by the extraordinarily wealthy Tata family, reactivated
(putatively) traditional Mughal design, in the form of a jewelry collection presented in the film by the proud Rajputen princess Jodhaa. The
jewelry was advertised both through the film posters and in glamor
magazines.[4] Although the focus here was certainly on a luxury good

---

[3] On the history of the gold mines in the Kolar region: M. A. Sreenivasan, *Labour in
India: Socio-Economic Conditions of Workers in the Kolar Gold Mines* (New Delhi: Vikas,
1980); C. P. Vinod Kumar et al., "Kolar Gold Mines: An Unfinished Biography of
Colonialism," *Economic and Political Weekly* 33, no. 24 (1998): 1467–74.
[4] Similar collaboration between the film and jewelry industries is evident in the film
Gentlemen Prefer Blondes (1953), whose production costs were substantially covered by

with an exclusive aura due to its material value (in the thousands of euros), Indian economic analysts who specialized in the gold market have repeatedly denied gold is such a good. In a publication of the Bombay Bullion Association we thus find the argument being made, in 1978, that "[g]old is not a luxury, it is not even an article of consumption. It is multipurpose, indestructible asset, and a necessity. Not a daily necessity but a life-time necessity, like life insurance. It is in universal demand, by all sections of the people, who prize gold as the most dependable form of saving."[5]

In this publication, the gold dealers defended state gold-auctions as offering legal access to gold – access not facilitated by smugglers – following the Indian government's Gold Control Rules of 1962, which strictly banned gold imports. In this context the authors pointed to other important functions gold had taken on for the Indian population: above all the function of economic safeguard and reliable form of investment. In India, readers were thus informed, gold was no luxury good but a necessity of life cutting across all social sectors. The extent to which this argument was steered by the interests of the gold dealers becomes clear with its inversion – defining gold purchasing as luxury consumption would hardly have been suited to liberalizing the gold trade, as the jewelers and dealers desired. But can the antigold laws of independent India be compared with the measures taken in other countries to dampen luxury consumption? To what extent did the relationship of the Indians to gold change together with independence and the spread of the money economy? This chapter will consider these questions in a series of steps: first, a brief overview of the symbolic significance and ritual use of gold in Indian society; second, a discussion of gold's social, communicative, and economic functions; third, a look at the hunger for gold in modern, postcolonial India, the failure of its policies regarding the precious metal import, and the shifting approach taken to the metal; and finally, an assessment of the extent to which Indian gold jewelry can in fact be

the de Beers (Oppenheimer) diamond firm. In the film, Marilyn Monroe sang "Diamonds Are a Girl's Best Friends."

[5] The Bombay Bullion Organisation, "Government's Gold Auctions – 1978," in *Aspects of Gold Policy*, ed. S. L. N. Simha (Madras, Bombay: Institute for Financial Management and Research, 1979), 59. In the World Gold Council's market overview, financed by the gold industry, the word *luxury* is decidedly avoided; instead the metal's function as jewelry and investment is emphasized. Nigel Desebrook and Jessica Cross, *An Introduction to the Indian Gold Market* (London and West Freemantle, WA (Australia): Virtual Metals Research and Consulting Ltd., 2002), 20.

characterized as a luxury good, its wearing as a manifestation of luxury (luxury understood here in the previously outlined sense).

THE RELIGIOUS AND RITUAL SIGNIFICANCE OF GOLD

Despite India's strong population growth, throughout the twentieth century more than three-fourths of all Indians lived in villages. Most gold was purchased from local goldsmiths, the raw material largely stemming from reused gold and gold imports reaching the villages from the harbor cities over the usual trading routes. As a result of middlemen, the price of the gold was often much higher in the country's interior than on the coast.

There is a limited, easily assessable body of historical research on gold in modern India. Scholarly research in general reveals a persistent difficulty in presenting a coherent picture of Indian society – something perhaps nearly impossible in view of the complex mix of languages, ethnicities, religions and forms of religiosity, local variants of the caste system, and economic structures. Even when scientifically solid statements can be made, counterexamples are often available. Nevertheless, when it comes to gold it is striking that although regional and social differences can be observed in its use, at the same time, everywhere in southern Asia – whether we are speaking of South Indian Hindus or the plain of the Ganges, Bengals, Ceylonese Tamils, or Bengalese Sikhs – the yellow metal was endowed with a ritual meaning – hence one going beyond pure economics.

Already in the classical Hindu texts, gold was ascribed with special significance (in the *Bhagavad Gita*) and seen as even standing for life itself, its luster being symbolically tied to the sun. It was considered particularly pure because it came from fire (the *Laws of Manu*) and was indispensable for a range of holy rites (the *Satapatha Brahmana*). Some of these texts were translated and edited in the framework of the Indology that first emerged in the nineteenth century.[6] At first, the previously mentioned coherency problem did not exist for this strongly philologically oriented discipline because its main interest was in these classical texts, written in Sanskrit, the discipline thus being oriented toward Brahman Hinduism. By contrast, both the popular, village-centered varieties of Hinduism and

---

[6] See, e.g., Max Müller, ed., *Sacred Books of the East in 50 Volumes* (Oxford: Oxford University Press, 1879–1910).

the many forms of religiosity manifest in the Hindu framework were widely neglected. More recently, researchers have begun to address this lacuna, reflecting, in particular, the influence of theoretical work in cultural and social anthropology.[7]

When it comes to sources, the situation is difficult: especially for rural India, except for land registries, the archives contain few written documents, even fewer have been examined; the few relevant oral history projects have been exclusively concerned with the independence and labor movements. Hence for a broad portion of the twentieth century, field studies by sociologists and social and cultural anthropologists form an important source type for historical research on India's rural society. This point of entry does have an advantage: researchers in these disciplines are especially interested in a society's rituals, but also study its material culture and the positions of its individual members. At the same time, in distinction to other sorts of sources with bureaucratic origins, it tends toward critical reflection on its own cognitive paths and their limits.

Findings from various regions indicate that in rites of passage (involving birth, initiation, marriage, and death) gold played an important role throughout India. For this reason, until sometime after the colonial period's end, one or several goldsmiths were active in nearly every village. In the local and regional hierarchy of the *jatis* (birth groups), marked by strong distinctions, they usually occupied the highest place of all craftsmen. It is the case that ethnological theory has long since left behind Louis Dumont's interpretation of the caste system as a hierarchical order grounded in an opposition between purity and impurity.[8] But it is nonetheless the case that the high position of goldsmiths – comprising the *sunar* caste – in the caste hierarchy resulted from the fact that the gleaming gold they processed was considered the purest of metals.[9] For that same reason, untouchables and casteless Hindus, considered impure, were forced over a long period to dispense not only with the wearing of certain articles of clothing but also with gold jewelry.[10]

---

[7] With its "Beiträge zur Südasienforschung" (Contributions to South Asian Studies), the South Asia Institute of the University of Heidelberg represents such a research orientation, as does the Centre of South Asian Studies at Cambridge University.

[8] Louis Dumont, *Homo Hierarchicus: The Caste System and Its Implication* (Chicago: University of Chicago Press, 1980), 59–61; Susan Bayly, *Caste, Society and Politics in India from the Eighteenth Century to the Modern Age* (Cambridge: Cambridge University Press, 1999).

[9] On the position of goldsmiths in the caste system of South India: K. Ishwaran, *Shivapur: A South Indian Village* (London: Routledge and Kegan Paul, 1968), 18–20.

[10] See John Henry Hutton, *Caste in India: Its Nature, Function and Origins* (New Delhi: Oxford University Press, 1963), 205; M. N. Srinivas, *India: Social Structure*

The Indian preference for especially high-carat gold was closely tied to such ideas of purity – in religious rituals in particular, the purity of the gold used was more important than either its form or objective value. In contrast, in Western counties gold was often combined with other metals to achieve greater firmness. (High-carat gold is very soft and can be formed and processed with a simple tool.)

Because gold was used in various rituals, an Indian goldsmith's traditional tasks were not limited to the manufacture and reworking of jewelry. Particularly in some rites of passage, the goldsmith played a direct role: one such smith was responsible, for instance, for the ceremonial piercing of the earlobes of three-to-four-month-old babies in villages in South Indian Mysore. For this ritual, he received not only gold but also traditional ritual payment in kind (*ulipi*: betel leaves and nuts, rice, beans, and brown sugar). Some years later he was called on for a similar task – piercing the nose of a five-year-old girl for a golden nose stud. After her marriage, the stud was replaced by another to mark her new status.[11] Women of advanced age would often decline nose studs and sumptuous jewelry, on grounds that displaying such items "doesn't look nice on an old woman." Older women heading households in any event relied less on jewelry because they already administered the family resources.[12]

The idea of "auspiciousness" – the belief that completing certain rites and acts of workmanship for specific fixed events promised special fortune – played a special role in fixing not only marriage dates but also the time for making the bridal jewelry – including the *tali* made by the goldsmith. In this way the goldsmith contributed to an auspicious Hindu ritual. But such belief also played a role in magic practices not directly tied to Hinduism's Sanskrit tradition, for example in the manufacture of talismans and amulets. In the 1960s, the Indian sociologist Karigoudar Ishwaran observed this process in a South Indian village – the highly discrete preparation of such magic objects by the local goldsmith,

(Delhi: Hindustan Publishing Corporation, 1980); Penny Vera-Sanso, "Increasing Consumption, Decreasing Support: A Multi-Generational Study of Family Relations among South Indian Chakkliyars," *Contributions to Indian Sociology (NS)* 41, no. 2 (2007): 237.

11 Other researchers likewise observed that many young women no longer had nose rings inserted at puberty but waited until just before their marriage. G.M. Ruma, "Caste Services in Rural Marriages: A Case Study from Mysore," *The Eastern Anthropologist* 21, no. 1 (1968): 4.

12 K. Ishwaran, *Tradition and Economy in Village India* (London: Routledge and Kegan Paul, 1966), 60–2; Doranne Jacobson and Susan P. Wadley, *Women in India: Two Perspectives* (New Delhi: Manohar, 1995), 209.

Narayan, accompanied by his explicit personal distancing from that sort of practice:

I am not a magician and I do not believe in magic. People come to me with all sorts of excuses to get one or more other magical ornament made. Illness, barrenness, rickets, misfortune in life etc., are believed to have been caused by evil spirits. It is also believed by the people that these could be removed by the mediation of a priest-cum-magician. The talismans etc. are used for this purpose. The magician spells a magical formula and places the talisman with the chanting of sacred verses.[13]

An amulet or talisman was manufactured strictly according to a magical formula involving the processing of five metals present in equal proportions – gold, silver, copper, iron, and brass. Following a sacred bath, the smith began his work, taking care that no hammer blow missed the metal, which was never to come into contact with the ground and with menstruating women, considered impure. The talisman was nearly always worn on the body, the exception here being on the occasion of burial ceremonies; preserved within it were seeds, sacred ashes, and a piece of paper or copper disc with sacred verses. In order to satisfy the local demand for talismans, Narayan maintained a broad network of ties with specialized priests and magicians in the village's wider environs.[14]

But also without special magic practices, gold was ascribed with effects fending off harm, with, for example, newborn children being decorated with gold in order to guard against evil spirits.[15] Following the death of a relative, the corpse was meant to have kusa grass (said to have originated in Vishnu's hair) and gold pieces placed in its body orifices, both the grass and gold representing immortality and imperishability. Within Hindu faith, they contributed to neutralizing death-bringing life forces, thus protecting both survivors and the deceased.[16] And gold was also used in priest-led religious rituals, gold disks and figurines thus being essential elements in constructing the fire altars.[17]

---

[13] Cited from Karigoudar Ishwaran, "Goldsmith in a Mysore Village," *Journal of Asian and African Studies* 1 (1966): 56.

[14] Ibid., 55–6.

[15] Nikila Mehrotra, "The Cultural Value of Gold," *The Eastern Anthropologist* 51, no. 4 (1998): 336, 343; Peter F. Seele, *Brains and Gold: Global Transformation Processes and Institutional Change in South Asia* (Sankt Augustin: Academia Verlag, 2007), 147.

[16] Jonathan P. Parry, *Death in Banares* (Cambridge: Cambridge University Press, 1994), 173–4. In practice, most families thought it sufficient to place one of these substances in the corpse's mouth. See Axel Michaels, *Der Hinduismus: Geschichte und Gegenwart* (Munich: C. H. Beck, 1998), 153, 160.

[17] Michaels, *Hinduismus*, 274. The special role gold took on in religious rituals and as a material in cultic objects was not unique to Indian Hinduism; there are many examples

For Hindus the initiation rite (*Upanayana*) was a second birth, so that through the rite one became twice born (*Dvija*) – the basis, from the Brahman Sanscrit perspective, for becoming a true Hindu. Having passed through the rite amounted to a genealogically determined authorization to learn the Veda, its visible sign was the "holy cord." Frequently this was made of cotton; but at least in some South Indian villages it was made of gold and was produced by the local smith. At the tonsure ceremony on the initiation's eve, a golden ring was woven into the remaining ringlet (*śhikā*) at the back of the head of the initiated party, a process meant to represent ancestral ties. Gold was also required for the ceremonial preparation of the sacrificial fire.[18] Beyond this, during pilgrimages and temple visits gold was donated to the temples as a sacrificial offering, although the extent to which this occurred is unknown because for a long time temple congregations avoided public transparency. According to Vedic theory, in sacrifices payment to the priest was to be made through a cow, gold, and a robe; if these were not available they could be replaced by edible fruit or roots.[19] The *doms*, whose caste in the *ghats* of Benares was responsible for the ritual burning of the dead, often received their agreed-on payment in gold. To this end, a piece of gold jewelry remained on the corpse during the burning, to be later washed clean from the ashes by the *doms*.[20]

There are good grounds for assuming that the rich gilding of the Venkateshwara Temple in Tirumala, the Golden Temple of the Sikhs in Amritsar, and many other temples represent a long tradition extending into the present. Hence the temples remain regular clients of gold-separation centers like National Refinery Pvt. Ltd. in Bombay, where they can hand over gold and silver offerings to be melted in exchange for their worth in rupees.[21]

In Hinduism, no special form of initiation was reserved for women; in essence the marriage ceremony served as a means of initiation,[22] with the symbolism of gold as an imperishable metal here playing an important

---

of this extending from antique Egypt and Persia to Christianity's sacred vessels. On the religious significance of gold in Southeast Asia, see Robert Wessing and Roy E. Jordaan, "Death at the Building Site: Construction Sacrifice in Southeast Asia," *History of Religions* 37, no. 2 (1997): 101–21.

[18] Michaels, *Hinduismus*, 85–114; Ishwaran, *Goldsmith*, 55.

[19] Brian K. Smith and Wendy Doniger, "Sacrifice and Substitution: Ritual Mystification and Ritual Demystification," *Numen* 63, no. 2 (1989): 199.

[20] Meena Kaushik, "The Symbolic Representation of Death," *Contributions to Indian Sociology (NS)* 10, no. 2 (1976): 269; see also Parry, *Death in Banares*, 91–3.

[21] Author's observation of the Zaveri bazaar and interview with Sonawala, September 15, 2008. It is highly striking that in both their market surveys and analyses of the Indian gold market, economists regularly ignore this phenomenon.

[22] Michaels, *Hinduismus*, 130.

role. Alongside many other rituals, such as the repeated walking around a holy fire by the bridal couple, the exchange of golden rings was part of a valid marriage.[23] In South India, the groom ceremoniously placed a golden chain (*mangalsutra*) or band with a golden pendant (*Tali*) around the neck of his bride.[24] Precisely as with the nose stud – or in the case of newly married Islamic couples in the marriage's first months, a chain extending from nose stud to ear – this piece of golden neck jewelry was a visible sign of the bride's new status for the entire village.[25]

Although these phenomena stem from different regional contexts, it is clear that everywhere gold was ascribed with a ritual significance distinguishing it from other metals. This was tied to a special appreciation of gold's high degree of purity. But beyond such ritual usage, the precious metal had an entire series of other functions, manifest particularly clearly in the framework of marriages, where the precious metal's ritual role tended to be relatively secondary.

GOLD JEWELRY AT WEDDINGS

In Indian village life, there were few opportunities to present gold and jewelry as openly as at wedding celebrations, which often lasted several days. Especially the bride wore as much precious jewelry as her family's economic circumstances allowed. The gifts to the bridal couple were exhibited to those attending the wedding to acknowledge and appreciate the gifts; gold jewelry being considered the most noble and prestigious of gifts was given a prominent place. The pieces of jewelry were scrutinized hand to hand, their weight and craftsmanship critically assessed by the women.[26] There would also be much gold jewelry to admire on the guests' ears, necks, arms, and fingers.[27] The relatives among both families

---

[23] Ibid., 130–6.

[24] See Ruma, *Caste Services in Rural Marriages*, 4; Holly Baker Reynolds, "The Auspicious Married Women," in *The Powers of Tamil Women*, ed. Susan Wadley (Syracuse, NY: Syracuse University, 1980), 45.

[25] In the poorer families, e.g., among the landless day laborers, this jewelry could be very small or simply be omitted; sometimes there was recourse to silver. Older sculpture suggests that nose studs were not part of traditional Hindu jewelry, see Anant Sadashiv Altekar, *The Position of Women in Hindu Civilization: From Prehistoric Times to the Present Day* (Delhi: Motilal Banarsidass, 1983), 301–2.

[26] See T. N. Madan, "Structural Implications of Marriage in North India: Wife-Givers and Wife-Takers among the Pandits of Kashmir," *Contributions to Indian Sociology (NS)* 9, no. 2 (1975): 234.

[27] Few Indian women did without jewelry on toes and ankles; the rings they wore here were mostly silver. In southern and central India, gold jewelry beneath the waist was taboo,

and all other guests would wear festive clothing. Not only the bride wore
ostentatious amounts of jewelry but all the women present, thus express-
ing the social rank and prosperity of their families. It was above all the
girls of marriageable age who wore strikingly rich items – the men hardly
wore any jewelry at all except a ring or neck chain, and sometimes a
golden watch.

In any case, gold jewelry, as suggested, was the visible sign of a family's
prosperity, with bridal jewelry often being saved up and invested in from
the daughter's birth onward. Parents, sometimes uncles and siblings,
would donate part of the jewelry, while also defraying a great portion
of the marriage costs. The bride's jewelry and the wedding arrangements
were the central measure of the social prestige of the two participating
families. The importance of the jewelry's communicative function is made
clear by the fact that not only the bride's own family members, but often
the future sister-in-law or mother-in-law was often ready – under strict
secrecy – to place part of her own collection at the bride's disposal for
the wedding ceremony. For the marriages of their daughters, entire families (not only parents) incurred debts extending over years; in interaction with bad harvests, others fell into debt traps from which they never
emerged or ruined themselves for the sake of marrying a daughter into
a higher caste. Hence not only the British colonial rulers but also pro-
gressive forces in the Indian independence movement were critical of the
opulence of marriage ceremonies and jewelry – the criticism revealing
parallels with the European discourse on luxury.[28]

Beyond its ritual function, the use of gold jewelry in Hindu marriage
ceremonies displayed many qualities typifying the use of luxury objects
in general. In the first place, the ceremonies were not everyday events
in which, as indicated, relative to their European counterparts unusual
amounts of gold jewelry were worn and prominently displayed. In the
second place, not everyone could afford an appropriate set of jewelry –
neck pendant, armband, earrings, rings; this was the source of its exclusivity. Women from less prosperous families resorted to borrowing jewelry,
especially when the marriage was not being held in the place they lived.[29]

---

while in Rajasthan and western parts of the country some castes claimed the privilege of
using gold rings on toes.

[28] See Matthew Hilton, "The Legacy of Luxury: Moralities of Consumption since the 18th
Century," *Journal of Consumer Culture* 4 (2004): 101–23; Jeremy Jennings, "The Debate
about Luxury in Eighteenth- and Nineteenth-Century French Political Thought," *Journal
of the History of Ideas* 68 (2007), 79–105.

[29] Ishwaran (*Goldsmith*, 51) indicates that in the early 1960s, during his field research he
could observe that the history of the jewels inherited by some village women was known
to them and could be narrated.

Or they used imitations: a feature, in the third place, of the communicative effectiveness of the gold jewelry and a confirmation of its function as a status symbol. In the fourth place, on account of its glimmer and artful manufacturing, in India gold jewelry was considered an especially beautiful and aesthetically pleasing gift. For the members of many *jatīs*, a bride without golden jewelry was simply unthinkable.[30] Within Hindu marriages, the role of gold was certainly that of a luxury object.

GOLD JEWELRY AFTER THE MARRIAGE CEREMONY

At first glance, it would seem that in marriages the gift of gold jewelry was not tied to any practical goal because it could not be used directly. It was useless for men immediately after the wedding – something reflected in many families selling gold given to the bridegroom very quickly. Otherwise than in the Mughal period, in colonial India it was increasingly considered in bad taste to wear large amounts of gold or jewels (a ring, a chain, or an armband clearly designed more robustly than for a woman were acceptable).[31] Hence in distinction to the bride's jewelry, which could function as a status symbol after the wedding, jewelry of the bridegroom had lost this function. It should be noted that with gold jewelry being an acknowledged surrogate for a gift of money, it could be converted into money without any loss of reputation or insult to the gift giver. But gold was preferred as a gift to money, for several reasons: the giver often preferred golden jewelry because of its higher prestige, and sometimes caste rules banned giving money as a gift.[32]

Gifts of gold to the bride, bridegroom, and his family were almost always agreed on when the marriage was arranged, with the weight of the gold fixed in English sovereigns. For the bridegroom's family, marriages were as a rule likewise tied to a certain financial expenditure, but nonetheless signified a clear economic gain: the bride's family had to bear most of the marriage costs, while at the same time also to pay

[30] There are various forms of marriage in Hinduism. The eight most important are described in the classical Hindu legal texts (including the *Laws of Manu*); the so-called Brāhma form, in which a daughter is given as a gift to a worthy man who is knowledgeable in the Veda, is considered a cultural norm. Other forms such as the sale or robbery of women are damned in the legal texts. Michaels, *Hinduismus*, 129.

[31] As buyers of gold, men are only mentioned as fathers of marriageable daughters. See Desebrook and Cross, *Introduction to the Indian Gold Market*, 114–27.

[32] Klaus W. Van der Veen, *I Give Thee My Daughter: A Study of Marriage and Hierarchy among the Anavil Brahmans of South Gujarat* (Assen: Van Gorcum and Company N.V., 1972), 26.

a dowry. This was determined according to both the rank of the bride-groom in the caste hierarchy and his economic situation. But in the colo-nial period it was only paid in a few *jatīs*; in the 1930s, the practice was being honored only among Brahmans, most of the other *jatīs* did not pay any dowry, some high castes even paid a bride-price.[33] In general, the dowry included gold jewelry for the bridegroom, and frequently for the bride's mother-in-law and sisters-in-law as well. Although there were many regional variants and caste differences in these marriage-linked gift relationships, what is relevant here is the crucial role gold often played in this context.[34]

In those *jatīs* maintaining the dowry system, the amount had great importance to the young wife. Particularly in extended families, being able to offer a large dowry meant an elevation of status among the women – and in face of her mother-in-law, whom she was obliged to obey.[35] In South India, after her marriage the only personal possessions a young wife was normally thought to own after her marriage were things directly given by her relations (money, clothing, and jewelry) – *strid-hanan*. In contrast, the dowry was a gift from her family to that of the bridegroom, not part of what she owned. As a rule, parents-in-law dis-posed of both the money and household items brought into the marriage, rarely the husband. Hence for the daughter-in-law, the question of who had given her what gifts and jewelry was decisive because different rights of ownership were tied to this. At least nominally, her husband and his

[33] In Gujarat, e.g., the elite Patidar, Rajpute castes, and the Desai Brahmans paid a pride price to receive a bride (while Anavil Brahmans continued to pay *dahej* in the 1930s). Although in individual cases they were still engaging in the practice in the 1960s, this was done in strict secrecy. Van der Veen, *I Give Thee My Daughter*, 46–7. A similar situation was reported for Orissa in the 1920s and 1930s: Bidyadhar Misra, *Village Life in India: Past and Present* (Delhi: Ajanta Publikations, 1988), 88–96.

[34] The term *dowry* is often used in a sweeping sense – one not distinguishing between, on the one hand, objects the bride brings into the marriage (e.g., household objects, clothing, and personal jewelry) and, on the other hand, payments or gifts required by the bride-groom's family, as agreed on in the marriage negotiations. In this regard Lionel Caplan has suggested stipulating the latter process as centered on "bridegroom-wealth" as opposed to the dowry proper; see Lionel Caplan, "Bridegroom Price in Urban India," in *Family, Kinship and Marriage in India*, ed. Patricia Uberoi (New Delhi: Oxford University Press, 1993), 358–9. But this narrower conceptualization has not become widespread. In our context what is above all important is the distinction between *stridhanan* and the other marriage gifts, so that "dowry" will continue to be used in the broader sense.

[35] Consistent with their approach to rural society in general, social scientists have tended to define extended or joint families as the norm in rural India. But microstudies have indi-cated that not even half of the rural population lived in such families, many households rather consisting of a married couple and children.

family had no right to her *stridhanan*, which thus, despite all subordina-
tion and economic inequality, offered married women a certain space for
action, when for instance her own money was needed in a crisis such as
divorce (rare) or in widowhood.[36] But the form of jewelry called *susral*,
that jewelry received by the bride from her husband's family, remained its
property, although the new family member was allowed to wear it.

The property question was handled in an entirely different way for
men. When it came to the jewelry he received as gifts, there was no comparable distinction between two forms of property according to origin.
Upon agreement of the extended family's head, he could freely dispose
over these gifts, and after a divorce all those he received at his marriage
remained his property.[37]

At Indian weddings, it became clear that gold jewelry could take on
several entirely different functions. As *mangalsutra* ("auspicious thread")
ceremoniously placed around the bride's neck, it had a ritual function.
In the same context, wedding rings, gold head-decoration (especially
for Muslims), and nose studs likewise had mainly symbolic significance,
rendering the woman's new status visible for all while communicating
(sometimes only apparent) prosperity. An opulent dowry proudly presented to guests was meant to reinforce the prestige of both families. The
economic value of gifts of gold could be appreciated by all involved. Gold
was a prestige-mediating sign for prosperity, thus displaying all signs of
being a luxury object. But at the same time, in South India, there were
property-centered legal questions tied to gifts of gold, questions above all
of great significance for the bride, because, as mentioned, she could procure certain possibilities of action through the *stridhanan*. The frequent

[36] Jacobson, *Woman in India*, 188, 197–203. Jacobson offers some examples of how women
used this space for economic action to pawn jewelry for cash or even to extend her own
credit. See also Charlotte V. Wiser, *Four Families of Karimpur* (Syracuse, NY: Syracuse
University, 1978), 215. Wiser describes the case of a wife from Uttar Pradesh, who on
her own initiative sacrificed her marriage jewelry to allow her man to complete his vocational training. The tradition of *stridhanan* has been confirmed principally for South
India; many studies of North India have not been able to confirm corresponding discre-
tionary power over their jewelry by young women. See Marguerite Roulet, "Dowry and
Prestige in North India," *Contributions to Indian Sociology (NS)* 30, no. 1 (1996): 91–2.
Many middle-class Indian women have defended the dowry system by arguing they
would receive nothing of the family inheritance otherwise; the system is here viewed as
a form of property transmission from one generation to the next. This view is strongly
refuted by Ursula Sharma, "Dowry in North India," in *Women and Property: Women as
Property*, ed. Renee Hirschon (London and Canberra: Croom Helm, 1984), 62–74.

[37] Jacobson, *Women in India*, 197–8; Ursula Sharma, "Dowry in North India: Its
Consequences for Women," in *Family, Kinship and Marriage in India*, ed. Patricia Oberoi
(New Delhi: Oxford University Press, 1994), 351–2.

quick sale of received gold jewelry by the bridegroom likewise points to the function – often overlooked within the debate on luxury – of that jewelry as a substitute for money. What was central here was thus not a display of luxury and expression of social prestige – a symbolically mediated message, but rather the high, and always realizable, exchange value of gold jewelry endowing it with a clear economic purpose.

THE ECONOMIC FUNCTIONS OF GOLD
IN EVERYDAY LIFE

The economic importance of gold jewelry in India becomes even clearer when we consider its function as an investment, on the one hand, and both a crucial source of credit and an object for pawning, on the other hand. Many peasants directly invested their crop earnings in gold jewelry that would be hidden at home in clay pots between the stored seed, buried in the soil, or placed within the clay walls of their houses. Even in the twentieth century, robber gangs would enter peasants' houses looking for hidden riches.[38]

In India's interior, a functioning bank system only existed in mid-sized cities; despite a massive effort by the British-Indian government to set up small banks as cooperatives, there were no other possibilities for investing. Because millions of peasants invested secure reserves in this manner, India's gold-import balance in a way mirrored the state of the rural economy. The interplay of (international) agricultural prices, the monsoons, and the harvest had a direct impact on the Indian import of gold. With the rise of agricultural prices and a good monsoon, the demand for gold jewelry quickly rose as well; the reverse situation could even lead to gold exports from India, as in the period of globally falling agricultural prices in the 1930s.[39] Clearly perceptible on the macrolevel, this purchase and sale dynamic shows the function of gold as a replacement for money in many areas of South Asia.

Gold was not only a form of monetary investment but often made it possible for the population of India's interior to borrow money. For in order to receive credit from a moneylender, a loan collateral had to be deposited. In most regions of India, landholding was strongly fragmented, so that most peasants only possessed a small – if intensely

---

[38] Such an attack was reported from Karimpur in the mid-twentieth century. Wiser, *Four Families of Karimpur*, 35–6.

[39] See Dietmar Rothermund, *India in the Great Depression, 1929–1939* (Delhi: Manohar, 1992), 33–57.

cultivated – amount of land. For both lenders and debtors, borrowing on the basis of jewelry instead of land had some advantages: if the debtor were to prove incapable of repayment, the lender could sell the jewelry elsewhere if necessary; in contrast, when land was involved a local purchaser had to be found – recovery of this credit enhancement was far more drawn out and uncertain. In such cases, a moneylender could have the land cultivated by landless peasants such as, for instance, his present debtors, but possibly he would bear the risk for the harvest. For peasants, the loss of one's own land meant a danger of having no income. In any event, landless families and village handworkers without their own landholding had no alternative to depositing jewelry when they needed a small amount of credit.

The special position of goldsmiths in many Indian villages often rested more on their trustworthiness and discretion than on their skilled craftsmanship. For example, married South Indian women could secretly use part of their *stridhanan* to obtain money from him and even offer someone a bit of credit without having to ask their mothers-in-law. The goldsmith also guaranteed the purity of the materials he used, although at times he tricked his clients.[40] As long as the families of the clients returned to the family of the goldsmith for reworking of the jewelry or a loan – the business relations had usually existed for generations – no damage was done through the petty cheating: the smith had to take the piece for payment according to the degree of purity, hence the value, he had originally indicated. The purchaser only suffered economic damage when the gold was given as a gift in another village or lent elsewhere – but it was not necessarily noticed. What we do find are expressions similar to those aimed at other castes, for example "a goldsmith would steal, if he got the chance, his own sister's gold."[41]

In colonial period India, gold was not only ubiquitous in celebrations and festivals but also in everyday life on the streets. As suggested, few women wore no jewelry, rather making do with imitations or with silver when they could not afford gold. A specific sort of jewelry – the

---

[40] Misra, *Village Life*, 38. As late as 2008, I could observe such cheating in a highly reputable gold dealership in Bombay, where gold earrings were being sold at one carat more than their actual degree of purity. Independent tests at, e.g., the Bombay Bullion Association bring such lesser and more serious cases to light (those involving about a carat are relatively frequent). In individual cases, the damage done the buyer is not great; but because of the high rate of sales involved here, the economic impact is presumably considerable. In this context it is worth noting that according to the *Laws of Manu* (XII 61), former jewelry thieves are reborn as goldsmiths.

[41] Ishwaran, *Tradition and Economy*, 102.

previously mentioned nose studs and gold pendants tied to the marriage ceremony, but also, for instance, colored glass armbands – was considered an indispensable attribute of married women, signaling her married status. If her husband died, the glass band would be broken, and the women would not wear jewelry (today sometimes only for several months). Hence for agrarian society, the lack of jewelry was viewed as the sign of a specific family status, the affected women approached with pity and sometimes stigmatized.[42] When a woman appeared in public without jewelry, this was usually taken as a sign of death and mourning or poverty, in precise reversal of the role of gold as a sign of prosperity, joy, and life.

It appears, then, that in daily life gold jewelry was not so much an expression of luxury as, for many women, an indispensable sign of family status: a reflection of the extent to which Indian women were defined through their family and status within it, and how removed this was from individualistic Western concepts of the self. Well past the mid-twentieth century, this marked an essential cultural difference in the cultural meaning of gold.

The economic transactions tied to gold jewelry, especially its pawning or sale, mostly took place in great secrecy, discretion being highly valued because of the prestige reflected in the metal's demonstrative wearing. Hence not only practices of display and demonstration were tied to that jewelry, but also their opposite: hiding, burying, and keeping secret. The opposition between these practices certainly contributed to the mysterious, symbolic aura of gold. Who owned – or seemed to own – what jewelry only could be seen on specific occasions such as marriage ceremonies.

THE HUNGER FOR GOLD IN MODERN INDIA

Indian nationalists repeatedly reproached the British colonial rulers for neglecting or even consciously hindering India's industrial development. Following independence, one of the most important goals of the Indian government was industrialization and modernization. From the perspective of economists, the population's uninterrupted hunger for gold was counterproductive because it bound up large quantities of capital, keeping it from being reallocated as investment credit. In addition, gold imports meant a continuous outflow of scarce foreign currency.[43]

---

[42] As late as the 1970s, when doing field research in a South Indian village Doranne Jacobson was repeatedly asked by interviewed women, with some trepidation, why she walked about "naked" in that she wore no jewelry on feet and toes. Jacobson, *Women in India*, 178.

[43] In May 1947, which is to say just a few months following independence, a "Committee of the Cabinet on the Control of Forward Trading in Bullion in the Bombay Province"

Against the backdrop of the military conflict with China in 1962, the Indian government thus decided to tackle what it at least viewed as the problem with gold. In January 1963, a supplement to the Defense of India Act took effect forbidding the import of gold and strongly regulating both its processing into jewelry and possession. Gold was no longer to play such a central role in the life of, above all, the rural population. On January 9, 1963, finance minister Moraji Desai declared on the radio that

I, for one, do not regard the demand for gold ornaments socially justifiable. I regard it as the moral duty of every patriotic citizen to refrain from buying gold in any form particularly in the present emergency. Even in normal times, it is not necessary to use gold for personal adornment. It is my earnest hope that every teacher in the country, every social worker and every leader of public opinion would make it his or her business to explain to the young and the old, the rich and the poor what the attachment to gold and gold ornaments means in terms of the strains it puts on the resources we need for defense and development. Let all young boys and girls growing up in the country be made to realize that they help built a safe and prosperous India by insisting that no gold be bought at the time of their marriages.[44]

In opposition to many early modern linkage between morality discourses on luxury and the nonnecessity of jewelry, in no passage of the new decree, the grounds offered for it, the connected parliamentary debates, or the accompanying press releases was there any condemnation of gold jewelry as an unacceptable luxury.[45] The government was not really intent on moral renewal; rather, the finance minister was simply using such a patriotically tinged rhetoric to move Indians to adjust their pattern of gold consumption so it would correspond better to the lack of foreign exchange and enduring dependency on imports. Interestingly, the economic as opposed to moral nature of what was finally at stake here offer a parallel to the European rejection of luxury.[46]

---

was convened. One of its main tasks was inquiring with gold dealers and goldsmiths regarding the possibilities for limiting gold imports and the consequences this would have. See Report of the Committee of the Cabinet on the Control of Forward Trading in Bullion in the Bombay Province, Bombay 1947.

[44] Reserve Bank of India, Central Records and Documentation Centre – F 14749 Papers Relating to Gold Board, Press Information Bureau Government of India, January 9, 1963, 4–5.

[45] See *The Gazette of India*, New Delhi, January 10, 1963, no. 8, 15–23; Lok Sabha Debates (Third Series), Vol. XXXVII, 1964, New Delhi 1965; Lok Sabha, ed., *The Gold (Control) Bill, 1963 (Report of the Joint Committee)* (New Delhi, 1964).

[46] The educational goals of gold control were also confirmed by an Informal Committee that grappled with its effects in 1966, declaring that "the ultimate goal is to wean people away from an age old habit, the harmful effects of which on the economy of the country are still not appreciated by the common man. For the time being, compulsion and

For the government, gold was now no longer to serve as the most important marriage gift and element of the dowry and as a replacement for money and security for credit; it was to lose its effect as a symbol for prosperity and happiness. As manifest in the preceding quotation, doing without gold marriage gifts was declared a patriotic duty serving national development and defense. It was clear to the Indian government that gold served in the country as far more than a luxury object. The desire was to directly break with tradition, with gold control designated as a "measure of far reaching social reform ... aimed at weaning people from centuries-old social habit."[47] But when it came to gold control, compulsory measures were unfeasible. While gold imports remained strictly forbidden – with refiners, gold dealers, and goldsmiths having to accurately declare their stock of the metal, private ownership of jewelry was allowed. The government was evidently aware that otherwise the executive would have been overburdened. There were, however, some limitations on privately owned gold jewelry. Most of what was already owned was twenty-two to twenty-four carats; it could continue to be inherited or given as a gift. But new jewelry was limited to fourteen carats. The first aim of this measure was to be able to distinguish imported gold traded on the black market from its legally declared counterpart. The second was to economize on the metal in this manner, making more jewelry from the available gold, thus satisfying the demand accompanying a growing population. This in any case created serious technical difficulties for the village goldsmiths because the fourteen-carat gold was much harder and could not be fashioned in the same skillful way as previously. Hundreds of thousands of goldsmiths lost their work; hundreds of them appear to have committed suicide.[48]

Nonetheless, it is very clear that, in this context, appeals to Indian patriotism went widely unanswered, the demand for highly pure gold jewelry being as strong as before. A brisk smuggling enterprise now emerged over the Indian Ocean, with Dubai becoming a juncture for

---

education have both to be employed to achieve results" (*Interim Report of Informal Committee on Gold Control*, ed. Ministry of Finance, Department of Revenue and Insurance [New Delhi, 1966], 8).

[47] Ibid., 4.

[48] Ishwaran, *Goldsmiths*, 59, following a report in the *Times of India* (Bombay), January 12, 1963. Contradictory data is also available concerning the number of effected goldsmiths. The 1961 census refers to 451,000 persons who lived from working on and trading in gold and silver, while later estimates range from c. 271,000 (finance minister T. T. Krishnamachari, Lok Sabha Debates XXXVII, December 21, 1964, cols. 5991f) to 300,000 (Interim Report of the Informal Committee, 6).

illegal deliveries using dhows to India's western coast. With a difference that often exceeded 75 percent between the international price of gold and the price on the Indian inland, the smuggling was lucrative.[49] It is estimated as having amounted to between 107 and 217 tons annually between 1968 and 1972.[50] In fact, the gold-control policy failed straight down the line, less because of the corruption of many customs officials than because of uninterrupted demand. Various modifications of the rules for control led to no great success – which is to say only in the 1990s – eventually prompting the government to bring the rules to an end.

For the most part, the Indian clientele for the goldsmiths and jewelers was not ready to accept fourteen-carat gold. Even ministers and parliamentarians were alleged to have insisted on giving only very pure, high-carat jewelry as wedding gifts.[51] Legally, the smiths could hardly purchase either enough gold from the central bank or sufficient old gold to manufacture the jewelry requested. For this reason, in the 1960s smugglers' messengers circulated each morning in the bazaars, collecting the daily orders of the gold workshops. A second courier usually took care of delivery on the same day; disguised as a fruit dealer or in another role he would hide his gold between his ware, which is what he would sell to the goldsmith or jewelry trader. The actual price would then be handed over to a third courier in the evening. When interviewed by this author, witnesses have indicated that in the end all the smiths and traders participated in the illegal trade in gold, although at present many notables would publicly deny the fact.[52]

Alongside this very professional cartel-driven smuggling, starting in the 1980s the many migrant workers from India's western coast, especially from Kerala, invested a portion of the pay earned in the Persian

---

[49] See Timothy Green, *The New World of Gold: The Inside Story of the Mines, the Markets, the Politics, the Investors* (Johannesburg: Jonathan Ball, 1981), 172–5.

[50] Atul Sarma et al., eds., *Gold Mobilisation as an Instrument of External Adjustment: A Discussion Paper* (Bombay: Reserve Bank of India, 1992), 29 (according to estimates of Consolidated Gold Fields Ltd.). In total illegal gold imports amounted to an estimated 4,770 tons of gold between 1958 and 1990. For comparison: at the end of 1991 the largest gold reserves in a central bank amounted to 8,146 tons (the United States), and the second largest 2.960 tons (Germany). See Gary O'Callaghan, *The Structure and Operation of the World Gold Market* (Washington, DC: International Monetary Fund, 1993), 11.

[51] See Lok Sabha Debates XXXVII, December 22, 1964; Prabhat Kar (MP, Hooghly constituency), 6216.

[52] Author's interviews in September 2008 in Karol Bagh in Delhi and at the Zaveri Bazaar in Bombay. Sometimes only through a specially broad grin, the notables confirmed this activity tacitly – but not when the conversation was being recorded.

Gulf in gold jewelry (for men). Through the distinctly higher price of gold in India, the gold they sold following their return home offered them a higher net income.[53] In turn, Indian Muslims used embarkations on the Hajj to purchase Arabic gold jewelry.[54] And as indicated by gold dealers in additional author's interviews in Durban, every year more than one hundred thousand South Africans with Indian roots were traveling to South Asia, covering themselves with large quantities of gold before the trip.[55]

In view of this massive smuggling process, it seems highly doubtful that the increasing unemployment of goldsmiths owed itself to the Gold Control Rules alone, as persistently argued by those who opposed them. In many places, local economic systems like the *Jajmani* system based on mutual economic and ritual obligations mutually tying members of the various castes, as observed by William Wiser in a village in the Ganges plain,[56] had already come under great pressure through political and economic changes. New earning possibilities and career paths outside the villages' narrow radius meant that increasing numbers of work and service relationships in the traditional village economy were becoming monetarized. Both longitudinal studies and microstudies have shown that this development affected all village handworkers, not just goldsmiths.[57] Increasingly, villagers not only used urban markets to sell their goods but to purchase jewelry from the gold dealers.[58]

---

[53] Suraj B. Gupta, *Black Income in India* (New Delhi: Sage, 1994), 93–4.

[54] Timothy Green, *Die Welt des Goldes: Vom Goldfieber zum Goldboom* (Frankfurt: S. Fischer, 1968), 216.

[55] Author's interviews in Durban, September, 2007.

[56] William H. Wiser, *The Hindu Jajmani System* (Lucknow: The Lucknow Publishing House, 1936).

[57] See Joseph W. Elder, "Rājpur: Change in the Jamāmani System of a Uttar Pradesh Village," in *Change and Continuity in India's Villages*, ed. K. Ishwaran (New York and London: Columbia, 1970), 105–27.

[58] Notably, the existence of *Jajmani* has been often thrown into doubt, its general applicability disputed, as a basic form of functioning of economic and ritual relations on both a local level and beyond caste limits. Recent research has approached the Jajmani system not as a centuries-old phenomenon, but rather as something only formed in the late nineteenth century – a "work of invention" of handworkers and untouchables. See Peter Mayer, "Inventing Village Tradition: The Late 19th Century Origin of the North Indian 'Jajmani System,'" *Modern Asian Studies* 27, no. 2 (1993): 357–95. But it is generally accepted that in most villages a local system of mutual dependencies existed, although the system may have functioned otherwise than what William Wiser suggested. See Denis Vidal, "Markets," in *The Oxford India Companion to Sociology and Social Anthropology*, ed. Veeda Das (New Delhi: Oxford University Press, 2003), 1342–60.

In India the growing spatial and vocational mobility was accompanied by growing social mobility. The economic ambition and success of members of relatively lower castes sparked widespread movement within a hierarchy whose stability and immutability had simply been a colonial construct. Aspiring groups took over the customs and mores of higher castes, in order to thus consolidate their newly won socioeconomic position on a symbolic level as well. This process of "Sanskritization,"[59] observable in many regions parallel to the increase of prosperity, was manifest in customs of eating and clothing and participation in religious rituals, but above all in the process of marrying by introduction of practices such as dowry. *Jatīs* who in the 1930s had paid no dowries now demanded considerable ones for their sons. The more families participated in the social and economic ascent, the stronger the dowry system spread, increasing in average size as well. With slowly rising prosperity, more money was needed, above all for marriage. Hence paradoxically, the dynamic of political and economic modernization catalyzed by independence strengthened a model of social behavior generally assessed as traditional.[60]

The pattern of gold consumption changed starting no later than the 1960s, in the cities earlier than in the villages. Especially for the urban middle classes, its function as a form of saving and as loan enhancement diminished substantially. Whoever had a regular income could receive credit with relative ease because the regular income served as a pledge. In addition, a range of banks competing in the credit market were located in the urban centers. In this respect, the situation was different in rural areas, where the efforts of first the British, then the Indian government to establish a banking system based on cooperatives frequently failed, meaning that it was impossible to do without investment in jewelry that could be pawned. Into the twenty-first century, supplying small farmers

---

[59] M. N. Srinivas, *The Cohesive Role of Sanskritisation* (New Delhi: Oxford University Press, 1989).

[60] See Siwan Anderson, "Why Dowry Payments Declined with Modernization in Europe but Are Rising in India," *The Journal of Political Economy* 111, no. 2 (2003): 269–310; K. N. Venkatarayappa, *Rural Society and Social Change* (Bombay: Popular Prakshan, 1973), 28–9; T. Scarlett Epstein: *South India: Yesterday, Today and Tomorrow: Mysore Villages Revisited* (Basingstoke, UK: Macmillan, 1973), 197–9. Even among Muslims, who originally did not have the dowry practice, it strongly increased, e.g., in Bihar: Nehal Ashraf, "Dowry among Muslims in Bihar," *Economic and Political Weekly* 32, no. 52 (1997): 3310–11.

and the rural underclass with sufficient credit would remain one of the unsolved problems in Indian economic policy.[61]

From an aesthetic perspective, women living in the cities tended to orient themselves to fashion more strongly than their rural counterparts. Their tastes in new jewelry now took in modern design together with more traditional and regional forms. For the upper and upper-middle urban social strata, design and craftsmanship had become more important than purely material value. The shift to a consumer society here took place more quickly and strongly than in the countryside, individual taste becoming an ever more important factor.[62] But in respect to marriage and official festivities, urban women continued to rely on family jewelry and traditional forms, various pieces thus now being worn according to the occasion.

Despite this basic pattern, by the 1970s at the latest even in South Indian villages such as Nimkhera, ethnologists could observe a beginning change of consumption patterns. In everyday life, relatively prosperous women who had previously worn traditional heavy jewelry had now begun to prefer less and lighter ornaments – and these, just as in the cities, in new designs. They continued to own collections of personal gold and silver jewelry (*maika*), thus preserving the economic possibilities tied to this. None of the women interviewed in this respect had sold their traditional gold jewelry, but they had occasionally borrowed against it.[63]

Alongside the two traditional purposes of wearing gold jewelry – to mark, indispensably, one's status as a married woman and to display a luxury object on special occasions – since the 1960s and more strongly in the following decades, the self-conscious wearing of new, in part modern pieces oriented around personal preference emerged on the scene. Women who preferred nontraditional jewelry tended to also dispense with what is widely thought of as typically Indian clothing such as the sari. But

---

[61] See A. G. Chandavarkar, "Money and Credit," in *The Cambridge Economic History of India 2, ca. 1757–1870*, ed. Dharma Kumar (Cambridge: Cambridge University Press, 1983), 762–803. The mistrust of these local cooperatives by many smaller farmers in particular was all too well-founded: in most cases control over the cooperatives fell into the hands of prosperous farmers, so-called local leaders, who thus furnished themselves with cheap credit while continuing to hand out overly expensive credit to small farmers, handworkers, and the landless. Interest rates of 50 to 75 percent per annum were not rare.

[62] This change already began at the end of the nineteenth century, with Bombay certainly being at the lead here. See Abigail McGowan, "An All-Consuming Subject? Women and Consumption in Late-Nineteenth- and Early-Twentieth-Century Western India," *Journal of Women's History* 18, no. 4 (2006): 31–54.

[63] Jacobson, *Women in India*, 212.

crucially, such public presentation showed more than personal taste and style, it staged autonomous individuality – without, however, having to break with the definitions of role in a patriarchally inclined society.[64] Hence at family celebrations and on religious occasions they continued to wear traditional jewelry, and the purchasing of more modern pieces and other similar luxury goods was only possible with the husband's understanding; it was far from being a genuine emancipatory act.

In any case, the luxury of a jewelry collection suitable for various occasions could only be enjoyed by India's upper classes. At the same time, at present we can observe how this double language of jewelry is starting to be imitated in lower-ranked social groups, albeit in more modest form, for instance as inexpensive fashion jewelry or as an imitation. It is highly likely that despite their low value, these objects are nevertheless perceived by their possessors as luxuries, precisely because they are economically useless, not being a substitute for money like real gold and silver. In this case, the actual material value is not the decisive factor in assessing jewelry wearing as a luxury-linked practice.

As already indicated, in the 1990s the Indian government annulled the ban on importing gold; it also repeatedly lowered the high import duty on precious metals. The growth that began with economic liberalization brought a marked rise in prosperity to the urban middle classes in particular. But despite new forms of jewelry and materials – as reflected in, for example, the increasing domestic demand for diamonds and platinum jewelry – the demand for gold did not sink. In fact, in the cities the number of gold dealers exploded; since the century's turn, India has developed into a global center of jewelry manufacturing.[65]

For the past few decades, different ways of using gold jewelry have coexisted in India. Members of the country's urban middle and upper social strata can draw on various sets of jewelry, traditional and modern – a situation most visible in shop displays and in the bazaars. But changes are also evident in the country; there as well, women who can afford it wear their jewelry according to the context, in the process applying

---

[64] On the ambivalence of female consumption in India see Nita Kumar, "Consumption and Lifestyle," in *Oxford India Companion to Sociology*, 675–94; Emma Tarlo, *Clothing Matters: Dress and Identity in India* (Chicago: University of Chicago Press, 1996).

[65] In the 1990s India became the second-largest manufacturer of gold jewelry after Italy. The value of Indian exports has increased from 304 million dollars in 1991–2 to more than 1.2 billion at present. Roughly 44 percent of the jewelry is manufactured in Mumbai's special economic zone, most of it being sold in the United States. Desebrook and Cross, *Introduction to the Indian Gold Market*, 136–41.

different social codes. Even in the villages, then, two forms of jewelry wearing have now come to exist side by side.[66]

CONCLUSION: THE QUESTION OF GOLD JEWELRY
AS A LUXURY IN INDIA

Within a global economic perspective, India was a developing and emerging country until the 1990s: a country on the periphery rather than at the center throughout much of the nineteenth and twentieth centuries. In the analysis of global flows of goods, India is mainly considered a producer, not a consumer. But this generality does not apply to gold because Indian men and women remain its most important private buyers, gold continuing to play a more important role than elsewhere, the demand for it enduring without interruption. At the same time, in India gold jewelry has meant something else than in Western societies, gold hardly being replaceable in many Hindu rituals. Gold did function as a luxury object in South Asia, but in this region that was one of various functions that had precedence according to the situation. It seems worthwhile to closely consider the recent past and present of an emerging country that not only serves as a producer of consumer goods then marketed in the West but also that represents the most important consumer of a scarce good – one considered a luxury in Western countries. The usual assumptions about economic influence within global markets, north-south imbalances, and the distribution of roles between center and periphery here come under sharp scrutiny.

A longitudinal historical examination of gold jewelry as a luxury good leads us to the basic question of whether the evaluation and categorization of certain objects and practices as luxurious in fact reflect Eurocentric perceptions. This would suggest that possibly our opening question was inaccurately posed and needs modification: To what extent is "luxury" a specifically European category, only transferable to other cultures and societies to a limited degree? In light of the complexly mistaken interpretations of foreign cultures stemming from the Europe-stamped view of colonial administrations, but also from scholarly research, the question seems called for.

At the same time, we could just as easily ask whether in Europe such multivalence and multifunctionality of objects, and such interpretability of practices assessed as "luxury" centered, do not display, with close

---

[66] See Misra, *Village Life*, 39.

scrutiny, a complexity similar to what is the case in South Asia. If we consider the separate contexts somewhat more closely, a far more differentiated picture emerges than what we tend to find, for instance, in studies of Europe's critical discourse on luxury.

The classification by economists of gold jewelry as a luxury good was actually responsible for the failure of India's gold-control policies. For most Indians the purchase of gold was anything but a useless outlay; in view of the adverse credit market – even according to the economists' academic models of a "homo oeconomicus" – it was a thoroughly sensible investment. As we have seen, in twentieth-century India gold had a wide range of functions: a religious function, stamped by Brahmanism, in rites of passage and initiation and as a fortune-granting talisman; a symbolic function as both an everyday marker of status for married women and as an expensive luxury object; a monetary function as a replacement for money and loan enhancement; and finally, an expressive function as a display of taste, style, and individuality. Just as gold's material condition could be transformed from a bar to a delicate piece of jewelry, then refashioned according to an older or newer design, in order to one day be again melted down into a gold bar, the metal's significance has also shifted from one social context to another, even if the material form of gold jewelry has not at all changed. The economically measurable exchange value of the material is not decisive for its assessment as either luxury object or social necessity. Paradoxically, precisely on account of its generally recognized high material value, in India gold is broadly no luxury good, while owners of less valuable jewelry like imitations can perceive them as a luxury.

For most twentieth-century Indians, gold was far more as merely a luxury object, rather having many functions. Nevertheless, in certain situations it was used as a luxury object and identified as such. Although in the twentieth century the approach Indians took to gold changed a great deal, one thing remained consistent: their preference for the precious metal. As late as 1999, it was estimated that Indians annually invested more in gold than in autos, bicycles, refrigerators, and televisions combined.[67]

---

[67] "India's Golden Tariffs," *The Economist*, January 16, 1999.

4

Chinese porcelain in local and global context:
The imperial connection

Anne Gerritsen

In the early thirteenth century, one man succeeded in uniting the disparate peoples of the Central Asian steppes. The consequences of the actions of this man, Genghis Khan (c. 1162–1227), were far-reaching. He and later his descendants established a vast land-based empire that stretched from China in the east to Iran, Iraq, and as far as Hungary in the west.[1] The Mongol invasions and conquests of first the Jin dynasty (1115–1234) in the north of China, and later the Southern Song dynasty (1127–1279) in the south, which lasted for most of the thirteenth century, drew China into a wider Central Asian realm. During the Mongol Yuan dynasty (1280–1368), this broader context meant a far greater movement of people throughout China and Central Asia, a flux of sociopolitical ideas, and, most importantly for us, the appropriation of new designs and techniques in the production of luxury goods. It was during the Yuan dynasty that the potters in one kiln town in southeastern China, a place named Jingdezhen, began to produce a luxury that had a truly global impact: porcelain. For centuries to come, the ceramics that the potters of Jingdezhen fired were whiter and harder than those produced anywhere else in the world. Jingdezhen's porcelains were also more striking and recognizable: the potters used Iranian cobalt to decorate their ceramics with patterns that initially pleased mostly their Central Asian consumers, but the creation of these white porcelains with blue decorations would eventually go on to transform the domestic interiors of seventeenth-century Europe (see Figure 8) and have an impact on the manufacture of luxury ceramics across the globe.

[1] Paul Ratchnevsky, *Genghis Khan: His Life and Legacy* (Oxford: Blackwell, 1991).

FIGURE 8. Anonymous painting (erroneously attributed to Francesco Fieravino, also known as Il Maltese), "Still life with fruit and dishes on a Smyrna tapestry," 1650–80.
Courtesy of Rijksmuseum, SK-A-2551.

This chapter seeks to explore the success of this luxury commodity produced in Jingdezhen and exported throughout the Chinese empire in three separate sections. It begins with a focus on the thirteenth and fourteenth centuries, when Jingdezhen's potters began to produce significantly different wares from other sites of ceramics manufacture. This section will compare Jingdezhen to the nearby production site of Jizhou, which, as we will find, had access to very similar resources, but lacked Jingdezhen's focus on a single product. Moreover, only Jingdezhen had an imperial manufactory. The presence of that imperial office, in charge of supervising the imperial kilns and selecting the finest pieces for use in the imperial palaces, had a significant impact on the quality of the production in Jingdezhen. The second section will explore the ways in which this imperial manufactory provided protection and stimulation to the potters in Jingdezhen, thereby contributing significantly to the success of Jingdezhen's porcelain both in terms of production methods and techniques and in terms of local and global export. The third section jumps from the beginning of Jingdezhen's dominance to its later stages. During the seventeenth century, the success of Jingdezhen's ceramics spread to Europe, when Europeans began to purchase these in large quantities. Changing consumption patterns of porcelain went hand in hand with growing curiosity about its place of origin and methods of production. The writings of European travelers to the Qing empire (1644–1911) in the seventeenth century did much to satisfy that curiosity and in the process enhanced the desire for these luxury wares. This final section explores some examples of seventeenth-century travel writings. Interestingly, the European writers, too, noted the presence of the imperial manufactory in Jingdezhen. Their awe-filled descriptions of the power of the emperor that stretched as far as the bricks of clay that formed the pots as much as the designs that graced them contributed a great deal to their appeal in the eyes of European consumers.

Overall, then, this chapter shows that porcelain was produced in vast quantities, for consumers throughout the Chinese empire and all over the world, and in a wide range of qualities, from fine wares for emperors and kings to daily wares for commoners. But it was the real or assumed association with the emperor that made Jingdezhen's wares exclusive, special, and, therefore, a desirable luxury.

COMPARING JIZHOU AND JINGDEZHEN

Before we explore the writings of seventeenth-century visitors to Jingdezhen, we return to the thirteenth century. When the Mongol forces invaded southern China, they encountered little effective resistance. One of the few to make his name in resisting the Mongols was a man named Wen Tianxiang (1236–83). Born in Jiangxi Province in southern China, he had been a brilliant student and had made his career in the imperial bureaucracy of the Southern Song. After the invasion, the Mongols tried in vain to co-opt him for their cause, but when Wen persisted in his refusal, the Mongols proceeded to capture and eventually execute him in 1283. Wen Tianxiang's martyrdom and the poetry he wrote in prison guaranteed his place amongst imperial China's most celebrated figures, his prominence in the literary record, and his appearance in numerous anecdotes.

One of the anecdotes in circulation about Wen Tianxiang features his hometown, a market town in Jizhou, located in Jiangxi Province, and known, amongst other things, for its manufacture of ceramics. Apparently, when news of the Mongol threat reached Jiangxi Province, Wen Tianxiang recruited troops locally to prepare to resist the Mongols. The potters of Jizhou abandoned their kilns en masse to join Wen Tianxiang's troops. Despite their efforts, Wen's troops were defeated comprehensively, and the kilns never recovered.[2] In this anecdote, the potters' departure from Jizhou and the failure of Wen Tianxiang's resistance serve to explain why ceramic production at Jizhou seems to have begun to decline around the middle of the thirteenth century. The material record confirms this. Jizhou ceramics from the Song and Yuan dynasties (or from the tenth to the thirteenth centuries) are abundantly represented in museum collections, but hardly anything exists from the establishment of the Ming in 1368. Somewhat inexplicably, from the middle of the thirteenth century, the production of ceramics in Jizhou begins to decline, and from the Ming onward, Jizhou's kilns seem to have produced next to nothing. It is probably unlikely that Wen Tianxiang's recruitment drive had any direct impact on the eventual decline of the Jizhou kilns, but perhaps his empirewide fame and his connection to Jizhou made him an appealing figure to use in the search for explanations for the decline of the Jizhou kilns.

Another anecdote highlights Wen Tianxiang's awesome presence in the area by claiming that with one glance Wen instantly turned all the pots in the Jizhou kilns to jade, which filled the potters with such fear that they fled to the nearby kiln town of Jingdezhen and continued their work there.[3] This story suggests that there was a connection between these two sites of ceramics manufacture: Jingdezhen and Jizhou. They were not exactly close; a river journey of nearly four hundred kilometers separated the two sites, but both were located within the same province, and both produced outstanding ceramic wares (see Map 2). Again, as the material record confirms, precisely at the point in time that Jizhou's kilns started to decline, Jingdezhen's kilns began to expand rapidly and produce ever-finer wares for consumers around the globe. Here,

---

[2] Yu Jiadong, *Jiangxi Jizhou yao* (Guangzhou: Lingnan meishu chubanshe, 2002), 19.

[3] Shi Runzhang (1619–83), *Juzhai zaji* (Congshu jicheng xubian edition), 19.10a–b. The translation of this text can be found in Stephen W. Bushell, *Description of Chinese Pottery and Porcelain: Being a Translation of the T'ao Shuo* (Oxford: The Clarendon Press, 1910), 48–9. See also Cao Zao, *Chinese Connoisseurship: The Ko Ku Yao Lun*, trans. Sir Percival David (London: Faber 1970), 141–2. In another explanation, a major, but unspecified, natural disaster had a devastating impact on the site of ceramic production. Yu, *Jiadong: Jiangxi Jizhou Yao* (Guangzhou Shi: Lingnan meishu chubanshe, 2002), 19.

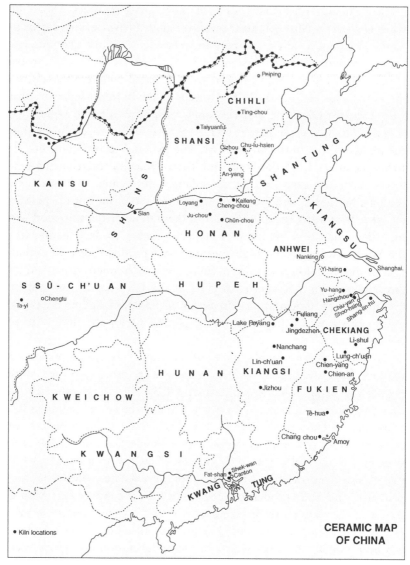

MAP 2. China.
Source: Map drawn by Cambridge University Press.

too, the anecdote does not so much provide an answer as pose a question: What, if anything, was the connection between the kilns at Jizhou
and Jingdezhen? Rather than focus on the specifics of the decline of the
Jizhou kilns and the connection to Jingdezhen, this chapter uses Jizhou as

a foil for understanding Jingdezhen as main producer of a luxury commodity that was highly sought after throughout the Chinese realm, as well as throughout the wider world. The wider question we would like to pose has to do with Jingdezhen's exceptionality. How can we account for the exceptional success of Jingdezhen's production? This chapter proposes that we should count the presence of the imperial manufactory, in place in Jingdezhen from the fourteenth century onward, among the factors that account for the success of porcelain by enhancing its exclusivity, and thereby its status as a luxury object.

The wider developments of the late thirteenth and early fourteenth centuries are undoubtedly significant here. During the Yuan dynasty, trade connections to Central Asia over land and throughout Islamic Southeast Asia by sea were strengthened. Islam was officially recognized as one of the religions of the Yuan, and for the first time given equal status next to Christianity, Buddhism, and Daoism. Merchants of the Muslim world were allowed to settle in Chinese territory, which they did mostly in the coastal regions, and control of trade lay largely in the hands of Persians, Arabs, Central Asians, and Uyghurs. These merchants had been given special privileges over the native Chinese officials and merchants who had held these positions during the Song dynasty. These non-Han Chinese merchants brought new techniques, ideas, and designs into the Chinese realm. In terms of ceramics, consumer tastes gradually began to shift away from the simple monochromes and dark-glazed tea wares so popular during the Song dynasty, to high-fired white ceramics decorated with underglaze blue patterns inspired by Central Asian designs.[4] Jingdezhen excelled at producing the wares that became known as "blue-and-whites," and began to cater to consumers worldwide, leaving behind centers of ceramics manufacture such as Jizhou that did not or could not modify their output. So from the fourteenth century, Jingdezhen's blue-and-white, the first "global brand" as Craig Clunas termed it, was treasured through time and space: from the fourteenth-century courts of Champa, Siam, and Cambodia, to the imperial kitchens of the Ottoman rulers as they settled in Istanbul during the fifteenth century to sixteenth-century imperial Iran under Shah Abbas, and, from the seventeenth century onward, also throughout Europe. This general narrative of the background against

---

4 Robert D. Mowry, "Chinese Brown and Black Glazed Ceramics: An Overview," in *Hare's Fur, Tortoiseshell, and Partridge Feathers: Chinese Brown- and Black-Glazed Ceramics, 400–1400*, ed. Robert D. Mowry, Eugene Farrell, and Nicole Coolidge Rousmaniere (Cambridge, MA: Harvard University Art Museums, 1996), 38.

which Jingdezhen's ceramics manufactures rose to global prominence is in many ways well rehearsed, but does not in itself fully answer the question of Jingdezhen's exceptionality. For that, we need to compare Jizhou and Jingdezhen in more detail.

JIZHOU AND JINGDEZHEN COMPARED: KILN TECHNOLOGY

There are many different ways in which one could go about comparing the two ceramic centers of Jizhou and Jingdezhen, starting with the necessary technology for the manufacture of high-quality ceramics. Creating a ceramic vessel required detailed knowledge of the methods of preparation for the different types of clay; recipes for clay mixtures and glazes and an understanding of kiln sizes and shapes; the effects of drafts and oxidization; the types of fuels; and the effects of different temperatures in the kilns. The kilns in use around 1300 in both Jizhou and Jingdezhen were so-called *longyao* or dragon kilns: narrowly shaped kilns built against the side of a hill with consecutive chambers between the fire at the lower end and a chimney at the higher end.[5] In these kilns, the draw was much stronger than in the coal-fired domed kilns in use in northern China at that time, because of the upward shape of the chambers. The temperature could easily be controlled because of the ports for side-stoking along the chambers, enabling a regulation of the oxygen levels. Constructed against scrubland hills that were mostly unusable for agricultural cultivation, dragon kilns were particularly suited to the southern conditions. From the mid-Ming onward, or from the fifteenth century, a technological innovation in the form of egg-shaped kilns appeared in Jingdezhen. Oval shaped and higher at one end than the other, these kilns were fast burning, with a significant drop in temperature between the high end with the fire box and the much-lower chimney end, a characteristic that could be exploited to fire a variety of wares at different temperatures simultaneously. By manipulating the varying oxygen levels inside the kiln, a variety of results could be achieved with simultaneous firing. Loading and managing the firing of such kilns thus became a demanding task that required the skills of experienced workers

---

[5] On the northern "*mantou*" kilns, see Rose Kerr and Nigel Wood, *Science and Civilisation in China*, Vol. 5: Chemistry and Chemical Technology, part 12, Ceramic Technology (Cambridge: Cambridge University Press, 2004), 314–34. Some *mantou* kilns were also found in the south, most notably in Sichuan. Ibid., 331. On the *longquan* kilns, see ibid., 347–59.

and suited the complex production systems gradually put in place in Jingdezhen.[6] Initially, however, the kilns at Jizhou and Jingdezhen used the same technologies to maximize the benefits of the local conditions to produce their highest-quality wares.

JIZHOU AND JINGDEZHEN COMPARED: CLAYS

Creating a vessel does not happen with technology alone; it requires the skillful hands of potters, and the ability of potters to adjust to the ever-changing environments in which they work. In both Jizhou and Jingdezhen, potters were able to adjust the materials they used for the construction of clay bodies, and to adapt to gradually changing local conditions and changing tastes. The earliest Jingdezhen ceramics, dating back to the Five Dynasties, had bodies of pure "kaolinized" porcelain stone (a locally mined stone with enough plasticity to enable the shaping of pots), and potters used this same material mixed with limestone to create the glazes.[7] Jizhou wares were glazed in the same way, although the clay Jizhou's potters used was slightly heavier. In both places, the limestone for the glaze was prepared for use by burning it with wood and bracken (fern leaves), creating a "glaze ash."[8] Both Jizhou and Jingdezhen had access to ready supplies of wood and ferns locally. Eventually, supplies of pure kaolinized porcelain stone ran out in Jingdezhen, and potters had to mix the porcelain stone with kaolin, found in the nearby Gaoling Mountains, to provide plasticity and refractoriness, and introduced a different material for the glaze. During the course of the Yuan dynasty, these new materials used in varying combinations in Jingdezhen could be fired at increasingly high temperatures, which created an opaque and slightly matte glaze that could cover up any impurities in the mixed clay the potters had started to use for the bodies.[9] During the Ming (1368–1644) and Qing (1644–1911) dynasties, the material for the bodies continued to contain mixtures of porcelain stone and clay, while the ingredients were gradually refined further and prepared to a higher

[6] Ibid., 366–78, 561.

[7] Clay referred to as "kaolin" is the product of the decomposition of feldspathic rock, and "kaolinization" is the process of decomposition of the feldspar that leads to the formation of kaolin. The porcelain stone used in these early bodies was highly "kaolinized," giving it plasticity and a highly refractory nature (i.e., able to withstand high temperatures). See ibid., 219.

[8] Ibid., 552–5.

[9] In Jingdezhen, the potters began to use a special "glaze stone" that was high in albite. The high albite content of the glaze stone enhanced its fusibility. Ibid., 229–33, 558–9, 443.

standard than beforehand, allowing the production of ceramic bodies of the purest white with extremely smooth and glossy glazes, known to us as porcelain. The ongoing refinement of ingredients and improvement of manufacturing technologies allowed Jingdezhen potters to produce a highly luxurious commodity: harder, smoother, and glossier than the potters in Jizhou could ever produce. Most elements, however, such as the shape of the kilns, the mixtures used to form the bodies and glazes, and access to elementary resources were surprisingly similar in both places.

JIZHOU AND JINGDEZHEN
COMPARED: LOCATION

In terms of the location of these kiln sites, too, similarities outweigh the differences. Both Jizhou and Jingdezhen were located along the banks of rivers that provided access to crucial transportation networks (see Map 2). Jizhou was located along the river Gan, which provided access northward to the provincial capital Nanchang, and from there via the Yangzi River to the capital of the Southern Song capital in Hangzhou, and southward to Ganzhou and to the coastal regions of Fujian and Guangzhou (Canton). Jingdezhen was located on the banks of the river Chang, providing easy transport to the county capital of Fuliang. The regional center of mercantile activity, Huizhou, was located just north of Jingdezhen. So from both Jizhou and Jingdezhen, people and goods could easily travel toward the economic center of gravity in the lower Yangzi valley, and from there northward along the imperial canal to the administrative center, or southward using Lake Poyang and the river Gan via the Meiling Pass to Canton, the center of overseas trade.

Jingdezhen's proximity to Huizhou Prefecture, bordering Jiangxi in the northeast of the province, is noteworthy. The Huizhou merchants were among the most active merchants in the Chinese realm, especially from the sixteenth century onward.[10] Among the goods the Huizhou merchants traded were locally grown tea; wood from the originally densely

---

[10] Harriet Thelma Zurndorfer, *Change and Continuity in Chinese Local History: The Development of Hui-Chou Prefecture, 800 to 1800* (Leiden, The Netherlands and New York: E. J. Brill, 1989); Michael Dillon, "Transport and Marketing in the Development of the Jingdezhen Porcelain Industry during the Ming and Qing Dynasties," *Journal of the Social and Economic History of the Orient* 35, no. 3 (1992): 278–90; Du Yongtao, *The Order of Places: Translocal Practices of the Huizhou Merchants in Late Imperial China* (Leiden, The Netherlands and New York: E. J. Brill, 2015); Antonia Finnane, *Speaking of Yangzhou: A Chinese City, 1550–1850*, Harvard East Asian Monographs (Cambridge, MA: Harvard University Asia Center, 2004), 57–68; Timothy

forested mountains; wood products such as ink, lacquer, and paper and printed materials; and numerous other locally crafted objects.[11] During the Ming dynasty, as the economy expanded, the number of Huizhou merchants grew rapidly, and throughout the Ming and Qing dynasties, the Huizhou merchants accumulated large profits through the process of buying and selling throughout the empire.[12] Initially, salt was the mainstay of their trade, but ceramics were also on their lists of profitable goods.[13] The proximity of Huizhou to Jingdezhen and the convenience of the access routes that connected these two places explain the active role of Huizhou merchants in the empirewide distribution of Jingdezhen's porcelain.[14] Nevertheless, even without Huizhou merchants championing their wares, Jizhou's ceramics did get widely distributed throughout the empire, so the proximity to Huizhou cannot be the single key to understanding why Jingdezhen's trajectory was so different from Jizhou's.

JIZHOU AND JINGDEZHEN COMPARED: PRODUCTS

If Jizhou and Jingdezhen did not differ greatly in terms of technologies, access to natural resources, and location, then the obvious point to compare would be the products. Seeing Jizhou and Jingdezhen wares next to each other immediately highlights some striking differences. Jizhou wares come in a wide variety. The Jizhou scholar Gao Liren distinguishes six main types of Jizhou wares: very early bluish-green wares and egg-white wares, the more common brownish black wares produced during the Song and Yuan dynasties, cream-colored painted wares, green glazed wares, and finally sculpted ceramics. Each of these are further subdivided; the black wares, for example, include not only deep black glazes, but also mottled glazes with evocative names such as "hare's fur," "tortoiseshell," and "partridge mottle," and black wares with paper-cut appliqué, leaf, and flower patterns. The painted wares include a wide range of motifs on glazed surfaces, and the sculpted wares include statuettes and animal

Brook, *The Confusions of Pleasure: Commerce and Culture in Ming China* (Berkeley and London: University of California Press, 1999), 126–9.

[11] Zurndorfer, *Change and Continuity*, 25–7, 41, 124–5. On the role of the Huizhou merchants in book making and book collecting, see Joseph McDermott, *A Social History of the Chinese Book: Books and Literati Culture in Late Imperial China* (Hong Kong: Hong Kong University Press, 2006).

[12] Zurndorfer, *Change and Continuity*, 64.

[13] Dillon, "Transport and Marketing," 285–6; Du Yongtao, *The Order of Places*.

[14] Zurndorfer, *Change and Continuity*, 18.

shapes.[15] The black wares in particular gained in popularity during the Song dynasty because of the growing popularity of the consumption of fine teas. Creamy white and light green teas were thought to taste best when served in simple dark-glazed bowls, not only throughout the Song and Yuan empires but also in Japan. Japanese tea consumption took on an increasing significance as part of the tea ceremony, and Jizhou's tea wares were highly sought after.[16]

Jizhou's production of highly varied wares was in part the result of the incorporation of design ideas from other kiln sites. Jizhou's potters were particularly adept at synthesizing ideas from other kilns. Ceramics known as Ding wares, and in particular purple Ding, the light-brown painted Cizhou wares (see Figure 9), the northern black wares, and the wares produced at the Jian kilns in Fujian were all closely connected to Jizhou wares.[17] Whether the potters traveled between these sites and transmitted techniques and designs in person, or whether the wares were transmitted along with migrants and travelers is difficult to ascertain, but Jizhou's strength undoubtedly was the ability of those working in Jizhou to respond to product innovations and consumer demands elsewhere.

Compared with Jizhou, Jingdezhen produced a rather narrower range of wares. The light clays combined with gradually more opaque glazes provided the perfect white underground for decorative patterns in color. During the Yuan dynasty, the introduction of cobalt blue applied to these clear white bodies created the stunning combination referred to as blue-and-white. From the introduction of cobalt to Jingdezhen, and the use of pencils to apply fine decorative patterns onward, Jingdezhen specialized in the production of blue-and-white, and from the fifteenth century onward, rapidly increased both the quality and the quantity of the production. The introduction and development of cobalt-based decorations on white wares was probably Jingdezhen's most significant innovation in terms of world ceramics, as can be seen in the many

---

[15] Ibid.

[16] Kerr and Wood, *Ceramic Technology*, 273. The consumption of tea in fine tea bowls is the subject of a number of famous poems, gathered together by the contemporary scholar Feng Xianming. See his "Cong wenxian kan Tang Song yilai yincha fengshang ji taoci chaju de yanbian," *Wenwu* 1 (1963): 8–16.

[17] Ding wares come from kilns in northern China (Hebei), and are usually dated to the Song dynasty, with fine ivory-white bodies decorated with engravings and later moldings under a colorless glaze. Mary Tregear, *Song Ceramics* (New York: Rizzoli, 1982), 63. The comparison between Ding and Jizhou wares was first made by Cao Zhao, author of "Essential Criteria of Antiquities" (*Gegu yaolun*), the influential fourteenth-century manual on the appreciation of arts and antiques.

FIGURE 9. Earthenware jar with dragon and phoenix design. Cizhou ware, Ming dynasty. H 40.5 centimeters × D 44.3 centimeters. Courtesy of Rijksmuseum, AK-MAK-110.

attempts to imitate this combination: the Isnik wares developed under the Ottomans, the Safavid ceramics produced near Isfahan, the luster-ware of the Hispanic world, Italian majolica, and the Dutch Delftware.[18]

This brief comparison between the various aspects of these two sites of ceramics manufacture, Jizhou and Jingdezhen, makes very clear that the greatest difference is in the wares. Jizhou produced a far wider range, but Jingdezhen had the edge in the production of fine wares of the highest

---

[18] The earliest surviving Western imitations of blue-and-white were made in Florence between 1575 and 1587. On the impact of Chinese blue-and-white after 1604 in the Netherlands, when the contents of the captured Portuguese ship were auctioned in Amsterdam, see Clare le Corbeiller, "China into Delft: A Note on Visual Translation," *The Metropolitan Museum of Art Bulletin* 26, no. 6 (1968): 269–76. John Carswell has charted the impact of blue-and-white ware from Jingdezhen on ceramic production throughout the globe, most notably in the Middle East and in Europe. John Carswell, *Blue and White: Chinese Porcelain around the World* (London: British Museum Press, 2000).

quality. It probably is not an exaggeration to claim that up to the end of the seventeenth century, the Jingdezhen "product" was more successful than what was produced at any other kiln in the world. For roughly three centuries, the potters at Jingdezhen produced high-quality luxury commodities that were desired both locally and globally. Moreover, they produced these wares in high enough volumes to satisfy much of their demand without compromising their high quality.

Of course, the success of Jingdezhen's ceramics manufacture has been the subject of a great deal of research, and undoubtedly multiple factors have to be taken into account to explain this success, but one of these factors may well have been the presence in Jingdezhen of an imperial manufactory. To understand the significance of this imperial connection to the kilns in Jingdezhen, we need to go back to the fourteenth century and the Yuan dynasty, and the time during which this connection became institutionalized.

THE SIGNIFICANCE OF MANUFACTURING
FOR THE COURT

The Yuan court's interest in extending control over the technologies of ceramic manufacture and the production of luxury porcelains for export fits into a wider context of the institutionalization of crafts under the Mongols. The Mongols' quest to legitimize their rule over Han Chinese territory, combined with their recognition of the efficiency of the extant structures, both feature in the Mongol decision to use the structures of the civil service bureaucracy to acquire luxury goods for the court. Near the highest echelons of the institutional hierarchy was the Imperial Manufactories Commission.[19] This commission was responsible for the supervision of artisans working in about twenty-five different workshops specializing in the manufacture of gold, silver, jade, and other luxury utensils for palace use such as crowns and belts, but also paintings and textiles. Many of the craftsmen that staffed these workshops had been captured by the Mongols on their campaigns in Central Asia, with those specializing in the making of weaponry sent off to accompany the troops, and those with skills in the production of luxury goods sent to richer and more peaceful areas. Only when Khubilai Khan (1215–94)

---

[19] There is some confusion in the Chinese sources over when the office was established. The *Yuanshi* states a later date than the biographies of officials who served in the commission would suggest. *Yuanshi, juan* 88, 2225–30. See also Anning Jing, "The Portraits of Khubilai Khan and Chabi by Anige," *Artibus Asiae* 1–2 (1994): 48 for details.

had established himself at the capital and founded the Yuan dynasty was the work of these artisans matched to the Han Chinese bureaucratic structure, and from then this structure grew rapidly, perhaps supervising as many as ten thousand artisan households.[20] The emperor relied heavily on the skills of the peoples he had subjected; the first, and probably most famous, incumbent was a Nepalese craftsman by the name of Anige (1245–1306), and later leaders were Persian and Mongolian. One of the workshops this commission supervised was the Supervisorate-in-chief of Metal Workers and Jewelers.[21] This, in turn, was responsible for the Fuliang Porcelain Bureau, established in the Fuliang county town of Jingdezhen at the site of production in 1278.[22] The fact that the Mongol rulers selected Jingdezhen for the location of this office is significant; it suggests that the wares produced there had the preference of the Mongol court over the wares produced at other sites such as Jizhou. The Porcelain Bureau, very small during the first years of its operation, increased in size in 1295, and flourished between 1295 and 1324. The bureau functioned until 1352, when the area fell into the hands of the rebel forces that would eventually establish the Ming dynasty. Through these institutions, the Mongols sought to use and modify the bureaucratic and administrative structures that were already in place to regulate the manufacture of court luxuries and to capitalize on the strength of the available craftsmen throughout the empire.

At the same time, the Mongol emperors sought to extend control over crafts by regulating the designs of these luxury wares. For example, they issued edicts intended to create "imperial" designs, setting them apart from designs that the wider population could use. In 1314, for example, the court issued an edict stating that no one but the emperor was allowed to wear clothing with the dragon or the phoenix pattern, nor use any ceramic implements (e.g., tea cups or wine cups) with the same.[23] The dragon that was out of bounds for anyone but the emperor was the dragon with five claws and two horns. After the Yuan dynasty, these rules were by no means consistently applied, but at least during the Yuan this

---

[20] Ibid. There are different figures in use for the conversion of households to population numbers, but 5.6 per household is sometimes used.

[21] It was called *Jinyufu* between 1261 and 1266.

[22] Shelagh Vainker, *Chinese Pottery and Porcelain* (London: British Museum Press, 2005), 179–80. The establishment of this office took the place of taking tribute from specific large-scale and high-quality kilns. During the early days of the imperial kilns, those kilns frequently did not produce enough, so luxury objects were taken from the folk kilns.

[23] Lian Song, *Yuan Shi (History of the Yuan)* (Beijing: Zhonghua shuju, 1976), 1942.

regulation is clearly documented.[24] Out of all the production of ceramic wares intended for the court, only a small percentage (between 10 and 20 percent) would actually be considered acceptable, but because these wares contained the imperial motifs they could not enter the commercial market, and had to be smashed and buried. The team working under the Jingdezhen archaeologist Liu Xinyuan has spent twenty years or so on the vast task of piecing together stores of cleanly broken pieces excavated in Jingdezhen, reconstructing rejected wares for the Yuan court.[25] These archaeological finds suggest that the imperial court commissioned blue-and-white pieces for the personal use of the emperor as early as the reign of Tugh Temur (the Wenzong emperor, who reigned between 1328 and 1332).[26]

This imperial control combined with imperial patronage had a significant impact on the development of the style and quality of Jingdezhen's wares. The refinement in Jingdezhen blue-and-white pieces over the course of the fourteenth century and throughout the Ming dynasty that followed the Yuan suggests the competitive advantage of imperial patronage. The pressure of having to produce wares of a high enough quality for use at the imperial court led to ongoing refinements in terms of the clays used, the cobalt used for decorations, glaze materials, and firing techniques. None of the other local kiln sites could keep up with the quality of Jingdezhen's imperial wares, and this may well have been one of the most significant factors in accounting for the fourteenth-century divergence between Jingdezhen and sites like Jizhou.

THE APPEAL OF JINGDEZHEN'S CERAMICS IN SEVENTEENTH-CENTURY EUROPEAN ACCOUNTS

Over the course of the fourteenth and fifteenth centuries, the processes of ceramics manufacturing in Jingdezhen developed further, becoming not only more refined, but also more differentiated. The increasing separation of the individual stages in the manufacturing processes led to an ever-increasing mass production in Jingdezhen. As the size of the imperial

---

[24] John Alexander Pope, *Chinese Porcelains from the Ardebil Shrine*, Smithsonian Publication (Washington, DC: Smithsonian Institution, Freer Gallery of Art, 1956), 35.

[25] Liu Xinyuan, "The Kiln Sites of Jingdezhen and Their Place in the History of Chinese Ceramics," in *Ceramic Finds from Jingdezhen Kilns, 10th–17th Century* (Hong Kong: The Fung Ping Shan Museum, The University of Hong Kong, 1992): 32–54.

[26] For a full discussion of the evidence used in dating these pieces, see Liang Sui, ed., *Jingdezhen chutu Yuan Ming guanyao waqi* (Yuan and Ming Imperial Porcelains Unearthed from Jingdezhen) (Beijing: Wenwu chubanshe, 1999), 14–16.

court grew, both in Beijing and in the princely courts throughout the empire presided over by the male relatives of the emperor, the demands on porcelain production in Jingdezhen also grew. Through mass production, dividing the production line into stages, and creating specialists for each stage – from gathering the wood for the fire to the delicate final touches on the decorations – Jingdezhen's potters could respond to imperial demand. But imperial demand could be fickle, so in times of high demand, orders were farmed out to private enterprises and, conversely, in times of low demand, workers in the imperial manufactory could produce for the commercial stream. During the fifteenth and sixteenth centuries, this commercial (i.e., nonimperial) production increasingly included production for export. Jingdezhen's blue-and-whites have been found along the African coast, throughout the Middle East and Central Asia, in South and Southeast Asia, and throughout East Asia. In fact, it is very hard to find a location that was never enticed by blue-and-white from Jingdezhen, and in many of the locations mentioned previously a local production of some kind of blue-and-white pottery followed the introduction of Chinese ceramics. The greatest increase in production for export, however, occurred when the Europeans appeared on the Chinese markets from the early seventeenth century, and began to order Jingdezhen's blue-and-whites in ever-increasing quantities, until eventually the European manufacture of porcelain overtook what was produced in China both in quality and in price.

Obviously, the seventeenth-century European consumers were by no means the first to hear about ceramics. As early as the fourteenth century, Marco Polo had enticed his readers with this description: "In a city called Tinju they make bowls of porcelain, large and small, of incomparable beauty. They are made nowhere else except in this city, and from here they are exported all over the world. In the city itself they are so plentiful and cheap that for a Venetian groat you might buy three bowls of such beauty that nothing lovelier could be imagined."[27] Polo's descriptions of porcelain and of the process of manufacturing (which included references to earth that had to be "stacked in huge mounds and left for thirty or forty years exposed to wind, rain, and sun" creating wares "of an azure tint with a very brilliant sheen") continued to fire the imagination of his medieval and early modern European readers. By the seventeenth century, however, detailed firsthand accounts of China started to appear in

---

[27] Marco Polo, *The Travels* (Harmondsworth, UK and New York: Penguin Books, 1958), 238.

print in Europe. The number of editions and translations of each of these accounts suggests they found an eager and growing readership. What had appeared in Marco Polo's account as a near-mythical realm now began to seem more "real"; beginning with the diaries of Matteo Ricci, the first Jesuit to live in Beijing until his death there in 1610, European readers had access to detailed descriptions of China's physical geography; illustrated narratives of towns and their inhabitants; and vivid accounts of the complex and awesome powers of the imperial court and its bureaucratic tentacles that regulated each aspect of society.

The awe in which European visitors held the imperial court is nowhere more visible than in the frontispiece of one of the most famous books about China of the mid-seventeenth century, Johan Nieuhof's *An Embassy from the East-India Company of the United Provinces, to the Grand Tartar Cham Emperor of China* (1669).[28] It was produced in Amsterdam, and based on lost diaries by Johan Nieuhof, a member of the first Dutch mission to the Chinese court between 1655 and 1657. This image says a great deal about the vision of China: the ever-imposing presence of the emperor, the number of people in his command, his perception of himself as possessor of the entire world, and the cruelty of that power represented by the men in stocks at the feet of the emperor. Because Nieuhof's writings had such a significant impact on the European imagination about China, they form a useful starting point in exploring European perceptions of the ceramics industry in seventeenth-century China.

This Dutch mission to the imperial court started in Canton, and the party traveled to the court in Beijing along the standard route used both by officials and travelers to journey between the north and the south, and by merchants transporting their wares south from the centers of silk and ceramics manufacture in Jiangnan and northern Jiangxi. The party proceeded northward on the Gan toward Lake Poyang, and stopped in the town of Wucheng, located on the western shore of the lake. Wucheng was a pivotal place along the route, providing access to crucial transportation routes in three directions. Nieuhof describes Wucheng as having a beautiful main street, full of shops of all kinds of trades, and as a better place to buy porcelain than the provincial capital (Nanchang). Wucheng

---

[28] Johannes Nieuhof, Pieter de Goyer, Jacob de Keizer, Athanasius Kircher, John Ogilby, and Johann Adam Schall von Bell, *An Embassy from the East-India Company of the United Provinces to the Grand Tartar Cham, Emperor of China*. London: Printed by the Author ... 1673. See also Leonard Blussé and Reindert Falkenburg, *Johan Nieuhofs Beelden Van Een Chinareis 1655–1657* (Middelburg: Stichting VOC publicaties, 1987).

served as the main ceramics distribution center; Jingdezhen's merchants brought their wares here for transportation in all directions.

Wucheng was the closest the party got to the center of ceramics production, and Nieuhof used the opportunity to inform the reader about the process of manufacture, so they would understand how the locally mined clays were turned into such fine ceramics. Nieuhof noted that the raw material, the clay, was sourced outside Jiangxi in Huizhou, "from whence it is brought in four-square clods to the above-mentioned Village (i.e. Jingdezhen), which have the Emperor's Arms stamp'd upon them, to prevent all manner of deceit."[29] The clay had to be transported to Jingdezhen, because this was the only place where potters had the skills to produce wares he describes as artfully worked, cleverly shaped, and with blue decorations that are easy on the eye. He also mentions the reduction firing process, whereby the ovens are sealed so tightly that no air can enter the kiln for fifteen days. When the firing is complete, "the Furnace is open'd in the presence of an Officer, appointed by the Emperor to take an Account of this Earthen Ware, and to receive his Duty, which is of each sort the fifth piece, according to the Laws of the Kingdom."[30] The remainder, Nieuhof adds, is sold not only throughout China but also "through the whole World."[31]

It is by no means an extensive account of the process of porcelain manufacture, but Nieuhof assumes his readers were already familiar with the material and would have shared his assessment that Chinese porcelain was unequalled. By this time, large quantities of porcelain were coming into the European markets, and especially the Dutch market, on a regular basis.[32] What his readers may not have known was how specifically local this process was, hence his emphasis on the location of the source of the clay and on the exclusivity of these skills. Only here do the potters have the knowledge of the firing process and the requisite skills to create such beautiful decorations. Considerable attention is given to the imperial connection; from the "Emperor's Arms stamp'd upon" the clay to the "Officer appointed by the Emperor" who oversees the opening of the furnace and the selection of the wares for the emperor, each aspect of the manufacturing process falls under imperial control.

---

[29] Nieuhof, *An Embassy*, 66.
[30] Ibid.
[31] Ibid.
[32] See on this the very recent volume, edited by Jan van Campen and Titus Eliëns, *Chinese and Japanese Porcelain for the Dutch Golden Age* (Zwolle: Waanders, 2014).

The second Dutch mission to China followed just more than a decade later. It was led by Pieter van Hoorn, took place between 1666 and 1668, and was described in full by a man named Olfert Dapper. Dapper's account appeared in Dutch in 1670, in English and German translations in 1671, and in French in 1680.[33] Dapper had never left Holland, but drew on the careful records kept by the members of Pieter van Hoorn's delegation and the records of an expedition along the Fujian coast by a Dutch admiral named Balthasar Bort (1626–84). "A Description of the Empire of China or Taising" accompanied the account of the mission. This included a segment entitled "Minerals, Stones and Earth," and here we find the fullest description of the process of manufacturing porcelain contained in Dapper's work. Dapper describes various kinds of porcelain, ranging from some "not much better than our Earthen Ware" to the "finest Porcelane we have in Europe." Wares of the highest quality is described "as fine and clear as Crystal, which on pain of Death may not be carry'd out of the Countrey, but must all be brought to the Court, and deliver'd to the Emperor and his Council."[34] The awesome power of the emperor and his exclusive control over all aspects of society and the economy were part of the general and long-lasting picture generated in these early European descriptions of China. The account goes on to describe where the earth used to manufacture porcelain is found (in Huizhou) and how it is transported to Jiangxi (by river "in square lumps or cakes").[35] And here the author finds another opportunity to remind the reader of the long arm of imperial control: "not one Lump may be carry'd away before it is mark'd with the Emperor's Arms, thereby to prevent the falsifying of it."[36] The wording may be slightly different, but in both accounts connections are forged between the high value of the porcelain and the imperial court. The same description even found its way into Dapper's account of Japan – again composed by him without ever having left Holland – where a reference to Japanese porcelain leads the author to a description of the clay used in China: the earth is "seal'd with the Emperors Arms" and "sold at a certain price."[37] And here too: "the Oven is open'd, in the

---

[33] The English version of this text appeared under the name of Arnoldus Montanus (1625–83), translated by John Ogilby. The English translation of the embassy's account is entitled *Atlas Chinensis: Being a Second Part of a Relation of Remarkable Passages in Two Embassies from the East-India Company of the United Provinces to the Vice-roy Singlamong*. Olfert Dapper, however, was the author of the original Dutch version.
[34] Dapper, *Atlas Chinensis*, 711.
[35] Ibid.
[36] Ibid., 712.
[37] Montanus, *Atlas Japannensis*, 434.

presence of one of the Emperors Officers, who narrowly looks on every Piece thereof, and, according to the Laws of the Countrey, takes away every fifth Piece of Porcelan to the Emperors use."[38]

If these Dutch writers seem mostly to repeat the same statements, the French Jesuit Louis le Comte (1655–1728), who traveled to China at the end of the seventeenth century, represents a slightly different view. The young Le Comte, born into a wealthy Bordeaux family, had joined the Society of Jesus at an early age, devoting himself to the study of mathematics, physics, and logic. In 1688, he traveled to the court of the Kangxi emperor, who sent him to the remote northern province of Shaanxi, where he remained until his return to France in 1691. The eight letters he sent to members of the French court upon his return were published in two volumes in 1696 and 1697, and reached a wide audience throughout Europe. Le Comte knew what interests were current amongst European consumers; he provided his readers with rich detail on the culture of the imperial court and the philosophy of the scholars; the daily lives of ordinary people; the urban and rural landscapes; and the mercantile activities he observed. Moreover, Le Comte included extensive detail on Chinese crafts in his letters; he wrote about porcelain, but also about lacquer, silk, paper, ink, and the casting of bells. His letter to the Duchess of Bouillon (Marie Anne Mancini, 1649–1714), which dwells extensively on porcelain, suggests that the European readers have come a long way since they were so in awe of the China conjured up in Polo's description. Porcelain surely could also be made by the French, if only "the Ingenious would please to make some Experiments, and operate diligently."[39] Le Comte's text dispels the myths that one or two hundred years were required "to the preparing the Matter for the Porcelain" as Marco Polo had suggested, and that porcelain was difficult to make. "If that were so, it would be neither so common, nor so cheap."[40] But Le Comte also had this to say about the role of the emperor in controlling ceramics manufacture: "The Emperor has constituted in the Province where the Manufacture chiefly is, a particular Mandarin, whose care it is to make choice of the fairest Vases for the court."[41] So far, so good. This statement matches the observations of Nieuhof and Dapper. But then Le Comte

---

[38] Ibid., 435.

[39] Louis Le Comte, *Memoirs and Observations ... Made in a Late Journey through the Empire of China* ... ([Nouveaux Memoires Sur L'etat Present De La Chine]: London trans., 1697, 1696), 160.

[40] Ibid., 158.

[41] Ibid.

claims that this mandarin "buys [these vases] at a very reasonable rate, so that the Workmen being but ill paid, do not do their best, and are not willing to take any pains for that which will not enrich them."[42] According to Le Comte, a potter working for a private employer "who would not spare for cost and charges"[43] would produce far better workmanship. It is an interesting view of the work of the potter; only with the incentive of good money would he produce truly outstanding pieces. Clearly, Le Comte's view of the imperial presence in Jingdezhen is not the same as the views of Nieuhof and Dapper. Le Comte sees the downside of imperial production, and considers it to be inefficient. It was precisely during this time that the European perception of China began to change more broadly from admiration and awe to ridicule and eventually contempt by the end of the eighteenth century.[44] Le Comte clearly had a more critical view of Chinese methods of production, and felt the French could easily match the Jingdezhen potters' skills. Even if Le Comte was less in awe, both of the production processes and the connection to the emperor, than Nieuhof and Dapper had been, he still observed the link between the two; the "fairest vases" in Jingdezhen were produced and selected for the court. By paying higher wages to a potter, one might obtain a piece of even higher quality, but the standard that quality is measured against remains the imperial court.

With the accounts of these seventeenth-century observers, we have moved a long way from Wen Tianxiang, the Jizhou potters, and the developments of the fourteenth century. The influx of designs and styles that accompanied the integration of the Chinese empire into the greater Central Asian realm; the establishment of the Imperial Manufactories in Jingdezhen during the first decades of the fourteenth century; and the creation of the striking combination of blue decorations on white porcelain together help to explain why Jingdezhen's production overtook the manufacture of ceramics at all other kilns. During the centuries that followed, the presence of the imperial manufactory in Jingdezhen continued to drive forward both the quality and the quantity of the Jingdezhen porcelain production. That presence also helps to explain how the Jingdezhen potters could respond so effectively to the vast increase in demand that occurred after the arrival of European travelers and traders. The surplus

[42] Ibid.
[43] Ibid.
[44] David Porter, *Ideographia: The Chinese Cipher in Early Modern Europe* (Stanford, CA: Stanford University Press, 2001).

of the imperial production, as well as the production of the private potters in Jingdezhen, supplied European homes with the blue-and-whites
that graced their domestic interiors from the seventeenth century. And
as the accounts of these early travelers also reveal, the presence of the
imperial manufactory did not go unnoticed by the Europeans. Perhaps
the appeal of these porcelain luxuries was even enhanced by the knowledge that they had been produced under the auspices of a very distant
emperor.

5

Luxury or commodity? The success of Indian cotton cloth in the first global age

Giorgio Riello

INTRODUCTION

Cotton textiles were in what is now called "the first global age" – the period spanning from the European voyages of discovery at the end of the fifteenth century to the period of divergence at the end of the eighteenth century – quintessential global commodities. Cotton cloth produced in the Indian subcontinent had already secured markets across the Indian Ocean in the centuries preceding the arrival of European traders – first the Portuguese and later the English, Dutch, French, and other East India companies on the shore of India. From 1500 onwards, Indian cottons conquered new markets, especially in Europe and the Americas, and made inroads into the habits of consumers almost everywhere in the world.[1] The age of "King Cotton," when plantations were set up in the Americas to produce raw cotton for the entire world was preceded by the age of "Queen Cotton" in which Indian cotton cloth was the most globally traded commodity.

This narrative appears particularly "modern" in the sense that it prefigures many of the traits that world trade came to assume in the period starting with European industrialization. The scale of the trade and its

---

[1] Giorgio Riello, "The Globalisation of Cotton Textiles: Indian Cottons, Europe and the Atlantic World, 1600–1850," in *The Spinning World: A Global History of Cotton Textiles, 1200–1850*, ed. Giorgio Riello and Prasannan Parthasarathi (Oxford: Oxford University Press, 2009), 261–87; Prasannan Parthasarathi and Giorgio Riello, "From India to the World: Cotton and Fashionability," in *Handbook of the History of Consumption*, ed. Frank Trentmann (Oxford: Oxford University Press, 2012), 145–70; *Interwoven Globe: The Worldwide Textile Trade, 1500–1800*, ed. Amelia Peck (New York: Metropolitan Museum of Art, 2013).

consequences both globally and within local markets is emphasized. Unlike the precious and expensive Chinese silks, Indian cotton textiles reached the most remote parts of the globe and changed the consuming habits not just of the elites but also of poorer consumers. They replaced traditional fibers such as arrowroot and linen as cottons were both cheap and available in large quantities. Rather than being expensive oriental luxuries in reach of the few, Indian cottons were the first cheap mass commodity satisfying the everyday needs of Chinese peasants, African slaves, and European housewives.[2]

This tension between "luxury" and "commodity" does not affect just cotton textiles but extends to the assessment of the nature of early modern global trade. Sanjay Subrahmanyam in a series of articles published in the 1990s encouraged historians of the Indian Ocean to look beyond the luxuries and rarities and to consider instead the role of widespread commodities such as rice.[3] Historians interested in chartering the trade between Asia and Europe encountered similar difficulties in defining the nature of those consumer goods traded back to Europe. While some have highlighted their potential to act as luxuries ensuring high profits, others have made the opposite claim counting, for instance, the millions of pieces of porcelain traded from China to Europe in the seventeenth and eighteenth centuries.[4]

One might conclude that, whatever the definition of *luxury* adopted, Indian cotton textiles did not fulfill well any of the criteria. This chapter argues instead that India's production of cotton textiles included not just cheap traded varieties but also a range of products that we could classify as luxuries. This chapter wishes to challenge the easy divide between luxury and commodity and claims that part of the success of cotton cloth as a global commodity was based on its luxury appeal. However, one might ask what luxury means and what a luxury

---

[2] See in particular my *Cotton: The Fibre that Made the Modern World* (Cambridge: Cambridge University Press, 2013), esp. chs. 4–6.

[3] Sanjay Subrahmanyam, "The Portuguese, the Port of Basrur, and the Rice Trade, 1600–50," *Indian Economic and Social History Review* 21, no. 4 (1984): 433–62. By comparison see Steensgaard's position on pepper and indigo, e.g., Niels Steensgaard, *Carracks, Caravans and Companies: The Structural Crisis in the European-Asian Trade in the Early 17th Century* (Copenhagen: Studentlitteratur, 1973), 174.

[4] Maxine Berg, "Manufacturing the Orient: Asian Commodities and European Industry 1500–1800," in *Prodotti e tecniche d'oltremare nelle economie europee: Secc. XIII–XVIII: Atti della Ventinovesima Settimana di Studi, 14–19 aprile 1997*, ed. Simonetta Cavaciocchi (Florence: Le Monnier, 1998), esp. 395; Robert Finlay, "The Pilgrim Art: The Culture of Porcelain in World History," *Journal of World History* 9, no. 2 (1998): 168.

product was in early modern global markets. I wish to consider the role of cotton textiles in three different areas of the early modern world: in South Asia, Southeast Asia, and Europe. I argue that in each of them Indian cottons were considered luxuries, though each case underlines a different definition of *luxury*. One might say that the true success of Indian cottons was their ability to embody different notions of luxury that I will illustrate through specific regional cases. In order to do so I first turn to a conceptualization of the different ways in which luxury operated in the early modern world.

A TYPOLOGY OF LUXURY IN EARLY MODERNITY

In the early modern period – and one might extend this statement to include the present – luxury was not a monolithic concept. There are different ways to categorize luxury, what I call a "typology of luxury" (see Table 2, page 168). A first broad differentiation should be made between "absolute" and "relative" luxury. There are mutually exclusive categories in which absolute luxury includes all goods that either because of rarity or material and conceptual worth cannot be provided in an assortment ranging from the inexpensive to the exclusive. A painting by Picasso or the 105-carat Koh-i-Noor diamond are absolute luxuries as one cannot get a Picasso for the price of a poster or the Koh-i-Noor for the price of glass. In fact, both belong to the subgroup of "unique" objects within absolute luxury. A great deal of the rarities and preciosities of the early modern world belonged to the category of absolute luxuries and inspired imitations, counterfeits, and copies. Different is, however, the notion of relative luxury, in which luxury is defined as "the best of" a range of specific goods. The definition of *relative luxury* better fits the case of Indian cotton textiles, in which only a small percentage of the best of them (for manufacture, materials, etc.) could be defined as luxuries. The vast majority of today's luxury goods ranging from clothing to bags, from cars to hotel stays, are quintessential examples of relative luxury.

More complex is the difference between what I define as "positional luxury," "ceremonial luxury," and "aspirational luxury" as the three main forms of luxury in the early modern period. It should be noted that this is a functional classification, that is, based on what luxury was used for, rather than a material one, based instead on specific goods belonging to one type rather than another. And this explains why cotton textiles could belong at the same time to all three types of luxury. My claim is actually that it was cotton cloth's ability to fulfill each of these types that made it such a successful product in the early modern period.

"Positional luxury" relates to those forms of luxury that are aimed at confirming one's social position within a specific hierarchy. A contemporary example might be the ownership of a yacht that allows entrance to a very restricted "social club" of multimillionaires. The value rests on the intrinsic worth of the object due to its rarity, cost of production, or material value. In the case of early modern cotton textiles, as we will see, could be used to indicate status – sometimes royal status – but they had to be the best and rarest among their category. We can think of similar positional luxuries in the early modern European courts ranging from enormous palaces to Boulle furniture and to the most splendid silks. These – like today's yachts and luxury cars – are part of conspicuous display and still remain intrinsically linked to complex and exclusive gifting practices. The social function of this type of luxury is to confirm one's position within a specific group, and it creates a relationship among people of equal status through the semiotic distinction brought about by extremely expensive objects. This is a type of luxury that works "horizontally," as it is aimed at a category of equals and attempts to exclude as many people as possible.

"Ceremonial luxury" refers instead to those luxury goods that mark special events or are part of rituality. A contemporary example is the conspicuous expenditure for weddings in the form of impractical dresses, expensive presents, and large banquets that amount to a considerable financial outlay. Their value is to mark a specific occasion in one's lifetime and in the family lineage. The goods become center stage in a social ritual and are often given profound meaning (that, e.g., leads people to preserve wedding dresses). In their long history, early modern cotton textiles played important roles in rituality, especially in Southeast Asia. Like today's wedding dresses, they were seen not as the most expensive, but the most special among a range of cloths. Liturgical vestments, court dress, and courtly processions were similar ceremonial luxuries in early modern Europe used to mark specific occasions and tie together communities. Their social function was often to connect people of different status and give material expression to family, community, and political ties. This is a "vertical" luxury as it tends to functionally distinguish different roles and mark specific relationships between parents and children or between ruler and subject, and so forth.

Finally, "aspirational luxury" includes a variety of forms of luxury that are more familiar to us. These are luxuries that tend to articulate social mobility and challenge social hierarchy. Contemporary examples are numerous and include the phenomenon of the luxury brand. This is a fetching example because the value of a Louis Vuitton bag or of a Chanel scarf is neither one of material worth, nor of deep meaning. Their value is often "extrinsic," based for instance on innovation, the exoticness of the product, its design and creative content, or simply the social value of a logo. Indian cotton textiles embodied many of the same characteristics that today we attribute to brands, competing among a variety of substitutes in terms of other materials and fabrics. A great deal of the early modern fashionable goods ranging from ribbons to wigs, from Wedgwood tea sets to mahogany chairs came to give expression – especially in Europe – to notions of fashionability and social distinction. These were not objects of indiscriminate use but things that people aspired to possess (often successfully). I call this "transversal" luxury because it creates social competition not just between people at different levels of society but also within specific groups (think about the competition to secure the latest Prada bag or the latest type of sneakers today). The appeal of this type of luxury often cuts across an entire society.

The rest of this chapter goes back to history, and in particular to the case of cotton textiles, in order to show how Indian cottons functioned as luxury goods according to all three different definitions here adopted. To do so, I wish to focus on the case of the consumption of cotton textiles in Mughal India as an example of positional luxury, moving to sixteenth- and seventeenth-century Southeast Asia to illustrate how cottons functioned as ceremonial luxury and finally to early modern Europe to show instead how cottons initiated a new form of aspirational luxury. The specific localization of my examples does not mean that cotton's typology was linked to a geographic specialization. All three definitions of luxury were present in all three areas; however, each example serves best to illustrate one aspect.

COTTON TEXTILES AS "POSITIONAL LUXURY" IN MUGHAL INDIA

The case for cotton textiles as positional luxury seems a difficult one. The great majority of the literature has claimed that cotton textiles had little value in marking social status and only rarely were used for conspicuous display. This is not just a Eurocentric perspective – that, as we will see, ignores a great deal of evidence related to Asia – but is also an interpretation confirmed in the papers of the European East India companies as well as in early modern travelogs. European travelers such as François Bernier and Jean-Baptiste Tavernier, for instance, emphasized the extent of the production and trade in cheap cloth in India as something much bigger than anything they had seen in Europe. The city of Sironj in Madhya Pradesh produced cloth that was – according to Tavernier – the favorite of "all the common people of Persia and Turkey" and for Bernier Bengal was the "common storehouse" of cotton cloth for the entire Asian continent.[5]

Yet the easy categorization of cotton as the cheapest and most common of the early modern global commodities is problematic for several reasons. First, as John Styles observed more than a decade ago, many historians – even those interested in understanding material change – have "treated objects principally as units to be counted." Price and quantities are one sort of criteria, but Styles observes that what is also needed is a "systematic understanding of the enormous range of variation and differentiation that lies concealed within each general category."[6] This becomes apparent in visiting one of the many museums and collections that show an astonishing range of beautiful, intricate, and, one might conclude, extremely expensive textiles. These are not just the silks of China but include a variety of seventeenth- and eighteenth-century Indian cotton textiles, sometimes impressive for their scale and their technical accomplishment. An appreciation of the range of products manufactured and the analysis of extant examples complicates the position of early modern Indian cottons.

One aspect that is often forgotten about the production of Indian cotton textiles is the sheer variety of cloths of different qualities produced in the many Indian localities. The Portuguese divided their cargoes of Indian cottons into high, medium, and low qualities. Among the expensive high-quality textiles one could find *semina*; *tafecira* (a striped textile produced in Sind); *salempuri* from the Coromandel Coast; and *percalos*, a very thin and tightly woven cotton also known as *malmal* produced either in Bengal or Gujarat.[7] A similar variety was encountered by the English when in 1603 John Saris named twenty-one varieties of Cambay and Coromandel cloth that were bartered for cloves in Malacca.[8] The

5 Tapan Raychaudhuri, "Inland Trade," in *The Cambridge Economic History of India*, Vol. I. c. 1200–c. 1750, ed. Tapan Raychaudhuri and Irfan Habib (Cambridge: Cambridge University Press, 1982), 332.

6 John Styles, "Product Innovation in Early Modern London," *Past and Present* 168 (2000): 126–7.

7 Afzal Ahmad, *Indo-Portuguese Trade in the Seventeenth Century, 1600–1663* (New Delhi: Gian, 1991), 92.

8 John Guy, "Sarasa and Patola: Indian Textiles in Indonesia," *Orientations* 20, no. 1 (1989): 49.

difference in price from one variety to another was staggering: a contract by the Dutch with the Queen of Achin (Aceh) in 1649 tells us that in order to acquire a Bahar of pepper (360 Dutch pounds) they had to give thirty-eight *Cannekeens*, but just six and a half broad *baftas*.[9] Of these, as for hundreds of other types of cloth, today we know just their names, making it all but impossible to appreciate their material qualities.

What is known, however, is that there was a clear hierarchy between the expensive Bengal muslin, the cheap Gujarati calicoes (at half the price of Bengal muslin), and the intermediate chintzes produced in Coromandel and elsewhere.[10] Gujarat specialized in the production of cotton textiles especially for the Indonesian market with Broach producing fine baftas at cheaper prices than anywhere else.[11] However Dutch traders remarked upon the fact that in places like Ahmedabad one could find much finer cloths such as "gold alcatifs, gold lakens, bright orhnis of gold and silver used by women to wrap around their heads in place of veils."[12] Tavernier, a great observer of textile production, tells us about the beauty and value of cotton textiles from Masulipatam and the Kingdom of Golconda as they were mostly "painted with a brush," whereas the chintzes from "the Empire of the Great Mogul" were printed. Cheap varieties of chintzes to be used as tablecloths, bedcovers, pillowcases, handkerchiefs, and waistcoats could be purchased in Lahore; more expensive varieties in Sironj; and the best colored in Berhānpur where one could also buy fine veils called *orhnīs* used by ladies as neck scarves. White cloth came from Agra, Lahore, Bengal, Baroda, and Broach.[13] European travelers to India were especially impressed by the whiteness and lightness of muslin, sometimes described in Mughal sources as "woven wind." Muslins of fine quality were produced in the Deccan and in Bengal. Varieties such as *betilles* (from the Portuguese "beatila" meaning "veiling") and *cassas* (from the Persian "khass" meaning "choice") were produced in cloths of fifty to sixty yards long with borders in gold or silver or embroidered with silk.[14]

[9] S. Sen, "The Role of Indian Textiles in Southeast Asian Trade in the Seventeenth Century," *Journal of Southeast Asian History* 3, no. 2 (1962): 106.

[10] K. N. Chaudhuri, *The Trading World of Asia and the English East India Company 1660–1760* (Cambridge: Cambridge University Press, 1978), 291.

[11] Om Prakash, "Archival Source Material in the Netherlands on the History of Gujarat in the Early Modern Period," in *Sources européennes sur le Gujarat*, ed. Ernestine Carreira (Paris: Société d'Histoire de l'Orient, 1998), 148–9.

[12] Cit. in ibid., 147–8.

[13] Jean-Baptiste Tavernier, *Travels in India*, ed. William Crooke, Vol. 2 (Oxford: Oxford University Press, 1925), 4–5.

[14] Mattiebelle Gittinger, *Master Dyers to the World: Technique and Trade in Early Indian Dyed Cotton Textiles* (Washington, DC: The Textile Museum, 1982), 147.

The cloth was so fine that a Portuguese commentator wrote that when "muslin of this kind is spread out on the grass to bleach, and when it is wet with dew, the cloth is no longer visible."[15]

Different types of cloths were used for skirts, turbans, sashes, handkerchiefs, bedcovers, pillowcases, bed hangings, tents, cotton carpets, and cheap sailcloth.[16] Prices ranged extensively: chintzes cost between sixteen to sixty rupees and *baftas* ranged from two to forty rupees.[17] Tavernier, yet again, discusses the different varieties and the price range of Indian cotton textiles and their different markets. In Baroda, for instance, white cloth sold for between two and twelve mahmūdīs depending on the size, but Tavernier says that finer cloth could fetch five hundred mahmūdīs, adding that: "In my time I have seen two pieces of them sold, for each of which 1,000 mahmūdīs were paid." And he recounts the story of the Iranian ambassador 'Alī Beg who, on his return to Iran from India, presented Shah Safavi II (ruled 1629–42) with "a coco-nut of the size of an ostrich's egg, enriched with precious stones; and while it was open a turban was drawn from it 60 cubits in length, of a muslin so fine that you would scarcely know what it was that you held in your hand."[18] Clearly this was no ordinary cotton cloth.

It is important to appreciate the superfluidity of types in order to see cotton textile's role as positional luxury. I decided to concentrate in particular on furnishing fabrics in a royal context although similar conclusions could be drawn by considering the fine muslin that we see adorning Indian emperors, princes, and their retinue in many Mughal miniatures (Figure 10). The luxurious use of textiles in Indian princely and royal courts was often commented upon by Europeans. Unlike the magnificent architecture of royal palaces in Europe, court life in India was peripatetic and characterized by the use of large and extremely luxurious tents.[19]

The scale of such tents made them worthy of attention. The Ain-i-Akbari (آئین اکبری) or the Constitution of Akbar, a sixteenth-century document detailing the administration of the emperor Akbar, provides a sense of the

---

[15] Cit. in H. Wescher, "Cotton in the Ancient World," *Ciba Review* 64 (1948): 2324.

[16] Tapan Raychaudhuri, "Non-Agricultural Production: Mughal India," in *Cambridge Economic History of India*, Vol. I., ed. Raychaudhuri and Habib, 270.

[17] These prices were for "the corge of twenty pieces" each. Raychaudhuri, "Inland Trade," 331.

[18] Tavernier, *Travels*, 2: 6.

[19] For an overview see John Irwin and Margaret Hall, *Indian Painted and Printed Fabrics* (Ahmedabad: Calico Museum of Textile, 1971), esp. 22–5 on "Tent Hangings, Floor Spreads and Coverlets."

FIGURE 10. "Emperor Babur receiving a visitor."
Source: Folio from a manuscript of the *Baburnama* (The Book of Babur), c. 1590.
Ink, opaque watercolor, and gold on paper. 35.6 × 22.8 centimeters.
Courtesy of © Metropolitan Museum, New York. Louis V. Bell Fund, 1967.
Accession Number: 67.266.4.

vastness of the royal compound as it required one hundred elephants, five hundred camels, and four hundred carts to be moved. It was said that the main tent could accommodate more than ten thousand people and needed a thousand men working for an entire week to set it up.[20]

If the scale was impressive, the same could be said of the textiles that formed it. Individual panels were made of finest cottons produced in Sironj and Burhanpur whose beauty did not escape foreign visitors (Figure 11).[21] The Frenchman François Bernier, for instance, described in detail the Mughal emperor Aurangzeb's tents. Although externally made of strong cloth, he noticed how they were lined "with printed Indian calico, representing large vases of flowers."[22] He also described the canopies of the Dīwān-i-'āmm (the audience space at the Red Fort at Delhi) as follows: "the outside of this magnificent tent was red, and the inside lined with elegant Maslipatam chintzes, figured expressly for that very purpose with flowers so natural and colors so vivid that the tent seemed to be encompassed with real parterres."[23] These chintzes were so rare and expensive that according to Tavernier "the quantity turned out is so small that when one makes requisition on all the workers who manufacture these cotton cloths it is with difficulty that he can obtain as much as three bales."[24]

This high-quality cotton production had a long tradition. In the thirteenth century, Marco Polo informs us that the area of Masulipatam already produced "the finest and most beautiful cottons found in any part of the world."[25] Particularly fine were the Golconda floor spreads and coverlets (*rumals*) produced in Petaboli, forty miles from Masulipatam and Palakollu which is eighty miles north (Figure 12).[26] Tavernier tells us that the decorations of these "chites or coloured calicoes" were all done by hand "which makes them more beautiful and more expensive than when printed."[27]

---

[20] Gittinger, *Master Dyers*, 82–3.
[21] Burhanpur was annexed by the Mughals in 1600 and its best products found their way into the imperial wardrobe (*toshkhanas*). Rosemary Crill, "Indian Painted Cottons," *Hali* 10, no. 4 (1988): 33.
[22] Bernier, *Travels*, 360.
[23] Ibid., 270.
[24] Tavernier, *Travels*, 2: 4.
[25] Marco Polo, *Travels*, book 3, ch. 21. Cit. in P. J. Thomas, *Mercantilism and the East India Trade* (London: Frank Cass, 1926), 32.
[26] John Irwin, "Golconda Cotton Paintings of the Early Seventeenth Century," *Lalik Kala* 5 (1959): 14. See also Francesca Galloway, *Islamic Courtly Textiles and Trade Goods, 14th–19th century* (London: Galloway, 2011): http://carpetour.com/Aphotos/IslamicCourtlyTextilesAndTradeGoods.pdf (accessed 30 January 2016).
[27] Tavernier, *Travels*, 1: 255.

FIGURE 11. Block-printed, painted, and resist-dyed cotton panel used for a tent hanging, produced in India, late seventeenth–early eighteenth century. Panels were joined together to form moveable screens (*qanats*) to provide privacy around the ruler's enclosures as in Figure 10. Hangings and *qanats* were also used as decorative items in palaces.

Courtesy of the Victoria and Albert Museum. V&A IM.29–1928.

FIGURE 12. Rectangular painted and resist-dyed cotton coverlet (*rumal*), produced in Golconda, c. 1625–50, dimensions 89.5 × 62 centimeters. The field shows scenes of courtly life involving figures in both Persian and Indian dress. Courtesy of Victoria and Albert Museum, IS.34–1969.

They were so fine that by the early seventeenth century Golconda floor spreads, bedspreads, and coat linings were key commodities in the ambassadorial relationship between the King of Golconda and the Shah of Persia, in exchange for which Golconda received supplies of horses for the kingdom's cavalry.[28] Equally appreciated were the expensive Deccani embroideries, cotton floor spreads embroidered in silk, and metal-wrapped thread.[29] These were produced by fine chain-stitch embroidery and were made by male professional embroiderers of the Gujarati Mochi community and sold across the empire as well as to Persia and Turkey.[30]

[28] Irwin, "Golconda Cotton Paintings," 5.

[29] Crill, "Indian Painted Cottons," 30.

[30] Yumiko Kamada suggests that the Dutch used Deccani embroideries in their private trade to Japan and as diplomatic gifts for high-ranking Japanese dignitaries. In 1774 one of these embroideries was acquired by Kyoto merchants to decorate their float for the Kyoto Gion Festival. This is a festival that celebrates since 869 the shrine of the god "Gion Tenjin." Yumiko Kamada, "The Attribution and Circulation of Flowering Tree and Medallion Design Deccani Embroideries," in *Sultans of the South: Arts of India's Deccan Courts, 1323–1687*, ed. Navina Najat Haidar and Marika Sardar (New York: The Metropolitan Museum of Art, 2011), 132–47.

Fine cotton textiles functioned as "positional luxuries" well beyond the borders of the Mughal Empire and its vassal states in South Asia. They were a "must" for the elites of central Asia, and therefore featured prominently as ambassadorial gifts. Shah Jahan's embassy to the Safavid Shah Safi included a gift of high-quality cotton textiles from Ahmedabad, Banaras, and Bengal. In 1621 Emperor Jahangir sent fifty thousand khāni worth of cotton cloth to the Sheikh of Bukhara (present-day Uzbekistan) through his ambassador Mir Bakara.[31] Considering the quantities involved, it is legitimate to think that such textiles were subsequently redistributed among the local elites. It might even be that they were used as ambassadorial gifts to other kingdoms as with the presents sent exactly half a century later, in 1671, by Khan Abdul-Aziz, the then-ruler of Bukhara, to Tsar Aleksei Mikhailovich of Russia that included not just the expected saddles, sabers, pelts, and tiger skins, but also a variety of cotton textiles ranging from locally woven to Indian varieties and fine cotton muslin.[32]

Trade and embassies brought such fine textiles to the courts of the Indian Ocean kingdoms as well. Masulipatam textiles were to be found in Thailand in the second half of the seventeenth century as remarked upon by French ambassadors who admired the beautiful painted cloths that they saw during their pageant entry into the Thai Capital of Ayutthaya.[33] The Frenchman Pyrand de Laval described the palace of the King of Maldives in 1610 with walls decorated with "hangings of silk or cotton, enriched with works, flowers and gold branches, and with colors dazzling to the view, such is the richness of the gold and colors exciting our admiration of the work."[34] These, according to de Laval, came not only from China, but also from Bengal, Masulipatam, and St. Thomas.

The Ottomans were so fond of Indian textiles that they often imitated them. Tents had pride of place not just among the Ottoman elite but also among Hungarian and Transylvanian princes who acquired theirs in Istanbul. One of these, acquired in 1638 for György Rákóczi II of Transylvania, is described as a tent "made of cotton fabric called

---

[31] Scott C. Levi, "India, Russia and the Eighteenth-Century Transformation of the Central Asian Caravan Trade," *Journal of the Economic and Social History of the Orient* 42, no. 4 (1999): 532.

[32] Richard Hellie, *The Economy and Material Culture of Russia, 1600–1725* (Chicago and London: University of Chicago Press, 1999), 294.

[33] Lotika Varadarajan, "Syncretic Symbolism and Textiles: Indo-Thai Expressions," in *Commerce and Culture in the Bay of Bengal, 1500–1800*, ed. Om Prakash and Denys Lombard (New Delhi: Manohar, 1999), 372.

[34] Cit. in Irwin, "Golconda Cotton Paintings," 28.

bogasia, both inside and outside. Its interior is decorated with flow-ers."[35] These were expensive objects. The tent belonging to Catherine Bethlen, widow of Michael Apafi II of Transylvania, and possibly acquired in the second half of the seventeenth century was similarly made of cotton with red backgrounds and "decorated with applied pic-tures of multi-colored fabrics, edged with white piping. Its umbrella or cover is made of sky-blue fabric with piping of the same color.... Twenty side walls of cotton belong to these, which form the 'court-yard' of the tent. Ten of these require twelve wooden poles, and the other ten require eleven poles."[36] This was a tent possibly made of Indian cloth and structured on an Indian model. The value of the tent amounted to an astonishing 416 gold florins.[37]

COTTON TEXTILES AS "CEREMONIAL LUXURY" IN SOUTHEAST ASIA

Fine Indian cotton textiles were key positional luxury items not just in the Subcontinent but across the Asian courts. Tents, coverlets, and hangings were indispensable items of courtly display and decoration and found markets as both "luxury commodities" and ambassadorial gifts. They were the top of an extensive market for Indian textiles that was extremely large and widely articulated and stretched back in time to Roman times.[38] By the ninth and tenth centuries, cloths of finer sorts reached the Middle East through the Gulf ports together with Islamic earthenware and glass and Chinese porcelain.[39] It was the finer cloth

---

[35] Cit. in Veronika Gervers, *The Influence of Ottoman Turkish Textiles and Costume in Eastern Europe, with Particular Reference to Hungary* (Toronto: Royal Ontario Museum, 1982), 8.

[36] Cit. in ibid., 9.

[37] Ottoman tents are an understudied topic, considering that extant examples of Ottoman tents can be seen in Istanbul (Topkapi and at the Military Museum), Vienna, Dresden, Venice (Museo Navale), Munich, and Cracow. Those in European collections were mostly captured by Christian forces in several battles against the Turks in the seven-teenth century. See Nurhan Atasoy, *Otağ-i Humayun: The Ottoman Imperial Tent Complex Nurhan Atasoy Aygaz* (Istanbul: Coach Publications, 2000). See in particu-lar on the Dresden Türckische Cammer: www.skd.museum/en/museums-institutions/residenzschloss/ruestkammer/tuerckische-cammer/index.html (accessed 19 January 2015).

[38] John Peter Wild and Felicity Wild, "Rome and India: Early Indian Cotton Textiles from Berenike, Red Sea Coast of Egypt," in *Indian Textiles in Indian Ocean Societies*, ed. Ruth Barnes (London and New York: Routledge, 2005), 11–16.

[39] N. Chittick, "East African Trade with the Orient," in *Islam and the Trade of Asia: A Colloquium*, ed. D. S. Richards (Oxford: Bruno Cassirer, 1970), 102.

that found easier markets across Asia. *Po-tieh* cotton varieties (fine muslin) were traded to Tang China and *his pu*, a cotton of special fineness, reached China using what Stephen Dale calls "the cotton Road" (the opposite direction of the East-West Silk Road). These fine Indian fabrics had names such as "rosy cotton" and "morning sunrise clouds" to indicate their light weight.[40]

China, like several other areas of Asia, produced cotton textiles on its own account, but finer and luxury products were almost entirely supplied by India.[41] Even Iran, with its long textile tradition in the production of silks and carpets, produced only mediocre cottons and imported finer qualities from India.[42] As early as the fourteenth century Ibn Battuta commented upon the fact that Indian cotton cloth was seen in Iran as superior to anything produced locally.[43] This was also the case in the Ottoman Empire where in the sixteenth and seventeenth centuries substantial quantities of luxury Indian textiles – mainly paid for in bullion and coins – were purchased by wealthy consumers.[44] By the seventeenth century, cloth produced in Sind with silver and gold stripes was traded to Ethiopia and several parts of East Africa.[45]

The very virtue of being imported made Indian textiles rare in Southeast Asia and more expensive than local varieties of cloth worn by the bulk of the population.[46] The display and wearing of foreign (Indian) textiles was

---

[40] Stephen F. Dale, "Silk Road, Cotton Road or … Indo-Chinese Trade in Pre-European Times," *Modern Asian Studies* 43, no. 1 (2009): 84. See also Rudolf Pfister, *Les toiles imprimées de Fostat et l'Hindoustan* (Paris: Les Editons d'Art et d'Histoire, 1938), 13–14.

[41] K. N. Chaudhuri, "The Structure of Indian Textile Industry in the Seventeenth and Eighteenth Centuries," in *Cloth and Commerce: Textiles in Colonia India,* ed. Tirthankar Roy (New Delhi: Sage, 1996), 33.

[42] Willem Floor, "Economy and Society: Fibres, Fabrics, Factories," in *Woven from the Soul, Spun from the Heart: Textile Arts of Safavit and Qajar Iran 16th–19th Centuries,* ed. Carol Bier (Washington, DC: The Textile Museum, 1987), 27.

[43] Joginder K. Chawla, *India's Overland Trade with Central Asia and Persia during the Thirteenth and Fourteenth Centuries* (New Delhi: Munshiram Monoharlal Publishers, 2006), 87, 96.

[44] Raymond W. Goldsmith, *Premodern Financial Systems: A Historical Comparative Study* (Cambridge: Cambridge University Press, 1987), 89.

[45] Shri Pramod Sangar, "Export of Indian Textiles to Middle East and Africa in the Seventeenth Century," *Journal of Historical Research* 17, no. 1 (1974): 5. For an overview of the Indian Ocean trade see Giorgio Riello and Tirthankar Roy, "The World of South Asian Textiles, 1500–1850," in *How India Clothed the World: The World of South Asian Textiles, 1500–1850,* ed. Giorgio Riello and Tirthankar Roy (Leiden, The Netherlands: Brill, 2009), 1–27.

[46] Anthony Reid, *Southeast Asia in the Age of Commerce, 1450–1680,* Vol. 1: The Lands below the Winds (New Haven, CT and London: Yale University Press, 1984), 90. See also Hema Devare, "Cultural Implications of the Chola Maritime Fabric Trade with Southeast Asia," in *From Nagapattinam to Suvarnadwipa: Reflections on the Chola*

seen as a sign of social prestige. Their value was one of "meaning" rather than simple consumption as it might be in a "modern" Western sense of the word. Imported artifacts – and textiles in particular – were central to the life of individuals and communities and were deployed in a variety of uses ranging from curing diseases, to death rites, the sanctification of icons, the payment of services and taxes, the decoration of royal compounds, ceremonial display, diplomatic exchange, and local mythology and for the narration of the passing of time.[47]

Because of their "deep meaning," they often served to mark status and were both treasured and handed down from one generation to the next. As curator and historian John Guy has observed, in Southeast Asian cultures *pukasa* (literally, heirlooms) comprised Chinese Indian textiles, glazed ceramics, bronze gongs, and other imported items that "were regarded as measures of value as well as barometers of wealth, social position and power."[48] Indian kalamkari (literally, "pen-work"), for instance, were found in many parts of Southeast Asia where they were known as *ma'a, mawa,* or *mbesa*. These tree-of-life cloths several meters long were not just items of furnishing but had specific symbolic value in their design and ownership.[49] Power and prestige was something that was transmitted from one generation to the next as textiles were handed down through the family tree; they were precious heirlooms.[50] The exotic hangings traded from India to the Toradja people of Southeast Asia were treasured over time and acquired sacred status.[51] Although their value as mediums of exchange and as trade items should not denied, many of these cloths from India were deemed to have a value of their own as they were widely believed to have magical properties and therefore acted as sacred heirlooms in many islands of Indonesia.[52]

Naval Expeditions to Southeast Asia, ed. Hermann Kulke, K. Kesavapany, and Vijay Sakhuja (Singapore: ISEAS, 2009), 178–92; Kenneth R. Hall, "The 15th-Century Gujarat Cloth Trade with Southeast Asia's Indonesian Archipelago," in *Gujarat and the Sea*, ed. Lotika Varadarajan (Vadodhar: Darshak Itihas Nidhi, 2011), 439–66.

47 Kenneth R. Hall, "The Textile Industry in Southeast Asia, 1400–1800," *Journal of the Economic and Social History of the Orient* 39, no. 2 (1996): 93–4.

48 Guy, "Sarasa and Patola," 49.

49 Robyn Maxwell, *Textiles of Southeast Asia: Tradition, Trade and Transformation* (Melbourne: Australian National Gallery and Oxford University Press, 1990), 26–7.

50 Lee Chor Lin, "Textiles in Sino-South East Asian Trade: Song, Yuan and Ming Dynasties," in *South East Asia and China: Art, Interaction and Commerce*, ed. Rosemary Scott and John Guy (London: Percival David Foundation of Chinese Art, 1995), 178.

51 Gittinger, *Master Dyers*, 146.

52 Fiona Kerlogue, "The Early English Textile Trade in South East Asia: The East India Company Factory and the Textile Trade in Jambi, Sumatra, 1615–1682," *Textile History* 28, no. 2 (1997): 151.

Anthropologically inspired studies have underlined how Indian textiles were also key to processes of noncommercial exchange such as diplomatic transaction and gift-giving practices that reinforced the relationship between people, in particular between superior and subordinate.[53] If one of the purposes of luxury – to use today's parlance – is to reinforce and mark distinction, then surely in this type of exchange textiles acted as luxury props that materialized and ritualized social hierarchy. This provides us with a notion of luxury that is not about individual expression but finds a definition in the structuring of social relations between people and across time. The sociologist Gilles Lipovetsky puts forward the argument that in its long history, luxury was not defined by the ownership of material goods, but by a spiritual and social component based on the exchange of gifts. Indian cloth shows that prestige was acquired through the circulation of specific goods that created ritualized relationships between individuals.[54]

An example of the role and function of such textiles can be found in the large-scale painted cloths produced on the Coromandel Coast of India and traded to Southeast Asia (Figure 13). They represent scenes from the battle between Rama and the monkey king and the ten-headed demon-king Ravana from the Ramayana epic. This was an expensive type of cloth that was particularly appreciated in Sulawesi and Bali.[55] It is thought that the Ramayana was subsumed into the Islamic culture of Bali and Indonesia as part of local theater. The five-meters-long cloth would have been placed between two scrolls and opened up to narrate the story.[56] Although the Hindu legend of Ramayana had no specific meaning among Southeast Asians, over time these types of cloths were given great ritual significance.[57] The scale and technical accomplishment of these cloths make them among the most sophisticated products traded from India to Southeast Asia in the early modern period. Yet, we know that this cloth was not unique. At least another fifteen identical or nearly identical versions survive in museums in North America, Europe, Asia, and Australia.[58] The value of this cloth lay not in its uniqueness as in the

---

[53] Lee, "Textiles in Sino-South East Asian Trade," 175.

[54] Gilles Lipovertsky, *Il tempo del lusso* (Palermo: Sellerio, 2007), 25.

[55] John Guy, *Woven Cargoes: Indian Textiles in the East* (London: Thames and Hudson, 1998), 115–17.

[56] *Féerie indienne: des rivages de l'Inde au royaume de France*, ed. Jacqueline Jacqué and Brigitte Nicolas (Paris: Somogy Editions, 2008), 93.

[57] Maxwell, *Textiles of Southeast Asia*, 155.

[58] Other examples of scenes from the Ramayana can be found at the Museum of Madras, the calico museum in Ahmedabad, the Australian National Museum in Canberra, the

FIGURE 13. Mordant-dyed and painted cotton ceremonial hanging produced on the Coromandel Coast of India in the eighteenth century, 450 × 95 centimeters. The cloth represents the scene from the Ramayana in which prince Rama and the demon king Ravana confront each other, together with their respective armies of monkeys and bears.
Courtesy of Victoria and Albert Museum. V&A IS.23–1996.

case of positional luxury but in its capacity to be recognized as an item imbued with a shared ritual value.

Ceremonial luxury cloth was not the prerogative of Southeast Asia. The use of Indian cloth could be found in ritualized practices across the Indian Ocean. Kalamkari were used as temple cloths in South India and derived from wall paintings.[59] In the Maldives, on the occasion of the festival of the Molids, the early-seventeenth-century traveler de Laval saw temporary temple structures "hung with cotton or silk cloths of all colour, and of the finest and richest description available" whose ceiling was made "of cotton cloth, very white and very fine, and to support them they run cotton cords, dyed black ... it is very neat."[60] As Lotika Varaderajan has shown, textiles produced in India for the Siamese court and social echelons were also made according to precise specifications and entered into the ritual of gift giving between the king and the nobility.[61] In Japan sarasa (Indian dye-patterned textiles) of fine quality were used in domestic tea ceremonies. This is why a

Tapi Collection in Delhi, the Metropolitan Museum in New York, and the Musée Guimet in Paris. See also "Catalogue," in *Féerie indienne*, 86.

[59] Crill, "Indian Painted Cottons," 28–9.
[60] *The Voyage of François Pyrard of Laval to the East Indies, the Maldives, the Moluccas and Brazil*, Vol. 1 (London: Printed for the Hakluyt Society, 1887), 146–7.
[61] Varadarajan, "Syncretic Symbolism," 368.

Thai embassy to Japan in the early seventeenth century thought it essential
to include ten pieces of chintz among his ambassadorial gifts.[62]

We must remember that the value of ceremonial luxury rests on its ability to make special occasions or to give meaningfulness to a social ritual.
This entails, if not rarity, the ability to closely monitor supply. Europeans
struggled to understand the logic of a market in which even tiny changes
rendered products worthless. English traders, for instance, were aston-
ished to find that Malay consumers would not accept any of the cloth for
sale because it had "a little narrow white edge, and the upright [correct]
Maley cloth must be without it." They concluded that if they had not seen
it firsthand they would have "never believed it, that so small a fault should
cause so great an abatement in the price."[63] The arrival of Europeans in
Southeast Asia markets also showed what we might define as the "fragility of luxury," that is, the fact that artifacts once prized as luxurious
might lose their value. In the culture of seventeenth-century Formosa, for
instance, textiles – both domestic and imported – played a significant part
as markers of wealth and status, especially in wedding and funeral rituals.
Rich parents owning 100 to 150 of cangan cloths could give twenty or
thirty to the bride's family. Fine textiles were used extensively in gift-giving
practices. But the arrival of the Dutch in the 1650s carrying a vast range of
fabrics, among them expensive and exotic textiles, cotton and silk coats,
as well as suits and hats, created an inflation of the value of existing textiles; they were no longer treasured.[64] Hsin-hui concludes that Formosan
societies could not escape consumerism; to which one might add that they
were in need of constructing new ideas of rarity and luxury.

COTTON TEXTILES AS "ASPIRATIONAL LUXURY" IN EARLY MODERN EUROPE

The arrival of European traders in the Indian Ocean in the sixteenth
century has often been interpreted as the beginning of a phase of
expansion for the sale of Indian cloth into European and Atlantic
markets. Yet the "globalization of cotton textiles" was not based on
simple commodification. Through cottons, Europeans elaborated and

---

[62] Ibid., 367.

[63] *Peter Floris: His Voyage to the East Indies in the "Globe," 1611–1615*, ed. W. H.
Moreland (London: Hakluyt Society, 1934), 71.

[64] Hsin-hui Chiu, *The Colonial "Civilizing Process" in Dutch Formosa, 1624–1662*
(Leiden, The Netherlands and Boston: Brill, 2008), 173, 175.

perfected a new notion of luxury that I call aspirational luxury. Indian cloth gave body and soul to a social process of sartorial mobility and competition that had already been evident since the later Middle Ages. By the time Indian cottons reached Europe in large quantities in the late sixteenth and in the following two centuries, sumptuary laws had given way in many parts of the continent to the realization that consumer goods – and fabrics in particular – were the new props of social competition.[65]

Novelty and fashion were linked to the emergence of demand for what Joan Thirsk calls "niceties": not the luxuries of the rich and powerful, but smaller and economical versions of goods that appealed to wider consumer groups.[66] This was the luxury of silk ribbons, comfy cushions on which to rest, and lace with which to decorate one's attire. Indian cottons with their exotic design, permanence of color, and their capacity to replace more expensive silks and linens slowly but steadily came to be integral to a notion of luxury to which people – even common people – could aspire. However, the question to be asked is why Indian cotton textiles did not become positional or ceremonial luxuries in Europe. My interpretation is that their success as aspirational luxuries in Europe was partly the result of their failure to achieve either ceremonial or positional status.

The Portuguese early trade in Indian textiles back to Lisbon was guided by the idea that these cloths belonged to elite luxury.[67] The traders bought expensive embroidered and painted bedspreads and hangings, sometimes of cotton, more often of mixed silk and cotton. These were very refined products traded in small quantities; the finest of these coverlets found markets in the entire Iberian Peninsula and beyond.[68] They competed with Italian, Chinese, and Persian silks for beauty though they were probably cheaper than comparable products consumed in Europe. Although

[65] Beverly Lemire and Giorgio Riello, "East and West: Textiles and Fashion in Early Modern Europe," *Journal of Social History* 41, no. 4 (2008): 887–916.

[66] Joan Thirsk, *Economic Policy and Projects: The Development of a Consumer Society in Early Modern England* (Oxford: Clarendon, 1978), 15–16.

[67] This established view has been partially revised by Maria João Ferreira's recent scholarship. See in particular Maria João Ferreira, "Asian Textiles in the Carreira da Índia: Portuguese Trade, Consumption and Taste, 1500–1700", *Textile History* 46, no. 2 (2015): 147-68.

[68] Om Prakash, *The New Cambridge History of India*, Vol. II, 5: European Commercial Enterprise in Pre-Colonial India (Cambridge: Cambridge University Press, 1998), 36. Before the 1550s textiles were hardly traded back to Europe. After that date, however, they constituted at least 10 percent of the cargoes. See also Beverly Lemire, *Cotton* (Oxford: Berg, 2011), 24; Riello, *Cotton*, 115.

they appealed to elite consumers thanks to their beauty and exoticness, they struggled to secure permanent markets. We must remember that elite taste in Europe was not geared toward innovation and many preferred the fine Dutch linens or the Italian silks to more exotic Asian textiles.[69]

Museums in Portugal, England, and other parts of Europe and North America show pieces of extremely refined workmanship that were produced in India and that Europeans bought in particular as ambassadorial gifts. English East India Company factors knew well the value of cloth as positional luxury; expensive Indian "scarlett and finest violett colour cloth" and "rich cloth of gold" was much appreciated by Indian rulers and they concluded that "[w]ithout presents nothing canne bee donne with these people."[70] Cotton carpets and quilts were also seen as fitting presents for service and as gifts back in Europe.[71]

Two objects might give a sense of how expensive furnishing textiles were deemed to be both positional and ceremonial luxuries. The first is the so-called Fremlin carpet, a woolen pile on cotton carpet produced in Lahore and commissioned by William Fremlin who served the East India Company in India between 1626 and 1644, and who was president of the Council of Surat at the end of his career (Figure 14). This carpet, which includes splendidly executed animal scenes, is one of only three known seventeenth-century South Asian carpets to bear European coats of arms, in this case that of the Fremlin family incorporated into the field and borders.[72] Clearly this was a positional luxury that celebrated both lineage and the connection to India. Equally important was the so-called Bell carpet, produced again in Lahore and now on display at the Girdlers' Company Hall in London.[73] This carpet was ordered by Robert Bell, one

---

[69] James C. Boyajian, *Portuguese Trade in Asia under the Habsburgs, 1580–1640* (Baltimore and London: Johns Hopkins University Press, 1993), 140.

[70] "President Wylde and Messrs: Skibbow, Page, Barber, Predys, Suffield, Mountney, and Norris at 'Sualy Mareene' to the Company, April 13, 1630," in *English Factories in India*, Vol. 1: 1618–21, ed. William Foster (Oxford: Clarendon, 1906), 28–9.

[71] "Captain John Sayers to be given two quilts for service done the Company in examining ships (19 Dec. 1645)" in *A Calendar of the Court Minutes of the East India Company, 1644–1649*, ed. Esthel Bruce Sainsbury (Oxford: Clarendon, 1912), 122.

[72] Daniel S. Walker, *Flowers Underfoot: Indian Carpets of the Mughal Era* (New York: Metropolitan Museum of Art, 1997), 17–19. The other two are the Girdlers' carpet, examined later, and the last one was putatively produced for Sir Thomas Roe, James I's ambassador to the Mughal court from 1615 to 1619. See *Arts of India: 1550–1900*, ed. Deborah Swallow and John Guy (London: V&A Publications, 1990), 157, plate 132.

[73] This is an artifact with a certified pedigree as it has been housed at Girdlers' Hall for nearly four centuries. We are sure of its provenance as we can read in the English East India Company Factory correspondence: "Four carpets sent home for Sir John

FIGURE 14. Detail of "The Fremlin Carpet," woolen pile on cotton carpet produced in Lahore in c. 1640. This was an extremely expensive object, made to order, and probably used as a table cover in Europe.
Courtesy of Victoria and Albert Museum. V&A IM.1-1936. Purchased with the assistance of The Art Fund and Mr. Frank Fremlin.

of the directors of the English East India Company, from the royal workshops in Lahore in 1634. In the same year it was given as a gift to the

Wolstenholme, and one for Mr. Bell." "President Hopkinson and Council at Surat to the Company, January 25, 1633," in *English Factories in India*, Vol. 4: 1630–3, ed. William Foster (Oxford: Clarendon, 1910), 277.

Girdlers' Company of which Bell was the master. In this case the carpet became a ceremonial luxury, a key heirloom for one of the most illustrious livery companies of London.

In the early seventeenth century, the English East India Company saw a commercial potential for high-quality Indian cottons. Between 1614 and 1620 the company acquired substantial quantities of Indian textiles such as coverlets, quilts, velvets, damasks, and carpets. Prices were very high and ranged from 19s to £4 for taffeta and damask cloths, from £6 to £30 for quilts embroidered on calico, and from £20 to a staggering £52 for coverlets.[74] Yet these were tricky commodities; it was difficult to buy them at moderate prices and supplies were erratic.[75] In Surat there was a lack of skilful tailors and, as a consequence, quilts were sent to England unmade.[76] It was no better for carpets: "Carpetts of such length and breadth as Your Worships desire them we shall hardly ever be able to procure" it was explained.[77] Similarly, at home, purchasers were not easy to find. With a price tag of £30 to acquire a set of Golconda hangings sufficient to decorate a gallery or room they were as expensive as silks.[78]

The English East India Company therefore embraced a different strategy. If Indian cottons seemed to have little potential as positional or ceremonial luxuries, they could be appealing to those strata of society that aimed at having something different, yet could not afford "top" money. It was no longer a matter of introducing precious Indian textiles among the choices of the elite, but of transforming them into commodities that suited the tastes and expectations of the mercantile and professional classes. By the 1680s, the English East India Company's directors in London were requesting hundreds of "Suits of painted Curtains and Vallances,

---

[74] K. N. Chaudhuri, *The English East India Company: The Study of an Early Joint-Stock Company 1600–1640* (London: Frank Cass, 1965), 199.

[75] Afzal Ahmad, *Indo-Portuguese Trade in the Seventeenth Century, 1600–1663* (New Delhi: Gian, 1991), 104.

[76] "Taylors in Suratt are not plentifull enough to worke what wee would sett them too, and time will not permit the making of any chintes into quilts; so they must be sent to England unmade. Urge the early dispatch of goods." "Thomas Kerridge at Broach to William Biddulph, Francis Fettiplace, &c., at Agra, July 14, 1619," in *English Factories*, 1: 108.

[77] And it continued by saying that "for of such sizes we find very few ready made, and we perceave, by experience of a few bespoken here, that the tardines, slownes and poverty of the workemen to be such that it is endles labour to bespeak them, and those bespoken to cost dearer then others ready made. Of th' ordinary syzes here made we have sent you of all sorts this yeare, and a good quantety, as herafter you will perceive and of other syzes then these you may never expect them, unles we can perswade the woorkemen of themselves to make them broader; which we will endeavor." "Thomas Rastell and Giles James at Surat to Thomas Kerridge at Broach, December 15, 1619," in *English Factories*, 1: 161.

[78] Irwin, "Golconda Cotton Paintings," 17.

ready made up of Several Sorts and Prices, strong, but none too dear, nor any overmean in regard you know our Poorest in England lye without any Curtains or Vallances and our richest in Damask."[79] The message was that these were products neither for the very poor nor for the very rich.

Next to cheaper "pindado quilts," more expensive Golconda chintzes, Masulipatam painted cottons, and large palampores (from palangpush, meaning "bed cover" in Hindi and Persian) were among the best commodities traded by the East India Company (Figure 15).[80] These still found purchasers among the aristocracy but were equally sought after by consumers further down the social ladder. To make them more appealing they were customized to suit the tastes of European consumers, thus including Chinese scenes, European roosters, and peacocks and other exotic birds.[81]

They were often set on a light background (much loved especially by English consumers) and were made exactly to fit European beds.[82] Their success, the directors of the East India Company explained, was totally dependent on fulfilling expectations and therefore had to follow exact specifications with the valances one foot high and six and a half yards long, the curtains eight to nine feet high. The counterpane had to be three and a half yards wide and four yards long, half quilted and half not. And each set had to have two small carpets and twelve cushions for chairs. They thought that these "may gain that repute here as may give cause of greater enlargement in them hereafter."[83]

The East India Company helped to forge a new notion of luxury, one in which luxury and commodity were not opposites. As early as 1623 the English East India Company's court book observed that "Callicoes are a commodity whereof the use is not generally known, the vent must be forced and trial made into all parts."[84] As observed by Jan de Vries, this

---

[79] India Office Records, British Library (hereafter IOR), Letter Book VII, f. 208. Cit. in John Irwin, "Indian Textile Trade in the Seventeenth Century. II. Coromandel Coast," *Journal of Indian Textile History* 2 (1956): 31–2.

[80] Satya Prakash Sangar, *Indian Textiles in the Seventeenth Century* (New Delhi: Reliance Publishing House, 1998), 29.

[81] "Catalogues," in *Féerie indienne*, 120–39; and Marzia Cataldi Gallo, *Mezzari and the Cotton Route* (Genoa: San Giorgio Editrice, 2007), 41–4; Pascale Gorguet Ballesteros, "Indiennes et mousselines: le charme irréductible des cotonnades, 1650-1750," in *Le Coton et la mode: 1000 ans d'aventures* (Paris: Musée Galliera, 2000), 47–8.

[82] Giorgio Riello, "Asian Knowledge and the Development of Calico Printing in Europe in the Seventeenth and Eighteenth Centuries," *Journal of Global History* 5, no. 1 (2010): 20–1.

[83] IOR, Letter Book VII, 208. Cit. in Irwin, "Indian Textile Trade," 31–2.

[84] IOR, Court Book, August 1623, 6: 89. Cit. in K. N. Chaudhuri, "Some Reflections on the World Trade of the XVIIth and XVIIIth Century: A Reply," *Journal of European Economic History* 7, no. 1 (1978): 224.

FIGURE 15. *Palampore,* a chintz hanging filled with beautifully drawn flowers. Produced on the Coromandel Coast of India, eighteenth century for either the Dutch or the Sri Lanka markets.
Courtesy of Victoria and Albert Museum, IS.132.1950 (given by G. P. Baker).

"new luxury" had an impact not on the rich but on modest and ordinary consumers.[85] What I call aspiration luxury included – according to Maxine

[85] Jan de Vries, "Luxury in the Dutch Golden Age in Theory and Practice," in *Luxury in the Eighteenth Century: Debates, Desires and Delectable Goods,* ed. Maxine Berg and Elizabeth Eger (New York: Palgrave Macmillan, 2003), 41–56

Berg – "fine but affordable consumer ware, marked by diversity, taste and fashion," especially those items produced in Asia for European consumers.[86] By engaging with these consumer goods, people aspired to "a civilized way of life."[87]

The attraction of Indian cottons was first provided by the fact that nothing of the kind could be produced in Europe. Unlike most places in Asia where a local cotton production provided cheap varieties for the masses, in Europe Indian cotton textiles had an "exotic" appeal due to their unfamiliarity. "Hitherto it is not known how the natives apply so successfully the colours to the 'soyes' and 'toiles peintes' in such a way that they lose nothing in the washing," explained the Frenchman Boullaye-le-Gouz, adding that "I showed some in France to several dyers, who were filled with admiration at them."[88] Others like Ovington claimed that it was the "ingenuity" of craftsmanship that made Indian cloth superior both in "brightness and life of colour."[89] There was enormous fascination not just with the products but also with the mysterious skills that had produced patterns, colors, and design that were unknown in Europe.[90]

Their appeal, however, was not just about their exotic provenance and making. As aspirational luxuries, Indian cottons came to challenge many of the established notions of what luxury was and what it meant. At the end of the seventeenth century, the commentator John Cary, puzzled to comprehend how products of no particular intrinsic value were craved and perceived as objects of worth: "He that considers how wonderfully Fashions prevail on this Nation," he commented "may soon satisfie himself how things of little value come to be prized, and to justle out those of greater worth."[91] Indeed cottons disentangled material worth from consumer value; a furnishing fabric could be appreciated as a luxury not on the grounds of its monetary value alone, but because of its capacity to act as a tool of social mobility, fashion, and "civilized living." Indian cottons now imitated more expensive silks and diffused the material expression of luxury across wider strata of society.[92]

[86] Maxine Berg, "In Pursuit of Luxury: Global History and British Consumer Goods in the Eighteenth Century," *Past and Present* 182 (2004): 104–5.

[87] Maxine Berg, "Asian Luxuries and the Making of the European Consumer Revolution," in *Luxury in the Eighteenth Century*, 239.

[88] Boullaye-le-Gouz, *Voyages et observations du Sieur de La Boullaye-Le-Gouz, gentil-homme angevin* (Troyes: Nicolas Oudot, 1657), 166.

[89] John Ovington, *A Voyage to Surat in the Year 1689*, ed. H. G. Rawlingson (Oxford: Oxford University Press, 1929), 167.

[90] Berg, "Asian Luxuries," 229.

[91] John Cary, *A Discourse Concerning the East-India-Trade* (London: Baldwin, 1699), 4.

[92] It was not just about competing with more expensive products. Beverly Lemire, e.g., by using a material culture methodology has shown the intricate ways in which printed

This was particularly the case when Indian cottons came to be adopted not just as furnishing fabrics but also for clothing in the last quarter of the seventeenth century. Daniel Defoe, in an often-cited passage, explained how the use of calicoes and chintzes had "advanced from lying upon [people's] floors to their backs."[93] In 1699 John Cary further explained that Indian fabrics had conquered consumers down the social ladder: "It was scarce thought about twenty years since that we should ever see *Calicoes* the ornaments of our greatest Gallants (for such they are, whether we call them *Muslins, Shades,* or anything else) when they were then rarely used ... but now few think themselves well dressed till they are made up in *Calicoes,* both Men and Women" (Figure 16).[94]

A contemporary treaties entitled *The merchant's ware-house laid open* (1696) detailed the variety of cloths imported from India now of everyday use. These ranged from muslin (*bettilies*) for "Cravats or Heads for women" to *chercanneys* and fine chintzes, "which are Painted with very fine Colours all of Indian Figures, either of Birds, Beasts or Imagery, which is washed never so often, still retain their colours till they are worn to pieces."[95]

These and other contemporary comments underline the degree to which Indian cottons – and increasingly copies produced at home – had made inroads into wardrobes.[96] Yet they also show how cotton was creating its own notion of luxury, less linked to the challenging, imitation, and replacement of more expensive fabrics and more to a hierarchy of its own based on several varieties destined for specific uses. Golconda muslins were thus "fine but thin" and never to be used for men's attire as they were "apt to be fray'd." "Origal" muslins were instead used only for the cravats of "ordinary Tradesmen" as "they are extream good, by reason they are not only strong but thick."[97] It was the existence of dozens

and embroidered Indian cotton replaced but also influenced and fostered the production of embroidered textiles in Europe. Already in the early sixteenth century a number of Indian embroiderers traveled to Lisbon to instruct local craftspeople in their art. By looking at surviving artifacts, one is conscious of the material "contamination" between indigenous and global, between the local idiom and foreign design influences. Lemire states that "a cross-cultural translation and reinterpretation of the Indian languages of design took place, materialized into curtains, hangings, and coverlets." Beverly Lemire, "Transforming Consumer Custom: Linen, Cotton, and the English Market, 1660–1800," in *The European Linen Industry in Historical Perspective*, ed. Brenda Collins and Philip Ollerenshaw (Oxford: Oxford University Press, 2003), 194–5.

[93] *Weekly Review*, 31 January 1708.

[94] Cary, *Discourse*, 4–5.

[95] *The Merchant's Ware-house Laid Open, or, The Plain dealing Linnen-Draper* (London: Bell, 1696), 5–8.

[96] The popularity of cotton textiles in seventeenth- and eighteenth-century Britain is a contested topic. For an overview see Riello, *Cotton*, 112–16.

[97] *Merchant's Ware-house*, 7.

FIGURE 16. Petticoat, visible underskirt of a woman's outfit made of mordant-dyed and resist-dyed cotton. Produced on the Coromandel Coast of India in c. 1750 for the European market.
Courtesy of Victoria and Albert Museum. V&A IS.19.1950 (given by G. P. Baker).

of varieties of cloth that allowed some to be more fashionable, finer, or simply more luxurious than others.

The potential of Indian cottons and other Asian commodities in challenging old notions of luxury in eighteenth-century Europe is a well-studied topic that had commercial, political, and philosophical implications.[98] By embracing increasingly large strata of society, aspirational luxury materialized by Indian cottons became a subject of both condemnation and approval. Yet one can also observe the maturing of

[98] See in particular Maxine Berg, *Luxury and Pleasure in Eighteenth-Century Britain* (Oxford: Oxford University Press, 2005).

new processes in which cotton was no longer the "challenger" but in turn stimulated new processes of innovation, substitution, and the creation of new(er) luxuries. Linen producers, for instance, started to adapt their products to resemble cottons by painting and printing them in the Indian manner with the result that by 1719 nearly three million yards of printed fabrics were produced in England and Wales.[99] Defoe, embracing a conservative stance, looked down on these painted linens that were so much in demand among "the poorer sort of people, the servants and the laboring poor who wear this new fangle are a vast multitude."[100]

Indeed, Defoe raised an important issue for us: Was the dynamism that aspirational luxury brought about going to lead to a debasement and a general loss of value of Indian cloth? Generally speaking, aspirational luxury seems to run into diminishing returns. Yet, cottons' success lasted several centuries thanks to its ability to maintain luxury status. Once their intrinsic qualities (newness of the material, permanence of color, and exoticness) were lost, cotton textiles acquired new characteristics. Consumers thought of them as fashionable items and generally superior to other competing products. As suggested by Natasha Coquery, the media advertising served to maintain the exotic allure and luxury façade that many Oriental commodities were fast losing in Europe in the eighteenth century. This is why shopkeepers emphasized provenance ("Robbe de chamber à la maniere des Indiens" or advertised that cottons "viennent des Indes orientales") through their own shop names ("A la flottes des Indes," "Au roi des Indes," etc.) and underlined quality ("de diverses couleurs et figures," "de toutes qualities et espèces," etc.).[101] The distinction brought about by these commodities was not permanent, nor was their luxury status. Yet this was exactly why they were fundamental to change, fashion, trade, and the expansion of production.

CONCLUSION

In this chapter I have provided three different notions of luxury. I have explained how Indian cottons were successful at a global level not just as commodities but also as luxuries. One might say that cotton textiles'

---

[99] Lemire, "Transforming Consumer Custom," 195.
[100] Daniel Defoe, *A Humble Proposal to the People of England* ... (London: Rivington, 1729), 50.
[101] Natasha Coquery, "Luxe, Orient, consommation: la boutique parisienne et la diffusion des indiennes au XVIIIe siècle," in *Féerie indienne*, 29.

versatility allowed them to be positional, ceremonial, and aspirational luxuries at the same time. They came in a variety of types that included splendid hand-painted coverlets and intricately woven carpets but also more mundane palampores and chintzes. In this context, the differentiation between commodity and luxury appears rather unhelpful because the two categories overlap. This is well illustrated both in the case of Southeast Asia where traded cloths were used for religious and social rituals or as heirlooms and in Europe where they decorated walls and eventually clothed fashionable bodies.

This chapter however needs two disclaimers. The first is that we should not see a scale progressing from positional, to ceremonial, to aspirational luxury. All three notions of luxury coexisted and are still with us. In India, cotton textiles were not just used as positional luxuries but also had ceremonial functions and to a certain extent acted as aspirational luxuries. One can also see the function of cottons as fashionable fabrics in places like Japan and West Africa, which makes the claim for a "modern" and "Western" form of aspirational luxury untenable. The second important point of the story is that the success of Indian cottons in creating new notions of luxury in Europe was partly based on their failure to fulfill more traditional notions of luxury both as ceremonial or positional items. From a European point of view, this is therefore as much a story of success as one of utter failure.[102]

[102] The research and writing of this chapter has been possible thanks to the support of the AHRC International Network 'Global Commodities: The Material Culture of Global Connections', the Philip Leverhulme Prize and the Leverhulme Network 'Luxury and the Manipulation of Desire: Historical Perspectives for Contemporary Debates'. Earlier versions of this paper were presented at the European Social Science History Conference, Vienna, 23-26 April 2014; at the Luxury Network's conference 'Luxury and the Ethics of Greed in the Early Modern World' held at Villa I Tatti, Harvard, and the European University Institute, Florence, 25-26 September 2014; and the 'Transcultural Objects: Exchanges of Ideas and Identity, c. 1000-1800' Seminar at Oxford University/The Ashmolean Museum. I would also like to thanks Maxine Berg, Anne Gerritsen and Luca Molà for their comments.

TABLE 2. *Typology: Positional, Ceremonial and Aspirational Luxury*

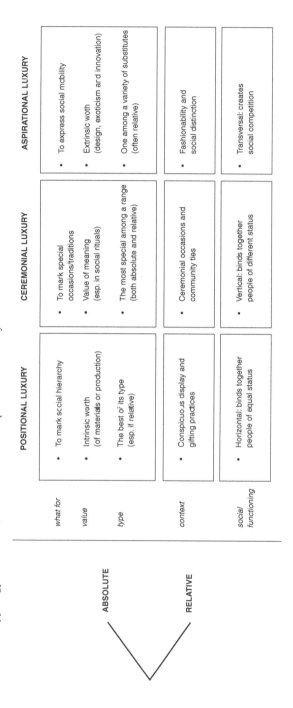

		POSITIONAL LUXURY	CEREMONIAL LUXURY	ASPIRATIONAL LUXURY
ABSOLUTE	*what for*	• To mark social hierarchy	• To mark special occasions/traditions	• To express social mobility
	value	• Intrinsic worth (of materials or production)	• Value of meaning (esp. in social rituals)	• Extrinsic worth (design, exoticism and innovation)
	type	• The best of its type (esp. if relative)	• The most special among a range (both absolute and relative)	• One among a variety of substitutes (often relative)
RELATIVE	*context*	• Conspicuous display and gifting practices	• Ceremonial occasions and community ties	• Fashionability and social distinction
	social functioning	• Horizontal: binds together people of equal status	• Vertical: binds together people of different status	• Transversal: creates social competition

6

The gendered luxury of wax prints in South Ghana: A local luxury good with global roots

Silvia Ruschak

One of the most obvious facts about West Africa is that there is a lot of cloth around.

John Picton (2001)

Ghanaian markets are known for cloth of complex designs and colors. Above all, industrially printed cotton, so-called wax prints of varied quality, dominate the market. The cloth is produced in African lands, Europe, and, since the start of the twenty-first century, in Asia. The illustrated material in Figure 17 mainly consists of wax block prints.[1] It is processed into clothing and worn mainly by women on an everyday basis and for festive events. But it also serves as a wedding gift, collection object, and investment.

Wax prints are precious – especially those manufactured by the well-known Dutch firm Vlisco.[2] In Ghana and broad parts of West Africa, Vlisco cloth is called "Real Dutch Wax" and is a familiar luxury good. It is used for all sorts of clothing, especially for women's clothing involving specifically woven combinations of a blouse-like top, a skirt, and

---

[1] On the categorization of the different types of cloth denoted in this chapter as wax prints see Silvia Ruschak, 2009. Stoffe die globale Geschichte machen. Stationen in der kulturellen Biographie von wax prints im urbanen, postkolonialen Südghana. Dissertation at the Department of History at the University of Vienna.

[2] See Robin van Koert, *Dutch Wax Design Technology from Helmond to West Africa* (Eindhoven: Lecturis, 2007), 10: "Originally established as NV P.F. van Vlissingen & Co's Katoenfabrieken, or P.F. van Vlissingen & Co [in 1846], on 1 June 1965, the company changes its name to Vlisco Textieldrukkerijen NV. In 1970 that name changes to Vlisco BV. On September 1964, a merger between P.F. van Vlissingen & Co, Ankersmit and Stoomweverij Nijverheid leads to the establishment of Texoprint NV as a holding company, which changes its name to Gamma Holding on 21 September 1972."

FIGURE 17. Mainly wax prints in a shop in Takoradi, Southern Ghana 2007.
Source: Silvia Ruschak.

an additional piece of cloth wrapped around the middle of the body. In Ghana, this combination is called "cloth." Often Real Dutch Wax is stored in six-yard or twelve-yard widths as an investment or heirloom, precisely because it is considered a timeless luxury good.

The cloth's designation as Real Dutch Wax sheds light on the entangled or interwoven global history of wax prints. The history's venues are not exclusively African, but are Dutch and Indonesian as well. Now thought of as characteristically African, the cloth is in fact the product of a global economic history and the result of a colonial trading network that only brought it to Africa in its present form at the end of the nineteenth century.

Real Dutch Wax cloth made by the oldest and most renowned firm, Vlisco, continues to be produced in the Netherlands.[3] Europe is not the consumer and processor of raw material (e.g., gold, diamonds, and ivory) gathered in Africa but the producer of luxury goods consumed on that

---

[3] See Immanuel Wallerstein, *The Modern World-System.* 3 vols. (New York: Academy Press, 1974–89).

continent. Above all, African women have been the consumers help-ing determine the shifting of this luxury-goods production from Africa to Europe.

The following example makes clear the extent to which Real Dutch Wax is presently considered a luxury good in Ghana. During a stay in London in 2006 for archival research, I lived with friends from Ghana. One day, the seventeen-year-old nephew in the family received a letter from a female Ghanaian friend, together with photos of the young lady that he shared with his aunt, his cousin, and myself. In one of these photos she was wearing a pinafore dress; this drew our attention and drew the women who were present into a lively discussion about whether the material for the teenager's dress was indeed Real Dutch Wax.

Both women were certain this was not the case. Betty, a nurse in her mid-thirties, explained as follows: "No, in fact we wouldn't sew that type of dress out of the expensive Holland prints. When we sew clothes out of the expensive fabrics we do styles that you can wear for a long time so it is worth it.... This is a fashionable style that is out of fashion soon again. We would not use the expensive prints to sew that."[4] Beyond this she felt that a young unmarried woman would never be able to afford such expensive material; and her mother would have better things to do with her money than spend it on Real Dutch Wax for her unmarried daughter. In short, the dress's form and both the age and social position of the young woman made it clear to my interlocutor that the cloth could not stem from the famous Vlisco Company.

The conversation shows that not every woman wears Real Dutch Wax cloth: both its social significance in the framework of southern Ghana's clothing-centered discourse and its economic relevance have rendered it into a luxury good only consumed by women of a certain age and socioeco-nomic status. Its name stands for high quality, high procurement costs, and a long tradition in Ghanaian cloth markets. But the conversation also offers insight into the sexually specific consumption of wax prints in general and Real Dutch Wax in particular. Whether produced in Europe, Africa, or Asia, wax prints are sold, worn, and collected in Ghana by women, a fact that will be looked at more closely in the following text. In the framework of a history of North American and European consumption, its connection with gender has been recognized and researched.[5] Although over the last

---

4 Betty Amoako, October 2006, London.
5 See Victoria de Grazia and Ellen Furlough, eds., *The Sex of Things: Gender and Consumption in Historical Perspective* (Berkeley, Los Angeles, and London: University of California Press, 1996); Emma Casey, ed., *Gender and Consumption: Domestic*

decade we can observe growing interest on the part of social and cultural anthropologists as well as historians in narratives of African consumption and in consumers of both sexes on that continent,[6] there have hardly been any sustained work in African gender and consumption history.[7]

Using the example of the luxury good Real Dutch Wax, the present chapter focuses on both the history of wax prints as played out in a global network and that history's sex-specific embedding in everyday Ghanaian life. We will begin with a look at the form and usage of this clothing, which is considered to be typical in Ghana. This is followed by a review of three stations in the cultural biography of wax prints.[8] The first station offers an overview of the global history of wax prints in the nineteenth century. The second explores the production history of wax prints in Ghana, using the Ghana Textile Printing Company as an example; this is set in relation to the development of the Vlisco Company, making clear that as a luxury brand Vlisco grew through successes and failures of Ghanaian cloth production. The third station involves a discussion of Vlisco's Real Dutch Wax and its significance as a luxury good in present-day urban southern Ghana. Here special attention will be paid to the cloth's economic, social, and cultural value; that of the clothing made from it; and the occasions on which it is purchased, given as gifts,

---

Cultures and the Commercialisation of Everyday Life (Aldershot, UK and Burlington, VT: Ashgate, 2007).

[6] Jeremy Prestholdt, Domesticating the World: African Consumerism and the Genealogies of Globalization (Berkeley: University of California Press, 2008); Hans Peter Hahn, ed., Consumption in Africa: Anthropological Approaches (Berlin: Lit, 2008); Timothy Burke, Lifebuoy Men, Lux Women: Commodification, Consumption and Cleanliness in Modern Zimbabwe (Durham, NC and London: Duke University Press, 2003); Margaret Jean Hay, "Hoes and Clothes in a Luo Household: Changing Consumption in Colonial Economy 1906–1936," in African Material Culture, ed. M. J. Arnoldi, C. M. Geary, and K. L. Hardin (Bloomington and Indianapolis: Indiana University Press, 1996); Jean Comaroff, "The Empire's Old Clothes: Fashioning the Colonial Subject," in Cross-Cultural Consumption: Global Markets, Local Realities, ed. D. Howes (London and New York: Routledge, 2000).

[7] Karen Tranberg Hansen, Salaula: The World of Secondhand Clothing and Zambia (Chicago and London: University of Chicago Press, 2000); Burke, Lifebuoy Men, Lux Women; Andrew M. Ivaska, "'Anti-Mini Militants Meet Modern Misses': Urban Style, Gender and the Politics of 'National Culture' in 1960s Dar es Salaam, Tanzania," Gender and History 14, no. 3 (2002): 584–607; Jean Allman, ed., Fashioning Africa: Power and the Politics of Dress (Bloomington and Indianapolis: Indiana University Press, 2004); Laura Ann Twagira, Women and Gender at the Office Du Niger (Mali): Technology, Environment, and Food, ca. 1900–1985 (New Brunswick: Rutgers, State University of New Jersey, 2011).

[8] See Arjun Appadurai, ed., The Social Life of Things: Commodities in Cultural Perspective (Cambridge: Cambridge University Press, 1988); Igor Kopytoff, "The Cultural Biography

stored, or inherited. The purpose of this discussion is to show that a type of African cloth widely thought of typical is in fact a luxury good with a complex global and gender-specific history: the history of a good produced in Europe and consumed by African women.

CLOTHING FROM WAX PRINTS: ITS
FORM AND USAGE

We encounter wax prints in Ghana not only as cloth sold in markets and shops but also in processed form, as women's clothing called *cloth*. *Cloth* is exclusively made to measure by local seamstresses. It consists of six yards or approximately five and a half meters of wax prints from which are sown a jacket-like blouse (a *kaba*), a skirt (a *slit*), and an extra piece of cloth (an *extra piece*). For a long skirt, a retracted cloth band takes care of individual fit, with a long slit of varied size offering desired freedom of leg movement. For the top many different classical and fashionable patterns are available. The extra piece of cloth is in any case always the same: roughly two yards long and usually worn around the waist in order to emphasize it and make it look fuller. But it can also be folded over the shoulders or used as a headscarf. The *extra piece* not only has an aesthetic purpose but is also functional: mothers carry their babies on their backs with it, and it is also used for protection from the sun and as a cover.

In Ghana, *cloth* is popular to the point of serving as a sign of national identity and tradition. Women, seen as the nation's guardians,[9] wear the material on a wide range of occasions. Especially women older than sixty make it part of their everyday clothing; at the same time, it is worn on festive occasions by women of every age and social standing – no woman would conceive of wearing something else at, for instance, a funeral. At the same time, *cloth* is by no means an a-historical material, rather reflecting changes in taste over time like all other clothing. Hence the usual form it presently takes is a product of the 1960s, although it also is subject to constant shifts in cut and interpretation.[10]

---

of Things: Commoditization as Process," in *The Social Life of Things: Commodities in Cultural Perspective*, ed. A. Appadurai (Cambridge: Cambridge University Press, 2005).

[9] See Nira Yuval-Davis, *Gender and Nation* (London: Sage, 1998); Anne McClintock, "'No Longer in Future Heaven': Gender, Race and Nationalism," in *Dangerous Liaisons: Gender, Nation, and Postcolonial Perspectives*, ed. Anne McClintock, Aamir Mufti, and E. Shohat (Minneapolis and London: University of Minnesota Press, 1997).

[10] According to Ghanaian accounts, the *slit* was made popular by Fathia Nkrumah, the Egyptian wife of Kwame Nkrumah, who led Ghana to independence in 1957 and was

Men wear *cloth* as well.[11] But other than is the case with women, it is not sewn for men but wrapped around the body. It is twelve yards long and worn in a way leaving the right shoulder free. Beneath it, men wear trousers or shorts. In contrast to women, men wear *cloth* only on special occasions like funerals and large family celebrations or political events. For that reason, Ghanaian men play a relatively minor role as consumers of the material.

Two central manufacturers of wax prints are, as indicated previously, the Dutch firm Vlisco and the Ghana Textile Printing Company, producer of what is known as GTP cloth. Although the two firms were joined in the 1960s, the different products continue to be easily distinguished by customers: at the lower border of each wax print, a label offers information on the type of material, how many dying stages it has undergone, and its brand. As a rule, the border of the sown clothing where the label is located is not hemmed but left visible as a status symbol – to show the material is expensive, the label respectably luxurious.

The more familiar and respected the label, the more expensive the material. Six yards of Vlisco cloth cost the equivalent of between fifty and eighty euros, while equivalent GTP cloth cost around thirty euros. How expensive this is becomes clear when juxtaposed with Ghana's minimum wage, 1.52 euros daily or 30.4 euros if the wage is monthly.[12]

A less expensive alternative to wax print is offered by so-called fancy prints; these undergo a printing process, on one side of the cloth. They have been both circulating and popular since the beginning of the twentieth century, because alongside their inexpensive procurement they offer possibilities for the detailed and precise printing of, for instance, images on the cloth. Nevertheless, they have never been able to compete with the desirability of wax prints. Both fancy prints and Chinese wax print imitations – the latter have become enormously popular over the past decade – can be bought for less than ten euros per six yards. This material is, of course, not tied to the

---

the country's first president. Beforehand, several widths of cloth were artfully wrapped around the body – a technique that Fathia Nkrumah is said not to have mastered, not being from Ghana. Her seamstress thus sewed long skirts for her that were similar to these "wrappers" and that became popular due to both her liking them and her medial presence.

[11] At the end of the 1950s and beginning of the 1960s, Kwame Nkrumah made wearing locally woven fabrics popular as a symbol of Ghanaian national identity; see Allman, *Fashioning Africa*.

[12] The legal minimum wage in Ghanaian new cedis is six. See http://en.wikipedia.org/wiki/List_of_minimum_wages_by_country (accessed November 25, 2014).

social capital contained in GTP or Vlisco cloth, although its price has made it popular with consumers.[13]

WAX PRINTS – A GLOBAL HISTORY FROM INDONESIA TO EUROPE AND ONWARD TO WEST AFRICA

West African countries are known for their wealth of textiles. In Ghana, alongside the *kente* and *adinkra* cloth, hand produced for centuries and only used for ceremonial and royal purposes,[14] industrially printed cotton is prized in everyday life, as mentioned, on account of its high degree of availability and simultaneous exclusivity. But how did this cloth arrive in West Africa? What global networks can be traced out in the history of material that has become so "typically African"?

As the first such cloth to do so, wax prints established themselves on the Gold Coast, present-day Ghana, in the second half of the nineteenth century. Their history emerges from centuries-old trade relations between Europe, India, Southeast Asia, and West Africa, and from industrialization within Europe.[15] The prints are the result of several techniques of

[13] As the example of the young woman shows, the price of a piece of cloth determines the way it is prepared. Pieces of clothing that are not classic *kaba-slit* combinations, e.g., skirts, blouses, and dresses like that of the young women, are made more easily from cheaper wax prints.

[14] On those types of cloth see Doran H. Ross, ed., *Wrapped in Pride: Ghanaian Kente and African-American Identity* (Los Angeles: Fowler Museum of Cultural History, Newark Museum, 1998); John Picton, "What to Wear in West Africa: Textile Design, Dress and Self-Representation," in *Black Style*, ed. C. Tulloch (London: V&A Publications, 2005); Vera Bendt, "Kente und Adinkra – Macht und Pracht einer matrilinearen Elite," in *Afrikanische Textilien: Aus der Sammlung des deutschen Textilmuseums Krefeld: In Memoriam Brigitte Menzel*, ed. V. Bendt (Krefeld: Deutsches Textilmuseum, 2007); Duncan Clarke, *The Art of African Textiles* (Rochester, UK: Grange Books, 2002).

[15] No detailed study of the emergence of wax prints and their complex global history has yet appeared, although work about individual aspects of it has been published since the 1960s. See Stuart Robinson, *A History of Dyed Textiles: Dyes, Fibres, Painted Bark, Batik, Starch-Resist, Discharge, Tie-Dye, Further Sources for Research* (London: Studio Vista, 1969); Ruth Nielsen, "The History and Development of Wax-Printed Textiles Intended for West Africa and Zaire," in *The Fabrics of Culture: The Anthropology of Clothing and Adornment*, ed. J. M. Cordwell and R. A. Schwarz (The Hague, Paris, and New York: Mouton Publishers, 1979); Christopher B. Steiner, "Another Image of Africa: Toward an Ethnohistory of European Cloth Marketed in West Africa, 1873–1960," *Ethnohistory* 32, no. 2 (1985): 91–110; John Picton, "Technology, Tradition and Lurex: The Art of Textiles in Africa," in *The Art of African Textiles: Technology, Tradition and Lurex*, ed. J. Picton (London: Barbican Art Gallery, Lund Hemphries Publishers, 1995); id., "Colonial Pretense and African Resistance, or Subversion Subverted: Commemorative Textiles in Sub-Saharan Africa," in *The Short Century: Independence and Liberation Movements in Africa, 1945–1994*, ed. O. Enwezor

textile printing developed in different locations in the world. Although the prints have been manufactured industrially since the late nineteenth century, and with the use of resin rather than wax, the word *wax* refers to the material's origins: batiks from Java, produced through negative printing just like the industrially prepared material for the Ghanaian market,[16] but differing in being prepared by hand and with wax.[17]

Indonesian batik, especially the cloth from the island of Java, has been famous for centuries. The elaborate handwork its manufacture depended on caught the attention of Dutch traders at the start of Indonesia's colonization in the seventeenth century. As the spice trade with Europe was booming, textiles were shipped there as well; but a market for Indonesian prints failed to develop, the designs being too exotic for European taste. Nevertheless, in the late eighteenth and early nineteenth centuries, European manufacturers began to take an interest in the methods used to produce the batiks so popular in Indonesia, a reflection of the increasing industrialization of the textile branch in particular.[18]

In the early nineteenth century, Java's governor general, Sir Thomas Raffles (1781–1826) wrote down a precise description of batik technique on the island for the use of European traders and textile manufacturers. Their interest in batik had shifted from the import to Europe of the handmade, expensive Indonesian product to the export to Indonesia of cheaper imitations machine-manufactured in Europe. But the British manufacturers had to quickly recognize that producing such duplicates was extremely time consuming and expensive. It seemed impossible to copy the unique colors and complex design of the material.

Dutch entrepreneurs likewise tried to reproduce Javanese batiks, but not yet by machine at the start of the nineteenth century. Rather, they did their best to learn and rationalize the techniques of the Javanese batik designers, using their own batik factories. The first of them was built in

---

(Munich, London, and New York: Prestel, 2001); id., "What to Wear in West Africa." The following overview constitutes a summary and critical reflection on that work.

[16] In negative printing, a pattern is not directly printed onto the cloth. The pattern becomes visible through the cloth being printed around a surface processed with a substance termed *reserve material*. The surfaces beneath the reserve material are not dyed through this process. Reserve material can consist of wax or resin, among other substances.

[17] The fact that the cloth had an English denotation in Ghana is a reflection of both colonial and global connections. The south of present-day Ghana became a British colony in the second half of the nineteenth century, with English naturally being the administrative language. From the south, those living in what is now Ghana came in contact with the industrially printed cloth from Europe known as wax prints; the English designation was retained without translation in local languages.

[18] See Nielsen, "The History and Development of Wax-Printed Textiles," 471.

1853 in Leiden, with others following in Haarlem, Rotterdam, Helmond, and Appledorn. In his *History of Dyed Textiles*, Stuart Robinson explains that "numbers of skilled craftsmen were brought to Holland and settled in specially built villages to teach the craft to Dutch workers, who then practiced in Holland before going to the East Indies to supervise the co-ordination of individual and family workshops into large State-controlled combines."[19]

In the period leading up to the mid-nineteenth century, the Dutch textile manufacturers also became increasingly interested in the machine production of batiks because block print in work by hand was only moderately successful – the quality was not nearly as high as that of the chintz fabrics produced in India.[20] Furthermore, manual production was too expensive in the Netherlands.

For these reasons, Dutch textile manufacturers began experimenting with the machine production of batik fabric. The firms included Previnaire & Co., which was originally based in Belgium but fused with the Haarlem Cotton Company (Haarlemsche Katoen Maatschappij) in the second half of the eighteenth century and from then on manufactured in Haarlem. As an alternative to the wax-filled pens used in handwork, a French money-printing machine was modified so that before the dyeing process a layer of resin could be pressed onto both sides of the cloth. The modified machine was called "la Javanaise"; but despite the evocative name it was soon replaced, as John Picton informs us, by a more efficient counterpart, "an adapted duplex form of the engraved-roller printing machine previously invented and patented by Thomas Bell, a Scotsman, in 1783."[21]

---

[19] Robinson, *A History of Dyed Textiles*, 41.

[20] See Rosemary Crill, ed., *Textiles from India: The Global Trade* (Calcutta, London, and New York: Seagull Books, 2006). The oldest example of block printing being used to imitate Javanese batiks is found in the Vlisco Museum; it is dated to 1846–9. See Picton, "Technology, Tradition and Lurex," 25. There has hardly been any research on the influence of European wax print firms in the nineteenth century. We do have some details on the history of Dutch presses. The role of British cloth presses in the development of wax prints for West Africa represents a fruitful avenue of research.

[21] Picton, "Technology, Tradition and Lurex," 25. We still lack precise historical information and sources. In this respect Picton confirms that "if documentary evidence exists, no one is letting on"; Picton, "Colonial Pretense and African Resistance," 160. Nevertheless, it appears that the Belgian J. B. T. Previnaire was responsible for the first machine production of a batik for the West African market, in 1893 for the *Haarlemse Katoen Maatschappij*. Which of the two sorts of machine was used is unknown. See Nielsen, "The History and Development of Wax-Printed Textiles," 474.

Although at the end of the nineteenth century it became technically possible to produce Javanese batik in Europe on an industrial scale, success was lacking: the cloth produced in Europe was simply not liked in the Southeast Asian markets around Java for which it was intended. When drying, the resin applied using the double-roller technique caused cracks through which places that were meant to be covered were dyed, resulting in cracks and breaches in the color boundaries. Application of a second layer of dye led to problems and imprecisions, so that the material produced by machine in Europe showed clear differences from the original Javanese batik. For Indonesian purchasers the imprecise dyeing had a highly unaesthetic effect. The market the Dutch had worked for in Indonesia was lost before it could be opened up.[22]

In any event the intense colonial trade meant that a new market soon opened up for the industrial imitations – in present-day Ghana rather than Indonesia. Even after the Dutch handed over their fort to the British in 1872, they had maintained their trading contacts in Ghana. As we have seen, the material became known there as wax print and gained a great deal of popularity – precisely the imprecise color boundaries, disliked in Indonesia were perceived by South Ghanaian customers as especially aesthetic. The blurred boundaries on each piece of cloth meant that each was unique, despite the same design and color; this rendered the cloth especially desirable.[23]

European traders and manufacturers quickly recognized the new West African market for the printed cloth and began to accommodate the new customers' needs. The reasons for the material and its patterns becoming so rapidly popular on the Gold Coast have hardly been researched. Two main factors were here at play. Alongside the intense trading activity in textiles taking place in both the British and Dutch Gold Coast trading outposts, young, unmarried European men who had emigrated there in the century's second half contributed to this development.[24] In Ruth

---

[22] See Picton, "Technology, Tradition and Lurex," 26; Picton, "Colonial Pretense and African Resistance," 160. In his description of the development Picton relies on orally transmitted company history. There is still no – badly needed – research on written sources.

[23] The so-called crackling effects are now deliberately produced to satisfy Ghanaian aesthetic expectations.

[24] See Femme S. Gaastra, *The Dutch East India Company: Expansion and Decline* (Zutphen: Walburg Pers, 2003); Désirée Marie Baumann, *The English East India Company in British Colonial History, 1599–1833* (Essen: Die Blaue Eule, 2007); Jaap R. Bruijn, and Femme S. Gaastra, eds. *Ships, Sailors and Spices: East India Companies and Their Shipping in the 16th, 17th and 18th Centuries* (Amsterdam: NEHA, 1993).

Nielsen's words, "As they settled down to trade, they quickly engaged ... African women in their businesses. The women taught them the language and received, in return sewing machines and instruction in how to use them, and before long the sale of the prints flourished."[25]

An additional factor in the immediate popularity of wax prints was the presence of West African soldiers recruited by the Dutch army for the war in Indonesia between 1810 and 1862.[26] When the Netherlands handed over Elmina fort to England in 1872, many of the surviving soldiers returned to the Gold Coast, settling in areas with a great deal of trading activity. They brought Indonesian batiks with them for their wives and families, thus contributing to the designs becoming familiar in what is now Ghana.

The Indian chintz cloth already widespread in nineteenth-century West Africa, hand printed with small flower motifs, contributed to the later popularity of prints in the area.[27] In addition, the prints were simply very practical: "The suppleness of the printed muslin," he observes,

allowed greater quantities of it to be worn without the weight of the indigenous weaving, hence it could be manipulated and tailored better to the human form, and its range of colors allowed greater individual aesthetic expression; and ... its laundering properties were better than the indigenous, woven cloth, especially during periods of drought when available water for washing is at a premium.[28]

Furthermore, Christian missionaries modified the attitude toward clothing on the Gold Coast. Their interest in what they considered proper women's clothing, in particular, played an essential role in the increasing wearing of wax prints. For these missionaries, that the female body was covered was a sign of women having moved away from "wild Africa" and being on the "path toward civilization."[29] Tied to this, seeing to a covering of the naked female body represented a form of control over it, and over sexuality.[30]

---

[25] Nielsen, "The History and Development of Wax-Printed Textiles," 470.

[26] See W. T. Kroese, *The Origin of the Wax Block Prints on the Coast of West Africa* (Hengelo: Smit, 1976). Kroese's history of wax prints and their establishment in present-day Ghana is inadequately researched and one sided in its company focus (the book has a foreword written by a Vlisco representative). Nevertheless, the study is cited in most subsequent treatments of the theme.

[27] See Picton, "Technology, Tradition and Lurex," 25.

[28] Justine M. Cordwell, "Appendix: The Use of Printed Batiks by Africans," in *The Fabrics of Culture: The Anthropology of Clothing and Adornment*, ed. J. M. Cordwell (The Hague, Paris, and New York: Mouton Publishers, 1979), 495.

[29] See Allman, *Fashioning Africa*, 147.

[30] On the role of sexuality and clothing in colonial societies see, among other works, Ann L. Stoler, *Carnal Knowledge and Imperial Power: Race and the Intimate in Colonial Rule*

By the mid-twentieth century, wax prints had penetrated so deeply into everyday culture that despite being manufactured in Europe they were viewed as Ghanaian and local. This is when they came to serve as a welcome supplement to the ceremonial *kente* and *adinkra* cloth. Women contributed significantly to the material's adoption to the needs of the Ghanaian market, communicating their likes and dislikes – above all "market women." European women sought out contact with consumers through the dealers who sold the cloth. The latter have always had a precise sense of the customers' preferences, and quite often they actively affected consumer behavior by promoting particular products.[31] From the end of the nineteenth century until far into the twentieth, market women had a particularly strong influence on the success or failure of cloth products: they gave names to specific designs for industrially printed cloth and designated them with adages, thus integrating them into local custom regarding cloth and clothing.[32]

In this manner market women served the purpose of conveying Ghanaian consumer needs and aesthetic taste to producers in the Netherlands. This process is the backdrop for the thesis of the historian of textiles and collector John Picton that wax prints are not merely a sign of (neo-)colonial exploitation but have art-historical and identity-founding significance, as well as contributing to a critique of colonialism.[33] In Picton's view, wax prints are "the outcome of a unique engagement between the Netherlands, Indonesia, and the Gold Coast, such that the design process in an industrial European context is driven by a very particular West African interest."[34]

VLISCO – THE LUXURY BRAND FOR WAX PRINTS

Until Ghana's independence from Britain in March 1957, wax prints were manufactured exclusively in Europe and sold in Ghana with the

---

(Berkeley and Los Angeles: University of California Press, 2002); Nira Wickramasinghe, *Dressing the Colonialised Body: Politics, Clothing and Identity in Sri Lanka* (New Delhi: Orient Longman, 2003).

[31] See Garcia Clark, *Onions Are My Husband: Survival and Accumulation by West African Market Women* (Chicago: University of Chicago Press, 1994); Jean Allman and Victoria B. Tashjian, *"I will not eat stone": A Women's History of Colonial Asante* (Portsmouth: Heinemann, 2000); Claire C. Robertson, *Sharing the Same Bowl: A Socioeconomic History of Women and Class in Accra, Ghana* (Ann Arbor: University of Michigan Press, 1990).

[32] See Picton, "Technology, Tradition and Lurex."

[33] See Picton, "Colonial Pretense and African Resistance."

[34] Ibid., 160.

help of distributors such as the United Africa Company (1929–87).[35] With political independence, Ghana also desired economic independence and the Nkrumah government instituted comprehensive industrialization policies. The projects tied to this included establishing the Ghana Textile Printing Company (short: GTP) in 1964 – a rather small undertaking when compared to, for instance, the Volta River projects of 1966. It was, however, rich in symbolism, reflecting the young nation's need for images and objects embodying its identity; wax prints were ideally suited to that end.[36] The country's economic ambitions in the realm of textile printing and the connected move away from European producers prompted fears on the part of Vlisco, in particular, of losing its preeminent West African position as a manufacturer of wax prints. But although massive losses were anticipated in the case of independent wax print production in Ghana, there was in fact inadequate know-how there regarding production, and inadequate machinery and raw materials for setting up a self-sufficient Ghanaian press. For these reasons, in 1964 GTP was established following tough negotiations, as a joint venture project between the Ghanaian state and the Anglo Dutch African Textile Investigation Group (ADATIG),[37] composed of representatives of Dutch and British firms, including Vlisco and the United Africa Company, owned by Unilever. With their 49 percent share of GTP, ADATIG was meant to contribute technical and business knowledge, thus maintaining a presence in the Ghanaian market while ceding a majority stake of 51 percent to the state of Ghana.[38] The founding of GTP was both a result of Ghana's political independence and a sign of persisting dependence on the former colonial powers.

The Vlisco Company had already been selling cloth to Indonesia in the mid-nineteenth century; it had been active in the West African market

---

[35] See David K. Fieldhouse, *Merchant Capital and Economic Decolonization: The United Africa Company 1929–1987* (Oxford: Clarendon Press, 1994).

[36] See Anne McClintock, "No Longer in Future Heaven"; Alison L Goodrum, *The National Fabric: Fashion, Britishness, Globalization* (Oxford and New York: Berg, 2005); Dominic Kofi Agyeman, *Ideological Education and Nationalism in Ghana under Nkrumah and Busia* (Accra: Ghana University Press, 1988).

[37] See Fieldhouse, *Merchant Capital*; id. *Unilever Overseas: The Anatomy of a Multinational, 1895–1965* (London and Stanford, CA: Croom Helm, Hoover Institution Press, 1978).

[38] In return for the 49 percent of GTP that the Ghanaian state relinquished to members of ADATIG it received 49 percent of a soap factory financed by Unilever and managed by Lever Brothers that was opened in 1963 east of the capital, Accra: a free adaptation, it seems, of the motto "Soap for the Ghanaians, textiles for the British and the Dutch"; see Koert, *Dutch Wax Design Technology*, 24.

since 1852; and it could now expand its position in the luxury textile segment. For even after the start of production by GTP in 1966, the rights to
Dutch knowledge of wax print production in Ghana remained hotly disputed.[39] The Vlisco Company wanted to only support the Ghanaian firm
in the production of fancy prints, which in their quality and popularity
could not compete with wax prints. This was already known to Vlisco's
management at the start of the 1960s. Not only sales numbers spoke
for that popularity, but also an internal report from 1960 on the social
embedding of wax prints in Ghana: "We have the impression that the
Wax Block prints ... are looked upon as the guaranteed quality, though
highly priced they are the backbone of the rather large assortment of
clothes, every woman has."[40]

Although economic pressure led to Vlisco declaring itself ready to
start producing wax prints at GTP in 1967, only certain patterns with an
extremely limited color selection could be directly manufactured there.[41]
Until the mid-1990s, GTP worked exclusively with indigo as a base color;
cloth with other base colors was occasionally produced in West African
factories that had emerged meanwhile, but mainly by Vlisco, whose
materials were highly attractive through quality and complexity of design
and color, in comparison to GTP cloth, which was treated as an inferior
product.[42]

The founding of GTP in 1964 was a sign of a tightening of the trading
networks tying together European trading firms and textile producers
and the Ghanaian government. The latter would institutionalize production of the material, already popular in Ghana by the mid-twentieth century, and firmly establish a local presence of global trading networks.[43]
But as the same time, as indicated, GTP's history shows the extent to

---

[39] For a more precise description of the history of the founding of the Ghana Textile Printing
Company between 1957 and 1967, see Silvia Ruschak, "Stoffe, die globale Geschichte
machen: Stationen in der kulturellen Biographie von wax prints im urbanen, postkolonialen Südghana" (PhD diss., University of Vienna, 2009), 125–208.

[40] Report of W. J. Boulman, "First Report Ghana Investigation, 5.12.1962," Vlisco Museum,
GTP file/ GTP folder, 1.

[41] In any case Vlisco took its time with technical preparation, only having enough work-
places for producing the wax block prints in 1971. See Koert, *Dutch Wax Design
Technology*, 64–5.

[42] Between 1994 and 1996 the majority shares of GTP were taken over by the Dutch holding society Gamma, which also owns Vlisco. Step by step after the takeover, and thirty
years after the founding of GTP, other basic colors were introduced at the latter firm.

[43] See Jürgen Osterhammel and Niels P. Petersson, *Geschichte der Globalisierung:
Dimensionen, Prozesse, Epochen* (Munich: C. H. Beck, 2003).

which Ghana remained caught in colonial economic structures. Political independence, in other words, did not lead to economic independence in the production of wax prints: as an initially majority state-run firm and then, after 1982, one that was entirely state run, GTP was not a success.[44]

Especially in the 1980s great difficulties emerged within GTP: after 1982 the distribution of its cloth completely collapsed. Market women stood in line the entire day to receive cloth for sale,[45] and even the small amount of cloth that could be produced suffered from the lack of raw materials. In the mid-1980s, a lack of dyes meant that only cloth with yellow as a base color could be produced, so that many Ghanaians recall the period as marked by "yellow fever." With quality and durability falling, the opinion of the material held by consumers fell drastically as well.

Vlisco textiles, by contrast, never lost their repute in the years of Ghana's political and economic crisis. It is the case that on account of high import duties, the company exported no cloth directly to Ghana in 1982, but the material was still smuggled into the country through Togo. In this period, being able to buy Real Dutch Wax was not only a sign of having money but also of being socially wealthy: one needed not only cash but also good contacts to get the highly desirable material from Holland. In the 1980s the high degree of demand and small degree of supply rendered Vlisco cloth into more of a luxury good than ever. That the scarcity of certain textiles and designs could lead to higher demand and thus a higher willingness to pay more for that textile, was already evident in Ghana in the 1960s, when the phenomenon was above all steered by female dealers conscious of the situation with wax prints: "The relative scarcity of a design, which often happens with new designs, increases its popularity to such an extent that the buyer keeps it for special occasions.

---

[44] Between the independence of Ghana in 1957, the founding of the first Ghanaian republic in 1960, and the constituting of the fourth, still extant republic in 1993, there were five putsches, four of these being led by the military. In the 1960s and 1970s Ghana's economic situation was serious, as a result of the political unrest and corruption, together with global developments such as the oil crisis in the 1970s and the fall of the price of cocoa, Ghana's main export.

[45] See Koert, *Dutch Wax Design Technology*, 71. The influence of military dictator Jerry Rawlings on market women trading in wax prints has not been researched in detail. See Kevin Shillington, *Ghana and the Rawlings Factor* (London and New York: Macmillan, 1992); Zaya Yeebo, *Ghana: The Struggle for Popular Power: Rawlings, Saviour or Demagogue* (London: New Bacon Books, 1991); E. Gyimah-Boadi, "The Search for Economic Development and Democracy in Ghana: from Limann to Rawlings," in *Ghana under PNDC Rule*, ed. E. Gyimah-Boadi (Oxford: Codersia, 1993); Paul Nugent, *Big Men, Small Boys and Politics in Ghana: Power, Ideology and the Burden of History 1982–1994* (London and New York: Pinter, 1995).

Maybe this explains the trade opinion here that one can overdo a design to such an extent that it will die.... If the trade wants to keep up the price he must give it a rest until it recovers its scarcity value."[46] Not every woman or man can have luxury. To retain its inherent value luxury has to be regulated, scarce, and not accessible to everyone. Ghana's political and economic crisis of the 1980s and the diminished supply of Vlisco cloth unintentionally increased its status as a luxury good.

In 1996, thirty-two years after GTP's founding, the firm's problems led to a majority takeover of its shares by Gamma, a Dutch holding company that belongs to Vlisco.[47] Since then there has been close cooperation between Vlisco and GTP.[48] After the takeover, regulation of cloth coloring and design was done away with, new machines brought to Ghana, and the quality of the material brought up to that of Vlisco's standards. Popular designs could now be printed in various colors under the GTP label – a change noted by the wax print saleswomen and their customers.[49] It is the case that many consumers are not aware that GTP belongs to Vlisco and speak of "our Ghanaian prints." While cheaper than Real Dutch Wax, the GTP remains among the most expensive wax print fabric in Ghana.

The development and maintenance of Vlisco as a luxury brand has been very positively influenced by the takeover and revitalizing of GTP. In any case, since the start of the millennium both brands, together with the rest of the West African wax print industry, have been in a highly difficult situation. More cheaply produced Chinese copies in favored designs have flooded the market, leading to an enormous fall in sales of the locally produced material.[50] As a response to this development, since 2006 textile

---

[46] Report of W. J. Boulman, 1.

[47] Other than was the case in the socialistically stamped Nkrumah's era, since the start of the 1990s state ownership of firms is not a precondition of economic independence for Ghana's political elites. Since 2007 Gamma Holding has owned 70.98 percent of GTP. See internal document, Tex Styles Ghana Limited, Tema (received January 25, 2008). It is unclear who owns the remaining shares.

[48] In 2004 the firm's name was changed to Tex Styles Ghana Limited. The brand name GTP was retained for the cloth because of its familiarity and popularity. See Koert, *Dutch Wax Design Technology*, 10.

[49] See the observation of one such seller in the Takoradi market in South Ghana concerning the GTP: "They have changed the quality. The quality is now more, it is among the best. Their cloth was not very nice cloth but now it is very beautiful. The colors are also different." GK 11.1.07.

[50] Since the beginning of this century the social anthropologist Nina Sylvanus has been working on the intensive trade in wax prints between West Africa and China. See Nina Sylvanus, "Negotiating Authentic Objects and Authentic Selves: Beyond the Deconstruction of Authenticity," *Journal of Material Culture* 15, no. 2 (June 2010): 181–203; id., "Chinese

imports have high import duties and can only be brought into Ghana using the Takoradi harbor. But despite these regulations, the development appears unstoppable and, also in 2006, already, Vlisco reacted with a shift in its approach to production: from that point onward, it has concentrated on the high-end/luxury textile segment, and now aims to produce not only cloth but also fashion. This decision was summarized as follows on the firm's homepage:

It was estimated at this point that 75 percent of all wax in Africa displayed Vlisco designs but only a proportion of this was authentic. Copies of the much loved designs have been made by many. To combat this trend, Vlisco decided to focus on becoming a leading fashion brand in Africa. This strategy forced Vlisco to adjust their ways of working. Part of this strategy was to produce fashion fabric collection with a quick turn around so they could not be so easily copied.

In 2007 Vlisco began with a production of four collections annually.[51] These are not tailored to the demands of specific regions or countries or coordinated with market women but rather produced for the entire African market. At the same time, a separate fashion line was introduced that for the first time features wax prints in the form of clothing and accessories to be sold in exclusive boutiques in Cotonou (Benin), Lomé (Togo), Abidjan (Ivory Coast), Calabar (Nigeria), Kinshasa (Democratic Republic of Congo), and Helmond (the Netherlands). Although Vlisco continues to produce some classical designs for different African countries in far lower quantities, the firm's new marketing strategy is clearly aimed at the growing elite population within those countries.

The specific impact of this shift in Vlisco's production cannot be predicted in our historical framework. What can be confirmed is that it represents a basic break with the previous history of wax print manufacturing. No longer do we find market women in Ghana and other African countries articulating the needs of consumers and transmitting their aesthetic preferences to wax print producers, but rather collections by the producers influencing and indeed determining the taste of specific consumers'

Devils, the Global Market, and the Declining Power of Togo's Nana-Benzes," *African Studies Review* 56, no. 1 (April 2013): 65–80; Nina Sylvanus and L. Axelsson, "Women Traders' Responses to the Entry of Chinese Wax Prints in Accra (Ghana), and Lome (Togo)," in *The Rise of China and India in Africa: Challenges, Opportunities and Critical Interventions*, ed. F. Cheru and C. Obi (London: Zed Books, 2010), 132–41.

[51] The collections follow the international fashion industry, which also produces new trends on a quarterly basis. The elaborately organized appearances on the web, advertising campaigns, and fashion shows deliberately recall the practice of large luxurious fashion brands. See www.vlisco.com/ (accessed June 21, 2010).

segments. The extraordinary ties between the Netherlands, Indonesia, and Ghana, with a design process within an industrialized European country depending on the taste of West African consumers, have been altered through Vlisco's new specialization in luxury fabrics designed uniformly for countries throughout Africa. In any event one thing has remained the same in face of the shift: a textile firm manufacturing in Europe is supplying various African countries with luxury goods. Our overview of the history of wax prints, especially those of Vlisco and GTP, has pointed to one more case, now, of the African continent not only producing raw materials for luxury goods generated and consumed in Europe but also consuming luxury goods produced in Europe.

FEMALE CONSUMERS GIVE THE CLOTH ITS MEANING

In the first two stations, of our cultural biography of wax prints, the role of women was repeatedly mentioned in marginal fashion: for example, women who were presented with industrially manufactured batiks destined for Indonesia at the nineteenth century's end, and saleswomen who supplied themselves with wax prints showing a range of designs in the twentieth century and integrated them into the local context under various appropriate names. A third station involves the significance of wax prints as a luxury good in South Ghana. Here women play a special role because they inscribe meaning into the material and the clothing made from it as its chief consumers.

Ghanaian women are often described as having a passion for as many wax prints and *cloth* outfits as possible. The number of such outfits and wax print clothing a woman possesses reveals something about her social status and wealth as seen in Figure 18. A fact not only confirmed by my interlocutors at the start of the twenty-first century[52] but also in mid-twentieth century sources. In the previously cited 1962 Vlisco report concerning the social embedding of wax prints in Ghana, we thus read as follows: "Estimates of what the average African woman spends on cloths run from 1/3 to 1/2 of her total expenditure. Naturally there are not factual data, fit to be checked, but they indicate the order of importance. There is a strong urge for possession of certain well known, accepted designs."[53]

---

[52] In a pair of two- to three-month research stays between 2003 and 2007, I engaged in conversations focused on the use and history of wax prints in the harbor city of Takoradi-Sekondi in South Ghana.

[53] Report of W. J. Boulman, 2.

FIGURE 18. A small selection of *kabas* owned by a woman in her mid-40s. Takoradi, Southern Ghana 2004.
Source: Silvia Ruschak.

But not every woman possesses wax prints with well-known and expensive labels. That a young, unmarried woman will wear a dress made of Real Dutch Wax will seem impossible to Ghanaian women as a result of the social, cultural, and economic meaning attached to the wearing in Ghana of expensive cloth from the Netherlands. Real Dutch Wax and expensive GTP wax prints not only say something about a Ghanaian woman's economic status but also about her social integration. They represent both a constituent feature of wardrobes and a form of wealth invested by married women and mothers. As a rule, the beginnings of a collection of wax prints and the *cloth* made from them later is constituted by a bridal gift offered by the future bridegroom's family. Alongside objects for everyday usage, brides are given trunks containing, among other things, at least six different six-yard pieces of wax print and/or fancy print.[54] The brands of cloth are agreed on beforehand and depend

---

[54] Frequently gifts are also made of underwear, perfume, soap, etc. It is clear when the shift took place from chests to trunks. The parallel between increasing migration, starting in the mid-1980s, of Ghanaian women and mothers to Europe, America, and Canada and

on the financial strength of the bridegroom's family. Middle-class families often opt for a mix of Vlisco, GTP, and other labels. Self-evidently, the more prosperous the family is, the more expensive and numerous the pieces of cloth given the bride. The gifts, after all, are meant to prepare the bride for the transition from single mother to wife, and on ceremonial occasions a socially anchored wife is expected to show herself in *cloth* made from material given by the husband's family.

Alongside the label and quality of material, colors are of central importance. Every bridal gift contains material in blue-white or black-white. Regardless of its label, this material is called "white cloth" and is worn for festivities such as marriages and the birth of a child, but also for ceremonies of thanks after funerals. At least one piece of cloth in a red-black or brown-black combination is also given because these colors represent mourning, for which the wife is also prepared. No South Ghanaian wife will go to a funeral in brightly colored material or in anything other than *cloth*.

Design also plays an essential role in purchasing the material – whether for bridal gifts or in individual purchases. Designs have names or a symbolic meaning allowing communication through the material. Hence as long as she is meant to be welcomed into the family, no women will be given material named, say, "everyone is mortal," whatever the brand. The name or adage represented by a certain type of cloth continues to strongly determine its sale together with the occasions on which it is worn.

Hence cloth given as a bridal gift has both practical value and a symbolic character. It stands for a wife's financial independence, with especially expensive material often being collected in trunks as seen in Figure 19 as an investment due to its material value, allowing women financial flexibility. The older a woman, the more material she owns, to be passed on to her daughters after her death. This social embedding of the cloth has contributed to designs being presently known that were first produced in the first half of the twentieth century.

Wax prints and the *cloth* sewn from them mark the transition to married status, rendering it externally visible. They are also essential in the transition to motherhood. In South Ghana, children are a sign of prosperity. The Fante term *mame*, mother, connotes prosperity and connected social status.[55] Motherhood also signifies a change in a woman's

the giving of trunks as gifts is presumably no coincidence. We have as yet no studies of the increasing popularity of trunks as containers of bridal gifts.

[55] Although in South Ghana marriage is inseparable from motherhood, motherhood is not always tied to marriage. There, as elsewhere, the proportion of women raising one or

FIGURE 19. The cloth chest of a circa forty-year-old cook. The material is not sewn and is stored as an investment. Takoradi, Southern Ghana 2007. *Source*: Silvia Ruschak.

clothing customs, at least in the period after the baby's birth. A teacher from Takoradi put it thus: "You are come to be a mother, so you start putting on our *cloth*, our native *cloth*. We carry our babies at the back and tie them with the *cloth*. So if you are in this short dress, ... the tight trousers, you cannot carry your baby, so you start sewing and using our native *cloth*."[56]

As mentioned, for mothers the *extra piece* in the *kaba/slit* combination has the extra function of serving as a carrying cloth for the baby. For this purpose, both the material's quality and its processing into *cloth* is a basic

---

more children without a partner is rising. Changes in the clothing of women who have become mothers are more visible by married women on account of larger family income, but should not be considered only in combination with marriage. Marriage and motherhood have been examined as a single unit in many anthropological studies – this was especially the case toward the end of the last century. See Ifi Amadiume, *Male Daughters, Female Husbands: Gender and Sex in African Society* (London and Atlantic Highlands, NJ: Zed Books, 1998), 69–88. On account of shifts in relationship patterns the connection needs to be loosened in future work.

[56] Mrs. Amadakah, Teacher Mary 22.3.2004, Takoradi, South Ghana.

matter: as my interlocutors insisted, a child simply cannot be carried in slacks or short skirts. But colors are also essential, as a sixty-year-old teacher explained: "If you give birth ... you put on white *cloth* for about three months, after that you change to yellow *cloth*, we call it gold *cloth*.... But if you give birth everything is white. Everything you go out with is white plus your hand bag."[57]

Wearing white-blue or white-black wax prints after a baby's birth designates the woman as a mother. This status becomes social capital communicated by wearing certain wax prints. A citation from Pierre Bourdieu is here apt: "From affiliation with such a group, material profits emerge, such as for instance the 'favors' often tied to useful relationships."[58]

Both in printed media and on television, as well as in daily conversations in the cities of South Ghana, there is repeated talk of a threatened collapse of morals and decline in evolved traditions, as seen in the manifest change on women's clothing: short skirts and low-cut narrow jeans as a sign of contempt for local values. Confronting these fears is the economic, social, and cultural embedding of wax prints in the daily clothing customs of Ghanaian women. Regardless of the fashions unfolding alongside wax prints, they remain closely connected to transitional life events and phases such as marriage, motherhood, and death – this being all the more the case with prints in specific colors and patterns. Especially festivities tied to such phases and events are attended in the prints, something underscored by many of my interlocutors. "We are the close family," one forty-year-old ordinary company employee thus explained, "so we are celebrating, as for that one you can't run away from it. No matter what you have in your suitcase you can't be part of it, unless you put on the *kaba* and the down white."[59]

CONCLUDING REMARKS

Wax prints play an essential role in textile consumption in Ghana and other West African countries. They have become an emblem for Africa, the material often being perceived as characteristically African both within

---

[57] Auntie Ama 14.5.2004, Takoradi, South Ghana.
[58] Pierre Bourdieu, "Ökonomisches Kapital, kulturelles Kapital, soziales Kapital," in *Soziale Ungleichheiten*, ed. R. Kreckel (Göttingen: Verlag Otto Schwartz and Co., 1983), 192. In Takoradi, mothers of babies are especially supported by both female and male family members. A woman spends the first weeks following birth with her mother or other female relatives, who take over care of both daughter and infant.
[59] Auntie Ama 14.5.2004, Takoradi, South Ghana.

and outside the continent. But as outlined in this chapter, the material has a complex global history tied in a unique way to the cultural and economic history, and that of textile production, in Indonesia, Northwest Europe, and West Africa. We have seen how the material developed into a characteristic object of Ghanaian identity through an accommodation of European wax print production to West African traditions; through denotation and integration, the material could be acculturated into numerous Ghanaian everyday and festive cultures.

As we have seen, this material is not only an object for everyday and regular festive usage, but, when produced by certain firms, a luxury good. But despite its high cost, Vlisco's Real Dutch Wax is hardly absent from the clothes chest of an married Ghanaian woman because the material is not *only* a luxury good, but also part of the cultural and social praxis supporting its consumption. This is the reason for almost every woman receiving at least one piece of Vlisco cloth in her life, as a wedding gift.

Real Dutch Wax, together with other wax print brands, is a sex-specific product, primarily purchased and worn by women. But the material has been far more clearly woven into the lives of women than of men. The changes in female lives – from woman to wife, woman to mother – are accompanied through the wearing of certain wax prints, so that the material seems destined to retain its popularity as long as it remains central to cultural practices surrounding women's distinct life phases. It is thus African women and women's lives that basically determine and maintain the consumption of wax prints. With African female consumers determining European production until Vlisco's production shift in 2006, what we have here is a unique chapter in both gender and economic history.

As I have emphasized, until the mid-twentieth century wax prints were only produced in Europe and only sold in West Africa. They are one of the few products to have broken open the economic-historical model for the relationship between center and periphery, identifying African countries as consuming countries with specific aesthetic needs fulfilled by European producers. In the case of Real Dutch Wax the connection between the European, Dutch producers and the African consumers is especially clear: a Real Dutch Wax has to be produced in the Netherlands because the place of production determines the tradition, significance, quality, and appearance inscribed in the material, and the luxury tied to this. The origin endows the material with its exclusive aura and – in a reversal of the term's original meaning – exotic potency.

7

From Venice to East Africa: History, uses, and meanings of glass beads

Karin Pallaver

Visiting Murano in 1828, a French traveler defined the local manufacturing of glass beads as an industry "that provides the mediocrity with the shimmer and apparent luxury of the rich," and "frivolous, like the fabrication of fashionable items, that can not be a viable resource of a country, as it does not satisfy any real and lasting need."[1] He was definitely wrong. On the one hand, he completely ignored how glass beads were used in many parts of the world not only as ornaments, but also as money. On the other hand, he was not aware of the fact that Venetian glass-bead production and export increased from the fifteenth until the end of the nineteenth century and largely sustained the local economy.

The fact that so many societies around the world so promptly accepted glass beads in exchange for precious commodities was deemed a clear demonstration of their "primitiveness," of their inability to distinguish between valuable and worthless goods. It is, in fact, not surprising that one of the founding myths about the United States is that the Isle of Manhattan was bought by Dutch settlers for $24 worth of beads and "other" trinkets, the very paradigm of a great deal, as it has been defined.[2]

---

[1] "[Q]ui permet à la médiocrité l'éclat et le luxe apparent de la richesse," and "frivole, comme la fabrication des ouvrages de mode, ne saurait être pour un Etat une véritable ressource, puisqu'elle ne satisfait point à des besoins réels et durables"; M. Valéry, *Voyages historiques et littéraires en Italie pendant les années 1827, 1827 et 1828, ou l'Indicateur Italien*, Vol. 1 (Paris: Le Nomant, 1831), 471, as quoted in Giuseppe Morazzoni and Michelangelo Pasquato, *Le conterie veneziane* (Venice: Società veneziana conterie e cristallerie, 1953), 66.

[2] David Graeber, "Beads and Money: Notes toward a Theory of Wealth and Power," *American Ethnologist* 23, no. 1 (1996): 4.

However, to really assess why so many people in different parts of the globe accepted beads as a means of payment it is necessary to study in depth the meanings and functions that glass beads acquired in the societies where they were used.

In the different stages of their biography commodities do not always have the same meaning and the perception of these goods in the places of production has limited our understanding of their role in African societies. At the same time, the value that some imported goods acquired when they entered African economic circles was connected to the ways in which they were locally perceived, as well as to ideas, often mythical, on how and where they were produced.[3] During his expedition in 1857, Richard F. Burton, the first European to travel into the interior of present-day Tanzania, was asked by some Gogo chiefs about Uzungu [the land of the whites] "the mysterious end of the world where beads are found underground...."[4] As we are going to see in this chapter, glass beads were used as currency in many areas of nineteenth-century East Africa and were coming, if not from the end of the world, from a place situated quite far from East Africa. They were therefore the result of a long commodity chain that posed a natural limit to the amounts in circulation, as well as restricted the possibility of counterfeiting or substituting them.[5]

The link between Europe and the rest of the world is often studied with Europe as the consumer of luxury commodities and with Africa, America, and Asia as the producers of exotic goods. As a consequence, very few studies have focused on Africans as consumers and very little attention has been paid to the ways in which consumer patterns in Africa were modified by the import of foreign goods, particularly by those commodities that crystallized

---

[3] Arjun Appadurai, "Introduction: Commodities and the Politics of Value," in *The Social Life of Things: Commodities in Cultural Perspective*, ed. Arjun Appadurai (Cambridge: Cambridge University Press, 1986), 3–63; Wim Van Binsbergen, "Commodification: Things, Agency and Identities: Introduction," in *Commodification: Things, Agency and Identities: The Social Life of Things Revisited*, ed. Wim van Binsbergen and Peter Geschiere (Münster: Lit, 2005), 9–52.

[4] Richard Francis Burton, *The Lake Regions of Central Africa*, Vol. 1 (London: Longman, Green, Longman and Roberts, 1860), 261.

[5] According to Gereffi and Korzeniewicz, a commodity chain is a network of labor and production processes whose end result is a finished commodity; each successive node within a commodity chain involves the acquisition and/or organization of inputs (raw materials and semifinished products), labor power and its provisioning, transportation, distribution, and consumption; see Gary Gereffi, Miguel Korzeniewicz, and Roberto P. Korzeniewicz, "Introduction: Global Commodity Chains," in *Commodity Chains and Global Capitalism*, ed. Gary Gereffi and Miguel Korzeniewicz (Westport, CT: Greenwood Press, 1994), 2–3.

into a monetary form, like glass beads.[6] As David Richardson has pointed out, the discussion on the exports from Europe to Africa has been "usually restricted to a cursory listing of certain well-known trade goods without a serious analysis of what this means."[7] This approach has favored the creation of the impression that Africans could not distinguish between valuable and worthless goods and is at the origin of what Philip Curtin has rightly defined the "gewgaw myth," or the widely accepted idea that Africans were economically naïve and accepted goods with no value, such as cheap knick-knacks, beads, or rum, in exchange for far more precious goods, such as slaves, ivory, or gold.[8] This has been the result of a lack of analytical studies on the actual use that African societies made of these imported commodities, and particularly on the values that these goods acquired when they entered African economic circles.

The main purpose of this chapter is to propose a biographical approach to the history of glass beads and to draw attention to the different functions and meanings that this commodity acquired in the historical, cultural, and economic contexts in which it was produced and used.[9] At the same time, this chapter adopts a commodity chain approach, focusing on the production in Venice and Murano and on the consumption in nineteenth-century East Africa, in order to explore how the various nodes of the commodity network were connected to each other, and how different patterns of interaction emerged. The resulting picture will reveal that Africa was not only a region where luxury goods were obtained for the European market, but also a place where European commodities were imported to satisfy a growing demand for foreign goods that profoundly transformed local economic practices.

The first part of this chapter will provide a brief history of the glass-bead production in Venice and in the Isle of Murano, with special reference to the connection between Venice and the foreign markets.

---

[6] Relevant exceptions on Africa are, among others, David Richardson, "West African Consumption Patterns and Their Influence on the Eighteenth-Century English Slave Trade," in *The Uncommon Market: Essays in the Economic History of the Slave Trade*, ed. Henry A. Gemery and Jan S. Hogendorn (New York: Academic Press, 1979), 303–30 and Jeremy Prestholdt, *Domesticating the World: African Consumerism and the Genealogies of Globalization* (Berkeley: University of California Press, 2008).

[7] Richardson, "West African Consumption Patterns," 304.

[8] Philip D. Curtin, *Economic Change in Pre-colonial Africa: Senegambia in the Era of the Slave Trade* (Madison: University of Wisconsin Press, 1975).

[9] This approach is used by Ogundiran to trace the biography of beads and cowries in the Bight of Benin; see Akinkumi Ogundiran, "Of Small Things Remembered: Beads, Cowries, and Cultural Translations of the Atlantic Experience in Yorubaland," *International Journal of African Historical Studies* 35, no. 2–3 (2002): 427–57.

The second part will set the historical context in which glass beads were traded and used in nineteenth-century East Africa.[10] The third part will then concentrate on the different uses of glass beads in East Africa focusing on their monetary functions as well as on the meanings that they acquired once they had left the economic circles. The fourth section will then explore how the demand for glass beads changed over time. The final section concludes with some remarks on the various uses and meanings of glass beads in nineteenth-century East Africa.

THE PRODUCTION SIDE: MURANO AND VENICE

At the end of the thirteenth century, according to the legend, the Venetian explorer Marco Polo returned to his hometown and informed his fellow citizens about the tremendous desire that the people of the Far East had for pearls, gemstones, and their imitations. Two ingenious glass manufacturers from Murano, Cristoforo Briani and Domenico Miotti, seized the opportunity and initiated the artistic technique of using glass to imitate the genuine pearls that Marco Polo had seen during his travels; the beads they created were the beginning of a lasting tie between Venice's history and the manufacturing of glass beads.[11] This account is not historically based, as several studies have demonstrated, because the production of glass beads was initiated in order to imitate the rosary grains made of amber, ivory, and rock crystal, which were largely in use in the Middle Ages. Nonetheless, the story of Marco Polo demonstrates how, since its origins, the history of glass beads has been deeply connected to foreign markets and desires.[12]

Glass beads began to be produced on a large scale in Venice during the fourteenth century. It was, however, only from the beginning of the fifteenth century that Venice obtained its supremacy in the world glass-bead

[10] In this chapter, with East Africa I intend, broadly, the area that in the nineteenth century became part of the commercial hinterland of Zanzibar and that comprised many areas of present-day Tanzania, Kenya, and Uganda, and part of the Democratic Republic of the Congo. Many of the examples given in the chapter refer to areas now located in the United Republic of Tanzania, but glass beads were widely traded and used in other areas of the Zanzibar commercial hinterland.

[11] Morazzoni and Pasquato, *Conterie Veneziane*, 8–9.

[12] For the origins of this myth and its meaning, see Francesca Trivellato, "Out of Women's Hands: Notes on Venetian Glass Beads, Female Labour and International Trades," in *Beads and Bead Makers: Gender, Material Culture and Meaning*, ed. Lidia D. Sciama and Joanne B. Eicher (Oxford and New York: Berg, 1998), 63–4; see also Elena Bertagnolli, Maria Teresa Sega, and Rossella Urbani De Gheltof, *Perle Veneziane* (Venice: Consorzio Venezia Perle, 1991), 27–8.

production, when Venetian glass-bead makers filled the void left by
the decline of Western Asian industries.[13] To establish and maintain its
supremacy, the government of the Venetian Republic established restrictive laws. The first one was issued in 1318, followed by a law in 1490
and another in 1547, in which all glass-bead makers were obliged not to
divulge glass-bead-making secrets and not to migrate abroad.[14] It was
deemed so important to preserve the secrets of the craftsmanship in the
bosom of Venetian families that a glass-bead maker who migrated abroad
could be charged with high treason. Emblematic in this sense is the case
of the glass-blower Giovan Antonio Vistosi, who, on account of his poverty, accepted the invitation of King Leopold II's ambassador to establish
a glass furnace in the Grand Duchy of Florence and thus migrated to
Florence in 1754. Because of the success of his activity he was followed
by three of his brothers at the end of the same year. In order to convince
Vistosi to go back to Venice, the Republic sent him several emissaries, but
to no avail. He was therefore accused of high treason and condemned to
death by poisoning. A hired killer was sent to Florence to find him, but
luckily Giovan Antonio became aware of the danger and thus escaped
death.[15] Despite the Venetians' attempts to keep the secrets of producing
glass beads at home, at the start of the seventeenth century they began to
be produced abroad, particularly in Amsterdam and Bohemia.[16]

From the thirteenth century until the end of the eighteenth century, the
methods of manufacturing glass beads in Venice and Murano remained
almost untouched.[17] In 1524, the guild of *perleri* (glass-bead makers)
was founded, and it regulated the access to apprenticeship and master-
ship and helped to regulate the production and to maintain the secrets of
glass-bead making.[18] The production of glass beads in Venice was more
complex than ordinary glass or mirror production. Glass canes could be
produced only in Murano, after a law of 1291 had established that all the
furnaces should be moved from Venice to the island of Murano for safety
reasons. Two different glass canes existed: solid rods (*canna massiccia*)
and hollow rods (*canna forata*). The manufacturing of glass beads from

[13] Lois Sherr Dubin, *The History of Beads: From 30,000 BC to the Present* (London: Thames
      and Hudson, 1987), 107.
[14] Morazzoni and Pasquato, *Conterie Veneziane*, 15. The visit to the glass furnaces was,
      e.g., forbidden; see ibid., 19.
[15] Ibid., 45–6.
[16] Bertagnolli et al., *Perle Veneziane*, 39; Trivellato, "Out of Women's Hands," 70.
[17] Trivellato, "Out of Women's Hands," 71.
[18] Francesca Trivellato, *Fondamenta dei Vetrai, Lavoro, Tecnologia e Mercato a Venezia tra
      Sei e Settecento* (Rome: Donzelli Editore, 2000).

a solid rod was an individual work in which the glass cane was melted on an oil lamp and beads were produced one by one.[19] In contrast, different stages were involved in the production of glass beads from hollow rods. To start with, glass canes were divided according to their thickness and then they were cut into small pieces. These pieces were again selected to sort out the broken ones. After that, they were transformed into beads through the use of fire. After being polished, the beads were strung together and were ready to be sold.[20] The ability to imitate nature was so great that, at the end of this process, glass beads did look like true pearls and gemstones. To avoid fraud, restrictive laws were issued that forbade setting the glass beads in gold and in 1445 the Republic enacted a law punishing those who tried to sell them as true pearls.[21]

Women were instrumental in the productive process as they generally performed the role of selecting the glass canes and the beads and of stringing them together.[22] Even though we do not have precise data on the number of women employed in the glass-bead industry, it is possible to estimate that several thousands were working in Venice in the eighteenth and nineteenth century.[23] This female labor force played an important role in the economy of the lower classes. The women working outside their homes earned a wage, even if very small, in exchange for their labor. The significance of their work was not only economic, but also cultural and social. The activity of stringing beads was performed individually with the bead stringers seated together in front of their houses, in the *calli* and *campielli* of Venice. This cemented neighborhood and social relationships.[24]

As a rich field of studies has shown in the last decades, the cultural, economic, and social role of commodities cannot ultimately be divorced from questions of technology, production, and trade.[25] The

---

[19] Trivellato, "Out of Women's Hands," 50.

[20] Ibid.; see also Morazzoni and Pasquato, *Conterie Veneziane*, 70–1.

[21] Morazzoni and Pasquato, *Conterie Veneziane*, 23; referring to glass in general, Maxine Berg underlines that its importance is not only determined by the value and rarity of its raw materials, but also by its potential for imitating nature; see Maxine Berg, *Luxury and Pleasure in Eighteenth-Century Britain* (Oxford: Oxford University Press, 2005), 117.

[22] Children of eight years and upward were employed in selecting the glass canes; see Morazzoni and Pasquato, *Conterie Veneziane*, 10.

[23] Nadia Maria Filippini, "Un Filo di Perle da Venezia al Mondo," *La Ricerca Folklorica* 34 (1996): 8; Trivellato, "Out of Women's Hands," 51.

[24] Filippini, "Un Filo di Perle," 9; on the role of women in the production of glass beads, see Trivellato, "Out of Women's Hands."

[25] Appadurai, "Introduction: Commodities and the Politics of Value," 35.

industrialization process that took place in the Western world in the nineteenth century created the conditions to produce and export great quantities of products, and Venice was no exception. From 1814 to 1848, there was a renaissance of the Venetian glass-bead production, with the increase in manufacturing, investments, and trade.[26] Improvements in the production techniques were introduced by new inventions, like a pipe to sharpen the beads (in 1817) and a machine to cut the glass canes (in 1822), which was later improved even more.[27] Then, starting from 1848, glass-bead manufacturing in Venice was subject to an extensive mechanization, with the reduction of the time needed to produce the beads and the subsequent decrease in the cost of production.[28] This significantly increased the output, and in the 1870s Venice obtained the monopoly of the world's production of glass beads.[29] This resulted in an increase not only in the quantities produced but also in the quality of the final products.[30] Another innovation, which was particularly important for the foreign markets, was the invention of new tints; for example, in 1866, a glass-bead maker first produced the golden bead, which was then requested all over the world, particularly to decorate sacred furnishings.[31] From contemporary reports, it is evident that one of the most important aspects of Venetian production was to offer new forms and new colors of beads to better satisfy the foreign demand.[32]

The major part of the production was, in fact, exported to distant foreign markets even though, in the sixteenth and seventeenth century, glass beads were also traded in Europe. In Milan, for instance, during the sixteenth century glass beads were widely used to decorate cloths and blankets. And in Naples in the seventeenth century, local women embellished their cloths with glass beads. However, from the seventeenth century onward, glass beads became mainly an export commodity, which

---

[26] Alberto Errera, *Storia e Statistica delle Industrie Venete* (Venice: Giuseppe Antonelli, 1870), 185.

[27] Sega et al., *Perle Veneziane*, 60–2.

[28] Errera, *Storia e Statistica*, 328.

[29] Sega et al., *Perle Veneziane*, 72. In the previous decades, Venice had suffered from foreign competition, particularly from Bohemia; for a work dealing with the glass-bead trade between Bohemia and East Africa, see Ulf Vierke, "Die Spur der Glasperlen: Akteure, Strukturen und Wandel im europäisch-ostafrikanischen Handel mit Glasperlen" (PhD diss., University of Bayreuth, 2006), 331–2.

[30] For a similar discourse on cotton production, see Giorgio Riello, *Cotton: The Fabric That Made the Modern World* (Cambridge: Cambridge University Press, 2013), 214.

[31] Sega et al., *Perle Veneziane*, 71.

[32] Cesare Vignola, *Alcuni Dispacci di Cesare Vignola Residente in Londra per la Repubblica di Venezia sull'Argomento delle Conterie di Venezia* (Venice: Tip. Cordella, 1884), 22.

was particularly important for the Venetian economy. At the end of the seventeenth century, they represented half of the total glass production of the Republic.[33] The seed beads, small glass beads obtained from hollow rods, were among the most requested of Venetian exports, particularly from African and Asian markets, and were called in Venice *conterie*. The origin of this name is uncertain. Some attribute its meaning to the Latin *comptus*, ornament; others consider it as deriving from the word *contare*, to count, as the seed beads were used as currency in many parts of the world.[34] No trader or explorer sailing to Africa would have left without a large supply of these glass beads. The small *conterie* became, among others, one of the privileged means of exchange to acquire slaves along the West African coast.[35]

The number of slaves exported from West Africa is still a matter of debate among scholars, but undoubtedly the second half of the eighteenth century was the period in which the largest number of slaves was exported to the Americas.[36] Data on the production and export of Venetian glass beads for the eighteenth century are fragmentary and often unreliable.[37] Nonetheless, the available data show that during the second half of the eighteenth century there was an increase in the export of glass beads from Venice both toward Europe (which was generally only an intermediate market) and to India and Africa, at least until 1784–5.[38] A source reports, for example, that from 1745 to 1754 Venice was so overwhelmed by the huge demand for glass beads coming from Paris, London, Spain, Portugal, and Alexandria that the local producers were not able to satisfy the demand, even though fifty-two new boys were hurriedly employed to increase the production.[39] The biggest part of the demand for Venetian glass beads came from the countries more involved in the slave trade, like Holland, England, Spain, and Portugal. Great Britain, France, and Portugal tried their best to reduce their dependence on Venice owing to

---

[33] Ibid.

[34] Morazzoni and Pasquato, *Conterie Veneziane*, 7.

[35] Stanley B. Alpern, "What Africans Got for Their Slaves: A Master List of European Trade Goods," *History in Africa* 22 (1995): 22–4.

[36] See, among others, Philip D. Curtin, *The Atlantic Slave Trade: A Census* (Madison: University of Wisconsin Press, 1969), esp. Tables 33 and 34; and Paul Lovejoy, "The Volume of the Atlantic Slave Trade: A Synthesis," *Journal of African History* 23 (1982): Tables 2–6.

[37] Adolfo Bernardello, "Venezia 1830–1866: Iniziative Economiche, Accumulazione e Investimenti di Capitale," *Il Risorgimento* 1 (2002): 4.

[38] Trivellato, *Fondamenta dei Vetrai*, Table 15, 230–1.

[39] Morazzoni and Pasquato, *Conterie Veneziane*, 29.

the extreme importance of glass beads in the trade with Africa. They attempted, for instance, to produce their own glass beads through the cooperation of expatriated Venetian glass-bead makers.[40] The glass canes were exported to London and Lisbon where the beads were then manufactured.[41]

Following the continuous increase in the glass-bead demand, interrupted only by short periods of crisis, the production in Venice reached its peak in the nineteenth century. During this century, the glass industry was affected by a severe crisis, which involved both artistic and ordinary glass production. This crisis was partly determined by the abolition of the guilds and partly by the Austrian dominion, which facilitated German and Bohemian competition.[42] Glass beads, however, were not involved and during a difficult period they largely sustained the Venetian economy. Thanks to the mechanization process previously noted and the continuous increase of foreign demand, glass-bead production remained, during the nineteenth century, the most trade oriented of all Venetian glass manufacturing, and was a major source of employment and profit.[43] In 1845 glass beads were the most important export article in Venice and represented 50 percent of the total production.[44] From 1860 to 1905 the average production was of 23,500 quintals per year, reaching a peak in 1867, with an export of 60,152 quintals. There were some years in which the production decreased (e.g., from 1857 to 1863),[45] but it remained generally high, due largely to foreign demand.[46]

During the nineteenth century, Venice did not export directly to Africa, India, and the Americas. The main destinations of Venetian glass-bead export remained England and France, which in turn shipped the beads to their colonies or to other parts of the world. This makes the reconstruction of the historical trajectories of glass beads particularly difficult because, once they had left Venice, glass beads were shipped to various destinations before reaching the consumption box of the commodity chain. Sometimes, however, Venetian traders were able to develop their

[40] It was very convenient to import the glass cane from Venice, as at the end of the eighteenth century its price was three times higher in London than in Venice; see ibid., 41.

[41] Ibid., 34.

[42] According to Trivellato, *Fondamenta dei Vetrai*, 54 and Sega et al., *Perle Veneziane*, 55.

[43] Trivellato, *Fondamenta dei Vetrai*, 54.

[44] Trivellato, "Out of Women's Hands," 78n60.

[45] Errera, *Storia e Statistica*, 87.

[46] A significant decrease in the glass-bead export began only after 1890, partly because of the increase of foreign competition, deriving from the establishment of new factories in Albania, Egypt, and Turkey; Morazzoni and Pasquato, *Conterie Veneziane*, 64.

own system of commercialization, particularly in Egypt and India.[47] The presence of a community of Venetian traders in Egypt facilitated the commercial relations with the Red Sea area, whereas Venetian traders settled in Bombay favored the commercial contacts with India and East Africa.[48]

Sources of information all over the world were another key factor in the success of Venetian glass beads and bridged, in Appadurai's words, the "knowledge and ignorance" that characterized different regimes of value, namely the production and the consumption sides.[49] Information on the types of glass beads in demand in the various foreign markets was obtained from different channels, both from Venetian traders operating abroad and from indirect sources of information. In 1843, for instance, a very long report written by a Venetian trader based in Suez, reached the head of the Vienna Chamber of Court, Baron Kübeck. The report underlined the rich potentialities of the Zanzibar market for the export of Venetian beads. A report written by a trader based in Zanzibar was attached, with a detailed discussion of the characteristics of the local glass-bead demand.[50] East Africa was, in fact, among the first destinations of Venetian glass beads during the nineteenth century. In the 1870s, for example, this area was the third destination of the direct Venetian bead export after India and England.[51] In many areas of East Africa glass beads acquired different roles and meanings, being widely used both as ornaments and as currency.

DIFFERENT CONTEXTS, DIFFERENT MEANINGS

Commodities do not always have the same meaning. In the different stages of their biography, their value and significance often change, as they circulate in different "regimes of value," which are the product of specific historical and cultural conditions.[52] As mentioned in the introduction

---

[47] Bernardello points out that a large community of Venetian traders was settled in Alexandria and Cairo in Egypt; see Bernardello, "Venezia 1830–1866," 31–2.

[48] According to Harding, Chinese and European glass beads were sent to East Africa through Bombay; see Joan R. Harding, "Nineteenth-Century Trade Beads in Tanganyika," *Man* 62 (1962): 104; on the use of glass beads in Ethiopia during the nineteenth century, see Richard Pankhurst, *Economic History of Ethiopia, 1800–1935* (Addis Ababa: Haile Sellassie I University Press, 1968), 465–6.

[49] Appadurai, "Introduction: Commodities and the Politics of Value," 42; this was crucial for items that were subject to rapid changes in the demand, like glass beads.

[50] Venetian State Archive, Chamber of Commerce, Busta 150, Fascicolo 1, 1843.

[51] First came India with 1,860,000 lire, then Great Britain with 1,470,000 lire, and then East Africa with 650,000 lire, followed by West Africa with 520,000 lire; data refer to 1874; see Filippini, "Un Filo di Perle," 6.

[52] Appadurai, "Introduction: Commodities and the Politics of Value," 4.

to this volume, patterns of consumption are geographically specific and heavily determined by cultural preference. This becomes particularly evident when we look at the commercial exchanges that developed between East Africa and the rest of the world in the nineteenth century, when glass beads and imported cloth entered local economic circles and were exchanged for ivory, gum copal, and slaves. Both ivory and glass beads had different meanings in the context of their production and in that of their consumption. Looking at the perception and uses of these commodities in distinct economic and social contexts allow us to see that Africa was not only a producer of exotic luxury goods for the European market, but also a consumer of imported goods that became valuable items in African markets and societies, though considered as just knickknacks in the places of production.

Asymmetry of exchanges is a recurrent theme in the reports of European travelers and missionaries in Africa, but it was not referable to the case of nineteenth-century East Africa. As an observer of the time writes, "In Europe it is generally thought that the savages of Inner Africa accept a string of beads or a yard of cloth as a sufficient recompense for dozens of elephants' teeth, and that the nourishment of a caravan is repaid by the honor of the visit. These happy days are long since passed."[53] The demand for glass beads, as we are going to see, was, in fact, very complex, and traders could not easily circumvent it.

At the same time as tons of glass beads were unloaded on the African coasts, European and American traders were competing against each other to get ivory, an East African commodity that for a long time had had no economic value among the societies of the interior. Tippu Tip, the famous slave trader, found that still in the 1870s, beyond the region of Manyema, in present-day Congo,

the locals did not use ivory as exchange. They hunted elephant and ate the meat but used the tusks in their homes for a stockade. With others they made pestles and mortars for their cooking bananas; these they made into a stew and ate. Others they made into flutes, and some they threw into the bush where they were eaten by animals, such as rats. Others rotted, giving off a stench as they decomposed.[54]

[53] Charles Rigby, "Mr. J. M. Hildebrandt on His Travels in East Africa," *Proceedings of the Royal Geographical Society* 22, no. 6 (1877): 452.
[54] Ḥamid ibn Muḥammad, al-Murjabī, *Maisha ya Hamed bin Muhammed el Murjebi Yaani Tippu Tip kwa maneno yake mwenyewe*, trans. W. H. Whitley (1902; repr., Kampala, Nairobi, and Dar es Salaam: East African Literal Bureau, 1959), 91.

Before the nineteenth century, ivory had almost only a symbolic value in the regions of the interior of present-day Tanzania. Some local chiefs, for example, wore ivory ornaments in order to distinguish themselves, and, in Unyamwezi, they were buried between two ivory tusks.[55]

It was only from the first decades of the nineteenth century that the value and significance of ivory changed, owing to the huge increase in the international demand for this commodity.[56] East African ivory was very valuable because it was particularly suitable for carving, being softer than West African and Indian ivory. In the nineteenth century, East African ivory began to be widely requested in Europe and America by a growing Western middle class, for which ivory-made luxury products, such as carved figures, parts of instruments, combs, billiard balls, and so on, became one of the symbols of a high standard of life.[57] The demand for ivory also came from India, where ivory-made jewelry was an important part of a girl's dowry.

The penetration into the interior by coastal traders was not only determined by the interest in ivory, but also by the increased demand for slaves coming from the clove plantations of Zanzibar and Pemba and the sugar-cane production of the Mascarene Islands. Other East African goods requested by the international markets were gum copal, which was used to produce varnishes, and hides, which were employed in American and European tanneries. All of these products had growing prices on the international markets during the nineteenth century, and this gave African producers and traders favorable terms of trade. Between 1826 and 1857 the price of ivory in Zanzibar doubled and it doubled again in the next thirty years.[58] The international demand for these products became a great stimulus for Indian, Swahili, and Arab traders operating on the coast to expand their commercial activities into the East African interior. Coastal traders were able to penetrate inland thanks to the Omani state, which supported their commercial enterprises and to the extremely favorable terms of trade that African commodities, particularly ivory, enjoyed

[55] Andrew D. Roberts, *Tanzania before 1900: Seven Area Histories* (Nairobi: East African Publishing House, 1968), 125; Père Mènard, *Journal de la Troisième Caravane*, 1880–81, White Fathers Archive, Rome (hereafter WF) C 11–48.

[56] Abdul Sheriff, *Slaves, Spices and Ivory in Zanzibar: Integration of an East African Commercial Empire into the World Economy, 1770–1873* (London: James Currey, 1987), 156.

[57] Raymond W. Beachey, "The East African Ivory Trade in the Nineteenth Century," *Journal of African History* 8, no. 2 (1967): 274.

[58] Francis P. Nolan, "Christianity in Unyamwezi, 1878–1928" (PhD diss., University of Cambridge, 1977), 43.

throughout the nineteenth century.[59] At the same time, African traders already operating in the interior organized their own caravans to the coast. Nyamwezi traders, in particular, pioneered the commercial routes to the coast (see Map 3), and with the development of the long-distance trade they began to enlist as porters in the Arab-Swahili caravans and organized their own caravans to the coast.[60]

The establishment of a strong commercial relationship with the coast led to a huge increase in the import of foreign goods, particularly cloth, glass beads, and metal wires, which were requested by African traders in exchange for their ivory and slaves. One of the results of this process was what has been called the "commodification" of the local economies.[61] The import of new goods created a strong link to the international economy that had profound implications on the patterns of local nineteenth-century economic change. From the intersection of formerly distinct economic orders – the coastal areas and the interior – glass beads and cloth started to be invested with new exchange value and emerged as new currencies.[62]

European travelers and explorers wondered where all the glass beads that "for centuries ton after ton" had been imported to East Africa ended up.[63] Richard Burton, for example, noticed that "though the people like the Indians carry their wealth upon their persons, not a third of the population wears any considerable quantity [of beads]."[64] The glass beads imported to East Africa were, in fact, not only employed to make ornaments, but also had ritual and monetary uses, that we are going to discuss in the next section.

[59] Sheriff, *Slaves, Spices and Ivory in Zanzibar*, 156.

[60] Andrew D. Roberts, "Nyamwezi Trade," in *Pre-colonial African Trade: Essays on Trade in Central and Eastern Africa before 1900*, ed. Richard Gray and David Birmingham (London and New York: Oxford University Press, 1970), 649–701; Stephen J. Rockel, *Carriers of Culture: Labor on the Road in Nineteenth-Century East Africa* (Portsmouth, NH: Heinemann, 2006).

[61] For a discussion on this issue, see Jonathon Glassman, *Feasts and Riot: Revelry, Rebellion, and Popular Consciousness on the Swahili Coast, 1856–1888* (Heinemann: Portsmouth, 1995), 36.

[62] Jean Comaroff and John L. Comaroff, "Colonizing Currencies: Beasts, Banknotes, and the Colour of Money in South Africa," in *Commodification: Things, Agency and Identities*, ed. van Binsbergen and Geschiere, 155.

[63] Ibid.

[64] Richard Francis Burton, "The Lake Regions of Central Equatorial Africa," *Proceedings of the Royal Geographical Society* 29 (1859): 424.

LUXURY ORNAMENTS AND SMALL CHANGE:
THE DIFFERENT USES OF GLASS BEADS

Glass beads have been imported to sub-Saharan Africa from before the Christian era, finding their way from the Mediterranean across the Sahara. In East Africa, glass beads of Indian origin have been excavated from archaeological sites on the coast and date from 200 CE.[65] From the coastal ports beads found their way inland through trade networks and this made people familiar with imported beads. At the same time, beads obtained from various materials (stone, ostrich eggshells, bones, etc.) had been locally produced for centuries.[66] When the first Portuguese arrived on the East African coast, glass beads of European origin were not accepted by the local traders.[67] In the following centuries, however, Venetian beads became extensively requested in exchange for ivory, slaves, and other goods. Where and when glass beads started to be used as currency in the interior is not clear. Glass beads undoubtedly had some characteristics that made them particularly suitable for being used as currency. As Graeber points out, glass beads fit almost all the standard criteria that economists attribute to money: they are highly portable, roughly commensurable, and do not decay.[68]

In the long-distance trade exchanges of nineteenth-century East Africa different commodity currencies were in use. The so-called Zanzibar hinterland (in the sense of the area where the goods sold in the Zanzibar market came from) was a huge area, which stretched across present-day Tanzania, Kenya, Uganda, and Congo. Cloth, glass beads, metal wires, and cowries were the currencies used in the interior, with some regional variations. For example, in Buganda cowries were the most accepted currency, whereas in the central regions of Tanzania cloth was the most requested means of payment and, elsewhere, among the Maasai and to the South of Lake Victoria, glass beads were the most widely accepted

---

[65] Dubin, *The History of Beads*, 125; see also Stephanie Wynne Jones, "Lines of Desire: Power and Materiality along a Tanzanian Caravan Route," *Journal of World Prehistory* 23 (2010): 219–37.

[66] For an overview, see Dubin, *The History of Beads*, 119–51.

[67] Wicher G. N. van der Sleen, "Ancient Glass Beads: With Special Reference to the Beads of East and Central Africa and the Indian Ocean," *The Journal of the Royal Geographical Institute of Great Britain and Ireland* 88, no. 2 (1958): 211–12.

[68] Graeber, "Beads and Money," 4.

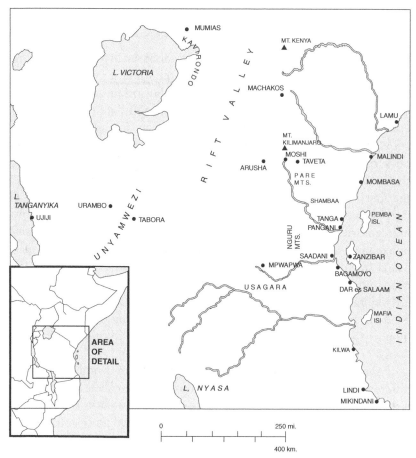

MAP 3. The Swahili Coast and the Interior.
Source: Map drawn by Cambridge University Press.

currency.[69] These commodities were requested by African traders in exchange for ivory and slaves; were used to pay porters' wages and to pay *hongo* (which were the taxes imposed by local chiefs on passing caravans); and were used to buy foodstuffs and water. Cloth, in particular, became, in nineteenth-century East Africa, the most widespread means of

---

[69] Carol J. Sissons, "Economic Prosperity in Ugogo, East Africa, 1860–1890" (PhD diss., University of Toronto, 1984), 34–68; on Buganda, see Richard Reid, *Political Power in Pre-colonial Buganda: Economy, Society and Warfare in the Nineteenth Century* (Oxford: James Currey, 2002), 144–5.

accumulating and storing wealth, as its possession was strictly related to political power.[70] Very often cloth was used in a complementary relationship with glass beads.[71] Even though cloth could sometimes be used to buy food, glass beads were often the more convenient currency. The availability of small change was, in fact, essential for these small transactions and because beads, as opposed to cloth, could be split up in small units, they became the most widespread means of buying food during caravan journeys. Daily food rations for porters were often paid in beads.

Another peculiarity of glass beads was that they were used as a recognized currency in the markets situated along the caravan roads, like Tabora and Ujiji. Owing to the different origins of the traders operating in these market towns, there was the need of a currency that could be accepted by all the traders attending the market and that could be used as the medium of the commercial exchanges.

In the market of Tabora, for example, tobacco was pressed and then cut into small cubes, each one equivalent to one string of glass beads, whereas thirty strings could be exchanged for an iron hoe.[72] Also in the market of Ujiji a bead currency was in use that consisted of cylindrical red and blue (or white and black) Venetian glass beads that were called *sofi*. The German explorer Hermann von Wissmann reports that in the Ujiji market the smallest coins were represented by red and blue glass beads; cotton cloth and copper crosses represented silver money and slaves; and cattle and ivory represented "European" gold.[73] The explorer Joseph Thomson also tells us that in the market of Ujiji "they have made the first advance towards the use of money in the adoption of a bead currency, which performs all the functions of our coppers, cloth being the medium for the larger purchases."[74] The existence in these market towns of a currency in beads was determined by the need to have a recognized exchange rate whereby the caravan roads of the interior and the different

[70] Sissons, "Economic Prosperity," 42–52.

[71] On the complementarity among monies, see Akinobu Kuroda, "What Is the Complementarity among Monies? An Introductory Note," *Financial History Review* 15, no. 1 (2008): 7–15.

[72] Mary A. Quiggin, *A Survey of Primitive Money: The Beginning of Currency* (New York: Barnes and Noble, 1970), 102.

[73] Hermann von Wissmann, *Unter deutscher Flagge quer durch Afrika von West nach Ost von 1880 bis 1883* (Berlin: Walther e Apolant, 1890), 235.

[74] Joseph Thomson, *To the Central African Lakes and Back: The Narrative of the Royal Geographical Society's East Central African Expedition 1878–1880*, Vol. 2 (1881; repr. London: Cass, 1968), 90.

types of currencies used were put in relation to one another.[75] During the early 1890s, at the beginning of the German colonial period, beads were still one of the most requested articles in the interior and were imported in great quantities every year to the colony. In the market of Tabora, for example, in 1891, red beads were still one of the most valued goods, followed by the white ones.[76] During the German colonial period, glass beads were still used in Ujiji as currency in the market and by Indian shopkeepers.[77]

Glass beads had some characteristics that made them particularly suitable for being used as currency. They were durable objects, almost impossible to counterfeit, and, being the result of a long network of supply, the amounts in circulation could be naturally limited.[78] Particularly relevant was the fact that glass beads had a very low unit value, which made them particularly appropriate where incomes and prices were also very low. In East Africa glass beads could be used to buy very small amounts of goods. Tippu Tip reported, for instance, that on Lake Kisale – present-day Congo – only one glass bead was needed to buy a small fish.[79] Being used to buy food in the markets and in many other small commercial transactions, glass beads reached a capillary diffusion in the interior. As a result, it is very likely that glass beads, very similarly to cowries in West Africa, affected the daily lives of people in East Africa much more than any other import.[80]

After being accepted as a means of payment, glass beads could be used in other commercial transactions or they could leave the economic circles.

[75] Beverly Brown, "Ujiji: History of a Lakeside Town" (PhD diss., University of Boston, 1973), 72; Karin Pallaver, "A Recognized Currency in Beads: Glass Beads as Money in Nineteenth-Century East Africa," in *Money in Africa*, ed. Catherine Eagleton, Harcourt Fuller, and John Perkins (London: British Museum Research Publications, 2009), 22–3.

[76] *Deutsches Kolonialblatt* 3 (1892): 165, and 4 (1893): 82. For an account of glass-bead import in German East Africa, see Vierke, *Die Spur der Glasperlen*, 319–42.

[77] Brown, "Ujiji: History of a Lakeside Town," 72.

[78] Paul Lovejoy, "Interregional Monetary Flows in the Precolonial Trade of Nigeria," *Journal of African History* 15, no. 4 (1974): 563–85.

[79] Ḥamid ibn Muḥammad, al-Murjabī, *L'Autobiographie de Hamed ben Mohammed el-Murjebi Tippo Tip (ca. 1840–1905)*, trans. François Bontinck (1902; repr., Brussel: Académie Royale des Sciences d'Outre-Mer, 1974), 81. In some areas of East Africa, glass beads were also an important part of the bride-price; see Philippe Broyon-Mirambo, "Description of Unyamwezi, the Territory of King Mirambo, and the Best Route Thither from the Coast," *Proceedings of the Royal Geographical Society* 22, no. 1 (1877–8): 34–5.

[80] Ogundiran, "Of Things to Be Remembered," 440. On cowries in West Africa see Jan Hogendorn and Marion Johnson, *The Shell Money of the Slave Trade* (Cambridge: Cambridge University Press, 1986).

Sometimes they could acquire ritual values. The explorers Cameron and Stanley both report on propitiatory sacrifices in beads made to gods on Lake Tanganyika. Stanley, for instance, was told by his guide that there was a custom, both among the coastal traders and the local people, of throwing white beads into the water to appease Kabogo, the god of the lake. His guide warned him that "those who throw the beads generally get past without trouble, but those who do not throw beads into the lake get lost and are drowned."[81] Lieutenant Cameron confirms this version, saying that at a certain point of his exploration of Lake Tanganyika, near the Machahezi River, two Jiji guides put three *fundo*[82] of beads into the water to appease Kabogo.[83]

Once they had left the economic circuits, glass beads could acquire some of the characteristics that, as explained in the introduction to this volume, make a commodity a luxury good. First of all, their use went beyond the realm of everyday practicality, as they were used to create a variety of ornaments, such as necklaces, bracelets, and belts, and were employed to decorate the body. In Usambara, for example, Burton found that "[t]he women are adorned with talismans in leather bags, and with massive collars of white beads, now in fashion throughout this region: a 'distinguished person' will carry from 3 to 4 lb. of these barbaric decorations."[84] Glass beads were also widely used to decorate beards and hair, or were embroidered in cloths or other objects, such as masks and dolls. Cameron reports that, on Lake Tanganyika, the women who had no children made a doll out of a calabash and decorated it with beads; they then tied it to their backs and carried it in the same way as children were carried in that country.[85]

Their special origin and their material characteristics produced special aesthetically pleasing qualities for those who wore them. After reaching Lake Victoria from the coast, the White Fathers had to wait for a long time to obtain the boats needed to cross the lake. While waiting, they

---

[81] Henry Morton Stanley, *How I Found Livingstone* (1872; repr., Vercelli: White Star, 2006), 347; Harding, "Nineteenth-Century Trade Beads," 106.

[82] A *fundo* was a unit of measure for beads; one *fundo* was equivalent to ten *khete* (or *kete*), a unit of measurement corresponding to the distance from the thumb to the elbow and back.

[83] Verney Lovett Cameron and Clement P. Markham, "Examination of the Southern Half of Lake Tanganyika," *Journal of the Royal Geographical Society* 45 (1875): 199; instead of god Kabogo, they call him "devil of Kabogo."

[84] Richard Francis Burton, *Zanzibar: City, Island and Coast*, Vol. 2 (London: Tinsley Brothers, 1872), 231.

[85] Cameron and Markham, "Examination," 212.

had to play up to the local chief (*manangwa*). They therefore made a necklace, with small and big blue beads, and then green, white, red, and yellow beads, symmetrically strung. When they gave it to the *manangwa*, he immediately put it on and started to look at himself. According to the missionaries: "He was delighted, he admired himself for several minutes."[86]

The possession and display of beads had also important symbolic and cultural values. As Lidia D. Sciama points out, "[B]eads, in their different colours, arrangements and styles, are important symbols of collective, as well as individual identity for many social groups."[87] There is a direct connection between being an object of desire and becoming a luxury object. The desirability of an object was conveyed not only by the object, but also by those who possessed or displayed it.[88] Wearing glass beads was a way of displaying a person's well-being, but was also a sign of being close to the ruling elite. In those societies in which glass beads were worn by local chiefs, beads were, in fact, considered as a sign of aristocratic status. In this sense, not only the physical characteristics of glass beads, but also "manners, gestures and style" made them a desirable object.[89] Cameron reported, for instance, that to the south of Lake Tanganyika, "Some of the people have their heads completely covered with sofi or pipe-stream beads, each strung on a separate tuft of hair.... Others who cannot afford beads imitate this by making their wool into blobs, and greasing it until one cannot detect the separate fibres."[90] Glass beads were therefore displayed as ornaments by those who could afford them for that purpose and imitated by those who could not.

Glass beads were also related to political power. Being rich in beads and cloth and having experience in the trade with the coast was fundamental for the maintenance and sometimes for the achievement of political power.[91] In some regions of the interior it was considered even more important than hereditary rights. As an example, before the 1840s, in the chiefdom of Unyanyembe (Unyamwezi), the succession to the throne

---

[86] "Il est ravi; il s'admire, se contemple pendant plusieurs minutes"; *Diaire du Nyanza*, WF C 11–26, entry of April 12, 1879.

[87] Sciama, "Gender in the Making," 18.

[88] Berg, *Luxury and Pleasure*; Christopher J. Berry, *The Idea of Luxury: A Conceptual and Historical Investigation* (Cambridge: Cambridge University Press, 1994), 3.

[89] Maxine Berg and Helen Clifford, eds., *Consumers and Luxury: Consumer Culture in Europe 1650–1850* (Manchester, UK and New York: Manchester University Press, 1999), 9.

[90] Cameron and Markham, "Examination," 213.

[91] Ḥamid ibn Muḥammad, al-Murjabī, *L'Autobiographie*, 86.

had been matrilinear. However, when chief Swetu died, the eldest son of Swetu's sister did not become the new chief; instead the son of Swetu, Fundikira, was elected. The local aristocracy preferred Fundikira to the heir apparent because he had visited the coast several times and had accumulated wealth in imported commodities. Since this election, the succession to the throne was no longer matrilinear, but was related to the commercial ability and wealth of the candidates.[92] With the commodification of the local economies, new men with new wealth could challenge the old political order.[93]

The commercial sphere that emerged in East Africa in the nineteenth century grew and extended its geographical range on the basis of indigenous transactional conventions.[94] These would not have been possible if not situated in a broader set of agreements concerning "what is desirable, what it is reasonable to sacrifice and who is permitted to exercise what sort of demand."[95] Being both used as currency and as ornaments, glass beads were critical in this process.

With the colonization of the area by the Europeans, the use of glass beads as currency started to slowly decline, and the money introduced by the colonial powers gradually took hold. The establishment of colonial borders and the introduction of metal coins in German East Africa, Uganda, and Kenya moved the use of beads as currency toward the Congo Free State, where in the first decade of the twentieth century they were still largely used to buy ivory. Nonetheless, during the colonial period glass beads continued to be used to produce ornaments and remained one of the main imports of the East African colonies.[96]

In nineteenth-century East Africa, glass beads were obtained through economic networks and were used as a means of payment and exchange. After leaving the trade circuits, they were widely used as ornaments and were socially important as a display of wealth, becoming objects of luxury used beyond the realm of everyday practicality.

---

[92] Alfred C. Unomah, "Vbandevba and Political Change in a Nyamwezi Kingdom Unyanyembe during 1840 to 1890" (paper presented at the Universities of East Africa Social Science Conference, Dar es Salaam, 27–31 December 1970); John Iliffe, *A Modern History of Tanganyika* (Cambridge: Cambridge University Press, 1979), 61–2.

[93] Ogundiran, "Of Things to Be Remembered," 446.

[94] Jane Guyer, *Marginal Gains: Monetary Transactions in Atlantic Africa* (Chicago: University of Chicago Press, 2004).

[95] Appadurai, "Introduction: Commodities and the Politics of Value," 57.

[96] In the early colonial period, glass beads were imported from Uganda to the Congo basin region, where they were used to buy ivory; see The National Archives, London, CO 536/2.

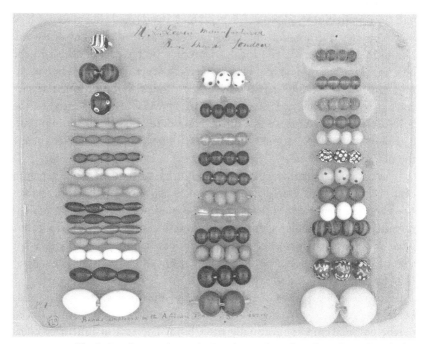

FIGURE 20. Trade beads sample card. "Beads employed in the African Trade for Ivory Presented by M. L. Levin, Manufacturer, London."
Source: M. L. Levin. Courtesy of © Trustees of the British Museum.

Hundreds of varieties of beads were in demand along the caravan roads and were produced in Venice especially for the African markets, as the sample card in Figure 20 shows. As we have previously noted, when we were discussing the production side, many different colors and sizes of glass beads had in fact to be produced in Venice to satisfy the foreign demand.

"THE FASTIDIOUS TASTES OF AFRICAN WOMEN": THE CHANGING DEMAND FOR GLASS BEADS

The ever-changing tastes for beads of the local populations were the subject of continuous complaints among the European traders and travelers of the time. The choice of the wrong types of beads could, in fact, determine the total failure of an expedition.[97] Stanley reports that Speke and

[97] The same situation could be found in West Africa, where only particular kinds of beads were accepted; see Pierre Edoumba, "Aperçu sur les monnaies d'Afrique," *Revue numismatique* 6, no. 157 (2001): 113.

Burton were obliged to throw away many beads considered worthless; on the coast they had purchased the wrong types of glass beads, beads that had no value in the interior and were not accepted even as gifts.[98] Traders and explorers going into the interior had therefore to pay particular attention to buying the right types of beads. Generally they consulted the recently returned caravan leaders, traders, or porters about the prevailing types of beads in demand among the populations living in the interior.[99] Here again, as in the case of the European consuls and traders on the coast who informed the producers in Europe on the types of beads in demand, special actors in the commodity chain made possible to bridge the "knowledge and ignorance" that characterized different regimes of value.[100]

But this was not always sufficient. Joseph Thomson, for instance, when organizing his caravan on the coast, asked Chuma, the chief headmen of his expedition, which kinds of beads were in use in the interior. Chuma listed all the colors and sizes of beads that were in use in the Lake Tanganyika region during the time he was residing there with David Livingstone. Trusting Chuma, Thomson "laid in a considerable supply of beads of the required size, composition and colour. When we arrived at the lake, we found beads of all kinds ignored, and coloured cloths in demand. The beads we had laboriously transported so far proved utterly useless."[101] According to Thomson, the "fashion" had changed, and it was not possible for Chuma to be aware of it. According to the sources, tastes and fashion might in fact change every year or even every month: Burton, for example, describing the bead currency of Msene, in Western Unyamwezi, explained that the information he was giving could be considered valid only for that year, 1858, because the kind of currency in use was continuously changing, causing severe losses to merchants, "who after laying in a large outfit of certain beads, find them suddenly unfashionable and therefore useless."[102]

Traders and explorers lamented that each population had its particular preference as to tint, color, and size. In Burton's times, for example, as

[98] Stanley, *How I Found Livingstone*, 32.
[99] Stanley, e.g., asked caravan leaders (Stanley, *How I Found Livingstone*, 204); Jerome Becker asked porters (Jerome Becker, *La vie en Afrique ou Trois Ans dans l'Afrique Centrale*, Vol. 1 [Paris and Brussels: J. Lebègue et Cie, 1887] 470); and Burton asked Arab traders (Burton, "The Lake Regions," 423).
[100] Appadurai, "Introduction: Commodities and the Politics of Value," 42.
[101] Thomson, *To the Central Lakes*, 1: 35–6.
[102] Burton, *The Lake Regions of Central Africa*, 1: 271.

many as four hundred different types of beads were in demand.[103] Later, in 1871, when Stanley was organizing his caravan on the coast to go in search of Livingstone, it took him a long time to decide which kind of glass beads to take with him. He decided, in the end, to buy eleven different types of beads among the great number in use, and he concluded:

> The various kind of beads [to be carried into the interior] required great time to learn, for the women of Africa are as fastidious in their tastes for beads as the women of New York are for jewelry. The measures also had to be mastered, which, seeing that it was an entirely new business in which I was engaged, were rather complicated, and perplexed me considerably for a time.[104]

According to many contemporary observers, the value of glass beads went hand in hand with their fashionable aspect. Père Livinhac of the White Fathers wrote that as barter goods glass beads were second in importance only to cloth, but were far more subject to the "caprice" of the people he met along the road.[105] Joseph Thomson was making the same point, when he wrote: "In one year a tribe goes mad for a particular bead; but the trader having supplied himself with the fashionable article, according to latest news, might, if his journey was long, arrive to find a fashion changed and his stock just so unmarketable rubbish."[106] Nonetheless, as I have discussed elsewhere, the limited flexibility of the demand should be attributed more to the fact that these items were used as currency and as a measurement of value rather than to the "fastidious tastes of African women" or their "caprice."[107] The circulation of currencies is based on their acceptability that, in the case of commodity currencies, could only be derived from their material characteristics.

The rapid changes in the demand for glass beads seemed to mainly affect seed beads. In contrast, it seems that beads that were particularly rare, and therefore more expensive, were not subject to these continuous changes. The coral red beads called *sami-sami*, for example, which were among the more expensive beads in nineteenth-century East Africa, were the most requested in Unyamwezi during Burton's travels in the 1850s. They also remained in demand during Stanley's first journey in 1871, and in 1878 the White Fathers found that these coral beads were still widely accepted along the central caravan road from Unyamwezi toward Lake

---

[103] Burton, "The Lake Regions," 424.
[104] Norman R. Bennett, ed., *Stanley's Despatches to the New York Herald, 1871–72, 1874–77* (Boston: Boston University Press, 1970), 5.
[105] Père Livinhac, S. Marie près de Roubaga, September 9, 1879, WF C 11–12.
[106] Thomson, *To the Central*, 1: 353.
[107] Pallaver, "A Recognized Currency in Beads."

Victoria.[108] That is why, after discovering that colored beads were preferred to the white ones he had brought with him, John Hanning Speke
reached the following conclusion:

> It is always foolish to travel without an assortment of beads, in consequence of
> the tastes of the different tribes varying so much; and it is more economical in the
> long-run to purchase high-priced than low-priced beads when making up the car-
> avan at Zanzibar, for every little trader buys the cheaper sorts, stocks the country
> with them, and thus makes them common.[109]

The same problem was reported by Venetian correspondents around the
world. An important trade company based in India wrote in the nineteenth century to some of the most influential glass-bead producers in
Venice, asking them to limit the shipping of beads, in order to avoid over-
stocking the local market and the fall of glass-bead prices.[110]

Even though we still do not have very detailed figures on the Venetian
glass-bead export for the entire nineteenth century in regard to both
direct and indirect exports, the information at our disposal confirms that
the East African market was extremely important for Venetian glass-bead
production during this century. Figures on the annual average of
glass-bead export from Venice to the main ports all over the world for the
period 1889–98 show that the main destinations were London (6,644 q)
and Liverpool (4,997 q), followed by India with Calicut (3,472 q) and
Bombay (3,154 q); then came two European ports, Antwerp (3,005 q)
and Marseilles (1,930 q), followed by Zanzibar with 1,215 q, which was
more important than Hamburg (1,074 q), Alexandria (612 q), Singapore
(304 q), Mombasa (170 q), Istanbul (430 q), and so on.[111] We also have to
take into consideration that these data refer only to direct exports, but we
mentioned that London, Marseilles, and Bombay were often only intermediate markets and reexported glass beads to various African ports. The
total amount of trade with East Africa was therefore much higher.

The ability of Venice to satisfy the expanding demand coming from
the foreign markets was due to its organizational flexibility and due
to the innovations that, in the framework of the nineteenth-century
Industrial Revolution, allowed the bead producers to mechanize the process and to reduce production costs. The Venetian manufacturing system

---

[108] See Pére Livinhac, S. Marie près de Roubaga, September 9, 1879, WF C 11–12; Harding,
"Nineteenth-Century Trade Beads," 104; Stanley, *How I Found Livingstone*, 32–3.

[109] John H. Speke, *What Led to the Discovery of the Source of the Nile* (Edinburgh: William
Blackwood, 1864), 281.

[110] Errera, *Storia e Statistica*, 681.

[111] C. Ricchetti, "L'industria delle conterie a Venezia," *La Riforma Sociale* 9 (1899): 989.

was particularly suited to satisfy the fluctuations of the demand. The work was, in fact, seasonal and the factories were closed during summer and other periods called *cavata,* which were scheduled according to the market trend.[112] Another peculiarity of the Venetian manufacturing system was the fact that the work of selecting glass canes and beads and of stringing beads was performed by Venetian women at home and assigned according to the factories' needs.[113] When the demand was particularly high, the final stages of the production could be therefore easily accelerated by the employment of a large body of temporary workers. This contributed to the organizational flexibility of the production, particularly in its final stages, which could be easily increased or diminished according to the fluctuations of the demand. This was one of the key elements in the ability of Venetian factories to satisfy the fluctuations in the demand.[114]

The adoption of a commodity chain approach is particularly effective in the analysis of the connection of the East African regions to the international economy. This was driven both by the development of new economic patterns in nineteenth-century East Africa and by the process of mechanization taking place in Europe. Through a commodity chain approach, we can understand how glass beads were valued and used in nineteenth-century East Africa and how they affected the daily lives of many people during a period of burgeoning relationships with the outside world. At the same time, the flexibility and the innovations that characterized the nineteenth-century production of beads in Venice, were key components in the organization of their global commodity chain and in the success of this commodity on the East African market.[115] Following the trajectories of glass beads from the production to the consumption produces a decentered and transcultural perspective of what luxury is – or is not – in the societies that used them.

LUXURY OR NOT? SOME CONCLUDING REMARKS

Glass beads had many of the characteristics that can be used to define an object as luxury. They had a special origin, were used beyond the realm

---

[112] Bertagnolli et al., *Perle Veneziane,* 77.
[113] Anna Bellavitis, "In Fabbrica e in Casa: Il Lavoro Femminile nelle 'Conterie' a Venezia," in *Perle e Impiraperle: Un lavoro di donne a Venezia tra '800 e '900* (Venice: Arsenale, 1990), 9–21; Bernardello, "Venezia 1830–1866," 5–66.
[114] Gereffi et al., "Introduction: Global Commodity Chains," 6.
[115] Ibid., 2.

of everyday practicality, became a way to accumulate wealth, and were a symbol of power and social status. Glass beads represent a good example of the way objects gain value thanks to the physical distance from the place of production to that of consumption. This gave them an "exotic" flavor, if this term is allowed, that made them an object of desire all over the world. Glass beads became luxury goods in many places situated far from the centers of production, not for their intrinsic value, but for their rarity, their material characteristics, and the uses that many societies in Africa, Asia, and the Americas made of the imported beads. The analysis of the different uses of glass beads in East Africa can help to better understand why glass beads were so requested in many parts of the world and what were the meanings that they acquired during their biographical life. The value of beads was related to their use as ornaments and to the meanings that were associated with the display of various glass-bead decorations. But glass beads were "more than luxury items ... for the personal indulgence of the ruling elite."[116] Once they were bought on the East African coast by traders going inland in search for ivory and slaves, glass beads acquired a recognized value and became part of a complex currency system, in which cloth was used as a higher unit of currency, whereas beads were used as small change. If we consider that in many regions of East Africa glass beads were commonly used to buy food, we can grasp how essential it was to acquire them for so many local societies. At the same time, being commodities, glass beads were also fungible items and once they left economic circles, they could acquire various social, ritual, and cultural meanings.

As mentioned at the beginning of this chapter, the fact that so many people around the world accepted glass beads in exchange for precious goods, such as land, slaves, and ivory, has become in the popular imagination a demonstration of their naivety, of their inability to distinguish between valuable and worthless goods. This assumption is based on how this commodity was perceived at the beginning of its biographical life, in the production centers, where a different "regime of value" was at place. However, in Africa, the perception of what was luxury could be very different from the perception in the places where African goods were heading to be used as luxuries.

---

[116] Edna G. Bay, *Wives of the Leopard: Gender, Politics and Culture in the Kingdom of Dahomey* (Charlottesville: University of Virginia Press, 1998), 123, quoted in Ogundiran, "On Things to Be Remembered," 428.

8

Imports and autarky: Tortoiseshell in early modern Japan

Martha Chaiklin

Plastics are an integral part of modern life, not a luxury. Most of the materials that plastic replaced, however, were expensive. Tortoiseshell, once used in hair clips, jewelry, and eyeglass frames; to make boxes; or to form handles for cutlery and instruments, has always been a luxury.[1] Luxury is an antonym for need, but to function as a part of society, need extends far beyond what is necessary to survive. It is fluid, changing as the position of the individual and society at large is transformed. Thus what was once a luxury becomes a necessity. For example, twenty-five years ago, cell phones were only owned by a few people; they were a luxury. In today's world they have become a necessity. Moreover, needs can be fulfilled adequately or well; one can have a basic phone or an iPhone. This is something like the trajectory of tortoiseshell in Japan. It began as a luxury confined to the uppermost echelons of the elite but as it was incorporated into the changing society of early modern Japan, tortoiseshell became a necessity for women of all statuses.

Tortoiseshell is beautiful, durable, lightweight, and waterproof. These characteristics made it the best possible natural material for myriad uses. Most of these applications could be satisfied with other materials, or through imitations, but tortoiseshell was the most elegant. The luxury did not lie in the impermanence but in the expense, because tortoiseshell had to be imported to many of the areas where it was consumed, and it required some skill to work. Thus, even today, it is characterized as "gem material."

In the West, the consumer revolution that brought luxury to the newly formed middle class is often seen as a corollary to the Industrial

[1] It was banned as an article of international trade in 1977.

Revolution. Technological progress resulted not only in increased production, but more efficient transport, which brought exotic goods, especially those from Asia, to Europe.[2] However, an examination of tortoiseshell in early modern Japan shows that protoindustrialization and a rise in the standard of living brought about a sense of luxury based on imports despite the lack of an industrial or transportation revolution and an official policy of autarky. Combs, writing boxes, and even dildos made of tortoiseshell, an imported material, proliferated by the eighteenth century. For women in particular, tortoiseshell became a need. Thus tortoiseshell provides a good case study for how changing perceptions of need subverted official and social sanctions against luxury and undermined trade restrictions in Japan.

THE NATURAL HISTORY OF TORTOISESHELL

When we speak of tortoiseshell we are actually speaking of turtles rather than tortoises – sea turtles to be exact. Although many kinds of turtle shell have been put to use at some time or another, the material most widely used in manufacturing luxury objects is comprised of the carapaces (shell top) or plastrons (shell bottom) of several species of sea turtle. True tortoiseshell is taken from the smallest of these species, the hawksbill turtle (*Eretmochelys imbricata*). The common name is derived from its beaklike nose, but the Latin species name was taken from the fact that the shell pieces are imbricated. Hawksbill shell is by far the most widely used and is highly valued for the quality and color of its shell. All of the turtle species used for their shell are found in tropical waters. Each is currently threatened or endangered, but the demand for tortoiseshell objects is only one contributing factor to a host of other threats to habitat and reproduction cycles.

Tortoiseshell is comprised of keratin and thus shares similar properties of thermoplasticity with other keratinous substances like horn and baleen. It is therefore used in some of the same ways. However, tortoiseshell also has some unique qualities. It can be peeled into thin sheets that can be joined to form veneer, yet it is hard enough to be turned on a lathe. As one might expect of the sea turtle, it is also resistant to damp. If broken, tortoiseshell can even be almost invisibly repaired by reapplying

---

[2] See Maxine Berg and Elizabeth Eger, "The Rise and Fall of the Luxury Debates," in *Luxury in the Eighteenth Century*, ed. Maxine Berg and Elizabeth Eger (New York: Palgrave Macmillan, 2003), 8–9.

FIGURE 21. Shibori *Kanzashi* benichoku.
Source: Horai Hidenobu 1818. Courtesy of the Library of Congress.

pressure and heat. This durability combined with its very light weight and warm, neutral colors were difficult to reproduce with other materials until plastics were developed. Limited supply and superior functionality combined with these fundamentally "pleasing" qualities made tortoise-shell a luxury.[3]

---

[3] Christopher Berry identifies "pleasing" as a requirement for luxuries. Christopher Berry, *The Idea of Luxury: A Conceptual and Historical Investigation* (Cambridge: Cambridge University Press, 1994), 12.

AN ABBREVIATED WORLD HISTORY OF TORTOISESHELL

The wide distribution of sea turtles with usable shells has ensured a long history for human utilization of tortoiseshell. In Southeast Asia and the Caribbean, where hawksbill is indigenous, it was used for jewelry and various implements and instruments. For example, pendants, carved ornaments, and bangles have been found in ancient gravesites in Thailand.[4] Tortoiseshell was equally treasured by the ancient Egyptians, who used it for jewelry at least five thousand years ago, in the Early Dynastic period.[5] Hawksbill objects have been found in Native American sites from about the same time period.[6] In ancient Greece, tortoiseshell was highly valued, being traded from the Red Sea region. It was even used to make lyres. Julius Caesar was so pleased by the seizure of warehouses of tortoiseshell in Alexandria that he made tortoiseshell a symbol of his triumph.

The Middle Ages must have cut off European craftsmen from the source of their materials because it was not widely used again in Europe until the early seventeenth century with the expansion of maritime routes to Asia. Thereafter, demand increased as the standard of living in Europe rose. It was used as a veneer on objects such as snuffboxes and tea caddies; to make spectacle frames; and to form handles and parts for scientific, medical, and musical instruments.

In East Asia, usage was equally ancient. Turtle carapaces were used for divination in Shang dynasty China. Tortoiseshell was used as one form of currency until currency was standardized under the Qin Emperor in the second century BCE.[7] Evidence that tortoiseshell was worked from ancient times can be found in *The Analects* of Confucius, embedded in a somewhat lengthy anecdote about the wisdom of waging war:

If when one's lord encounters danger his ministers do not support him, or when he is about to fall his ministers do not catch him, then what on earth are his

[4] C. F. W. Higham and R. Bannanurag, *The Excavation of Khok Phanom Di: A Prehistoric Site in Central Thailand* (London: The Society of Antiquaries and Thames and Hudson, 1990).

[5] See, e.g., Tine Bagh, "Jewelry and Amulets: Finds from the Royal Naqada Tomb," in *Egypt and Its Origins*, ed. Stan Hendrichs (Leuven: Peeters Publishers, 2004), 599. Some scholars dispute whether these objects were made from hawksbill shell. See Peter L. Lutz and John A. Musick, eds., *The Biology of Sea Turtles* (Boca Raton: CRC Press, 2003), 22.

[6] James Spotila, *Sea Turtles: A Complete Guide to Their Biology, Behavior and Conservation* (Baltimore: Johns Hopkins University Press, 2004), 66.

[7] Nishijima Sadao, "The Economic and Social History of Former Han," in *The Cambridge History of China*, Vol. 1, ed. by Denis Twichett and John F. Fairbank (Cambridge and New York: Cambridge University Press, 1986), 579.

ministers for? ... When a tiger or a rhinoceros escapes from its cage, or when a precious tortoise shell box or piece of jade is destroyed in its case, who is to blame for this?[8]

As this quotation indicates, in China tortoiseshell was valued as a jewel, and significant quantities were imported. It was used as inlay in musical instruments and to ornament court clothing and utensils.[9] Canton (Guangzhou), where the Supervisorate of Maritime Trade was located, was an important carving center from at least Tang (618–907) times.[10]

Tortoiseshell combs have been excavated from Korean tombs dating from circa 45 CE.[11] Tortoiseshell, therefore, had the international appeal of other gem materials and precious metals. Nevertheless, despite frequent contacts with both these nations and the adoption of many elements of political, religious, and material culture from abroad, the people of the Japan did not adopt tortoiseshell until significantly later.

TORTOISESHELL IN JAPAN

Turtle was eaten in Japan, but not very widely or often. The most widespread custom involving turtle ingestion was probably the drinking of the blood of the snapper turtle, which is still consumed as an energizer and aphrodisiac. The shell, however, was more important. Scapulimancy using turtle shells was one of many divination techniques practiced in ancient Japan. This practice has continued into modern times in some areas.[12] Turtle shell was also valued as medicine. It was believed to cool fevers and was used to treat the kidneys. However, in spite of the availability of sea turtles and the technological ability to work horn and other materials, tortoiseshell was not worked in ancient Japan. The earliest

---

[8] Roger T. Ames and Henry Rosemont, trans., *The Analects of Confucius – A Philosophical Translation* (New York: Ballentine Books, 1998), 195.

[9] See Edward Schafer, *The Golden Peaches of Samarkand* (Berkeley: University of California Press, 1963), 115, 135.

[10] Roderich Ptak, "China and the Trade in Tortoise-Shell (Sung to Ming Periods)," in *Emporia, Commodities and Entrepreneurs in Asian Maritime Trade, c. 1400–1750,* ed. Roderich Ptak and Dietmar Rothermund (Stuttgart: Steiner Verlag, 1991), 203.

[11] Sarah M. Nelson, "Bound Hair and Confucianism in Korea," in *Cultures,* ed. Alf Hiltebeitel and Barbara D. Miller (Albany: State University of New York Press, 1998), 114.

[12] On Tsushima see Ozaki Takashi, "Japan and the Continent," in *Cambridge History of Japan,* Vol. 1, ed. Delmer M. Brown (Cambridge: Cambridge University Press, 1993), 292.

reference is found in an early-ninth-century history. This work recorded a jeweled tortoiseshell belt in an entry for 799, but the singularity of the object suggests it was from China.[13] Similarly, the Shōsōin, an imperial treasure house built in 756, holds tortoiseshell objects such as a box and a plectrum for a lute (*biwa*) – but all these objects appear to have likewise originated from China.[14]

By the Heian period (935–1185), the word for hawksbill turtle appeared in Japanese-language dictionaries.[15] However, the absence of any mention of tortoiseshell object in works of literature such as the *Tale of Genji* or the *Pillowbook of Sei Shonagon*, which detail the dress of the aristocracy in minute detail, suggests that tortoiseshell still played no part in the lives of even the wealthiest consumers of Heian Japan. Foreign trade with China and other countries in East and Southeast Asia increased over the next half millennium, but there is no significant record of tortoiseshell use in Japan before the seventeenth century.

ATTITUDES TOWARD LUXURY

The late seventeenth century was a time of rapid economic growth in both the agrarian and the industrial spheres. Tokugawa Japan has sometimes been characterized as protoindustrial, but it did not experience an industrial revolution. Although there was no transportation revolution either, larger and better ships were built for coastal trade, and barriers that had impeded domestic transit such as toll roads were removed. The growing economy resulted in a significantly higher standard of living and the resulting discussion of the moral impact of luxury flourished in eighteenth-century Japan much as it did in Europe, for many of the same reasons.

In eighteenth-century Europe, luxury was negatively associated with femininity and weakness.[16] This was no less true in early modern Japan.[17] Austerity was an ideal promoted by the upper echelons of the warrior class. It enabled discipline and focus. From its very founding the Tokugawa shogunate was known for frugality. Neo-Confucianism,

---

[13] *Nihon kōki* (Enreki 18).

[14] Schafer, *Golden Peaches*, 245.

[15] *Iroha Jiruisho* (1144–81).

[16] Berg and Eger, "Rise and Fall," 18.

[17] Tokugawa Ieyasu was described as parsimonious by nature. This was in stark contrast to his predecessors in the process of unification, who were known for extravagances that included luxurious clothing and opulent castles. See Donald Shively, "Sumptuary

the predominant intellectual trend in early modern Japan, reinforced these ideas. The culture of shame, pressure to adhere to the group, and respect for hierarchy fed into a disdain for luxury.[18] Thus many writers during the Edo period (1603–1868), which was a time of peace, emphasized these values. Influential Neo-Confucian scholars also promoted this viewpoint. Ogyū Sorai (1666–1728), for example, wrote that "frugality is the way of great rulers, and the great virtue of kings."[19] Daidōji Yūzan (1639–1730), author of a popular primer for the warrior class, expanded on this concept by suggesting that frugality was one way that loyalty should be shown to one's lord.[20] Similarly, Yamamoto Tsunetomo (1659–1719), author of another influential tome, *Hagakure* (Hidden Leaves), stated that "much *sake*, self-pride and luxury are to be avoided by a samurai."[21] The doctor and scholar Kaibara Ekiken (1630–1714), who wrote a number of influential texts, even believed luxury was detrimental to health, writing: "When you have no self-control over your appetites and latch onto pleasures with greedy abandon, you will exceed your natural limits, damage your body, and thus exhibit a lack of common decency."[22]

Similar ideals of austerity were common among the merchant class, albeit for slightly different reasons. On the one hand, excess by the merchant class was regulated by the government in accordance with Confucian ideals that placed them at the bottom of the social scale. When merchants failed to live up to these ideals, their assets could be, and occasionally were, seized. On the other hand, thrift was promoted by the merchants to ensure the economic continuity of their family enterprises. Codes issued by merchant houses stressed frugality above all. Although these are individual documents with a great deal of personal variation, essentially for each writer the goal was the continuity of the house. One early code, by Shimai Sōshitsu, admonished his heirs to refrain from a huge number of leisure activities, including moon viewing, go games, and

Regulation and Status in Early Tokugawa Japan," *Harvard Journal of Asiatic Studies* 25 (1964–65): 138.

[18] Pierre Xiao Lu, *Luxury Consumer Behavior in China* (Singapore: John Wiley and Sons, 2008), 6–7.

[19] Ogyū Sorai, "Benmei," in *Ogyu Sorai's Philosophical Masterworks*, ed. John A. Tucker (Honolulu: Association of Asian Studies and University of Hawaii Press, 2006), 244.

[20] Daidoji Yuzan, *Budoshoshinshu*, trans. William Scott Wilson (Santa Clarita, CA: Ohara Books, 1984), 65–6.

[21] Yamamoto Tsunetomo, *Hagakure: The Book of the Samurai*, trans. William Scott Wilson (Tokyo and New York: Kodansha International, 1979), 71.

[22] Kaibara Ekiken, *Yojokun-Life Lessons from a Samurai*, trans. William Scott Wilson (New York and Tokyo: Kodansha International, 2008), 12.

tea ceremonies.[23] The Mitsui family code of 1722 similarly emphasized thrift, if not in such a rigid way. Author Mitsui Takafusa (1684–1748), suggested that allowing one's house to decline condemned one to eternal hell.[24]

The works of Ihara Saikaku(1642–93), a realist novelist of the merchant class who wrote for his peers, are littered with similar didactic parables and sayings that expound the value of thrift and the danger of luxury. For example, in the story of a wealthy merchant who forces his son to learn to make his own money, he wrote:

A young man succeeding at making a living by using a present of cash from his parents is exactly the same as a samurai warrior living off his hereditary stipend. If a person were to save just one *mon* each day from the day he was born, after one hundred days the money could be deposited in a bank at ten percent interest, and after sixty years he would have sixty *kanme*. When you stop to think about it in these terms, there is no excuse for not making every effort to economize.[25]

Women were frequently seen as a cause for extravagance, who prevented thrifty husbands from progressing. Saikaku frequently makes comments such as: "Ever since the evening he proposed to his wife, this man knew, sad as it might sound, that if he married a woman with expensive tastes, he would never make his fortune, no matter how hard he worked."[26] Or, "In recent years, … almost all housewives have waxed extravagant."[27] The security of the house was seen to rest on the frugality of women. This can be seen, for example, in the influential *Onna Daigaku* (Greater Learning for Women), which is attributed to the Confucian scholar Kaibara Ekiken. The text admonishes the woman of the house as follows: "In everything she must avoid extravagance, and both with regard to food and raiment must act according to her station in life, and never give way to luxury and pride. If the wife be evil and profligate, the house is ruined."[28]

Most human beings desire comfort, however, and moral strictures against luxury did not prevent it from flourishing. Extravagance was almost a sort

[23] J. Mark Ramseyer, "Thrift and Diligence: House Codes of Tokugawa Merchant Families," *Monumenta Nipponica* 34, no. 2 (1979): 209–29.

[24] Ichirou Horide, "The House of Mitsui: Secrets of Its Longevity," *Journal of Marketing Theory and Practice* 8, no. 2 (2000): 31–6.

[25] Ihara Saikaku, *Some Final Words of Advice*, trans. Peter Nosco (Rutland, VT and Tokyo: Charles E. Tuttle, 1984), 84.

[26] Ibid., 102.

[27] Ihara Saikaku, *This Scheming World*, trans. Masanori Takatsuke and David C. Stubbs (Rutland, VT and Tokyo, 1965).

[28] L. Kranmer-Bing and S. A. Kapadia, eds., *Women and Wisdom of Japan* (London: John Murray, 1909), 41.

of rebellion. The popular culture of the city dweller, especially the popular culture of Edo, therefore conversely admired the spendthrift. It was seen as the height of cool to come home at the end of an evening out with no money left in your pockets. The saying went, "Daimyo on departure, beggar on return."[29] Saikaku, from Osaka, where people were reputed to be thrifty, commented, "In Edo, not only the lords, but also the townspeople are extremely openhanded."[30] It was this environment that allowed handicrafts such as tortoiseshell to thrive.

THE LUXURY OF IMPORT

Although hawksbill turtles are found within the borders of modern Japan, this was not the case for much of the pre-modern period. The origins of the present Imperial State formed in the area around Nara, far north of the closest source for hawksbills. There is no clear-cut reason why tortoiseshell suddenly became a craft practiced in Japan in the seventeenth century. Etchū Tetsuya, a scholar of Nagasaki, has theorized that the craft of tortoiseshell work was transmitted by Portuguese merchants, basing his arguments on the fact that some Portuguese tortoiseshell objects were brought to Japan in the sixteenth century, and that knowledge of tortoiseshell craftsmanship existed, as is indicated in a Japanese-Portuguese dictionary compiled by missionaries. Although this theory has gained some acceptance, Edo period writers had another explanation, suggesting that the tortoiseshell use came by way of the Kingdom of the Ryukyus, the group of islands that is now incorporated into Japan as Okinawa Prefecture.[31] Although there is little hard evidence to support either theory, a number of reasons suggest the correctness of the latter argument in favor of Ryukyus. First, sea turtle habitat was only incorporated into the Japanese state in the early seventeenth century. The Satsuma domain on the southeast corner of the Island of Kyushu made the Kingdom of Ryukyu a vassalage in 1609. In part to reduce dependence on the Portuguese trade in Chinese goods, Ryukuan trade was especially encouraged in the early seventeenth century.[32] Second, Portuguese, Spanish, Dutch, or English ships might have carried objects of tortoiseshell, but it is highly unlikely that they would have carried

---

[29] *Edoko wa yoigoshi no zeni wa motanu; Edoko no yuki wa daimyo, kaeri kojiki.*
[30] Saikaku, *Scheming World,* 126.
[31] *Nakayama denshinroku,* and cited in Kitamura Nobuyo, *Kiyūshōran,* 2 vols. (Tokyo: Nihon zuihitsu taisei kankokai, 1929), 134.
[32] Richard Sakai, "The Satsuma-Ryukyu Trade and the Tokugawa Seclusion Policy," *Journal of Asian Studies* 23, no. 3 (1964): 391–2.

craftsmen of tortoiseshell. The finished object is distinct enough from the shell in its natural state to suggest some form of transmission rather than trial and error was necessary. A half-century of contact with the Spanish and Portuguese did not leave physical or written evidence of tortoiseshell in Japan before the seventeenth century. The single exception, of dubious veracity, is in a legendized account of the notorious bandit Ishikawa Goemon (1558–94), who reputedly stole some tortoiseshell hair ornaments in 1592.[33] Finally, the primary products that tortoiseshell came to be used for in Japan, hair ornaments, were worn by Ryukuans, but not by European sailors. Moreover, there is a precedent from about the same time period of Ryukuan influence reaching the main islands of Japan in the samisen, a three-stringed fretless musical instrument played with a plectrum sometimes made of tortoiseshell. It was developed in Japan in the seventeenth century from a snakeskin-covered instrument played in the Ryukyus.

Tortoiseshell is worked in a very similar manner in both East and West so that the processing does not supply a clue to origin. For example, in Noël Pluche's *Spectacle de la Nature* of 1733 the common method used in the West is described:

His shell ... is fashioned as the Workman pleases, by softening it in warm Water, after which it is clapped into a Wood Mould, whose Impression it immediately takes, by the Assistance of a strong Iron Press; they afterwards polish and adorn it with Chasings of Gold and other Embellishments.[34]

The Japanese craftsman similarly used heat, water, and metal clamps to weld the laminae into a thick piece to work. Shears were used to cut the pieces. Sometimes the pieces were pressed into wooden molds. The shell is softened in warm water and dry heat so that the shell pieces can then be stretched, bent, formed, split, or welded together. Files, saws, chisels, and iron pincers with smooth broad jaws were then used to work the shell.[35] The Japanese craftsman usually received the plates of the shell already removed from the turtle's back. It made more sense to transport them this way, and the separated shells were also the basis for the assessment of quality when the shells were purchased at the source.

---

[33] Shimada Tadamasa, "Edo jidai no Nagasaki to bekkō," *Nagasaki chihoshi dayori* 11 (1978): 7. There is no evidence that hair ornaments were even worn in this period.

[34] Noël Antoine Pluche, *Spectacle de la Nature, or, Nature Display'd*, trans. Samuel Humphreys (London: J. Pemberton, 1733), 474–5.

[35] J. J. Rein, *The Industries of Japan: Together with an Account of Its Agriculture, Forestry Arts and Commerce* (Surrey: Curzon Press, 1995), 422.

Imports to Japan were almost exclusively of hawksbill turtle shells.[36] Although hawksbills could be obtained from the Ryukyus, there was a preference for larger shells that could only be found even further south and consequently had to be imported.[37] Size was important because the correspondingly thicker shell allowed more versatility in type of production. Moreover, larger shells were believed to have better color, supposedly being lighter and clearer. It was believed that the hotter the climate from which the turtle originated, the shinier the shell would be.[38]

Nagasaki, as the point of entry for most foreign goods, both European and Ryukyuan, became the center for tortoiseshell craftsmanship, rather than, say, ports in the Satsuma Province. Even today it is the largest consumer of tortoiseshell. In a pattern replicated in crafts such as glass blowing, the new craft began in Nagasaki, where imported goods and information entered, and spread from there to the other major population centers in Kyoto, Osaka, and Edo (now called Tokyo). Unlike most crafts in Japan, which emphasized secrecy in the transmission of the important aspects of the craft, the need for cooperation in the production of tortoiseshell work, which required one man to apply heat and another to bend the shell, meant that the techniques of the craft spread relatively rapidly.[39]

THE CONTRADICTIONS OF TRADE

The late seventeenth century was a time of sharp economic growth but declining income for the shogunate. Foreign trade, one source of this growth, was purposefully undercut by shogunal policy. Declining output from gold and silver mines had led to currency debasement and inflation within Japan. Most foreign trade consisted of consumables such as medicine and textiles that were exchanged for gold and silver. Arai Hakuseki (1657–1725), an influential government official in the late seventeenth century, successfully advocated trade caps to reduce the exportation of precious metals. In addition, Hakuseki advocated self-sufficiency to reduce reliance on imports. It was in this period, however, that the use of tortoiseshell spread.

---

[36] Ibid., 421–2. Rein states that the loggerhead was used, but this may have been a misunderstanding or a supply issue unique to his time.

[37] Kajishima Takao, *Nihon dōbutsushi* (Tokyo: Yasaka Shobo, 2003), 356.

[38] Santō Kyōsan, *Kinsei rekise josoko*, Nihon zuihitsu taisei series 1, Vol. 6 (Tokyo: Yoshikawa kobunkan, 1976), 212.

[39] Ibid., 210.

By 1639, the only major foreign traders in Japan were Dutch and Chinese. An early encyclopedia, *Wakan sansai zue* (1713) identifies tortoiseshell as a Dutch import, but as trade relations were reestablished with China after the collapse of the Ming dynasty in 1644, the Chinese also became important suppliers, possibly more significant than the Dutch. It is difficult, however, to the compare quantities of tortoiseshell brought to Japan by each of these trading nations. Although the Dutch recorded what the Chinese brought, after about 1680 Dutch shipments of tortoiseshell were sold in private trade auctions known as *kambang*. The Dutch East India Company frowned on its servants trading on their own account, fearing this would compete with its own markets. In Japan, however, the Company was forced to accept a compromise in which certain products were reserved for the Company, and the rest could be traded privately. These practices continued even after the demise of the Dutch East India Company in 1799. Because tortoiseshell was sold privately, records are rather scarce. We know that in 1836, for example, about sixty catties[40] of tortoiseshell was imported by the Dutch traders.[41] Tortoiseshell could be lucrative, as the following excerpt from a memorandum from former Opperhoofd Isaac Titsingh sent to Captain Henry Zelar advising what to bring for sale in Japan in 1801, shows:

Loggerhead or Hawksbill turtle shell – thick pieces, as white as can be found, gathered in bunches of 1 ¼ or of 5 cd.

Hawksbill tortoiseshell heads or feet, the thicker they are the better. In my time they paid from 12 to 18 *koban*[42] per cattie in private trade – they are best in America, especially those found around Canada – these articles rise steeply in price when supplies are lean.[43]

The rationale for making tortoiseshell a private trade good is not clear but there was a consistently strong demand in China and other areas negating the need to take risks in Japan. While figures for Chinese traders are not available in this year, in 1832 164 catties and 2,906 catties of "nails" (smaller shell-edge pieces) were brought by Chinese traders. One catty of tortoiseshell could, for example, produce about fifteen hair

---

[40] One catty equals about 625 grams or 1.1 pounds. Based on Malay or Javanese, this measurement was widely used in Southeast and East Asian trade.

[41] See Martha Chaiklin, *Cultural Commerce and Dutch Commercial Culture* (Leiden, The Netherlands: CNWS, 2003), 179, 182.

[42] A Japanese gold coin.

[43] Frank Lequin, ed., *The Private Correspondence of Isaac Titsingh*. 2 vols. (Amsterdam: J. C. Gieben, 1992), 2: 755. Letter 294. It is not clear why Tisingh thought the turtle came from northern waters.

ornaments, so import numbers, while variable, suggest that fairly large quantities of crafts could be produced.[44]

Traders obtained tortoiseshell by trading with local hunters in various tropical ports in sea turtle habitat, including, for example, sea nomads around Makassar and Bugis along the Malay Peninsula. Chinese traders even gave credit a year in advance to ensure a supply.[45] In Ceylon, occupied by the Dutch until 1798, a completely different method was used. According to J. W. Bennett, a British government official, the Singhalese hunted sea turtles during the mating season, when they came ashore. The fishing rights renter of the district would assemble his people near the mating grounds, and temporary huts and a bazaar for daily necessities were erected. The turtles were left to lay their eggs in peace, but when that process had been completed, a signal was given:

by whispering along the whole line of the ambuscade; from whence a simultaneous onset is made by the whole gang, each carrying a stout Bamboo pole, and ligatures of the twisted bark of certain jungle trees, for the purpose of securing the turtles, as they are turned upon their backs, by tying the opposite fins, or rather *feet*, together....[46]

Once the turtles were secured:

Fires are lighted upon the spot; a bamboo pole is then passed longitudinally between the tied feet and the breastplate of each turtle, by which it is suspended over the blazing fire, until the dorsal plates ... become heated and start from their horizontal position, when they are rapidly stripped off, beginning with the plate nearest the head, which is the largest, until the while thirteen plates that cover the disk, are removed ... as soon as the stripping is over, the despoiled animal is liberated, and allowed a free egress to the sea.[47]

Apparently this ritual did not deter the turtles from returning, which they did each year. This was verified by:

A Dutch gentleman, who had charge of the district in 1794;[48] who to satisfy his doubts upon this point, caused brass rings, marked with the dates for the capture of the turtles, in Dutch and Malay, to be attached to a fin of a certain number selected for this purpose.[49]

[44] Shimada Tadamasa, "Edo jidai no Nagasaki to bekkō," 7.
[45] Gerrit Knapp and Heather Sutherland, *Monsoon Traders: Ships, Skippers and Commodities in Eighteenth-Century Makassar* (Leiden, The Netherlands: KITLV Press, 2004), 40, 98–9.
[46] J. W. Bennett, *Ceylon and Its Capabilities* (London: W. H. Allen, 1843), 273–5.
[47] Ibid.
[48] Either Willem Jacob van de Graff who was governor from 1785–94 or Johan Gerard van Angelbeek who was in charge from 1794–6.
[49] J.W. Bennett, Ceylon and Its Capabilities (London: W.H. Allen, 1843), 273–275.

One of the fishers brought Bennett a ring from a four-hundred-pound turtle in 1826, and according to the fisherman, the same turtle had returned to the same cove for thirty-two years.[50] As inhumane as this seems, it allowed the extraction of tortoiseshell without killing the turtle. If the animal was dead for too long, it affected the color of the shell.[51] This is a stark contrast to, for example, the practice in the Celebes, where the turtle was merely smashed on the head and then boiled to remove the plates.

The restrictions on trade at the beginning of the eighteenth century certainly did not deter trade in tortoiseshell. They did, however, ensure that prices never dropped too low. The unreliability of supply, difficulties involved in trade, and exotic origins added to the functionality and "pleasing" qualities to make tortoiseshell a luxury in the eyes of the Japanese consumer.

GENDERED CONSUMPTION

The spread of tortoiseshell occurred conjointly with a rise in the standard of living. This economic growth resulted in an explosion of material culture that parallels the development in Western Europe. Consumerism was based on increased income and leisure rather than industrialization. Luxury was based on imported materials and time-consuming, fine local production. Significantly different were the consumers of tortoiseshell, who were predominantly women.

Tortoiseshell came to be favored by women because imports of tortoiseshell, the rise of luxury, and changes in women's hairstyles all occurred at the same time. Moreover, women's rights to inheritance and other methods of wealth accumulation had gradually deteriorated since the rise of warrior society in the late twelfth century.[52] Therefore, personal goods were one of the few ways women could legally hold property. Until the seventeenth century, women generally wore their hair long, and simply bound. From the mid-seventeenth century onward, a woman's hair was bound in a variety of elaborate chignons that were decorated with a number of ornaments.[53] Although these ornaments were produced from

---

[50] Ibid.

[51] James Emerson Tennent, *Ceylon: An Account of the Island* (London: Longman, Green, Longman, Roberts, 1859), 190.

[52] See Hitomi Tonomura, "Women and Inheritance in Japan's Early Warrior Society," *Comparative Studies in Society and History* 32, no. 3 (1990): 592–623.

[53] See Martha Chaiklin, "Up in the Hair – Strands of Meaning in Women's Ornamental Hair Accessories in Early Modern Japan," in *Asian Material Culture*, ed. Marianne Hulsbosch et al. (Amsterdam: University of Amsterdam Press, 2009), 37–64.

a wide range of materials, including wood, ivory, and coral, by about the 1660s tortoiseshell became favored because it has many of the properties desirable in a hair ornament: beauty, durability, and lightness.[54]

It was also an advantage that, should an ornament fall and break, it could be repaired, which was not the case for most of the other materials used for this purpose. A preference for tortoiseshell was further stimulated by a ban on silver and gold implements in 1744.[55] Silver and gold were also appreciated, but exports and constant demand had an effect on currency supplies. Therefore, the shogunate responded by trying to keep precious metals in circulation by banning them from extramonetary use. Tortoiseshell, which did not have such a direct impact on the economy, was not subject to the same sort of restrictions.

Fashion for clear tortoiseshell and shell with spots waxed and waned. However, solid-colored ornaments were generally seen as better for formal occasions.[56] Although initially restricted to the upper class, the custom of wearing tortoiseshell hair ornaments trickled down. As early as 1719 Confucian scholar Nishikawa Joken (1648–1724) complained not only of the extravagance of tortoiseshell hair ornaments and the fashion for them even though they were not used in the past, but of the fact that even low-class women wore them.[57]

Courtesans, who were exempt from many sumptuary laws, became the greatest consumers of tortoiseshell through the number of hair ornaments they wore. It is possible, but not documented, that the fashion originated in Nagasaki, which had a famous red-light district known as Maruyama, which catered to foreigners. Ironically perhaps, most courtesans in early modern Japan were sold into servitude to help their destitute families, but to their patrons they were a luxury. This perception was cultivated through the physical environment, the training of the women, and the way they dressed. Therefore, while normal women might have a comb and a bodkin or two, by the late eighteenth century courtesans might have half a dozen. As one Western observer noted:

The abundant hair of the woman is arranged into the form of a turban, and stuck full of pieces of fine tortoiseshell, fifteen inches long, of the thickness of a man's finger, highly wrought, and polished to look like gold. They are said to be

---

[54] Katō Eoin, "Ware koromo," in *Nihon shōkumin seikatsu shiryō shūsei*, 31 vols. (Tokyo: Sanichi shobo, 1968–1984), 15: 13.

[55] Ibid., 16.

[56] Kitagawa Morisada, *Morisada mankō*, 5 vols. (Tokyo: Tokyodo shuppan, 1990), 2: 104.

[57] Nishikawa Joken, *Chōnin bukuro, Hyakusho bukuro, Nagasaki yobanshi gusa* (Tokyo: Iwanami Shoten, 1942), 66.

FIGURE 22. *Courtesan* Takao of Miura-ya wearing three combs, eight *kanzashi*, and an extra-long kōgai of tortoiseshell. "Miuraya Takao."
Source: Utagawa Sadakage, c. 1818–1830.
Courtesy of Library of Congress Prints and Photographs Division, no. 1928.

extremely costly; and the more of them project from a lady's hair, the better she is dressed.[58]

Sometimes these combs were elaborately lacquered and could cost as much as two gold coins (*ryō*).[59] Because the primary consumers of tortoiseshell were women, who were already seen as luxury-loving creatures that could cause a man's downfall, tortoiseshell hair ornaments were often used to symbolize this vice. Saikaku, in *Some Final Words of Advice*, used tortoiseshell combs twice as proof of the extravagance of women. In the first case, a parable about the dangers of a bad marriage, the mother-in-law describes the extravagance of her daughter-in-law in three paragraphs, including the fact that "[f]or two *chokin* [a silver coin] she had a pocket comb made to order from the translucent bits of the finest tortoiseshell...."[60] This was the sort of wife who would bring a merchant house down, and the story is about the cost of divorce. In the second, a maid seeking a temporary placement strolled into an employment agency dreadfully overdressed, sporting a "translucent tortoiseshell ornamental comb."[61] In this case, the implication was that she had turned to tempting men with sex to support her taste for luxury.

The same qualities that made tortoiseshell appealing for personal ornaments also made it desirable for less public use in the bedroom. While defining a dildo as a luxury might depend on one's definition of human sexual behavior, one made of tortoiseshell was a luxury. Phallic worship has existed in Japan since Neolithic times and remains a viable tradition today. Whether this was related to dildo use, or dildos were first imported from China as one scholar suggests, is a matter of speculation.[62] What is certain is that from the late seventeenth century, literary and pictorial references to them increase dramatically. Increased leisure promoted literacy, causing a greater demand for books, which in turn led to more venues and improved printing techniques. More books meant lower prices that resulted in more pornography.

Tortoiseshell was regarded as the preferred material for dildos. Illustrations show carefully crafted pieces with ridges in the shaft.[63] The

---

[58] *Japan and the Japanese in the Nineteenth Century: From Recent Dutch Travels, Especially the Narrative of von Siebold* (London: John Murray, 1852), 22.
[59] Katō, *Ware koromo*, 16.
[60] Ihara, *Final Words*, 62.
[61] Ibid., 198.
[62] Tanaka Yūko, *Harigata to edo onna* (Tokyo: Yosensha, 2004), 25. Tanaka suggests they came from China, but offers no real supporting evidence.
[63] Yasaburō Ikeda, *Seifūzoku*, 3 vols. (Tokyo: Yuzankaku, 1989), 2: 386.

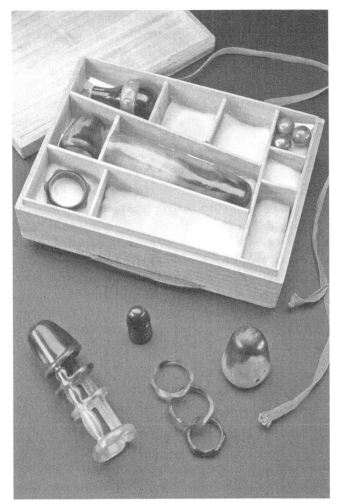

FIGURE 23. Four penis sheaths, four penis rings, one finger sheath (all made from tortoiseshell).
Source: Arita Drug and Rubber Goods Co, Kobe, Japan. Courtesy of Science Museum/Science & Society Picture Library, A641105.

advantages of tortoiseshell over less expensive options were numerous. It was unlikely to splinter. In its polished state it was very smooth, reducing the potential for drag and friction. It was lightweight. Finally, it could be warmed before use by putting hot water into it. On account of these same properties, a hard sheath of horn or tortoiseshell was sometimes used as a condom as well.[64] It has been suggested that these condoms served double duty as dildos when a male companion was not present.[65]

Certainly, tortoiseshell was used in gender-neutral ways or even for objects used only by men, such as *inrō*.[66] The most significant of these was probably for spectacle frames. For example, Tokugawa Ieyasu (1543–1616), founder of the Tokugawa shogunate, owned a pair of eyeglasses with tortoiseshell frames that are preserved in Toshogu Shrine. According to import records, however, the most-favored material for imported spectacle frames was ivory or bone, with only occasional reference to tortoiseshell or silver.[67] Other things, such as ink boxes, sweet trays, and letter boxes, were all made out of tortoiseshell. Tortoiseshell was also combined with other materials. An antique piece, supposedly from the early Edo period, was shown at the Centennial Exposition in Philadelphia in 1876. "It was a nest of jewel cabinets set in a frame of beautifully carved tortoise shell. The four cabinets that filled this frame were made in the four main styles of lacquerwork...."[68] Nevertheless, none of these objects have survived in anywhere near the quantities that exist for hair ornaments, an object likely to receive more wear and tear, so the largest group of consumers of tortoiseshell was almost certainly women.

WHAT'S IN A NAME? POLITICS, ECONOMICS, AND SUMPTUARY LAWS

Sumptuary law has been called "one of the oldest, most important, and most pervasive negative principles for organizing society Western history has known."[69] In Japan, sumptuary laws for tortoiseshell were utilized for a variety of reasons that included but were not solely for the purpose of social stratification. Rather, they were often applied as austerity measures against the promotion of luxury in general. The

---

[64] T. Scott Matsumoto, Akira Koizumi, and Tadahiro Nohara, "Condom Use in Japan," *Studies in Family Planning* 3, no. 10 (1972): 251–5, esp. p. 251.

[65] H. Youssef, "The History of the Condom," *Journal of the Royal Society of Medicine* 86 (1993): 227.

[66] A sectioned box hung from the belt. Originally it contained a seal and vermillion but was also used to carry around medicine.

[67] Chaiklin, *Cultural Commerce*, 132–3.

[68] J. S. Ingram, *Centennial Exposition: Described and Illustrated* (Philadelphia: Hubbard Bros., 1876), 562.

[69] John Sekora, *Luxury: The Concept in Western Thought, Eden to Smollett* (Baltimore: Johns Hopkins University Press, 1977), 2.

Neo-Confucian ideology applied by the government ensured a paternalistic approach to morality that included the promulgation of sumptuary laws. Such laws were issued in the twilight of the shogunal system, as late as 1862.[70]

In older texts, the hawksbill turtle and its shell are known as *taimai*, a word taken from Chinese. It is found in the oldest Japanese dictionary of Chinese compounds, the *Wamyosho* of 938. *Taimai* was the common appellation until the early seventeenth century, when *bekkō*, the term still used today, was popularized. Writers of the Edo period believed this change in terminology was an attempt to avoid a government prohibition of tortoiseshell imports because the first character in the second term refers to a domestic snapping turtle. However, the term predates any trade regulation by the Tokugawa shogunate and can be found in the Japanese-Portuguese dictionary compiled by missionaries in 1603.[71] Nevertheless this shows a public perception of luxury enforced by luxury laws.

The earliest prohibitions regarding turtles were in regard to consuming the meat. In 1630, turtle was prohibited in certain months in order to comply with cosmological dictates.[72] A half-century later, in 1687, consumption was entirely forbidden as a part of the so-called Laws of Compassion issued by shogun Tokugawa Tsunayoshi (1646–1709). This series of edicts were intended to enforce a Buddhist compassion for life by forbidding the use, consumption, and killing of animals. It is interesting to note that no animal products such as tortoiseshell or leather were directly prohibited. In 1683, however, a general ban on imported goods was issued as a way to raise the standard of morality. While the impact was great during Tsunayoshi's lifetime the edicts were repealed in 1709, immediately upon his death.

When prohibitions on tortoiseshell were issued, they were directly tied to ideas about luxury. This stands out among other regulations regarding personal accoutrements that primarily limited the use of precious metals to prevent depletion of supplies, thus affecting the economy as a whole. Conversely, an edict regarding tortoiseshell issued in 1743 was typical of sumptuary law regarding tortoiseshell. It railed against the selection

---

[70] Ishii Ryōsuke, ed., *Tokugawa Kinrekō*, 11 vols. (Tokyo: Sobunsha, 1959), 5: 272.

[71] Etchū Tetsuya, *Nagasaki no bekkō* (Nagasaki: Privately printed, 1983), 21.

[72] Hans Krämer, "Not Befitting Our Divine Country: Eating Meat in Japanese Discourse of Self and Other from the Seventeenth Century to the Present," *Food and Foodways* 16, no. 1 (2008): 39.

of high-quality, expensive tortoiseshell to be made into hair ornaments and sold at high prices, requiring that hair ornaments return to the more modest sizes and styles of the past.[73] This sumptuary law was issued as part of a series of laws known as the Kyōhō reforms. A response to famine and financial crisis in the shogunate, the reforms included a series of sumptuary laws that led to a scaling back on personal accoutrement of all sorts.[74]

The next restriction on tortoiseshell was the result of similar governmental overhaul. Natural disasters such as the eruption of Mount Asama in 1783, the resulting famine, and the depletion of the shogunal treasury led to a new round of reforms (Kansei Reforms) in the last decades of the eighteenth century. In the third month of 1789, an edict was issued mandating that the size of tortoiseshell hair ornaments should not be excessively large.[75] Matsudaira Sadanobu (1759–1829), the shogunal official responsible for this legislation, presumably targeted tortoiseshell for two reasons. First, he generally sought to curb the activities of merchants and to limit foreign trade as part of an economic retrenchment based on Confucian principles that sought to restrain the merchant class. Second, he wanted to promote a general climate of austerity. As a result, later in the year all the employees in the shogunate were warned that their wives and children should not "wear any silk clothes, hair ornaments made of tortoiseshell or silver, worsted or other Dutch or Chinese cloth on penalty of being put in prison." The prohibition was extended to the entire town of Nagasaki.[76] It was enforced initially as can be seen in the case of one woman dressed in silk and wearing tortoiseshell combs who was required to undress completely; the offending goods she had been wearing were then confiscated.[77] Moreover, the requested supplies of tortoiseshell for the following year were canceled. The loss of this profitable source of income caused severe hardship for the factory members, who had made ends meet with private trade.[78] The ban was maintained until 1799, but once it had been repealed, the shogunate made efforts to control the prices by requiring that tortoiseshell be sold through a government agency rather than freely at auctions.[79]

[73] Ishii, *Kinreikō*, 5: 366.

[74] Katō, *Warekoromo*, 16.

[75] Ishii, *Kinreikō*, 5: 381.

[76] Cynthia Vialle and Leonard Blusse, eds., *Deshima Dagreisters*, Vol. X (Leiden, The Netherlands: University of Leiden, 1997), 8.

[77] Ibid., 9.

[78] Ibid., 64.

[79] Ibid., 155.

Efforts at controlling prices over the long term were fruitless, however. Less than a decade after the tortoiseshell prohibitions were passed, larger and thicker tortoiseshell combs than ever before were fashionable.[80] Despite government efforts at containment, prices on tortoiseshell combs dropped throughout the Edo period. As a result, they became more and more of a necessity and less and less of a luxury.

FAKES AND FORGERIES

A corollary to luxury is forgery, and the diversity of tortoiseshell imitations confirm that it was a desirable luxury. Knockoffs were endemic. Such fakes could have been produced to defraud the consumer, but in most cases the intent was more likely to have been to fool the observer. By the late eighteenth century, tortoiseshell combs had arguably passed from the luxury to the need category for married women on formal occasions.[81] Tortoiseshell had become a part of social identity, but it was too expensive for everyone, which would explain the plethora of fakes.

Originally Chōsen (Korean) tortoiseshell referred to lower quality loggerhead or green tortoiseshell. However, from the 1770s, so-called Chōsen (Korean) tortoiseshell referred to reproductions produced from water buffalo horn. Within ten years, the amount of suitable water buffalo horn available declined and the price went up. The horns of Japanese oxen and horse hoof were substituted. Horses from flat areas without stones in the road were reputed to have especially clear hooves, and thus horse hoof from Nerima was particularly valued.[82] A horn or hoof core was sometimes enveloped in a veneer of genuine tortoiseshell. The thermoplastic nature of these materials meant that they could be welded together seamlessly enough, so that it was difficult for an amateur to discern their falsity.[83] In the mid-eighteenth century, fake tortoiseshell was made from quail eggshells.[84] Another technique, which came to be known as the "Nagasaki technique," reproduced the visual

---

[80] Kitagawa, *Morisada mankō*, 2: 103.

[81] Ibid., 2: 117.

[82] In the early modern period, this was a village outside Edo, but is presently within the Tokyo city limits. Tamura Eitarō, *Nihon shokunin gijutsu bunkashi* (Tokyo: Yuzankaku, 1984), 2: 693.

[83] Ibid., 72, 103.

[84] *Rekisei fūzokshi*, *Nihon shokunin gijutsu bunkashi*, 2: 693.

characteristics of tortoiseshell in lacquered wood.[85] Even fakes could have a touch of luxury.

CONCLUSIONS

Tortoiseshell has many properties to recommend it, but it did not become a luxury in Japan until the seventeenth century for three reasons. First, a transportation revolution in Europe and commercial expansion in Japan allowed larger quantities to be brought to Japan than ever before. Second, a higher standard of living gave more people the income to invest in luxuries. This was accomplished without an industrial revolution. Finally, the most demand for tortoiseshell arose among women who had gradually lost other ways to accumulate wealth. Although Japan did not experience an industrial revolution until the end of the shogunal system in the late nineteenth century, a growing economy resulted in the spread of luxury and attitudes toward it that parallels developments in industrial Europe. Similar parallels can be found in the Confucian-based condemnation of luxury as a moral deviation. Women, who were regarded as morally deficient in Confucian thought, became the biggest consumers of tortoiseshell because it was well suited for personal items that they used, resulting in gendered-oriented consumption patterns. These conditions made tortoiseshell a necessity for the social identity of women in early modern Japan.

The end of isolation in 1859 meant the end of any delusions of self-sufficiency. Japan was flooded with cheap manufactured products from Europe. Tortoiseshell craftsmanship thrived because handicrafts were promoted to counteract the negative balance of trade. In this new world order, tortoiseshell was predominantly used to create souvenirs for wealthy travelers and eyeglass frames. The demand for hair ornaments gradually declined because traditional hairstyles were largely replaced by Western ones. As Japan industrialized along Western patterns, traditional lifestyle became something of a luxury, as kimonos were not suitable for factory work. Shortly afterward, plastics replaced tortoiseshell for many of its uses, including the production of hair ornaments, to such an extent that in 1907 Fredrich Böckman wrote: "Celluloid constitutes the most

---

[85] Raymond Bushell, *Inro Handbook* (New York: Weatherhill, 1979), 129–30. It is not clear whether this technique was developed to replace tortoiseshell during times of prohibition or merely for the joy of executing a difficult technique to produce an aesthetically pleasing pattern.

suitable imitation of tortoise-shell that has ever been devised...."[86] We have replaced most uses of tortoiseshell with plastic. Plastic can look like tortoiseshell but it can never feel like it, so there remains a small but steady demand for tortoiseshell. Thus, tortoiseshell, which was a luxury that had become a necessity, reverted from a necessity to a luxury as a direct result of industrialization.

---

[86] Friedrich Böckmann, *Celluloid: Its Raw Material, Manufacture, Properties and Uses* (London: Scott, Greenwood and Son, 1907), 97.

9

Tickling and clicking the ivories: The metamorphosis of a global commodity in the nineteenth century

Jonas Kranzer

On the Internet page of House of Staunton, an American manufacturer of chess articles, we are offered a wide choice of different chess pieces. The most inexpensive pieces are made of plastic and cost about four dollars. The most expensive are made of wooly mammoth ivory and go for $12,995.[1] The use of ivory chess pieces has a long tradition. Napoleon, for instance, is said to have had them,[2] and in Washington's Smithsonian Museum of American History we can admire an ivory set that belonged to John Quincy Adams. Alongside an abundance of toilet articles such as combs and brushes, the catalog of the ivory-worker F. J. Kaldenberg contains ivory chess pieces.[3] For the game, the material made use of is insignificant. Hence those purchasing ivory chess pieces are not concerned merely with owning chess pieces, but rather with an aura of exclusivity not least of all involving the high price. For the use of ivory chess pieces undoubtedly moves past everyday life; consequently, their main function is not use but rather to stage the game of chess – the game of kings – as something special. In this way, they exemplify the fact that ivory objects have always been luxury goods.

In the nineteenth and twentieth centuries, ivory was thus a highly prized material. In this chapter its history will be reconstructed in a series

---

[1] "Chess Sets, Chess Pieces." The House of Staunton, www.houseofstaunton.com (accessed November 8, 2014).
[2] "Napoleon's Unique Ivory Chessmen," *American Chess Bulletin* 17, no. 8 (1920): 174–6.
[3] The National Museum of American History, Archives Center, "Kaldenberg, F. J., 1875–1880? Manufacturer of Ivory Toilet Articles, Stationary and Fancy Goods, New York," Warshaw Collection of Business Americana: Business Ephemera: Ivory, box 1, folder 5.

of steps that will include its global dimension, value regime, material qualities, uses, and shifting values.

THE GLOBAL DIMENSION OF IVORY

In London at present, very little evokes the past trade in ivory. Still, if moving from the Tower of London, we follow the signposting beneath the Tower Bridge and reach St. Katherine's Dock. If we step onto the dock from the north side, we pass through a large iron gate upon whose two side pillars sit elephants. Walking from the gate, we move directly to an L-formed brick building with a tower clock: the Ivory House. The building still has its name from the time when ivory was a raw material in strong demand in Europe, with London possessing, as the British Empire's fulcrum, a central position in the ivory trade. Pictures in the Museum in Docklands archives show the upper floor of the Ivory House, the floor covered everywhere with enormous amounts of ivory.[4] At the height of ivory trading between the second half of the nineteenth century and the Great War, this Ivory Floor was at the activity's center (it had its counterpart in the Antwerp ivory auction). Here potential buyers could inspect the wares before their auctioning; and here the supply chain of ivory, spanning the globe, came together in one place.[5]

In Africa elephants were hunted by various tribes. In East Africa, they were hunted by the Makua tribe in particular; "Makua" thus becoming a collective term for elephant hunters over time.[6] The tribes exchanged the collected ivory for cloth, glass pearls, copper wire, weapons, and alcohol;[7] the caravan trade was basically controlled by Arabic traders from Zanzibar. Efforts by the Europeans to break up the dominant position of the Arabs ended in failure – as seen in the case of the Hamburg firm of the ivory dealer Heinrich Adolph Meyer, sometimes spectacularly and tragically: on the trip from Tabora to Bagamoyo, one of three caravan routes leading from the East African coast to the interior,[8] Meyer's agent

---

[4] Museum of London Docklands Archive, Photo Cab 2.3, Ivory Folder.

[5] The building that housed the Ivory Room still exists and now contains a restaurant and luxury apartments.

[6] Oscar Baumann, *Durch Massailand zur Nilquelle: Reisen und Forschungen der Massai-Expedition des deutschen Antisklaverei-Komite in den Jahren 1891–1893* (Berlin, 1894), 62.

[7] On caravan trade see in detail Michael Pesek, *Koloniale Herrschaft in Deutsch-Ostafrika: Expeditionen, Militär und Verwaltung seit 1880* (Frankfurt: Campus, 2005), 40–101.

[8] There were three caravan routes: (1) a southern route over Lindi and Kilwa to Lake Nyasa; (2) a central route from Bagamoyo and Pangani over Tabora to Ujiji on Lake

was murdered. The Arab dominance would last until the construction of a railway.[9]

For its part, transcontinental trade was dominated by Indian merchants based in Zanzibar, who served as the main sources of credit for the caravan traders. Their defining role in the ivory trade was grounded in India being another important country for purchasing raw ivory, together with Europe and America.[10] European and American trading houses were also active in Africa, dealing with ivory and other colonial goods. As suggested, most of the ivory making its way toward the United States and Europe was first auctioned in Antwerp and London. In a certain way, the auctions had the role of a raw-goods exchange in which countries without their own ivory deposits could cover their needs. There were important centers for ivory processing in Ivoryton, Connecticut, and Erbach in the German Odenwald. There and elsewhere, the raw material was made into piano keys, billiard balls, knife handles, and carvings – all very much in demand within Western middle-class consumer societies.[11]

Nevertheless, the trade in ivory was not a phenomenon limited to the nineteenth century and emerging from the colonial division of Africa. Already in antiquity, ivory was a coveted raw material and luxury good, its trade mentioned in the first reports of geographers and travelers.[12] During the reign of Amenophis III (c. 1388 to 1351 BCE), Egyptian merchants with trading contacts extending down to the East African coast regularly imported ivory; that it was prized within Egyptian culture is revealed in many grave objects discovered in excavations in the Valley of the Kings. Following expansion of the Roman Empire to North Africa, Roman traders likewise had trading contacts extending into East Africa – for members of the Roman upper class, ivory was a favored way of demonstrating wealth and power. The chair of the Roman magistrates known as the *sella curulis*, was, for example, partly made of ivory.[13]

Tanganyika; and (3) a northern route from Tanga over Moschi and Arusha to Lake Victoria.

[9] Normann R. Bennett, *Arab versus European: Diplomacy and War in Nineteenth-Century East Central Africa* (New York: Africana Pub. Co., 1986), 211–13.

[10] Abdul Sheriff, *Slaves, Spices and Ivory in Zanzibar: Integration of an East African Commercial Empire into the World Economy, 1770–1873* (London: Currey, 1987), 108.

[11] For an overview see Ruth Rempel, "Trade and Transformation: Participation in the Ivory Trade in Late 19th-Century East and Central Africa," *Canadian Journal of Development Studies* 19 (1998): 529–52.

[12] R. W. Beachey, "The East African Ivory Trade in the Nineteenth Century," *The Journal of African History* 8, no. 2 (1967): 269–90, esp. p. 269.

[13] Edward A. Alpers, "The Ivory Trade in Africa: A Historical Overview," in *Elephant: The Animal and Its Ivory in African Culture*, ed. Doran H. Ross (Los Angeles: Fowler Museum of Cultural History, 1992), 352.

In any case trade in ivory was by no means limited to the Mediterranean region, rather taking in, above all, the Indian Ocean area. Since roughly the seventh century CE, dhows belonging to Indian and Arabic merchants followed the monsoon winds. In this period, only a small portion of the ivory made its way to Europe.[14] Over a number of centuries, most of it was processed and consumed in India and China.[15] The stream of ivory goods would only be redirected from its standard routes to the North Atlantic realm in the nineteenth century, in the course of the colonial partitioning of Africa.

THE VALUE REGIME OF IVORY

Ivory's global supply chain thus extended from the Makua in East Africa, by way of Arabian caravan traders and Indian and European merchants based in Zanzibar to auctions in Antwerp and London, and onward to ivory carving in Erbach and piano-key manufacturing in Ivoryton. It seems likely that all the people involved here, interconnected through the supply chain, shared a strong interest in ivory. But in view of their anchoring in various highly different sociocultural contexts, their sharing of a common value regime when it came to ivory would be highly improbable.[16] For on its way from the elephant to the piano key, ivory circulated in highly disparate value frameworks. Along this path, we can observe how ivory was transformed from an everyday, useful instrument to an important element in luxury goods.

For the African elephant, the value of ivory – more precisely, of its tusks – lay in its function as a tool in the search for food and water[17] and as a weapon for fighting with both other elephants and with human and other outside enemies. For the African hunters who killed elephants, often at risk to their lives, ivory first of all had ritual value: in many areas of East Africa, it was usual to deliver the so-called ground tusks – the single

[14] In the Middle Ages, ivory was mainly used in Europa in the manufacture of sacred objects. See, e.g., Johannes Duft and Rudolf Schnyder, *Die Elfenbein-Einbände der Stiftsbibliothek St. Gallen* (Beuron: Beuroner Kunstverlag, 1984).

[15] Abdul Sheriff, "Ivory and Commercial Expansion in East Africa in the Nineteenth Century," in *Figuring African Trade: Proceedings of the Symposium on the Quantification and Structure of the Import and Export and Long Distance Trade of Africa in the 19th Century 1800–1913*, ed. Gerhard Liesegang et al. (Berlin: Reimer, 1986), 415–42.

[16] On the concept of the value regime see Arjun Appadurai, "Introduction: Commodities and the Politics of Value," in *The Social Life of Things: Commodities in Cultural Perspective*, ed. Arjun Appadurai (Cambridge: Cambridge University Press, 1986), 3–63.

[17] Because African elephants eat about two hundred kilograms of food and drink one hundred liters water daily, the tusks are an indispensable tool.

tusks with which each elephant first touched the ground while dying – to the chief in the framework of a ritual aimed at propitiating the spirits of the land.[18] In Africa, ivory initially had relatively little value, the explorer Richard Burton thus reporting on tusks used as pasture fences or for decorating graves.[19] Horns carved out of tasks were also widespread.[20] But the elephant was far more important: the large animals could become a mortal threat to entire villages when they ravaged whole fields in their search for food. The repute of hunters in the different tribal societies was correspondingly great, with repeated examples of chiefs who had been successful hunters.[21] The first thing removed from a dead elephant following a successful hunt was its tail tassel, not its tusks – the tassel served as proof of both the animal's death and the hunter's success. The elephant was then nearly completely made use of: its flesh being eaten, clothing made from its skin, and so forth.[22]

The entry of the Arabic trading caravans meant a change in ivory's value regime in Africa. Alongside its ritual value for chiefs and hunters, it now had exchange value. In his autobiography, Tippu Tip, one of the most important Arabic caravan traders, describes the exchange of goods for ivory[23] – a process that was not always peaceful. Tippu Tip thus also reporting with remarkable openness on a violent plunder of ivory in the course of which he subjugated entire villages and tribes, henceforth forced to deliver ivory to him.[24] This example makes very clear how both caravan trade and access to its goods, especially guns, called traditional forms of rule into question and led to their replacement with new forms.[25]

For the Indian and European traders, ivory's value lay in the high prices that could be fetched for it in Zanzibar or in the London auctions. Small deviations put aside, the price of raw ivory rose in the auctions

---

[18] Bernhard Gissibl, "Jagd und Herrschaft: Zur politischen Ökologie des deutschen Kolonialismus in Ostafrika," *Zeitschrift für Geschichtswissenschaft* 6 (2008): 508.

[19] Richard Francis Burton, "The Lake Regions of Central Equatorial Africa," *Journal of the Royal Geographical Society* 29 (1859): 441.

[20] Doran H. Ross, "Imagining Elephants: An Overview," in *Elephant: The Animal and Its Ivory in African Culture*, ed. Doran H. Ross (Los Angeles: Fowler Museum of Cultural History, 1992), 24. The tone produced by these horns is said to be very similar to an elephant's trumpeting.

[21] Burton, *Lake Regions*, 126.

[22] Paul Reichardt, "Das afrikanische Elfenbein und sein Handel," *Deutsche Geographische Blätter* 12 (1889): 144–5.

[23] Wilfred Howell Whitley, ed., *Maisha ya Hamed Bin Muhammed el Murjebi, yaani Tippu Tip: Kwa maneno yake mwenyewe* (Nairobi: East African Literature Bureau, (1966), 61.

[24] Ibid., 69, 75.

[25] Pesek, *Koloniale Herrschaft*, 49, 72, 91.

from year to year. Because correspondingly the prices of the caravan trade's exchange goods had become much cheaper because of industrial manufacturing methods, the profit margin was large enough to finance the transport of ivory by porters to the coast from the interior. In turn, craftsmen working with ivory prized its suitability for carving, a result of its blend of elasticity and hardness and its general warmth. And Western consumers of ivory products saw their value less in, for instance, playing upon ivory keys than in possessing a product worthy of their aspirations and serving – like the piano in the middle-class salon – as a means of distinction.[26]

THE MATERIAL DIMENSION OF IVORY

In his book on ivory, Benjamin Burack defines it very broadly as "a modified kind of dentin in certain types of teeth, usually one pair of tusks that extend outside the mouth and are adapted for use in obtaining food; they are also used sometimes for attack or defense."[27] If we follow this definition, then walrus and narwhal tusks, for instance, are made of ivory. But usually ivory is understood to come from the tusk of the African elephant, an understanding mirrored in the etymology of the English word (together with its Romance-language counterparts): it stems from Latin *ebur*, signifying both "elephant" and "ivory" and apparently derived from Egyptian *abu*.[28]

As with the teeth of all other mammals, ivory largely consists of dentin, with both inorganic (approximately 35 percent) and organic (approximately 65 percent) components. The organic portion basically consists of the protein collagen, which endows ivory with its elasticity, the inorganic portion of calcium phosphate, providing for its hardness and stability.[29] The hardness of elephant tusks varies according to area of origin, with a

---

[26] Gissibl, *Jagd und Herrschaft*, 230–1.

[27] Benjamin Burack, *Ivory and Its Uses* (Rutland, VT: Charles E. Tuttle, 1984), 28. The main focus will be on African ivory here. In the period covered by this chapter predominately ivory from Africa was used in Europe and America for various purposes. The Asian elephant was used widely as productive livestock and also hunted for its ivory. Widespread poaching led to the decline of the Asian elephant. See, e.g., Daniel Stiles, *The Elephant and Ivory Trade in Thailand* (Petaging Jaya [Malaysia]: TRAFFIC Southeast Asia, 2009), 1.

[28] *Oxford English Dictionary*, 2nd ed. 20 vols. (Oxford: Oxford University Press, 1989). In German, the word *Elfenbein* is derived from Old High German *helfantbein/helphan(t) bein*, literally *elephant bone*.

[29] Erika Fischer, *Ägyptische und ägyptisierende Elfenbeine aus Megiddo und Lachisch: Inschriftenfunde, Flaschen, Löffel* (Münster: Ugarit-Verl., 2007), 54.

distinction emerging between soft and hard ivory. The composition of an elephant's food here plays a considerable role in tusk hardness. Recent research has isolated seventeen different chemical elements in elephant tusks, allowing relatively precise conclusions about the region in which the animal lived[30] (this capacity is potentially valuable in combating ivory smuggling).

The tusks of African elephant bulls can reach a length of more than three meters and a weight of more than 110 kilograms, although at present tusks weighing more than twenty kilograms hardly reach the market – the average is 6.7 kilograms. Tusks that are around 1.6 to 1.7 meters in length have a diameter of around sixteen centimeters at the base. The tusks of females are considerably shorter and slimmer than those of bulls.[31] Cavities called pulpa are located at the base of the tusks. At their outset they are very broad, continuing as a fine channel until almost the end of the tusk, in this way nearly a third of the tusk is markedly hollow. In the past the broad hollow portion – in Zanzibar it was called *bamboo* – was often sawed through and segmented at African trading places, the sections of tusk then shipped to India for the manufacture of bangles.[32]

In Zanzibar the ivory would be divided into different classes oriented toward the possibilities for later use. Tusks weighing more than forty pounds were designated as large, prime ivory (*pempe bab-ulya*); a weight between twenty-five and forty pounds was medium prime ivory (*bab cutch*); and below twenty-five pounds was termed "ball ivory" (*pembe calasia*). In turn, ball ivory was divided into three classes depending on diameter: number 1, between 2.5 and 3.5 inches; number 2, between 2.25 and 2.4 inches; and number 3, less than 2.25 inches. Damaged ivory was termed *bab china*. Alongside the division into weight classes, distinguishing between hard and soft ivory was also usual.[33]

---

[30] E. J. Raubenheimer et al., "Geographic Variations in the Composition of Ivory of the African Elephant (Loxodonta africana)," *Archives of Oral Biology* 43 (1998): 645.

[31] Bundesamt für Veterinärwesen BVET/Artenschutz. Elfenbein, 2–3. www.blv .admin.ch/themen/handel_wild/05116/05144/05158/index.html?lang=de&downl oad=NHzLpZeg7t,lnp6IoNTUo42l2Z6ln1acy4Zn4Z2qZpnO2Yuq2Z6gpJCDdn 95gWym162epYbg2c_JjKbNoKSn6A-- (accessed November 8, 2014).

[32] *Zanzibar Gazette*, December 5, 1894, 4. In many areas of India these rings were a fixed element in the engagement ceremony. Today plastic or other synthetic material has replaced the ivory. Prem H. Bhalla, *Hindu Rites, Rituals, Customs and Traditions* (Bangalore: Hindology Books, 2009), 103.

[33] *Zanzibar Gazette*, December 5, 1894, 4.

But the material requirements placed on ivory could be far more differentiated, as we see in the five-page classification found in the papers of the American ivory dealer Ernst R. Domansky.[34] Domansky worked for some years in Africa, including a period in Zanzibar. Presumably he thought out the classification on his return from Africa, on the basis of his experiences and an informational brochure of the London ivory brokers Lewis & Peat Ltd. Domansky first distinguished seven weight classes: prime, cutch, bangle, light bangles, small bangles, scrivelloes with an average weight of seven pounds, and scrivelloes with an average weight of 3.5 pounds. In addition, he proposed adding tusk quality to the classification spectrum, distinguishing between sound, good defective, defective, poor defective, and diseased tusks. For precise division into the individual quality classes, he even developed a point system, according to which, for example, cracks in the upper area of the tusk led to one or more points being removed. In this system, a completely sound tusk had one hundred points, a sick one less than eighty-nine. And Domansky also worked with percentages, beginning with a basis of 25 percent suitable for rendering fine ivory into piano keys.[35] In any event Domansky's classification schema was never applied, rather remaining a former trader's purely private matter. We may presume it was too detailed and complicated.

For the London auctions, the ivory brokers operated with the following schema: the ivory was first divided into its place of origin (Zanzibar, Abyssinia, Mozambique, Egypt, or African West Coast), and then separated into soft and hard ivory, and according to both size (tusk, scrivelloe, points, bangles, etc.) and weight. The auction reports also contain information about the tusk's condition (sound, nearly sound, defective, etc.).[36] To this end trained personnel in Saint Katherine's Dock carefully inspected, measured, and weighed the tusks before providing each with a stamp.[37] Old photos in the *Museum of London Docklands* archive repeatedly show dockworkers inspecting tusk pulpae with lamps: according to a report in the Port of London Authority's journal, this was to see

---

[34] Domansky later took the last name of his uncle Dwight Moore, henceforth calling himself Ernst D. Moore. He published *Ivory: Scourge of Africa* (New York and London: Harper and Brothers, 1931) under this name; the book treated his time as an ivory dealer in Africa. The E. D. Moore papers are kept in the National Museum of American History, Archives Center, "Ernst D. Moore Papers, 1888–1932."

[35] "E. D. Moore Papers," 312, box 4.

[36] Auction reports of the firms, ibid.

[37] The assessment and measuring of the tusks can be seen very clearly in old photos stored in the Museum of London Docklands, where the collected documents of the Port of London Authority are kept.

whether anyone had inserted stones, metal objects, or other heavy things into the cavity to falsify the tusk's weight and gain a higher price.[38]

Before the auctions in the London Commercial Sales Rooms in Mincing Lane, the ivory was spread out on the Ivory Floor in the London docks, to be assessed by potential buyers. The ivory's classification was aimed, first and foremost, at making it easier for buyers to seek out the ivory most suitable for their specific needs. Hence billiard ball manufacturers chose tusk tips possessing the rough diameter of the balls, in order to end up with the least possible loss. Because the entire tusk could be used to manufacture piano keys, in this case buyers inspected entire tusks.[39]

The ivory's precise classification can be understood as an attempt at fixing purchasing norms or establishing a product line, against the backdrop of the function of ivory products as elements in various products that were mechanized and marked by a division of labor. Whether used for knife handles in Solingen or Sheffield or for piano keys in Ivoryton, ivory was needed in consistent quality and sufficient quantities to maintain ongoing production.[40] But as with other natural products, the classification efforts could not assure that a tusk had the desired quality; a final assessment was only possible when the ivory was carved into shape for its intended purpose. The classification's chief aim was thus organizational simplification, facilitating an overview of the stock by both suppliers and purchasers – in this way also facilitating price comparison and trade.[41]

Along with walrus and narwhal tusks, those of mammoths, together with hippopotamus and sperm whale teeth, have also been treated as forms of ivory. Since ratification in 1989 of the international ban on elephant ivory, mammoth tusks – so-called fossil ivory – has been the material's principle source. In the past, narwhal and walrus tusks were particularly used in Northern Europe, where there were no elephants. But these variants of ivory were also prized outside the northern regions; sixteenth-century English buyers thus paying twice as much for ivory from walrus as from elephants.[42]

---

[38] For research on his article in the *PLA Monthly*, the editor A. G. Linney spoke with a qualified worker who told him that in twenty years he had seen only a single tusk prepared in that way. But the same worker is said to have once found a petrified frog in a tusk. In *PLA Monthly*, March 1927, 146.

[39] Ibid., 148.

[40] Ludwig Trainer, "Das Elfenbein im Welthandel" (PhD diss., Universtität Berlin, 1935), 19. Trainer estimates the need for ivory by the knife industry in Sheffield and Solingen as amounting to nearly a third of the entire European need.

[41] "E. D. Moore Papers," 312, box 4, General Information regarding Ivory, 3.

[42] Burack, *Ivory and Its Uses*, 31.

A special characteristic of luxury goods is that they are subject to repeated efforts at imitation or at replacement by similar things. This was also the case with ivory. Substitute materials were, for example, bone, horn, and the dried fruit of *phytelephas aequatorialis* (i.e., vegetable ivory from the tagua nut of the ivory-nut palm). Without question, such materials had some disadvantages vis-à-vis ivory – or else they had qualities deviating from it. For a start, there was the problem of size: on account of their length and diameter, elephant tusks offered far more complex processing possibilities than, for instance, fist-size tagua nuts, which thus ended up being used mainly to manufacture buttons.[43] In addition, the chemical composition of elephant ivory made it a material coveted by carvers. Its combination of hardness, density, and elasticity allowed far more detailed work than was possible with bone because of bone's greater hardness. Ivory is also far more translucent than bone, so that the material is endowed with a living warmth. In addition, ivory can be polished in a manner giving the surface a special luster that together with its translucency endows it with a unique, inimitable appearance. Furthermore, ivory is a poor heat conductor, making it highly suitable for all sorts of handles. Finally, the material is tied to an aura of exclusivity, and to an exoticness it already possessed in antiquity.[44]

TICKLING THE IVORIES

In the classic edition of the popular detective game called Clue, players try to find the murderer of Mr. John Boddy. To do so, they move through the victim's mansion, looking for the possible weapon and room in which the deed took place – one possibility being the billiard room.[45] For traditionally whoever has thought highly of himself and could afford it has had a billiard room to confirm his status. Beginning in seventeenth-century France, the game of billiards spread out through Europe. While initially the balls were made of wood, in the nineteenth century ivory became the favored material, as during play they generated the ideal "click."[46]

---

[43] Alan W. Meerow, "Phytelephas spp. tagua," in *The Encyclopedia of Fruit and Nuts*, ed. J. Janick et al. (Wallingford: CABI Publishing, 2008), 151–3.

[44] Fischer, *Ägyptische und ägyptisierende Elfenbeine*, 55; BVET, *Elfenbein*, 3.

[45] In some of the later versions the rooms have changed and the billiard room is no longer included. Instead a movie theater is included.

[46] Later manufacturers would especially emphasize the click as an important quality, e.g., the Albany Billiard Company in its catalog of 1899. The National Museum of American History, Archives Center, "Albany Billiard Ball Company Records, 1869–1973."

To be sure, music was more important than billiards for the Western bourgeoisie.[47] The piano played a central role within its musical culture, as directly mirrored in rising production numbers for the piano manufacturers: in 1859, Bechstein produced a mere 176 instruments in Berlin; twelve years later the figure was 4,855.[48] Similarly, between 1860 and 1909 the number of American piano manufacturers nearly tripled, from 110 to 294, with production numbers rising correspondingly from approximately 20,000 to approximately 374,000 instruments a year.[49] In this manner, during the course of the nineteenth century the piano became ubiquitous, having a presence in salons, coffeehouses, schools, and hotels, and onward to hospitals and ocean steamers. The instrument thus turned into a favorite distinguishing mark of the cultivated middle class, as evident in the advertising brochures of the manufacturers. In its brochure, Bechstein addressed the women in potential purchasing households as follows:

Beautiful woman! These pages very specially apply to you, because you give the home a breath of the beautiful and personal. For the piano is more than a musical instrument to you. You know that even if you do not yourself play music, the piano belongs in your home for the sake of your guests, and you feel its artistic effect on space, which renders it a part of the whole, your home's adornment.[50]

At a price that after World War I lay between one thousand and five thousand reichmarks, the piano's role as a status symbol received further emphasis.[51] The piano in the parlor became an important status symbol for the middle class.[52]

In early-twentieth-century America, "tickling the ivories" emerged as an expression for piano playing. The Ivoryton firm that manufactured piano keys was Pratt, Read & Co.[53] After being delivered there in raw

---

[47] This central aspect of middle-class living was often underscored. See, e.g., Volker Kalisch, "Studien zur 'bürgerlichen Musikkultur'" (PhD diss., Universität Tübingen, 1990), 1.

[48] Numbers from Hagen W. Lippe-Weißenfeld, "Das Klavier als Mittel politischer Distinktion im Zusammenhang mit der Entwicklung des Klavierbaus in London und Berlin an den Beispielen Broadwood und Bechstein" (PhD diss., Freie Universität Berlin, 2006), 193. Parallel to this, the number of employed workers rose.

[49] Cyril Ehrlich, *The Piano: A History* (Oxford: Clarendon, 1990), 129.

[50] Cited from Lippe-Weißenfeld, "Das Klavier," 211.

[51] Trainer, "Elfenbein im Welthandel," 27.

[52] Craig H. Roell, *The Piano in America, 1890–1940* (Chapel Hill: University of North Carolina Press, 1989), xii. By 1915 the majority of middle-class families owned a piano (ibid., 70).

[53] The National Museum of American History, Archives Center, "Pratt, Read Corporations Records, 1838–1990." Originally the company was named Comstock, Cheney & Co. In 1936 the company merged with its rival Pratt, Read & Co. from nearby Deep River, adopting the name of the latter.

condition, the ivory was first placed in storage to assure enough available ivory in the event of delivery problems. Processing the tusks then began in the Ivory Shop, the objects being first sawed into roughly four-inch pieces that were then marked transversally by foremen. The markings corresponded to the size of one white key – the black keys were made out of ebony and were applied in circular form, in order to produce the least possible loss of material. The piece was then sawed through along the markings, the resulting pieces cut into thin plates eventually serving as the key's ivory veneer. The plates were now bleached in a solution of hydrogen peroxide and water, then washed. Following this process, the plates were brought to specially constructed bleaching houses on the company grounds; these houses looked like hothouses with a triangular cross section. In the bleaching houses, the keys were placed in wooden racks and then bleached for approximately two weeks in the sun. When the bleaching was finished, the plates were sorted according to quality and color and divided into six classes, then dried in special boxes for about three days, until no more shrinkage was evident. The key's veneer had two portions: a head and tail. These were now glued together and then again stored, with careful control of temperature and humidity to prevent warping – until finally being glued onto the keys in the Ivory Laying Department.[54]

The use of ivory for piano keys was considered completely normal and went unchallenged. Indeed, in caricatures the theme was approached humorously. Hence in 1949 Walt Disney presented a smiling elephant, behind whom two apes discussed why he was so happy. The answer: "He's going to make music his career."[55] And until the 1970s, even after Pratt, Read & Co. no longer used ivory, the firm's logo still showed an elephant head with tusks.[56]

The use of ivory for billiard balls was also an object of caricatures. In a brochure of the billiard manufacturer Brunswick-Balke-Collender published in December 1901, we see two elephants playing billiards, alongside a price list for ivory balls.[57] As indicated, ivory had already become the chief material for the balls many decades earlier. Because a complete billiards set – table, balls, and sticks – was relatively expensive, the game

---

[54] "Pratt, Read Corporations Records, 1838–1990," series 3, box 51, folder 7.
[55] The caricature is found as a newspaper clipping in the documents of Pratt, Read & Co., ibid., series 3, box 35, folder 3.
[56] Ibid., series 3, box 42, folder 10.
[57] The National Museum of American History, Archives Center, "Albany Billiard Ball Company Records, 1869–1973."

had long since been played chiefly on coffeehouses, hotels, and other public places. (After the Great War, a set cost between 1,000 and 1,600 reichmarks.) In Paris at the start of the nineteenth century, approximately 1,500 billiard tables were accessible in this way[58] – coffeehouses represented an especially favored venue. (This had its reflection in painting of the period, with works such as Van Gogh's *Night Café* and Gauguin's *In the Café* being two well-known examples.)

Starting in the mid-nineteenth century, Europe's material culture possessed many other luxury uses of ivory alongside piano keys and billiard balls. These included knives with ivory handles and all possible sorts of "fancy goods." In the Warshaw Collection of the Smithsonian, the file on ivory contains a catalog from the F. J. Kaldenberg firm. In the catalog, we find nearly everything that could be made out of the material, extending from a toilet mirror with an ivory handle to a thermometer.[59]

We should note, as well, that accompanying this – in the broadest sense – bourgeois consumption of ivory there was its use as decoration by scattered eccentrics. Wild Bill Hickok and George Patton might here serve as examples – both figures carried ivory-handled guns. Patton is said to have even clarified things for a confused reporter with the words "They're ivory. Only a pimp from a cheap New Orleans whorehouse would carry a pearl-handled pistol."[60]

SUBSTITUTES

In a commentary to a lecture by Professor Richard Owen of the Society of Arts in December 1856, a certain Mr. Coleman indicated that

I'm far from considering the subject exhausted and believe it would well repay the attention of any chemist who would make a series of experiments with the view of producing an artificial ivory, even if at cost of 20s. or 40s. per lb.... That our necessities will one day demand such a substance, I believe, notwithstanding the remark of Dr. Livingstone, that in Africa the supply of elephants appears almost inexhaustible, for it seems reasonable to suppose that, as civilization advances, and the demand for dentine increases, seas, rivers, and plains will become exhausted of the ivory-producing inhabitants. As the coal-fields has supplied the deficiencies of the forest, and as the pump will probably someday supply the deficiencies of the coal cellar, so doubtless artificial dentine will supply

---

[58] Franz Schiffer, *Billard: Pool, Snooker, Karambol: Regeln, Technik, Geschichte* (Munich: Hugendubel, 1994), 13.

[59] The National Museum of American History, "Kaldenberg, F. J.," Ivory, folder 5.

[60] The quote is from the movie Patton directed by Franklin J. Schaffner. If Patton really said those words, is unclear.

the place of natural, and a great benefactor will he be to the toothless community who first produces it.[61]

In his expression of concern at the possibility of a decline of ivory through overhunting, Coleman was certainly ahead of his time. The very considerable killing of elephants was also noted some decades later by Heinrich Adolph Meyer, who expressed the concrete fear that the high American and European demand would quickly exhaust the source of the raw ivory supply. In a brochure published by his firm in 1876, Meyer even spoke of a war of extermination against the elephants.[62] And already in 1891, the explorer Oscar Baumann demanded a trading ban on ivory, for the sake of recuperation of the stock of African elephants.[63] Finally, in a travel report published two years later, Joseph Thomson indicated that the area between Lake Tanganyika and the East African coast, twenty years earlier still rich in tusks, was now almost bereft of them. Evidently in some regions of East Africa the elephant stock had been decimated.[64]

Nevertheless, if we look at the statistics for London's and Antwerp's large auction houses, then the situation seems to have been very different, with, essentially, a strong increase in the quantities traded extending to World War I and relatively stable prices. Quantities and prices only sank, and then rapidly, after the war. Hence against the opinions of Coleman, Meyer, and others, we cannot really speak of an ivory problem in the nineteenth century. The emerging search for artificial materials that could replace ivory in fact was only superficially tied to the fictional ivory problem, rather having its origin in a very real and different problem: the unsuitability of ivory's material qualities for billiard balls.

It is the case that because of its elasticity it was, in an essential way, superior to the types of wood that had been used previously; but it also had decisive disadvantages. Above all else, ivory balls were extremely temperature sensitive, manufacturers thus expressly advising their customers to take great care in that respect in their treatment of the balls. In its December 1901 price list, the Brunswick firm thus included full-page

[61] Richard Owen, "Ivory and Teeth of Commerce," *Journal of the Society of Arts* 5 (1865): 73.

[62] Heinrich A. Meyer, *Ivory* (Hamburg: G. J. Herbst, 1876), 11.

[63] Oscar Baumann, *Usambara und seine Nachbargebiete: Allgemeine Darstellung des Nordöstlichen Deutsch-Ostafrika und seiner Bewohner auf Grund einer im Auftrag der Deutsch-Ostafrikanischen Gesellschaft im Jahre 1890 ausgeführten Reise* (Berlin: Reimer, 1891), 283.

[64] Joseph Thomson, ed., *To the Central African Lakes and Back: The Narrative of the Royal Geographical Society's East Central African Expedition, 1878–80.* 2 vols. (London: Sampson Low, 1881), 2: 17–18.

"Advice on the Purchase and Care of Ivory Balls." Most of the advice concerned the balls' temperature sensitivity: they needed at least a week of acclimatization to their place of usage before play began; otherwise they could develop cracks, especially in cold weather. For this reason, it was best to purchase the balls in summer, and if they were ordered in winter, claims for damages tied to the cold would be rejected. In general, then, although they were only prepared from the best soft ivory from Zanzibar, changes of temperature seem to have represented a serious problem for the billiard balls. Accompanying warnings about winter damage were others about exposing the balls to drafts during play, because the air in drafts, readers were informed, was the most dangerous of all. Finally, oil was not to be used to clean the balls, which would absorb it, because it would render them heavy and cause early disintegration. Instead, following each game they were to be washed with a damp cloth, then rubbed dry with a leather cloth.[65] In view of the plethora of negative material qualities, it is not surprising that the New York wholesale billiards dealer Phelan observed that "[i]f any inventive genius would discover a substitute for ivory, possessing those qualities which make it valuable to the billiard player, he would make a handsome fortune for himself, and earn our sincerest gratitude."[66] And he backed his words with a prize offer of $10,000 for the discoverer of such a substitute.

One of the inventors spurred on in this manner was John Wesley Hyatt,[67] who together with his brother Isaac founded the Albany Billiard Ball Company in 1869. That same year, he applied for a patent for an "improved method of composition to imitate ivory." Some of his experiments in that framework were with nitrocellulose (known informally as guncotton). But use of the substance for billiards proved seriously unsuitable: following an explosion in Hyatt's factory, an anonymous *New York Times* writer commented on September 16, 1875, under the heading "Explosive Teeth," that "No man can play billiards with any real satisfaction, if he knows that the billiard-balls may at any moment explode in a series of three closely-connected explosions, thereby spoiling a promising run, and burying the players under the wreck of table and cues."[68] In later catalogs of the Albany Billiard Ball Company, references to celluloid

---

[65] The National Museum of American History, Warshaw Collection (60), Billiard, folder 5.
[66] Michael Phelan, *The Game of Billiards* (New York: H. W. Collender, 1858), 34.
[67] On its home page, the German Museum of Synthetics even has an entry on Hyatt: "John Wesley Hyatt," Deutsches Kunststoffmuseum, www.deutsches-kunststoff-museum.de/rund-um-kunststoff/erfinder/john-wesley-hyatt-celluloid/ (accessed November 9, 2014).
[68] "Explosive Teeth," *New York Times*, September 16, 1875.

products are replaced by those to "composition balls"[69] – guaranteed, in stark contrast to the ivory balls, for a period of three years. Alongside the guarantee, the firm offered an assurance that the composition balls were the only perfect substitute for ivory. At the same time, the special material qualities of the artificial balls were underscored: even balance, and the same click, hardness, weight, and elasticity as ivory.[70]

The Albany Billiard Ball Company was naturally not the only firm in the market. The Eburnea Coy's Works in Lancaster presented its own synthetic ivory under the name Eburnea (Latin for ivory); this company placed somewhat more emphasis on the chemical composition of their material than did Albany – it was, the company indicated, superior to the original and took three to four weeks to manufacture.[71] In this way, the new materials were not only superior to ivory in their qualities but also far more quickly available, as the manufacturers tirelessly explained. A direct comparison is hardly possible any more, but their assessment does seem plausible: for one thing, ivory traveled over a long time from Africa's interior to Europe and America before undergoing its elaborate processing; for another thing, its sensitivity to temperature and typical disadvantages of a natural product were permanent, repeatedly generating problems.

In any case the main factor involved in the increase demand for balls made from artificial material was price. Even after World War I, a complete set of ivory balls cost 120 reichmarks, representing 10 percent of the cost of a complete billiard set (table, sticks, and balls). In addition, the balls had a life expectancy of 1.5 years, meaning that in ten years the money spent on balls equaled that spent originally on a complete set.[72] Plastic balls cost a fraction of their ivory counterparts and lasted much longer (three years were guaranteed).

The same pattern was at work in respect to the piano. Here as well the price difference between plastic and ivory keys was great. A complete set of keys cost thirty reichmarks on average; keys using artificial materials cost a tenth of this. In a steadily shrinking market, this was a serious factor for piano manufacturers. Hence in the period between 1913 and 1929, the production of pianos in Germany shrank from 140,000 to 65,600 instruments, with the percentage of white keys made of ivory

[69] These were produced from cellulose, but that was not made clear in the product's name on marketing-technical grounds.
[70] The National Museum of American History, Warshaw Collection (60), Billiard, folder 1.
[71] The National Museum of American History, Warshaw Collection (60), Ivory, folder 9.
[72] Trainer, "Elfenbein im Welthandel," 35.

being 75 percent in 1913 and 35 percent in 1929.[73] Ivory continued to be used only on especially valuable pianos because many pianists felt plastic veneer to be too hard and cold. In this regard, when in 1989 a complete trade ban on ivory took effect and there was a total shift to plastic white keys, researchers developed a special artificial material duplicating ivory's uneven surface structure, thus offering pianists the friction resistance they desired; the impossibility of distinguishing this material from ivory was confirmed in blind experiments.[74]

PROTECTION FOR ELEPHANTS

Parallel to the development of artificial replacements for ivory, at the end of the nineteenth century hunting laws were put into effect in the African colonies. An agreement was signed at an international conference on hunting limitations held in London on May 9, 1900, with the signatories obliging themselves to, among other things, see to the protection of female elephants and the young.[75] However, what at first view would appear a measure for the sustained use of a threatened resource reveals itself with closer inspection as the strategy of a European elite to shape hunting in Africa according to its needs. Four years earlier, the governor of German East Africa, Herrmann von Wissmann – an enthusiastic hunter – had issued a "decree on preserving the stock of wild animals" in the colonial possession. This decree made a license necessary for every hunting expedition. The fee was five rupees for Africans, twenty for sports hunters, and five hundred for professional elephant hunters. Although the fee for Africans may seem small, such a sum was extremely hard to come up with for the vast majority, being more than their annual tax fee. For the European sports hunters, the fee was relatively small.[76] For German East Africa, the corresponding hunting decrees of November 5, 1908 and December 30, 1911 contained the following rules: hunting elephants was only allowed to those possessing the "big game certificate," which cost 450 rupees, with an additional shooting fee of 150 rupees being charged for the first elephant, the second costing an additional

[73] Ibid., 28–9.
[74] "Plastik statt Elfenbein," *Der Spiegel* 23 (1993), 194.
[75] Franz Stuhlmann, "Elfenbein," in *Deutsches Kolonial-Lexikon,* ed. Heinrich Schnee, 3 vols. (Leipzig: Fines Mundi, 1920), 1: 556–8.
[76] Conradin von Perbandt, *Hermann von Wissmann: Deutschlands größter Afrikaner* (Berlin: Schall, 1906), 439–44.

400 rupees. More elephants could only be killed with special permission from the German government.[77]

But these hunting laws only superficially involved species protection. In actuality, the interests of the big-game lobby stood behind them. The lobby exerted particularly great influence on legislation in Germany, thus seeing its approach to hunting and sport for a prosperous upper class realized in various decrees. Hence the focus here was on an exclusive enjoyment of luxury by privileged Europeans. With the introduction of the hunting laws, that activity underwent a deep transformation in Africa: because of the prohibitive fees, African hunters were either forced to the margins or criminalized. In their place came increased numbers of European big-game hunters for whom East Africa, with its new hunting laws, was a kind of El Dorado.[78]

METAMORPHOSIS OF THE ELEPHANT: FROM SUPPLIER OF RAW MATERIAL TO CHARISMATIC ANIMALS

Alongside ivory's replacement by artificial materials and the transformation of hunting into an elite sport, there was a third notable change in the realm of ivory: that of the elephant's image.[79] Before the nineteenth century, elephants were a curiosity – a sight that could rarely be wondered at by a broad public. With the arrival of circuses and zoos, this situation rapidly altered. The precursor of the modern zoo was the nobility's menagerie, in which scattered exotic animals could also be admired – by, to be sure, a blue-blooded public alone.[80] In Germany it was above all the Hamburg animal-dealer Carl Hagenbeck who imported exotic animals in great style from all over the world for a broad general public.[81] In the United States, Jumbo the Elephant created a great deal

---

[77] Stuhlmann, "Elfenbein," 557.

[78] John M. MacKenzie, *The Empire of Nature: Hunting, Conservation and British Imperialism* (Manchester, UK: John MacDonald, 1988), 149; and Juhani Koponen, *Development for Exploitation: German Colonial Policies in Mainland Tanzania; 1884–1914* (Hamburg and Münster: LIT, 1995), 536.

[79] This change can be illuminated by the research field of animal studies. See Mieke Roscher, "Forschungsbericht Human-Animal-Studies," *Informationen zur modernen Stadtgeschichte* 2 (2009): 94–103; Pascal Eitler, "In tierischer Gesellschaft: Ein Literaturbericht zum Mensch-Tier-Verhältnis im 19. und 20. Jahrhundert," *neue politische literatur* 54 (2009): 207–24.

[80] Eric Baratay and Elisabeth Hardouin-Fougier, *Zoo: Von der Menagerie zum Tierpark* (Berlin: Klaus Wagenbach, 2000).

[81] Lothar Dittrich and Annelore Rieke-Müller, *Carl Hagenbeck, 1844–1913: Tierhandel und Schaustellungen im deutschen Kaiserreich* (Frankfurt: Lang, 1998).

of excitement – P. T. Barnum had purchased the elephant from the zoo in London for $10,000; it arrived in the New World on April 9, 1882. Accompanied by a gigantic media echo, Barnum toured the country with Jumbo and Tom Thumb, a dwarf elephant. During their three-year tour, about nine million people wondered at Jumbo, although he was untrained and could perform no tricks. The tour had a tragic end at the Ontario train station on September 14, 1885: Jumbo crashed directly into a moving train, news of his death then spreading throughout North America and the wider world by telegraph. The elephant had been called the "giant pet of two nations," and his demise sparked especially great grief in the United States and England.[82] A monument was established by Walt Disney in 1941 with his animated film *Dumbo* (whose actual name in the film is Jumbo Jr.), its story – of a flying elephant with huge ears – being loosely based on Jumbo's real narrative. Through such films, elephants were increasingly distanced from their natural African environment, to be represented as lovable house pets.[83]

Alongside *Dumbo*, the *Babar* stories of Jean de Brunhoff had a particularly strong influence on the evolution of the elephant's image. The first of the series, *L'histoire de Babar*, appeared in 1931.[84] Here the elephant child Babar flees to Paris after his mother is killed by a hunter. In the French metropolis, he is taken in by a friendly old woman who raises him like a human being. He even wears clothing made for humans: green suit, bowler hat, and shoes with spats. After the death of the old elephant king, he returns to the jungle to become the new ruler, founding the city of Celesteville, where elephants live according to the human model. After Jean de Brunhoff's death in 1937, his son Laurent continued the *Babar* series. In 1989 the movie arrived, along with a seventy-eight-part TV series shown in 150 countries; at present more than 120 million books have been sold worldwide.[85]

As the largest land mammals, elephants were studied with increasing scientific intensity in the course of the twentieth century. Researchers

---

[82] Stephan Oettermann, *Die Schaulust am Elefanten: Eine Elephantographia curiosa* (Frankfurt: Syndikat, 1982), 184–90.

[83] Eric Scigliano, *Love, War, and Circuses: The Age-Old Relationship between Elephants and Humans* (Boston: Houghton Mifflin, 2002), 213.

[84] Originally Jean's wife Cecile de Brunhoff told their children a bedtime story about an elephant. Her husband later reworked and expanded that story and added the colorful illustrations. She even had her name removed from the title of the first Babar book because she thought she played only a minor role creating it. See Paul Lewis, "Cécile de Brunhoff, Creator of Babar, Dies at 99," *New York Times*, April 8, 2003.

[85] Dan Wylie, *Elephant* (London: Reaktion, 2008), 97.

such as Cynthia Moss and Ian and Oria Douglas-Hamilton published books about their lives with elephants. There was here a strong emphasis on the animals' social capacities (and no mention made of the threat they posed for places of human settlement), with calls for their special protection.[86] In the conservation context the work of Bernhard Grzimek, director of the Frankfurt zoo, was particularly influential. Produced in 1957, his documentary *Serengeti Shall Not Die* was presented in theaters two years later and became an international success, winning the Oscar for best documentary film in 1960. A book with the same title (the German edition having a subtitle translatable as "367,000 animals seek a city") had been translated into nineteen languages by 1974, with 735,000 copies sold in Germany alone.[87] Grzimek explained his intentions as follows:

> Books, even when bestsellers, are only read by several ten thousands or perhaps hundred thousands of people. But we would like to make it clear to millions of Europeans and Americans that lions and elephants, rhinoceroses and giraffes – creatures everyone admires – are increasingly vanishing; and that their last places of refuge, the national parks, are steadily smaller. But we can only reach millions through film, television, and glossy magazines.[88]

In respect to elephants, the strategy of mass mobilization turned out to be very successful. In the 1970s, African elephants were poached for their ivory on a massive scale. The Western media reacted with horror, and with emotive photos of bloody elephant cadavers. Finally, in 1989 elephants were taken up in Appendix I of the Washington treaty on species protection known as Convention on International Trade in Endangered Species (CITES), which marked the beginning of the still-existing total ban on trade in ivory.

The ban, however, has not meant an end to the story of ivory. The twin problems of poaching and smuggling persist, their source being now as before the ban the demand for ivory in China and Japan – despite prices of more than $300 a kilo.[89] At the 2010 Doha conference of the CITES signatory states, Tanzania and Zambia failed in their proposal to have

---

[86] Ian and Oria Douglas-Hamilton, *Wir kämpfen für die Elefanten* (Munich: Droemer Knaur, 1994); Cynthia Moss, *Elephant Memories: Thirteen Years in the Life of an Elephant Family* (New York: W. Morrow, 1988).

[87] Johannes Paulmann, "Jenseits von Eden: Kolonialismus, Zeitkritik und wissenschaftlicher Naturschutz in Bernhard Grzimeks Tierfilmen der 1950er Jahre," *Zeitschrift für Geschichtswissenschaft* 56 (2008): 549–50.

[88] Bernhard and Michael Grzimek, *Serengeti darf nicht sterben: 367 000 Tiere suchen einen Staat* (Berlin: Ullstein, 1959), 12.

[89] Wylie, *Elephant*, 159.

ivory trading partly allowed again.[90] Since the ban's introduction, there have been repeated efforts of that sort, some successful. Hence in 2007 (the most recent such case) South Africa, Namibia, and Botswana were together allowed to sell sixty tons of ivory to Japan, where small ivory stamp seals are carved to be used in the signing of all sorts of everyday contracts (e.g., for house purchases); these enormously elevate the prestige of their owners.[91] Until today, it is thus impossible to speak of the arrival of a "post-ivory age," as was fearfully looked forward to by a German ivory dealer. Ivory objects remain coveted luxury goods, even if the demand has been geographically displaced.

---

[90] "CoP15 Committee I Results," Convention on International Trade in Endangered Species of Wild Fauna and Flora, www.cites.org/eng/news/meetings/cop15/Com-I_results.pdf (accessed November 9, 2014).

[91] Judith Raupp, "Der Lockruf des weißen Goldes," *Süddeutsche Zeitung*, June 4, 2007.

10

The conservation of luxury: Safari hunting and the consumption of wildlife in twentieth-century East Africa

Bernhard Gissibl

The organized cultural practice of hunting or viewing wild animals commonly known as safari has been one of the most persistent legacies of European colonial rule in East Africa. Combining African cultures of travel and hunting with the material and symbolic significance of big-game hunting in the imperial expansion of Europe, the East African big-game safari emerged as a thoroughly ritualized and commercialized luxury practice in the first decade of the twentieth century. Royal, aristocratic, and wealthy elites from Europe and North America expressed class and status, whiteness, masculinity, worldliness, and authority by turning elephants, lions, rhinoceroses, or buffaloes into various forms of trophies. Hunting as a luxury indulgence prompted the development of a wildlife tourism sector that linked the continents, popularized East Africa as the paradise of the big-game hunter, and created imaginaries of a primeval wildlife that proved remarkably stable throughout the twentieth century. Africans, by contrast, were gradually excluded from access to wildlife by restrictive game laws that turned their hunting, often undertaken for subsistence, into poaching. Safari hunting as a conspicuous leisure pursuit of the rich and mighty reached its heyday between the 1930s and 1950s, to be gradually complemented, morally ousted, and ultimately eclipsed by the merely visual consumption of game in wildlife tourism. Since the 1960s, the term *safari* has become firmly associated with such nonconsumptive visual encounters with wild animals, and complete hunting bans enacted in Tanzania and Kenya in 1973 and 1977 appeared to terminate the glamorous era of the East African hunting safari.[1]

[1] The author wishes to thank Thomas Lekan, Katharina Niederau, Anna-Katharina Wöbse, and the editors of this volume for valuable comments and critical queries on earlier drafts.

Trophy hunting has remained prohibited in Kenya ever since, but the ban in the iconic homeland of the safari only marked a new beginning in other sub-Saharan countries. They expanded their hunting sectors in the absence of East African competition, often with the help of safari operators and professionals who had been put out of business in Kenya and Tanzania. In East Africa, the readmission of tourist hunting in Tanzania just one year after the enactment of the Kenyan ban paved the way for the gradual "return of the great white hunters."[2] Since the late 1980s, state control of the hunting sector in Tanzania was attenuated to encourage foreign investment and private enterprise,[3] and the last decades have witnessed the return of trophy hunting as a key instrument of community-based resource management across Southern Africa. Couched in concerted efforts to decentralize wildlife sectors, enhance community participation in wildlife management, and harness conservation to rural development by the sustainable utilization of the wildlife resource,[4] big-game hunting, once the "quintessential symbol and activity"[5] of European imperialism, has been reframed as an inconspicuous form of high-end niche tourism and a philanthropic tool of pro-poor conservation. The recreational killing of wildlife is now conceptualized as

---

Edward I. Steinhart, *Black Poachers, White Hunters: A Social History of Hunting in Colonial Kenya* (Oxford: James Currey, 2005); see also John M. MacKenzie, *The Empire of Nature: Hunting, Conservation and British Imperialism* (Manchester, UK: Manchester University Press, 1988); Kenneth Cameron, *Into Africa: The Story of the East African Safari* (London: Constable, 1990). Popular accounts that relish largely uncritical in the heroism and adventure of big-game hunting, but contain valuable details include Bartle Bull, *Safari: A Chronicle of Adventure* (New York: Viking, 1988); Brian Herne, *White Hunters: The Golden Age of African Safaris* (New York: Holt, 1999).

[2] Antony Barnett, "The Return of the Great White Hunters," *The Observer*, October 12, 2003.

[3] For surveys of the legal development of hunting in Tanzania see Fred Nelson, Rugemeleza Nshala, and W. A. Rodgers, "The Evolution and Reform of Tanzanian Wildlife Management," *Conservation and Society* 5 (2007): 232–61, and Nigel Leader-Williams, "The Effects of a Century of Policy and Legal Change on Wildlife Conservation and Utilization in Tanzania," in *Wildlife Conservation by Sustainable Use*, ed. Herbert H. T. Prins, Jan Geu Grootenhuis, and Thomas T. Dolan (Boston, Dordrecht, and London: Kluwer Academic Publishers, 2000), 219–45.

[4] See David Hulme and Marshall Murphree, eds., *African Wildlife and Livelihoods: The Promise and Performance of Community Conservation* (Oxford: James Currey, 2001); J. Peter Brosius, Anna Lowenhaupt Tsing, and Charles Zerner, eds., *Communities and Conservation: Histories and Politics of Community-Based Natural Resource Management* (Lanham, MD: AltaMira Press, 2005).

[5] Harriet Ritvo, "Destroyers and Preservers: Big Game in the Victorian Empire," *History Today*, January 2002, 34; Bernhard Gissibl, "Hunting and Empire", *The Encyclopedia of Empire*, eds. John M. MacKenzie et al. (Hoboken: Wiley-Blackwell 2016), DOI: 10.1002/9781118455074.wbeoe403

"high value consumptive use of wildlife"[6] and marketed as a significant contribution to the alleviation of rural poverty.[7] To put the paradoxes of African trophy hunting at the beginning of the twenty-first century differently: killing specimens of charismatic wildlife is an integral instrument of conservation and sustainable utilization. As a form of luxury tourism, trophy hunting is also supposed to alleviate the plight of the rural poor.

This metamorphosis of trophy hunting from a core performance of imperial power into a tool of local empowerment is remarkable. Yet, the more astonishing aspect of East Africa's wildlife history throughout the twentieth century is the apparent persistence of the ritualized hunting of wild animals as an indulgence of the rich. The increasing rehabilitation of trophy hunting as a legitimate form of utilizing wildlife defies the moral progressivism that has been implicit in the "standard historical narrative"[8] of East Africa's conservation history. Taking its cue from the wildlife history of Kenya, this standard narrative has focused on the rise of preservationism and the proliferation of national parks.[9] It portrayed big-game hunting as a first profligate, then sportsmanlike, and ultimately

---

[6] Peter Rosa and Patricia Joubert, "Entrepreneurial Wildlife Exploitation in Sub-Saharan Africa," in *Tourism and Entrepreneurship: International Perspectives*, ed. Stephen Page and Jovo Ateljevic (Oxford: Butterworth-Heinemann, 2009), 189.

[7] Vernon R. Booth, *A Comparison of the Prices of Hunting Tourism in Southern and Eastern Africa* (Budapest: FAO/CIC, 2009); Nigel Leader-Williams, J. A. Kayera, and G. L. Overton, eds., *Tourist Hunting in Tanzania: Occasional Paper of the IUCN Species Survival Commission (SSC)*, no. 14 (Gland: IUCN, 1996); P. A. Lindsey, P. A. Roulet, and S. S. Romanach, "Economic and Conservation Significance of the Trophy Hunting Industry in Sub-Saharan Africa," *Biological Conservation* 134 (2007): 455–69; Barney Dickson, Jon Hutton, and William M. Adams, eds., *Recreational Hunting, Conservation and Rural Livelihoods: Science and Practice* (Chichester, UK: Blackwell Publishing, 2009).

[8] William M. Adams, "Sportsman's Shot, Poacher's Pot: Hunting, Local People and Conservation," in *Recreational Hunting*, ed. Dickson, Hutton and Adams, 127.

[9] The terms *conservation* and *preservation* are used according to their established meaning in international environmental history, i.e., conservation denoting measures of nature protection that allowed for management and sustainable utilization to ensure the continued use of animals through humans, as opposed to preservation as noninterventionist forms of protection predicated upon assumptions of ecological integrity and natural balance, see Libby Robin, "Conservation and Preservation," in *The Palgrave Dictionary of Transnational History*, ed. Akira Iriye and Pierre-Yves Saunier (Basingstoke, UK: Palgrave Macmillan, 2009), 191–4. The terms *game* and *wildlife* are used interchangeably, although it must be noted that early conservationist efforts aimed almost entirely at animals classified as "game," i.e., those that were actually hunted, whereas *wildlife* is the later and more comprehensive term, see Mark Cioc, *The Game of Conservation: International Treaties to Protect the World's Migratory Animals* (Athens, OH: Ohio University Press, 2009), 5–7; Etienne Benson, "From Wild Lives to Wildlife and Back," *Environmental History* 16, no. 3 (2011): 418–22.

marginalized way of relating to the continent's larger fauna.[10] The unbridled game slaughter of the years of colonial conquest spawned a conservationist ethos among penitent sportsmen whose advocacy prompted the introduction of restrictive game laws and reserves since the 1890s. From the 1930s onward, this ethos was gradually supplemented and ultimately replaced by a concern over the preservation of East Africa's unique wildlife heritage for future generations in inviolable national parks.[11] As a consequence, the rise of preservation, scientific game management, and the politics of protected areas in East and Southern Africa were high on the academic agenda. Whereas environmental historians and political ecologists have been busy revealing the violence and exclusions associated with "fortress conservation" in national parks, the fate of wildlife outside of them, alternative forms of its conservation, the persistence of luxury hunting, and its varying compatibility with conservationist thinking and practices throughout the twentieth century have remained largely neglected.

This chapter rethinks East Africa's wildlife history by using luxury as an analytical entry to the history of its appropriation and conservation. Poised between anthropology, economy, and ethics, luxury is a consequence of human inequality, a scale of economic value, and a means of social communication. Luxuries allow individuals to communicate identity, status, and difference through the consumption of things and practices that are deemed dispensable, yet desirable in a given society. They are characterized by a relative scarcity that restricts access to them to social or financial elites. As a marker of class and status, luxury consumption is a contested form of social distinction. It is emulated by aspiring social inferiors and rejected as morally inacceptable by critical or envious nonpractitioners. Among its practitioners, luxury consumption is bound in a spiral of constant refinement and commoditization. The unceasing quest for the ultimate distinction produces different and more refined practices or accoutrements that become emulated and commoditized and set a new cycle of refinement in motion.[12]

---

[10] Steinhart, *Black Poachers*, 3, 212; MacKenzie, *Empire of Nature*. Cf. John S. Akama, "Controversies Surrounding the Ban on Wildlife Hunting in Kenya: An Historical Perspective," in *Tourism and the Consumption of Wildlife: Hunting, Shooting and Sport Fishing*, ed. Brent Lovelock (London and New York: Routledge, 2008), 73–86.

[11] Studies following this narrative include MacKenzie, *Empire of Nature*; Steinhart, *Black Poachers*; Thomas P. Ofcansky, *Paradise Lost: A History of Game Preservation in East Africa* (Morgantown: West Virginia University Press, 2002).

[12] See Christopher J. Berry, *The Idea of Luxury: A Conceptual and Historical Investigation* (Cambridge: Cambridge University Press, 1994); Tobias Thomas, *Luxus: Statusstreben und demonstratives Konsumverhalten* (Marburg: Tectum, 2007).

The first association that comes to mind is probably the luxury-in-the-bush, personal chef, air-conditioned tent, and iced sundowner sort of safari that encapsulates the awkward yet defining alliance of the decadent with the archaic. But safari as a luxury goes beyond the accoutrements of its performance. It pertains to the exclusive status of long-distance travel in Western societies as well as to the economy of wildlife. Bringing luxury into the analysis of African conservation serves to highlight that, since around 1900, the future preservation of Africa's wildlife has not only been driven by a civilizing discourse "against extinction,"[13] but also was intricately entwined with various forms of its consumption as a luxury, above all by members of Western societies. Luxury did not give birth to conservation, but it has been an indispensable element of its political economy.

Safari as a luxury practice thrived upon the fascination of seeing charismatic wildlife "in its place." Only a small number of species mobilized an infinitesimal yet growing number of Westerners to travel to East Africa in order to hunt or view these animals, or otherwise donate considerable amounts of money for their protection in national parks and other protected areas. The charisma of species like lions, elephants, rhinos, hippos, buffaloes, and zebras is produced both by "the agency of the nonhuman being witnessed and the social structure in which the witness is enmeshed."[14] Elephants, for example, were charismatic in an African context, too, but it is their "Western" charisma that mattered for their luxury consumption and became their global trademark. The animals' visibility and morphology; their alleged and, in the course of the twentieth century, scientifically substantiated behavioral patterns; and their geographies and temporalities all played a role. So did the cultural values and backgrounds of visitors, discourses of scarcity and uniqueness, and the multisensory and emotional appeal of the embodied encounter. Without the elements of embodied experience, thrill and adventure, heat and sweat, expectation, exhaustion, awe, disappointment, and triumph, it is impossible to explain why people found it so important to engage with potentially dangerous animals "at home" and document this encounter in some form of tangible proof.

[13] William M. Adams, *Against Extinction: The Story of Conservation* (London: Earthscan, 2004).
[14] Jamie Lorimer, "Natures, Charismatic," in *International Encyclopaedia of Human Geography*, ed. Rob Kitchin and Nigel Thrift, 12 vols. (Oxford: Elsevier, 2009), 7: 324–5; see also id., "Nonhuman Charisma," *Environment and Planning D: Society and Space* 24 (2007): 911–32.

The corporeal encounter with wildlife at home necessarily involved transcontinental travel and required an interlocking chain of divided labor that gets the hunter there and the trophies back. As in the case of other luxury commodities procured from the Global South, the "production" of wildlife linked Western consumption with the radical transformation of ecologies in colonial settings – the difference being that in the case of wild-life, production and consumption were not spatially disjointed. Consuming wildlife by hunting and viewing not only utilized what is "naturally" there but also fundamentally transformed its object: the Western desire to have recourse with wildlife in its authentic, natural surroundings gave rise to a complex environmental legislation and geography of protected areas that, in the case of Tanzania, comprises up to a third of the country's territory. Conserving and preserving wildlife was a genuine form of productive land use, an important element of nation branding in a global economy of places and images, and it was inexorably entwined with forms of transcontinental tourism that were a luxury for its practitioners.

The following analysis of the hunting safari as a luxury proceeds in six steps. After an initial sketch of the nineteenth-century hunting world I will situate the making of the East African safari in the colonial globalization around 1900. The chapter then discusses the political economy and the ele-ments of luxury involved in safari hunting before it charts the erstwhile end of the "classic" East African safari through the moral hegemony pres-ervationism achieved thanks to decolonization and the global rise of the national park ideal. A final section discusses the insights that the history of conservation gains from attention to its association with luxury.

GLOBE-TROTTING FOR TROPHIES:
THE NINETEENTH-CENTURY HUNTING WORLD

Albeit the most famous, the East African safari was but one regional ema-nation of the broader cult of big-game hunting that paralleled the height of European imperialism between the middle of the nineteenth and the middle of the twentieth century. As early as 1808, Thomas Williamson's voluminous *Oriental Field Sports* popularized pigsticking, the use of tamed cheetahs, and the tiger hunt in British India. Here, the necessities of predator control merged with British notions of sport and Mughal traditions of hunting and elephant taming in the transcultural pageant of the Indian *shikar*.[15] In Southern Africa, the northward extension of

---

[15] Thomas Williamson, *Oriental Field Sports*, 2 vols. (London: William Bulmer and Co., 1808), 1: v; Julie E. Hughes, *Animal Kingdoms: Hunting, the Environment, and Power*

white settlement in the first half of the nineteenth century provided the stage for the self-fashioning of profligate hunters like Roualeyn Gordon Cumming or Frederick Courteney Selous as empire builders.[16] Hunting in the North American West "flavored the English tradition of genteel sport with the American tradition of frontier self-reliance," attracting East Coast industrialists and visiting European aristocrats to reenact the frontier encounter with big game.[17] In British Columbia, the Canadian Pacific Railway appropriated the images and stereotypes of big-game hunting and deployed them for its corporate interests. Since the 1880s, the area was marketed as a "sportsman's paradise" to lure wealthy hunters with buffalo, grizzly bear, and moose.[18] The inclusion of the Arctic and Spitsbergen, but also southeastern Europe and Scandinavia, into the regular itineraries of globe-trotting hunters from the middle of the nineteenth century shows that, although largely an accompaniment of Europe's commercial and political expansion overseas, the hunting cult flourished wherever human-environmental relations had left room for the survival of animals regarded as "big game."[19] The appearance of the mobile, transnational class of globe-trotting hunters indicated that an area was already past its frontier phase, rendered accessible through the routes of global transport, and controlled enough to allow for voluntary and recreational hunting in the wake of conquest. The worldwide leisure hunting of Westerners relied upon the paradox that only the exported structures of Western modernity – the colonial state and a globalized logistic network – provided hunters with the opportunity to encounter the wilderness presumed to exist beyond the steamship line, the railway station, and the last European outpost.

   in the Indian Princely States (Cambridge, MA: Harvard University Press, 2013); Kevin Hannam, "Shooting Tigers as Leisure in Colonial India," in *Tourism and the Consumption of Wildlife*, ed. Lovelock, 99–111; Anand S. Pandian, "Predatory Care: The Imperial Hunt in Mughal and British India," *Journal of Historical Sociology* 14 (2001): 79–107.

16 William Beinart and Peter Coates, *Environment and History: The Taming of Nature in the USA and South Africa* (London: Routledge, 1995), 17–33; MacKenzie, *Empire of Nature*, 85–119.

17 Daniel Justin Herman, *Hunting and the American Imagination* (Washington, DC: Smithsonian Institution Press, 2001), 125; Harry Liebersohn, *Aristocratic Encounters: European Travelers and North American Indians* (Cambridge: Cambridge University Press, 1998).

18 Greg Gillespie, *Hunting for Empire: Narratives of Sport in Rupert's Land, 1840–1870* (Vancouver: University of British Columbia Press, 2007); Karen Wonders, "Hunting Narratives of the Age of Empire: A Gender Reading of Their Iconography," *Environment and History* 11 (2005): 269–91.

19 Pia Sillanpää, "The Scandinavian Sporting Tour 1830–1914," in *Tourism and the Consumption of Wildlife*, ed. Lovelock, 59–72.

Big-game hunting as a tourist practice thrived upon the charged metaphorism of hunting as a complex and multifunctional performance of white, masculine power over the nonhuman and human inhabitants of "wild," colonial spaces. Hunting had provided the protein subsidy for the conquering vanguard of European expansion, cleared the land for European settlement and cultivation, offered rare diversion on imperial duty, and helped colonizers to familiarize with unknown environments. If hunting contributed to empire building, empire undeniably "modernized" hunting, for it was also a critical source of "scientific" knowledge. Disciplines as diverse as early ecology, veterinary science, and tropical medicine drew upon hunting in one way or another. So did the visual representation of taxonomy, evolution, and zoogeography in the natural history museums that mushroomed throughout North America and Europe and its empires.[20]

Occasional female and non-European interlopers notwithstanding, the obsession with the hunting of big game was a white and male phenomenon. It was thoroughly tainted by the culture, ideology, and practice of British imperialism, respectively the North American frontier. The intimate association of big-game hunting with the politics and culture of empire gave rise to an ideal of "imperial man the hunter" that encapsulated the virtues and values deemed necessary requirements for the men that made and ran the empire – courage, self-organization, endurance, individualism, resourcefulness, sportsmanship, marksmanship, and environmental mastery. This ideal type was enshrined in a myriad of travelogs and adventure stories; it informed the Boy Scout ideal; and it was admired, envied, emulated as well as caricatured and criticized beyond the borders of the British Empire.[21] The "heroic" exploration that preceded the establishment of European rule in East Africa, as well as the ivory hunting that supported it, lent the model of "imperial man the hunter" new vigor. It also inspired leisurely travelers to trail the vanguard of official imperialism and relish in the ritualized, imaginary reenactment of first contact with the wild.

---

[20] John M. MacKenzie, *Museums and Empire: Natural History, Human Cultures and Colonial Identities* (Manchester, UK: Manchester University Press, 2009); Susanne Köstering, *Natur zum Anschauen: Das Naturkundemuseum des deutschen Kaiserreichs 1871–1914* (Cologne, Weimar, and Vienna: Böhlau, 2003).

[21] John M. MacKenzie, "The Imperial Pioneer and Hunter and the British Masculine Stereotype in Late Victorian and Edwardian Times," in *Manliness and Morality: Middle-Class Masculinity in Britain and America, 1800–1940*, ed. J. A. Mangan and James Walvin (New York: Manchester University Press, 1987), 176–98.

THE MAKING OF THE EAST AFRICAN SAFARI

Developing in the wake of Anglo-German colonial conquest since the 1880s, the East African safari was a comparatively late addition to the global geography of sporting countries. But by the eve of World War I, it had become the most conspicuous and commercialized local and trans-cultural adaptation of the imperial hunting cult. If the extension of colonial rule into sub-Saharan Africa mobilized administrators, militaries, missionaries, settlers, and scientists, the revolutions in communication and transport as well as social and economic transformations in Western societies constituted particularly powerful push factors that facilitated the emergence of a new type of leisurely traveler: the globe-trotting sports-man.[22] The opening of the Suez Canal, regular steamship connections, and the extension of railways in colonial territories resulted in a considerable shrinkage of travel time, which brought East Africa ever closer to Europe. When a weekly imperial air service opened from London in the mid-1930s and regular jet plane connections brought Nairobi within twenty-four-hours reach from London and Frankfurt another two decades later,[23] a hunting trip that previously consumed three months could now be done within two weeks to match the tightest business schedule. Moreover, the global network of telegraph lines and submarine cables was extended to East Africa since the 1880s, allowing for effective advance organization and short-term arrangements on part of both hunters and safari outfitters.[24] The second wave of industrialization in Europe and the United States augmented wealth, changed leisure and consumption patterns, and meant that a growing number of bourgeois industrialists and upwardly mobile members of the middle classes commanded both disposable time and income necessary for nonoccupational

---

[22] There exists no collective biography of the globe-trotting sportsman, but many biographies of big-game hunters testify to the pervasiveness of transcontinental trophy hunting of which the East African safari was only one part. See for early examples of such journeys the account of Paul Niedieck, a German hunter-adventurer from a dynasty of velvet manufacturers in the Rhineland: Paul Niedieck, *With Rifle in Five Continents* (London and New York: Rowland Ward, 1909); similarly, Max C. Fleischmann, *After Big Game in Arctic and Tropic: A Sportsman's Notebook of the Chase off Greenland and Alaska; In Africa, Norway, Spitzbergen, and the Cassair* (Cincinnati, OH: The Jennings and Graham Press, 1909).

[23] Robert McCormack, "Imperialism, Air Transport and Colonial Development: Kenya, 1920–46," *Journal of Imperial and Commonwealth History* 17 (1989): 374–95.

[24] Dwayne R. Winseck and Robert M. Pike, *Communication and Empire: Media, Markets, and Globalization, 1860–1930* (Durham, NC and London: Duke University Press, 2007), 105–10.

voyaging. This enabled them to emulate what had heretofore been privileged aristocratic patterns of travel, diversion, and gentlemanly conduct, such as hunting and its century-old association with aristocratic
exclusiveness, worldliness, and power. At the same time, aristocrats, the
members of Europe's royal families, and leading politicians discovered
big-game hunting as a way to cast a key habit of their landed lifestyles
into colonial space and symbolically stake their claim to social and political leadership.[25] An armed and transcontinental extension of the Grand
Tour, globe-trotting for trophies took up from established aristocratic
practices and "modernized" them through the association with popular
contemporary agendas, such as scientific exploration and the extension
of empire.

Big-game hunting's popularity and entry into the repertoire of plu-
tocratic leisure activities was further promoted by changing cultures of
nature in turn-of-the-century Europe and North America. The cult of wilderness and the frontier in the United States; the growth of nature conservation and naturist reform movements on both sides of the Atlantic;
mountaineering and outdoor-oriented movements such as the Boy Scouts
all testify to a widespread uneasiness about industrial modernity that
articulated itself in various forms of getting "back to nature."[26] Unsettled
by mass society's challenges to paternalist social models, hunting was
portrayed as an antidote to the emasculating complexities of urban and
industrial modernity and the nerve-taxing speed of progress, in short, to
"ultra civilization."[27] Stalking the big game of Africa was about the closest to "nature" contemporaries could imagine to get, and hunters understood the encounter with Africa's game as an educative instance that
activated and restored the "natural" manhood that had been civilized
away in Europe. A vulgarized Darwinism encouraged such understandings of hunting as an atavistic natural instinct that linked contemporary
men to humankind's remote ancestry,[28] while a seemingly antediluvian

---

[25] Roderick P. Neumann, "Dukes, Earls and Ersatz Edens: Aristocratic Nature
Preservationists in Colonial Africa," *Environment and Planning D: Society and Space* 14
(1996): 79–98.

[26] See, e.g., Nash, *Wilderness*; John Alexander Williams, *Turning to Nature in Germany:
Hiking, Nudism and Conservation, 1900–1940* (Stanford, CA: Stanford University Press,
2007); Robert H. MacDonald, *Sons of the Empire: The Frontier and the Boy Scout
Movement 1890–1918* (Toronto: University of Toronto Press, 1993).

[27] Clive Phillipps-Wolley, "On Big Game Shooting Generally," in *Big Game Shooting*, ed.
Clive Phillipps-Wolley (London: Longmans, Green, 1895), 3.

[28] The evolutionist understanding of hunting as an atavism and the transient pleasure of
being "Palaeolithic" has received philosophical sanction by the Spanish philosopher

megafauna appeared to embody deep time and render the East African savannah the living Pleistocene. There is hardly a travelog that did not portray a safari in East Africa as an experience of unrestrained freedom, a holiday from "civilization," and a travel across time into the dawn of mankind.

Developments outside Africa help explain the phenomenon of the globe-trotting hunter, but they fall short in accounting for the particular form, organization, geography, and political economy of the hunting safari as a genuinely transcultural practice of encountering wild animals. Its African roots must be sought in the long-distance caravan trade for slaves and ivory that generated a distinct culture and infrastructure of porterage and travel in East Africa and turned the governance of hunting into a key mechanism of political authority.[29] Edward Steinhart has identified the "size of the entourage, the military demeanour of the caravan, and the central role of hunting in the daily operation" as the main elements the imperial hunting safaris incorporated from the trade caravans of the nineteenth century.[30] Yet, their legacies went further and pertained to terminology, personnel, and geography, too. British and German colonialists incorporated the Kiswahili term *safari* as a technical term into colonial parlance, narrowing its original meaning of "travel" or "journey" to denote a journey undertaken in the company of porters for the mere sake of hunting. Erstwhile ivory hunters, "professional" porters, and caravan headmen transferred the skills, values, hierarchies, and masculinities of the caravan trade into colonial expeditions and the commercialized safari, while specialized hunter-foragers like the Waata developed a reputation as outstanding scouts and trackers. The outfitters of hunting safaris inherited and profited from a culture of porterage and occupational migration that constituted an often-overlooked complementary mobility to the long-distance voyaging of the tourist hunter, at least until the 1930s, when the use of motorcars rendered porters increasingly superfluous.

The fusion of the voluntary long-distance mobility of Western travelers with the regional mobilities and local expertise contributed by indigenous

---

Ortega y Gasset, see his *Meditations on Hunting* (Belgrade, MT: Wilderness Adventures Press, 2007), 125 [first published in Spanish in 1944].

[29] For a comprehensive discussion of these continuities see Michael Pesek, *Koloniale Herrschaft in Deutsch-Ostafrika: Expeditionen, Militär und Verwaltung seit 1880* (Frankfurt and New York: Campus, 2005); Stephen J. Rockel, *Carriers of Culture: Labor on the Road in Nineteenth-Century East Africa* (Portsmouth, NH: Heinemann, 2006).

[30] Steinhart, *Black Poachers*, 113–14.

porters, trackers, and headmen was part of the safari's allure as well as a
cause for severe tensions. There was an apparent discrepancy between the
sovereign mastery European hunters ascribed to themselves in the narratives and visual iconography of the hunt, and the social relationships
within the microcosm of the safari, which were characterized by the visiting hunters' almost complete dependence on the skills, guidance, and
superior knowledge of his local companions. These asymmetries were a
constant threat to the racial hierarchies upon which colonial rule rested.
Therefore, commercial outfitters introduced the role of the professional
"white hunter" as the intermediary who spared racist visiting hunters the impertinence of entrusting themselves directly into the hands of
"natives."[31] The "white hunter" was as much a continuation of the earlier
caravan trade as an attempt to transform and appropriate its established
roles and institutions. In addition to his taking over the logistic, organizing, and negotiating duties of the nyampara-headman in the caravan
trade, the "white hunter" served as translator and personal counselor,
mapped out itineraries, and was responsible that the client encountered all
the desired trophy animals in situations of "safe danger."[32] His knowledge
about seasonal game movements and areas best suited for hunting made
his services indispensable, even before it became mandatory for overseas
visitors to hire a professional white hunter after World War II.

The precolonial caravan trade also determined the geographies of the
commercial safari as it emerged after the turn of the century. Because the
majority of trade routes that connected the Congo Basin and the Great
Central African Lakes with the Swahili Coast ended up in port cities that
came under German rule after 1885, Kenya inherited a smaller share of
the trade in ivory, East Africa's most important export commodity of
the time. The will to tap the ivory stocks of the African interior was one
reason behind the construction of the Uganda Railway, which, upon its
completion in 1901, turned out a perfect motor for the fledgling hunting
tourism. Finally, the ever-increasing intensity of ivory hunting had taxed
the elephant herds in the British and German colonial territories in East
Africa to a degree that authorities on both sides were convinced by the
middle of the 1890s to risk the species' regional extinction if the wanton
destruction was not halted by concerted efforts.[33] Only the introduction

---

[31] See Cameron, *Into Africa*, 158–72; Steinhart, *Black Poachers*, 131–7.
[32] Steinhart, *Black Poachers*, 132.
[33] See Bernhard Gissibl, "German Colonialism and the Beginnings of International Wildlife
Preservation in Africa," *GHI Washington Bulletin Supplement* 3 (2006): 121–43; Cioc,
Game of Conservation, ch. 1.

of game laws made access to charismatic game exclusive enough to allow for the ritualized distinction of the hunting safari.

GAME AS LUXURY: THE POLITICAL ECONOMY
OF SAFARI HUNTING

Both British and German East Africa featured similarly scenic landscapes and the charismatic species of big game desired by hunters, and in both colonies the much-deplored unbridled slaughter of big game for primarily commercial purposes was tackled by legal regulations since the middle of the 1890s. But it was the combination of political will, a tradition of imperial hunting, a legal framework that encouraged entrepreneurship, and tourism with the advantages of infrastructure and biogeography that gave Kenya the upper hand as East Africa's foremost hunting destination. British authorities soon realized that, compared to the German regulations, it was more promising to design the Kenyan game laws "slightly more favourable to wealthy sportsmen who bring money into the territory, and who ... should be encouraged rather than otherwise to visit it."[34] German authorities, by contrast, still reckoned with the commercial exploitation of ivory as a source of revenue in the late 1890s and underestimated the potential of tourist hunting. The German hunting ethics of *Weidgerechtigkeit* had evolved with an emphasis on sustainable game management on small estates in central Europe and was less conducive to a business-like approach to game than British understandings of hunting as sportsmanship. But it was the opening of the Uganda Railway that gave the British colony the decisive infrastructural advantage. When the Germans in Tanganyika finally adopted game laws geared to attract wealthy leisure hunters in 1912, the safari business in Kenya had already boomed for a decade.[35] While the oft-complained "underachievement"[36] of Tanzania in realizing its tourist potential had deep roots in German colonial policies, the conservationist regime that ensued in Kenya favored the nonutilitarian, recreational, and ritualized hunt of gentlemanly "settler hunters" and visiting sportsmen from Europe and North America. They

[34] PRO FO 403/302, no. 31: Hardinge to Salisbury, Zanzibar, 27th August 1897.
[35] For a comprehensive discussion of Tanganyikan game legislation under German rule, see my *The Nature of German Imperialism: Conservation and the Politics of Wildlife in Colonial East Africa* (New York and Oxford: Berghahn, 2016).
[36] See, e.g., Vojislav Popovic, *Tourism in Eastern Africa* (Munich: Weltforum, 1972); for a survey Noel B. Salazar, "A Troubled Past, a Challenging Present and a Promising Future: Tanzania's Tourism Development in Perspective," *Tourism Review International* 12 (2009): 259–73.

blended the ideology of frontier hunting with the habit, social bias, and exclusive tradition of the aristocratic hunt from Europe and created the big-game safari as "Kenya's most distinctive contribution to the venatic tradition."[37]

Historians have duly emphasized the emotional and psychological significance of wildlife as a core motif behind conservationist policies. They have also stressed the metamorphosis of erstwhile ivory harvesters into "penitent butchers" who sounded the alarm bell of rapid game depletion and lobbied for restrictive game legislation.[38] But they have often overlooked that luxury, too, stood at the cradle of the wildlife conservation regime in East Africa. The new discourse of species and nature protection may have emphasized the intrinsic value of wildlife, but its market value was of at least equal importance. So was the degree to which colonial administrations constructed game laws that emphasized this market value by reserving charismatic game for luxury consumption. Setting the stage for the commercialization of safari as leisure was less moral improvement on part of individual hunters, but rather a legislation that, since the late 1890s, aimed to reconcile conservation and colonial development through creating an exclusive market for trophy hunting.

Undeniably a lesson learnt from the devastations wrought by hunters on other imperial frontiers in North America and Southern Africa, the Kenyan Game Ordinances gazetted in 1897 and 1899 introduced an expensive "sportsman's licence" (later: visitor's license) that enhanced the exclusiveness of big-game hunting in two important ways. First, it reserved the hunting of elephants, rhinoceroses, hippopotami, buffalo, and giraffe entirely to those capable of affording this license. By implication, all other forms, traditions, or entitlements to hunt these animals, be it by Africans or European settlers, were made unlawful and turned into poaching. The will to preserve the most charismatic species for the luxury consumption of sportsmen was inextricably entwined with the creation of the poacher as the heroic sportsman's evil twin.[39] Second,

---

[37] Steinhart, *Black Poachers*, 69–77, 91 (quotations); similarly, John M. MacKenzie, "Chivalry, Social Darwinism and Ritualised Killing: The Hunting Ethos in Central Africa up to 1914," in *Conservation in Africa: People, Policies and Practice*, ed. Richard Grove and David Anderson (Cambridge: Cambridge University Press, 1987), 41–61.

[38] David K. Prendergast and William M. Adams, "Colonial Wildlife Preservation and the Origins of the Society for the Preservation of the Wild Fauna of the Empire, 1903–1914," *Oryx* 37 (2003): 251–60; Richard Fitter and Peter Scott, *The Penitent Butchers: 75 Years of Wildlife Conservation* (Reading: Collins, 1978).

[39] On the recent discursive history of the poacher, see Roderick Neumann, "Moral and Discursive Geographies in the War for Biodiversity in Africa," *Political Geography* 23

the ordinance created an artificial scarcity by restricting the hunting of these species to no more than two heads under one license.[40] At first sight, it appears counterintuitive that such a restriction may have made a journey of several thousands of miles more appealing. But unlike in German East Africa, where the lack of a ceiling on elephant hunting attracted a rough lot of ivory hunters before World War I, the artificial scarcity created an environment of distinction: hunters came because it was exclusive.

Circumventions, exceptions, and alterations to these game laws notwithstanding, their overall thrust was clear: the code of the gentleman hunter had become law, visiting hunters received preferential treatment, and legal regulation, above all, civilized hunters into the exertion of restraint. The most charismatic species of Africa's fauna had been transformed into a commodity through which the inequalities of race, wealth, and status were expressed.

Imperial wildlife conservationists enthusiastically embraced the link established between luxury and conservation and were untiring in their emphasis that the sale of licenses made big game an "asset of large pecuniary value." "This is a utilitarian age," one hunter-conservationist argued in 1906, and the public "might like to be satisfied that it is, besides being a matter of public sentiment, commercially and financially advantageous to preserve the game ... and that the revenue derived therefrom may very well be utilised in enforcing and carrying out the laws and regulations for their preservation."[41] The business approach to conservation – that game could and should pay for its conservation by restricting access to wealthy trophy hunters – has appealed already to cash-strapped colonial administrations around 1900. In the decades that followed, the revenue derived from visiting leisure hunters provided a powerful and convincing economic justification for game conservation, especially against the continuous demands by European settlers and veterinary officials to remove

---

(2004): 813–37. A social and discursive history of the "poacher," perhaps the most evocative and least decolonized moral stereotype of Africa's social and environmental history in the twentieth century, is a pressing requirement.

[40] *Correspondence Relating to the Preservation of Wild Animals in Africa* (London 1906) (= Parliamentary Papers, Vol. lxxix, 25), enclosure in no. 36: Game Regulations of the East Africa Protectorate 1899, § 4. The same conditions applied to a cheaper public officer's license.

[41] "Recommendations of the Society Sent to the Secretary of State for the Colonies in June 1906," *Journal of the Society for the Preservation of the Wild Fauna of the Empire* 3 (1907): 14–15; "Minutes of Proceedings at a Deputation from the Society for the Preservation of the Wild Fauna of the Empire to the Right Hon. The Earl of Elgin, His Majesty's Secretary of State for the Colonies, June 15, 1906," ibid., 27.

wildlife that was host to livestock diseases and an obstacle to agricultural development. Although varying in its discursive purchase and often honored merely in the breach, the argument that revenue from tourist hunting paid conservation remained valid throughout the century. The currently widespread implementation of the *"use it or lose it"* approach to conservation into schemes of sustainable hunting is but a rediscovery of one of the oldest rationales behind colonial game policies.

Surviving sources and figures from the early 1900s indicate that the enthusiasm of the wildlife conservationists was not unfounded. The revenue derived from the sale of sportsmen's licenses rose from £ 1,600 in 1902 to more than £ 9,000 in 1906.[42] Part of this revenue was invested into conservation through the creation of a Game Department that remained, however, chronically understaffed and underfunded. Hunting safaris boomed and were so popular by 1907 that the Colonial Office soothed concerns about overexploitation with the argument that no more than five hundred sportsmen licenses would be issued annually.[43] When Ruprecht Böcklin von Böcklinsau, a German baron and peer of the Baden Parliament, returned to Nairobi from a three weeks' safari in January 1911, he found "about 80 safaris" ready to venture out – "Lucky man I am that I got out ahead of them! I got all my big game – après moi le déluge! – It's going to be like Picadilly a couple of miles behind me."[44]

The reservation of the spectacular species of game for wealthy hunters was enmeshed in the overall contestation over access to, respectively, "ownership" of wild animals among various interest groups in East Africa's colonial societies. Settlers of more modest means were bitter about their exclusion from a charged ritual. Gentlemanly settlers, however, were often involved in the hunting business as professional hunters and profited from the boom. As owners of extensive lands, they were also among the first critics of the extent, geography, and concrete means of

---

[42] *Correspondence Relating to the Preservation of Wild Animals in Africa* (London 1906) (= Parliamentary Papers, Vol. lxxix, 25), enclosure in no. 220: Memorandum of Deputy Commissioner Frederick J. Jackson on the question of game preservation, February, 1906; the figures ibid., enclosure in no. 203, Commissioner Jackson to CO, August 25, 1905, and no. 224, Colonel Hayes Sadler to Earl of Elgin, Secretary of States for the Colonies, June 9, 1906.

[43] *Further Correspondence Relating to the Preservation of Wild Animals in Africa* (London 1909), Enclosure to no. 5, Report by Arthur Blayney Percival, 19; ibid., no. 23: Colonial Office to SPWFE and the editor of *The Field*, May 22, 1907. A German hunting entrepreneur guessed the number of shooting parties visiting British East Africa at three hundred to four hundred in 1913, see Friedrich Wilhelm Siedentopf, "Deutsch-Ostafrika und Britisch-Ostafrika," *Wild und Hund* 19 (1913): 335.

[44] Staatsarchiv Freiburg U 101/1, No. 9: Diary entries January 12 and 14, 1911.

game conservation for the hunting of wealthy outsiders. While the game laws became slightly more accommodating to white settlers, for example, by introducing a traveler's license that enabled settlers to invite tourists to hunt on their estates, Africans remained excluded from access to wildlife until more participatory schemes were introduced in the 1950s.

The conservation of big game for the consumption by Western hunters reshuffled the relationship between luxury and necessity. The unavoidable exclusion to render game a luxury for the visiting hunter often increased the necessity of hunting for those who bore the brunt of exclusion in their everyday coexistence with large predators and herbivores. Not only did exclusive hunting rights interfere heavily with local subsistence hunting, but also the transmission of dangerous diseases as well as crop damage through wildlife constituted a structural conflict between wildlife conservation and land use for agriculture and cattle farming. Moreover, the competing claims of humans and animals to land and water increased in frequency and intensity as a consequence of population growth and the extension of agriculture. From the 1920s onward, one of the Game Department's main tasks was the mitigation of crop predation through large-scale schemes of wild-animal control.

Human-wildlife conflicts were particularly fierce in the vicinity of game reserves, which had been introduced in both German and British East Africa since the 1890s. Established above all as sanctuaries for the game and thus for the sake of preservation, reserves did equally form part of the economic rationale behind safari hunting. From the outset, they were assigned the purpose to produce overflow populations that could be hunted in their immediate surroundings. This said, we know surprisingly little about the concrete spatial ecology of safari hunting – the changing boom-regions and how outfitters tailored their target destinations according to the wishes of their clients; how visiting shooting parties interacted with local communities; and how their off take of game influenced local ecologies and the degree to which tourist hunting was, for example, associated with game-control schemes to mitigate crop damage by wildlife.[45] For decades, the Athi Plains outside the Southern Reserve in Kenya counted among the foremost destinations for shooting parties, and many of the hunting blocks and wildlife management areas that were earmarked as target zones for hunting safaris since the 1950s followed

[45] The 1921 Game Ordinance, e.g., granted additional entitlements to wildebeest if license holders shot them in the Southern Maasai Reserve, probably in order to diminish a source of infection and competition for grazing for both the cattle of Maasai and white settlers in the vicinity.

a similar complementary logic of preservation and utilization. The most popular among them were often situated as buffer zones just outside national parks.[46]

THE DECADENCE OF THE ARCHAIC: SAFARI AS A LUXURY PRACTICE

The East African safari combined the archaic drama of life and death in the hunt with lavish expenditure that seems, at first sight, out of place and unfitting to the illusion of the primitive. However, it is exactly this characteristic juxtaposition of decadence with the archaic that made the safari a luxury, despite itself. There was a constant tension between hedonistic amenities and ascetic naturalness. Safari hunters and their admirers were untiring throughout the decades to portray their activity as a necessary return to the authentic, primitive, and simple, "a grand corrective", as one sympathetic observer put it, "to super-refinement and luxury run riot."[47]

It is not without irony that the safari, hailed here as a remedy against effeminating luxuries, itself increasingly became associated with luxury. But where did necessity end and luxury begin? The answer to this question did not only depend on individual judgment and hunting socialization. It was subject to constant transcultural negotiation and the ongoing politics of distinction that characterized the safari. For hunters "accustomed to the rough camping of North America," for example, "the idea of having from twenty-five to forty porters besides a cook, headman, and a tent boy, to say nothing of a couple of Askaris" may have appeared "positively ridiculous" at first encounter.[48] Such distinctions between the pragmatic American frontier hunter and the extravagance of the pampered Briton point to the importance of different cultural and ideological frames in which hunting abroad was made meaningful. In their mixture of criticism and envy, they were exactly the stuff on which discourses of luxury thrived. In actual practice, however, the line between necessity and

---

[46] For a critique see Roderick P. Neumann, "Primitive Ideas: Protected Area Buffer Zones and the Politics of Land in Africa," *Development and Change* 28 (1997): 559–82.

[47] See, e.g., Hilda V. Moffat, "On Safari," *Cornhill Magazine* 12 (March 1902): 376.

[48] Arthur Radclyffe Dugmore, *Camera Adventures in the African Wilds, Being an Account of a Four Months' Expedition in British East Africa for the Purpose of Securing Photographs of the Game from Life* (New York: Doubleday, Page and Company, 1910), 200; see also Stewart Edward White, *The Land of Footprints* (London et al.: Doubleday, Page and Company, [1912]), 443–7.

amenity was always blurred. Aspects and items that were frowned upon as superfluous by outside observers, such as a large entourage, bathtub, cutlery, or the white dinner jacket, were regarded as indispensable in practice, especially as the use and display of these amenities marked the hunters as "civilized."[49] The constant tensions and negotiations arising from rivaling and shifting assumptions about what was morally acceptable and what was not, what constituted a necessity, and what constituted an indulgence contributed to the allure of the safari as a distinctive practice as well as to its moral dubiousness that would increasingly prevail in the second half of the twentieth century.

Other elements that rendered safari hunting a luxury practice were rather straightforward. In the 1890s as well as in the 1960s, leisure travel to East Africa constituted a luxury, accessible only to the privileged few who commanded the wealth to indulge in such practice. Often, the emulative and conspicuous consumption of a luxury sooner or later results in the percolation of its consumption down the social scale. To a certain degree, this was also true of big-game hunting. The safety of travel guaranteed by colonial rule together with the ever-more comprehensive packaging by outfitters allowed for the occasional adolescent to be initiated into the hunt by his father in Africa. Honeymoon safaris, too, increased in popularity. The appearance of women and spouses on the hunting scene, while unable to undermine the discursive hegemony of man the hunter, at least contributed to expose the constructed character of claims about the "natural" masculinity of hunting.[50] The postwar safari boom of the 1950s and 1960s, also attracted a growing number of "people who had little or no interest in the hunt" and merely followed a fashion "to get out of the rut."[51]

However, social emulation had its clear limits. The individualistic nature of hunting, the unavoidable disturbance of wildlife, and the overall imperative not to tax game populations too heavily all put a structural ceiling on the number of customers that could be admitted per season.

---

[49] Helen Callaway, "Dressing for Dinner in the Bush: Rituals of Self-Definition and British Imperial Authority," in *Dress and Gender: Making and Meaning in Cultural Contexts*, ed. Ruth Barnes and Joanne B. Eicher (Providence: Berg, 1992), 232–47.

[50] Cf. Kenneth P. Czech, *With Rifle and Petticoat: Women as Big Game Hunters, 1880–1940* (Lanham, MD and New York: Derrydale Press, 2002), 123–60; Andrea L. Smalley, "'I Just like to kill things': Women, Men, and the Gender of Sport Hunting in the United States, 1940–1973," *Gender and History* 17 (2005): 183–209.

[51] Elspeth Huxley, "The Safari Business Is Booming," *New York Times*, June 19, 1960, SM11, 23, 25; Stephen R. Conn, "Safaris Give the Social Set Another Way to Get Out of the Rut," *New York Times*, April 28, 1968, 84.

Socialization into hunting was another important predisposition. But the most important restriction remained capital. Depending on individual requirements and indulgences, the aggregate cost of travel, equipment, taxes, license, and shooting fees could achieve forbidding dimensions. In the early twentieth century, British sources estimated the necessary expenses between one hundred and two hundred pounds per month, including the journey from London or New York.[52] Contemporary German sources reckoned it cost between 8,000 and 10,500 Marks for a three-month safari – at least eight times the average annual income of a contemporary German worker.[53] The introduction of motorcars and wireless as standard equipment of safaris after World War II made prices go up further. Around 1960, the expenses for U.S. hunting clients were guessed at around $8,000 for a safari of one month.[54] "If a fellow makes up his mind when he's 20 to go on safari," one U.S.-safari organizer commented arrogantly in the late 1960s, "he can do it by the time he's 40 – if he saves his money."[55]

It was, however, not only the gatekeeping effect of wealth that created luxury, but the desire of aspirants to do as the wealthy do. From the outset, this envy was fanned by corporate marketing that equally created, exploited, and reinforced the safari's exclusiveness. Safari became a luxury also because it was marketed as such by shipping and railway companies and a fledgling safari industry consisting of a handful of enterprising British, Germans, and Americans plus the Australians Newland and Tarlton, who became the prime outfitter in Kenya before World War I. Together with the transport companies, these business pioneers commercialized big-game hunting and unfolded an astonishingly elaborate corporate marketing that successfully branded Kenya as the land of "safari."

Probably the first on the market in late 1905 was a voluminous brochure on "Big Game Shooting in East Africa" issued by the Mombasa (B.E.A.) Trading and Development Syndicate.[56] One year later, German

---

[52] Cameron, *Into Africa*, 57–8.

[53] A. Hauter, "Einiges über Jagdreisen nach Ostafrika," *Deutsche Jägerzeitung* 60 (1912–13): 681–2; "Zoologie und Sport, Löwenhöhe (Britisch-Ostafrika)," *Deutsch-Ostafrikanische Zeitung* 10, no. 88 (14 November 1908), 12; Chas. A. Heyen, "Kosten einer Jagdexpedition in Britisch-Ostafrika," *Wild und Hund* 13 (1907): 539–40.

[54] Ibid. and Huxley, *The Safari Business*; Robert M. Lee, "Safari Costs," *New York Times*, July 10, 1960, SM 2. See also "Easier Tracks to Big Game," *The Times*, June 14, 1958, 7. The figures provided by Bull, *Safari*, 295, are even higher.

[55] Conn, *Safaris*, 84.

[56] A copy of the brochure is held, e.g., in Bundesarchiv Berlin-Lichterfelde R1001/13, enclosure to fol. 59, Mombasa Trading and Development Syndicate to German Foreign Office, Colonial Department, February 16, 1906.

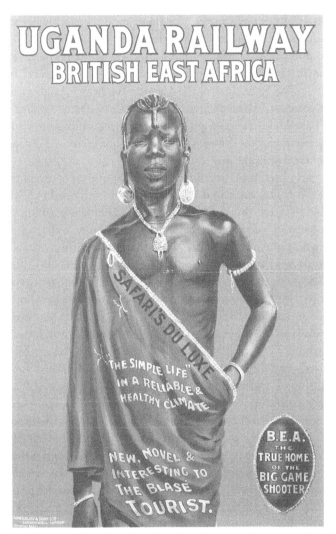

FIGURE 24. An exotistic and racist advert for big-game hunting in Kenya by the Uganda Railway Company, pre–World War I. "Uganda Railway."
Source: Stationers' Company. Courtesy of Jon Williamson, www.jonwilliamson .com/template_permalink.asp?id=5841.

expatriate Richard Huebner, having established a base for hunting expeditions in Kibwezi along the Uganda Railway, brought his "Notes for Hunting Expeditions to British East Africa" to the attention of the German-speaking hunting world. His brochure resonated particularly well among landed aristocrats in the Austro-Hungarian Empire. From 1908 onward, the Uganda Railway Company issued its famous posters advertising the railway journey "through nature's zoo" and "safaris de luxe" with "a maximum of comfort and a minimum of risk."[57] Another brochure published by the company in 1909 or early 1910 featured a lioness on the frontispiece and promised hunters "real sport" by taking "a 303 or a 450 Express over the Uganda Railway." At about the same time, the company also coedited a forty-page booklet together with the German East Africa Steamship line to advertise hunting safaris in Kenya on the German market – a remarkable instance of business cooperation across imperial boundaries.[58]

These early brochures and adverts of safari outfitters reveal that it did not take the transcontinental media coverage of Theodore Roosevelt's safari in 1909–10 to throw East Africa into the limelight of hunting tourism. The Kenyan safari business had achieved an astonishing degree of packaging and integration before, and already the early touristic encounters with the wild were occasions of organized uniqueness – thoroughly rationalized undertakings enabled by a globalized logistic network and the achievements of Western modernity. The flurry of brochures of the 1900s also shows how the corporeal mobility of hunters was preceded by the mobilization of imaginaries that shaped powerful and lasting "destination images."[59] All of them deployed the myths of the unchanged, the unrestrained, and the uncivilized, which have been identified as central to the marketing of tourism in so-called Third World countries,[60] but are in fact deeply anchored in imperial narratives of hunting and exploration. The illusion of an archetypical, first encounter between man and beast in a landscape of deep time was one of several pasts that safari marketing exploited. Later advertising also capitalized on colonial nostalgia and marketed the reenactment of the allegedly authentic experience that had been available to pioneering safari hunters. The imaginaries of place and practice that characterized the publications of hunters and safari operators were readily taken up in the mass media who responded to the news values of exoticness, celebrity involvement, and strong emotions. Popular illustrated or lifestyle magazines, like the *Illustrated London News* or the

---

[57] *Deutsche Ost-Afrika-Linie, Uganda Railway: Die Uganda-Eisenbahn, Britisch-Ostafrika* ([London, around 1908]), adverts following p. 31.

[58] Copies of these brochures are held, e.g., in Staatsarchiv Freiburg U 101/1, Papers of Rupert Böcklin von Böcklinsau.

[59] See Salazar, *Envisioning Eden*, and Andrew Norton, "Experiencing Nature: The Reproduction of Environmental Discourse through Safari Tourism in East Africa," *Geoforum* 27 (1996): 355–73.

[60] Charlotte M. Echtner and Pushkala Prasad, "The Context of Third World Tourism Marketing," *Annals of Tourism Research* 30 (2003): 660–82.

U.S. *Life* and *Esquire*, repeatedly covered the "bringing down of dangerous giants" approvingly as a desirable form of masculine leisure.[61] Also
the travel sections of West German quality newspapers kept providing a
forum for elite hunters and promoted safaris as the "greatest attraction"
on the international tourism market throughout the 1950s.[62] Thereby,
they did not only help recruit new customers, but also created the cultural
background necessary for the functioning of the safari and its trophies as
forms of social communication.

The commercialization of the safari as a luxurious yet standardized
leisure practice triggered an autopoietic process of inventing, redefining,
and shifting forms and practices of distinction and singularity. As soon
as railway and commercial outfitters had turned the Kenyan safari into
a reliable and comfortable affair, hunters began to displace the "real"
and "authentic" safari experience elsewhere, within Kenya and beyond.
Thereby, other places were colonized as primitive and wild and brought
into the purview of international tourism. In the 1960s, a U.S.-couple
preferred Chad over East Africa because, amongst others, "We eat with
our hands there; in the east, they use a knife and fork"[63] – the more primitive, the more refinement. The quest for distinction did not only work
through places, but equally through time, practice, or prey: the packaged
safari of three months was trumped by the luxury of an even longer version; the introduction of motorcars created the niche of the authentic
foot safari; and the voraciousness that often accompanied licensed trophy hunting enabled distinction through selectivity. In the 1960s, Toddie
Lee Wynne Jr., President of the American Liberty Oil Company of Dallas
and part owner of the Dallas Cowboys football team, took pride from
being allegedly the first person "ever to shoot a bongo and a situtunga"
on one and the same safari.[64] Even the most unlikely "first" could be utilized as a marker of distinction.

Distribution through travel agents and taxidermists ensured that the
early efforts to market safari hunting as a luxury reached their target
audience. Marketing brochures advertised with the names, trophies, and

---

[61] See, e.g., "Helicopter Safari in Africa," *Life*, June 10, 1957, 80–93; "A Sentimental
Safari in 'T.R.' Tradition," *Life*, November 10, 1961, 52–8; "A Sentimental Safari," *Life*,
April 19, 1963, 88–99; cf. Bill Osgerby, *Playboys in Paradise: Masculinity, Youth and
Leisure-style in Modern America* (Oxford: Berg, 2001).

[62] See, e.g., "Heia Safari: Auf Jagd mit Büchse und Kamera," *Frankfurter Allgemeine
Zeitung*, September 6, 1958, 45; "Eine Safari ist kein Spaziergang," ibid., January 12,
1955, 8; "Elefanten sind billiger als kapitale Hirsche," ibid., November 17, 1958, 12.

[63] Conn, *Safaris*, 84.

[64] Ibid.

praise of distinguished customers, who often not only lent their names but acted as honorary representatives of safari companies in Europe. Marketing efforts of safari operators interacted with other arenas of upper-class conviviality and exclusive networks of communication. Many a safari originated in aristocratic, business, or professional elite networks; personal acquaintances; or the cosmopolitan atmosphere of London's gentlemanly clubs.[65]

Indeed, the desire to bag a lion did not spring from an individual want of experience alone, but also because those acknowledged as socially equal or superior used it to communicate status and distinction. In addition, celebrity sanction bestowed respectability upon a practice that increasingly begged justification in the face of decreasing wildlife numbers and growing demands for complete preservation. The list of political leaders, society celebrities, writers, business tycoons, and millionaires who came after Roosevelt is so extensive that it is impossible to name but the most conspicuous ones. Before World War I, the safari bore a decidedly aristocratic stamp. Representatives of virtually all European royal houses partook in imperial expansion by proxy of a hunting expedition into the tropics. Members of the British royal family, like the Prince of Wales (later Edward VIII) in 1928 and 1930[66] or Princess Elizabeth and Prince Philip in 1952, went on safari as a leadership-confirming conduct, but also as part of sampling and integrating the empire. European lifestyle celebrities and gentleman playboys of the 1950s, like Gunter Sachs or Prince Ali Khan, reanimated the dazzle of the Kenyan safari after it had lain dormant during the war. The examples of the big-game hunting Prince Philip in the United Kingdom and Prince Bernhard of the Netherlands illustrate the shifting relationship between celebrity and wildlife in Europe since the 1960s: the hunting networks of both have been imperative in enlisting business circles and social elites in the founding of the World Wildlife Fund (WWF) in 1961, and many national chapters of the fledgling WWF were headed by men whose interest in the preservation of the more spectacular species of wildlife had been mediated through hunting. Within a few years, however, both luminaries had to abandon their controversial pastime as it became increasingly irreconcilable with the preservationist

---

[65] Cf. Amy Milne-Smith, "Club Talk: Gossip, Masculinity, and the Importance of Oral Communities in Late Nineteenth-Century London," *Gender and History* 21 (2009): 86–106.

[66] The Prince of Wales' safari triggered a veritable rush of emulation in the early 1930s, see Kenya National Archives DC/TTA/1/1, Annual Report, Taita District 1931, 28.

mission and public image of the organization.[67] In the United States, a not yet fathomed number of industrial magnates and millionaires followed Roosevelt, including George Eastman of Kodak; *LA Times* publisher Otis Chandler; Edgar M. Queeny, the longtime board chairman of Monsanto Chemical; or millionaire sportsman George Vanderbilt, who afforded his own little plane for game spotting on his 1935 honeymoon safari.[68]

And then, of course, there was Ernest Hemingway. Apart from adding psychological self-exploration and a sexually charged metaphorism to big-game hunting, his writings elevated the subject from the depth of often-sensational travel accounts into the realm of high literature. Together with the romanticization of hunting and professional white hunters in Karen Blixen's *Out of Africa* and other Kenya novels of the 1930s, Hemingway forged a sentimentalized image of the safari as an outlet for adventurous masculinity in a paradise of wildlife. These writings nourished the East African safari boom in the United States after 1945 and invited followers like the newspaper columnist Robert Ruark. His account, published under the title *Horn of the Hunter* in 1953, turned into one of the most successful hunting books ever and continued the boost that the safari received from literature.[69]

Leaving aside the nexus of emulation and social distinction, the changing social composition of safari hunters as well as the geography of their origins need yet to be substantiated by empirical research.[70] European aristocrats surely dominated the scene before 1914, supplemented by American millionaires and industrial tycoons since the interwar years, while American wealth provided an estimated "nine customers out of every ten"[71] in the 1950s and 1960s. Yet, the concrete motifs and values of all those "Texas oilmen, the German noveaux riches, the occasional French president, various forms of multi-nationalist wealth or leisured and superannuated aristocrats"[72] beg further investigation. They may have engaged in the same practice, but what did it mean

---

[67] On Prince Bernhard and the European royalty in the founding generation of the WWF, see Alexis Schwarzenbach, *Saving the World's Wildlife: The WWF's First Fifty Years* (London: Profile, 2011), 77–81.

[68] Czech, *With Rifle and Petticoat*, 154.

[69] Terry Wieland, *A View from a Tall Hill: Robert Ruark in Africa* (Camden: Countrysport Press, 2000), 115.

[70] Steinhart, *Black Poachers*, 136 provides a few hints, but his approach is predominantly typological.

[71] Huxley, *The Safari Business*, SM11, 23, 25.

[72] MacKenzie, *Empire of Nature*, 308–9.

for British imperial elites to hunt in a colony on the verge of independence, a *Wirtschaftswunder* German industrialist to hunt over the former "German East," or for that "Memphis, Tennessee cotton man" who encouraged his fourteen-year-old daughter to shoot one of the biggest elephants in postwar Kenya and turn it into a wastebasket?[73] Equally uncharted are the cultural politics behind the safari of non-Western luminaries who inscribed their own values into a cultural practice of Western supremacy. Sultan Muhammad Shah, the third Aga Khan and imam of the Ismaili Muslims, combined his visits to the Ismaili communities in East Africa with the opportunity of a hunting safari since the early 1900s,[74] and he was followed by the Maharajas of Datia or Umaid Singh of Jodhpur. King Mahendra of Nepal went hunting in Kenya incognito in the late 1950s, while Prince Abdorreza Pahlavi, a member of the Persian royal family, became one of the most prolific global hunters of the second half of the twentieth century.[75] Their repeated high-end safaris in Kenya show that the celebrity effect was by no means restricted to Europe and the United States. The safari commended itself not only as a practice to claim belonging to an international elite, but also as a continuation of Asian traditions of royal and elite hunting; as a stage for the display of lavish splendor and nonindustrial wealth; and, for the hundreds of Indian princely rulers, an ostensible compensation for the loss of political status after the formation of the Indian Union in 1947. Indeed, the combination of primitive outdoor life with champagne and whisky on the rocks, a trademark of Western safaris, appears frugal compared to the pomp one Indian Maharaja unfolded, probably in the 1950s. Perhaps a sign of overcompensation, he mobilized a fleet of vehicles from Europe and America to carry a "mobile wireless receiving and transmitting station, a van for cinematography which included a screen and projector and armchair seats from which the Maharajah could watch wild animal films [!], an elaborately equipped kitchen, generating plants" and further lorries

[73] "Speaking of Pictures ... a 14-Year-Old Big-Game Huntress Poses with Her Trophies," *Life*, September 29, 1947, 18–20. The uncritical picture story of the "Diana heroine" evoked some disgusted letters to the editor, see *Life*, October 20, 1947, 12, 14.

[74] "The Aga Khan's Tribute to British Rule," *The Times*, March 13, 1937, 11; [Muhammad Shah], *The Memoirs of Aga Khan: World Enough and Time* (London: Cassell, 1954), and picture opposite p. 271. On his membership in London clubs and his passion for gentlemanly British endeavors like horse racing see Anne Edwards, *Throne of Gold: The Lives of the Aga Khans* (London: Harper Collins, 1995). The fourth Aga Khan would become a major investor in high-end safari lodges in East African National Parks.

[75] William R. Quimby, *Royal Quest: The Hunting Saga of H.I.H. Prince Abdorreza Pahlavi of Iran* (Long Beach, CA: Safari Press, 2004).

with an X-ray unit, a drawing room with piano, and, last but by no means least, several chemical lavatories.[76]

Apparently, even a portaloo could become a distinguishing feature on safari, but the more usual media to render conspicuous what hunters did "in the bush" were text, picture, and trophy. Since the late nineteenth century, photographs had served as the visual complement to textual representations of hunting, and the image of imperial man the hunter, perched atop the body of a slain animal and surrounded by African bystanders, certainly counts among the lasting generic icons of the imperial age.[77] In as far as the camera captured the vanquished animal opponent a second time after its death, photographs were a derivative form of the ultimate and most tangible objective of the hunters' desire: the body of the hunted prey as the actual trophy and proof of the hunters' victory and mastery over the game. Depending on purpose and financial input, trophies were prepared in a variety of forms. Not only body parts, such as horns, tusks, and skins, but also mounted heads or the "fictions of liveness"[78] created by real size, reanimated dermoplastic models still communicated the association of the hunter with the characteristics and values ascribed to the vanquished opponent. These trophies tried to restore a minimum of dignity to the killed specimen that was entirely missing in cases in which the body parts of wild animals were transformed into household decor and furniture, such as elephant feet worked into umbrella stands, sofas upholstered in zebra skins, zebra-skin watch straps and wallets – or the leopard-skin lining in the Rolls Royce of the Maharaja of Baroda.[79]

Tourist hunters working their trophies into souvenirs that deindividualized the original prey became more widespread in the broader context of the postwar safari boom. Yet, they remained the exception rather than the rule because hunters usually respected the trophy as a unique material reference to a particular personal encounter with one particular specimen of game. It was taken as the result of a "fair" contest and should preserve

[76] J. A. Hunter, *Hunter's Tracks* (New York: Appleton-Century-Crofts, 1957), 212.

[77] James R. Ryan, *Picturing Empire: Photography and the Visualization of the British Empire* (Chicago: University of Chicago Press, 1997); Dunaway, *Hunting with the Camera*; Wonders, *Hunting Narratives*; Bernhard Gissibl, "Exotische 'Natururkunden': Tierfotografie im Kontext des deutschen Kolonialismus," in *nützlich, süß und museal: Das fotografierte Tier*, ed. Ute Eskildsen and Hans-Jürgen Lechtreck (Göttingen: Steidl, 2005), 60–9.

[78] Jane Desmond, "Displaying Death, Animating Life: Changing Fictions of 'Liveness' from Taxidermy to Animatronics," in *Representing Animals*, ed. Nigel Rothfels (Bloomington: Indiana University Press, 2002), 159–79.

[79] "Maharaja's Birthday," *Life*, May 24, 1948, 40–1.

FIGURE 25. The East African trophy exhibition of German Colonial Official Fritz Bronsart von Schellendorff (Karlsruhe, 1903).
Source: Koloniales Bildarchiv. Courtesy of Koloniales Bildarchiv, Universitätsbibliothek Frankfurt/Main, 011-1200-1.

as much as possible of the characteristics of the individual animal.[80] A trophy could not be bought, but had to be gained, and its value was personal, exclusive, unique, and, therefore, inconvertible into cash. If a trophy was put on display, it was always the hunter who was on display, too.[81] What remained usually eclipsed was the whole chain of transcontinental mobilization and organization of labor that enabled the trophy's acquisition, including the work of trackers, skinners, and porters. Instead,

[80] The broader trend of the safari's entering the world of commodities, complementary to the rise of the photo safari as a leisure practice of the middle classes, lies beyond the purview of this chapter. Starting with outdoor clothing, the term *safari* came to bestow an aura of adventure, exoticness, and sport to things as diverse as TV sets, typewriters, station cars, and a pen that could be loaded with "two cartridges of liquid ink," as contemporary adverts for these products show, e.g. in *Life* magazine. Safari-style interior decoration as a commodity beyond the trophy rooms of individual hunters was part of this process and would warrant further research.

[81] See Linda Kalof and Amy Fitzgerald, "Reading the Trophy: Exploring the Display of Dead Animals in Hunting Magazines," *Visual Studies* 18 (2003): 112–22; Wonders, *Hunting Narratives*.

the trophy conflated hunter and hunted in a symbolic relationship that could almost be described as sympathetic magic,[82] indicating as it did the hunter's appropriation of the qualities ascribed to the respective species and its habitat. It is, therefore, no coincidence that those body parts were turned into trophies that expressed the strength and fitness of sexually dimorphic species, such as the horns or the mane of a lion.

The material exploits of safari hunters became, first and foremost, part of private collections and adorned the walls of stairways, entrance halls, or separate trophy rooms in landed estates as well as banker's apartments in downtown New York. They served private delectation, memory, and self-affirmation, and marked their owner as virile, close to nature, and widely traveled in the eyes of visitors. And while a lion or a zebra rug could add a tactile and sensual dimension to the memory and experience enshrined in the trophy, the predominant effect of a wall of horns and heads was the creation of an atmosphere that sympathetic observers often described as sacral and awe inspiring.[83] Put up in other contexts, trophies could convey a multiplicity of further messages. In colonial and international exhibitions, they accrued cultural capital and social recognition for the hunter at the same time as they asserted imperial domination, reduced colonial rule to an exotic adventure, promised rich natural resources, or expressed the revisionist romanticism of a lost colonial paradise, as was the case with trophies from Tanganyika or Namibia displayed in German colonial exhibitions after World War I. Finally, trophies that ended up as dermoplastic models or part of habitat groups in natural history museums, bestowed an aura of scientific purpose upon the hunter that was often used as an apology for the act of killing the animal in the first place.

Since World War II, exhibitions, but also natural history museums, ceased to provide a context for putting trophies on display for broader audiences. The consumption of trophies became an increasingly private affair, at least, until the Internet provided a new arena for hunters' exchange and communication. Yet, there has been one continuous and entirely virtual platform for the display of trophies that can hardly be

---

[82] In its classic definition by anthropologist James George Frazer, sympathetic magic implies that "like produces like" and that "things which have once been in contact with each other continue to act on each other at a distance after the physical contact has been severed," see James George Frazer, *The Golden Bough: A Study in Magic and Religion, Abridged Version* (New York: Macmillan, 1922), 11.

[83] See, e.g., Lutz Heck, Vorwort (Foreword) to *Auf großer Pirsch in Eis und Tropen*, by Carl Horst Andreas (Gütersloh: S. Mohn, 1965), 5; see also Donna Haraway, *Primate Visions: Gender, Race, and Nature in the World of Modern Science* (New York and London: Routledge, 1989), 26.

overestimated in its significance for hunters: Rowland Ward's authoritative *Records of Big Game*. First published in 1892,[84] the book has served ever since as a handbook that informed hunters about the geographic distributions and characteristics of all species that were hunted as game worldwide. But above all, it compiled the benchmark data for what constituted a trophy in terms of size, weight, and measurement in the respective game species, and the description of each species and its trophies is followed by long lists of those hunters who have obtained the biggest trophies in recorded hunting history. Hunters measured prowess in size, and, undeniably, Ward's recording motivated hunters' chasing for records and guided their actions in the field. Although professional hunters occasionally complained about clients trying to assemble "as many world records as could be managed,"[85] they had a vested interest that their customers obtained the best possible trophies. Between 1955 and the disintegration of the association in 1977, the East African Professional Hunters' Association (EAPHA) annually awarded the prestigious Shaw & Hunter trophy to the professional hunter whose client shot the most outstanding game trophy of the season.

A PASTIME OF THE IMPOTENT? THE END OF SAFARI HUNTING

Safe in the knowledge that preservationism would ultimately prevail, Edward Steinhart's social history of Kenyan hunting makes virtually no mention that after World War II, three decades of safari hunting actually preceded the ban of 1977. If we avoid such reading of history backward, a different picture emerges. Despite the slumps during postwar recovery and the Mau Mau Uprising, more hunting safaris visited Kenya than ever before. EAPHA membership reached new heights, and the development and planning onslaught of the late colonial state resulted in a "postwar conservation boom" that reverberated beyond the establishment of the first permanent national parks in Kenya.[86] The multifaceted efforts to reconstruct imperial legitimacy also included elaborate land planning

---

[84] The first edition of 1892 was entitled *Horn Measurements and Weights of the Great Game of the World*, being a record for the use of sportsmen and naturalists (London 1892). From 1896 onward, the book retained the title *Records of Big Game*, with subtitles varying in subsequent editions.

[85] Hunter, *Hunter's Tracks*, 213.

[86] Roderick Neumann, "The Postwar Conservation Boom in British Colonial Africa," *Environmental History* 7 (2002): 22–47. On the framework of postwar development and planning see Frederick Cooper, "Reconstructing British and French Empire after 1945," *Past and Present* 210, no. 6 (2011): 196–210.

for tourist hunting and attempts at sharing some of the benefits from wildlife utilization with African communities. During the 1950s, Game Controlled Areas (GCAs) were created in both Kenya and Tanganyika. Further subdivided into hunting blocks, they pursued the aim to generate revenue also in peripheral areas and encourage African residents' concern for game conservation on their land. Any of the eighty-eight hunting blocks all over Kenya needed to be booked well in advance, and one of the aims was to diversify the income from safari hunting and direct tourist hunters into regions off the beaten safari tracks. The constant assessment of game stocks by wardens should guarantee sustainable off-takes, and the fees levied for permits to enter the GCAs were supposed to end up in the coffers of the respective African District Council. It is hard to assess if such plans in fact entailed tangible benefits for communities, especially as government authorities were determined to reclaim trophy hunting as "a Central Government responsibility"[87] after independence. Nonetheless, the hunting block system remained in operation, and in 1972, tourist hunters contributed 9 percent of Kenya's tourist revenues, although they made up less than 1 percent of all visitors.[88] Undeniably, tourist hunting provided an incentive to conserve game beyond national parks, as well as it helped keep populations in check in these areas. Planners stressed the potential for further extension of GCAs, and pilot projects funded by the United Nation's special agencies strove to strengthen the link between tourist hunting, wildlife utilization, and local communities.[89] As late as 1975, a governmental paper warned "that the potentially large and secure export market[s] for the products of consumptive wildlife utilization" should not be "foreclosed through ignorant 'preservationist' pressure."[90]

---

[87] *Ramogi Achieng Oneko, Minister of Information, Broadcasting and Tourism, in the Kenya National Assembly, August 1, 1963* (= Official Report, Vol. I, Pt. II), 1624.

[88] Philip Thresher, *Some Economic Problems of Wildlife Utilisation in Kajiado District.* Working Paper 124 (Nairobi: Institute for Development Studies, University of Nairobi, 1973).

[89] Ibid.; Wendell Swank, *Cropping, Processing and Marketing of Wildlife in Kajiado District, Kenya* (Nairobi: FAO, 1974); Reuben M. Matheka, "Antecedents to the Community Wildlife Conservation Programme in Kenya, 1946–1964," *Environment and History* 11 (2005): 239–67.

[90] Quoted after Ngeta Kabiri, "Historic and Contemporary Struggles for a Local Wildlife Governance Regime in Kenya," in *Community Rights, Conservation and Contested Land: The Politics of Natural Resource Management in Africa*, ed. Fred Nelson (London: Earthscan, 2010), 136; Nigel Leader-Williams, "The Effects of a Century of Policy and Legal Change on Wildlife Conservation and Utilization in Tanzania," in *Wildlife Conservation by Sustainable Use*, ed. Prins, Grootenhuis, and Dolan, 219–45.

The ongoing flow of trophy-doting hunters, the realized revenue, the planning invested into reconciling safari hunting with sustainable wildlife management and community development as well as the growing popularity of private game ranching and other schemes to utilize and manage wildlife beyond parks in many Southern African countries[91] should all caution against reading too much inevitability into the enactment of hunting bans in both Kenya and Tanzania in the 1970s. Of course, preservationist critique and humanitarian condemnation of "the silliest form of luxury – the killing of animals for the mere amusement of rich people" had accompanied the hunting safari since the late nineteenth century.[92] Rampant urbanization and the further dissociation of Western societies from "nature," the new and leftist environmentalism of the 1960s, advances in the wildlife-related sciences, and impending decolonization all contributed to the further sacralization of allegedly pristine wildernesses and a general revaluation of wildlife as a unique heritage beyond tangible consumption. Rising incomes enabled a growing number of tourists the embodied close-up encounter with wildlife from the safety of a four-wheel drive, while hugely popular wildlife films enabled those staying at home an even closer virtual intimacy with Africa's wildlife that subverted the hunters' framing of their charisma. The image of the threatening brute was replaced by the fascination with harmless, petlike creatures who had complex social lives and personalities and were threatened by human greed and folly.[93]

The degree to which this revaluation undermined the legitimacy of big-game hunting as a form of heroic masculinity is perhaps best

[91] Jane Carruthers, "'Wilding the Farm or Farming the Wild?' The Evolution of Scientific Game Ranching in South Africa from the 1960s to the Present," *Transactions of the Royal Society of South Africa* 63 (2008): 160–81.

[92] Henry Salt, "The Sportsman at Bay," *International Journal of Ethics* 16 (1906): 491; cf. Ernest Bell, "Big Game Hunting," in *Killing for Sport: Essays by Various Writers*, ed. Henry S. Salt (London: G. Bell, 1914), 101–15; Dan Weinbren, "Against All Cruelty: The Humanitarian League, 1891–1919," *History Workshop* 38 (1994): 86–105; Mieke Roscher, *Ein Königreich für Tiere: Die Geschichte der britischen Tierrechtsbewegung* (Marburg: Tectum, 2009).

[93] Greg Mittman, *Reel Nature: America's Romance with Wildlife on Film* (Cambridge, MA: Harvard University Press, 1999); id., "Pachyderm Personalities: The Media of Science, Politics, and Conservation," in *Thinking with Animals: New Perspectives on Anthropomorphism*, ed. Lorraine Daston and Greg Mittman (New York: Columbia University Press, 2005), 176–95; Franziska Torma, *Eine Naturschutzkampagne in der Ära Adenauer: Bernhard Grzimeks Afrikafilme in den Medien der 50er Jahre* (Munich: Martin Meidenbauer, 2004). For a recent review of the literature, see William Beinart and Katie McKeown, "Wildlife Media and Representations of Africa, 1950s to the 1970s," *Environmental History* 14 (2009): 429–52.

encapsulated by a controversy of international celebrity conservationist Bernhard Grzimek with two members of Germany's trophy-hunting industrial and political elite in the second half of the 1950s. The latter invoked the established stereotypes of the civilized white hunter and the barbarous black poacher and rehearsed all arguments of hunting as a form of conservation funding and management. Their doubts about an overall decrease of wildlife were probably more to the point than the undifferentiated and gloomy "No Room for Wild Animals" alarmism of Bernhard Grzimek, at least at that time.[94] Yet, it was Grzimek who left the debate victorious. He stripped big-game hunting of its heroic antics and framed it as an instance of psychological inferiority and moral degeneration: "Nowadays," he wrote in 1959, "rich business men can feed on the fame of the real hunters of the past century or politicians out for cheap publicity can buy a mantle of bravery and daring by going big game hunting. I believe that many of them suffer more often from impotence than is common among ordinary men. They have to compensate for their inferiority complexes by making themselves known as courageous lion killers."[95] Grzimek was certainly not the first to shame hunters in this way, but he was the first who reached a mass audience through several books, a regular series on German TV, and two wildlife documentaries that found international resonance in the 1950s, above all the Academy Award–winning *Serengeti Shall Not Die*.[96]

Such changing sensibilities in Western societies motivated the withdrawal of the WWF's royal luminaries from conspicuous hunting because of the "possible repercussions on the reputation of the WWF as a conservation organization" in the early 1960s.[97] Still, they did not automatically

---

[94] Manfred Behr and Hans Otto Meissner, *Keine Angst um wilde Tiere: Fünf Kontinente geben ihnen Heimat* (Munich et al.: BLV Verlagsgesellschaft, 1959); see also Walter Frevert and Henry Makowski, "Zu Großwildjagd in Afrika," *Wild und Hund* 62 (1959–60): 330–7. See Neumann, *Postwar Conservation Boom*, 25–7 for contemporary estimates that testify to "a great deal of species and geographic variability between and with colonial territories" rather than universal degradation.

[95] Bernhard Grzimek, *Serengeti Shall Not Die* (London: Hamish Hamilton, 1960), 234; see also id., "Zeitvertreib für schwache Männer: Löwenjagd," *Die Welt*, June 6, 1959. For East African elites reciprocating this view, see, e.g., the opening address of the Kenyan Minister of State Joseph Murumbi, in *Proceedings of the Eighth General Assembly of the IUCN, Nairobi, Kenya, September 1963* (Morges: IUCN, 1964), 37–8.

[96] For a broad contextualization of Grzimek's activism in late colonial and early independence Tanzania, see Thomas Lekan's *Saving the Serengeti: Tourism, the Cold War, and the Paradox of German Conservation in Postcolonial Africa, 1950-1985* (forthcoming with Oxford University Press)

[97] Schwarzenbach, *Saving the World's Wildlife*, 81.

translate into East African politics. Rather than the inevitable triumph of preservationism, the hunting bans in Kenya and Tanzania were a product of conjunctures and constellations that linked East Africa and the wider world.[98] Sentiments of postcolonial retaliation and a general thrust toward Africanizing the wildlife sector eased the decision to do away with the obstinate racism of white hunters and a practice rife with the symbolism of the imperialist past.[99] Concrete cases of corruption, abuse of the hunting system, and elite involvement in illegal ivory exports played an important role. Ultimately, however, it was the conjuncture of preservationist pressure, a booming industry of wildlife tourism, and the escalating problem of poaching that made trophy hunting morally unacceptable, politically untenable, and economically dispensable for the elites of the East African gatekeeper states.[100] The revenue derived from trophy hunting was infinitesimal compared to the foreign exchange brought into the country by the hundreds of thousands of wildlife lovers who flocked to East Africa's national parks on photo safaris. Economists figured that the very lion that earned $8,500 as a target for a sport hunter on a safari of three weeks could draw $515,000 in foreign exchange by being on view for safari tourists for a minimum of six or seven years.[101] Doubts about the destructive consequences of mass tourism for fragile ecosystems notwithstanding, the promising economics of nonconsumptive utilization of wildlife brought in line the interests of the conservation-related sciences, the whole wildlife tourism business, and those international environmental and animal welfare organizations, who lobbied African governmental elites for strict wildlife preservation. Pointing to the Convention on International Trade in Endangered Species agreement of 1973, they pressurized governments into curbing the trade in wildlife products, coming down on poaching, and saving the remnants of charismatic wildlife in national parks as their last refuge. Transnational nongovernmental organizations, like the WWF, the International Fund for Animal Welfare, or Bernhard Grzimek and his Frankfurt Zoological Society, combined the

[98] For discussions of the Kenyan ban, see Raymond Bonner, *At the Hand of Man: Peril and Hope for Africa's Wildlife* (New York: Knopf, 1993), 235–50; Steinhart, *Black Poachers*; Akama, *Controversies*; Kabiri, *Struggles*.

[99] For Tanzania, see Elizabeth Garland, "State of Nature: Colonial Power, Neoliberal Capital, and Wildlife Management in Tanzania" (PhD diss., University of Chicago, 2006).

[100] On the notion of the postcolonial gatekeeper state that derived its sovereignty above all from the control of outside resources and capital flows see Frederick Cooper, *Africa since the 1940s: The Past of the Present* (Cambridge: Cambridge University Press, 2002), ch. 7.

[101] Philip Thresher, "The Economics of a Lion," *Unasylva* 33, no. 134 (1981): 34–5.

stick of pressure and shaming with the carrot of substantial funds for antipoaching measures and the management of national parks. Above all, the bans appeared necessary to address the escalating problem of poaching, both practical and as a symbolical gesture of preservationist commitment. Poaching, an inevitable complement of exclusive game laws, achieved a new quality since the 1970s through park-related evictions and skyrocketing prices for ivory, rhino horns, and skins, mainly due to new forms of luxury consumption in Japan and Hong Kong.[102] This commerce-driven hunting did not only result in rapidly declining elephant and rhino populations – contemporary estimates assumed a drop from 167,000 elephants in Kenya in 1973 to 65,000 by the end of 1977[103] – but created a climate of anxiety in which the fortressing of parks and the extinction of markets for wildlife products appeared imperative. Not only was it hard to disentangle a market for legitimate trophies from illegitimate trade, but it became virtually impossible to communicate that the select shooting of individual specimen could contribute to the overall preservation of a threatened species. The opposition between the cruel and wasteful poacher and the restrained and sporting trophy hunter, for decades a core rationale to justify exclusion and privilege, collapsed under the discursive hegemony of preservationism between the 1960s and 1980s, giving way to the homogenizing assumption that any hunting ultimately entailed extinction. Safari hunting came under the verdict of sacrificing the universal heritage of African wildlife to the satisfaction of a morally depraved, wealthy minority.

CONCLUSION: FROM CONSPICUOUS TO CONSCIOUS CONSUMPTION?

Bringing luxury to bear on the analysis of East Africa's conservation history yields at least five insights. First, the conservationist regime that was established in East Africa after 1900 entailed not so much the withdrawal of wildlife from the unbridled extension of markets for wildlife, but the creation of new and controlled markets for their consumption

---

[102] See Chapter 9 in this volume and, for a survey, Thomas Princen, "The Ivory Trade Ban: NGOs and International Conservation," in *Environmental NGOs in World Politics: Linking the Local and the Global*, ed. Thomas Princen and Matthias Finger (London and New York: Routledge, 1994), 121–59.

[103] "Conservationists Win Important Victories in Battles to Save Wildlife," *The Times*, November 23, 1978, 13.

as a luxury.[104] The moral imperative of preventing Africa's charismatic fauna from extinction may have been a novel and powerful idealist motif behind the establishment of wildlife conservation regimes in Southern Africa. Yet, its putting into practice always operated through the starker realities of economics and the market. From the vantage point of economics, the aesthetic, moral, and ecological values of wildlife in preservationist discourse only added to its value as one of the colony's "best capital assets."[105] Thus, wildlife conservation was also born from and thrived upon the spirit of privilege and luxury. Second, the commodity status of game as a luxury to be exploited by hunting and wildlife tourism made it possible for colonial and postcolonial elites and decision makers to conceive of "development" as a process in which wildlife was a constitutive agent rather than an obstacle to be colonized away. Third, seen throughout the twentieth century, hunting and preservation were by no means successive or mutually exclusive forms of relating to wild animals, as the standard narrative suggests. Although often conflicting, they coexisted as spatially demarcated, alternative forms of utilizing the wildlife resource. Fourth, awareness to the commodity status of game draws attention to the fact that from the origins of organized safari tourism in the early 1900s, the commercial marketing of wildlife appropriated and redeployed core elements of the imperial hunting discourse. Indeed, tourism, alongside conservation, became the main agency for the perpetuation of images and imaginaries of African nature and wildlife that were essentially colonial in origin. And finally, the charisma of big game that animated various forms of luxury tourism in East Africa was an essentially Western construct. Although the elements of this charisma as well as the ethical obligations derived from it were subject to change during the twentieth century, it was marked by Western sensibilities that tended to efface other representations and ideas about the same animals. Luxury in one society is subject to completely different regimes of value in another: one man's charismatic object of a lifetime safari is another man's crop-raiding pest. There is a tension between the values of international tourism and conservation, on the one hand, and the values of everyday coexistence, on the other, that is not easily reconciled.[106]

---

[104] The market relationship behind game conservation is emphasized in particular by Lance van Sittert, "Bringing in the Wild: The Commodification of Wild Animals in the Cape Colony/Province c. 1850–1950," *Journal of African History* 46 (2005): 269–91.

[105] *The Official Gazette of the Colony and Protectorate of Kenya*, January 30, 1951, 200.

[106] See also Annu Jalais, "Unmasking the Cosmopolitan Tiger," *Nature and Culture* 3, no. 1 (2008): 25–40.

This said, the hunting bans of the 1970s were as much a decisive water-shed in the history of trophy hunting as they marked new beginnings. "Safari" retained a close association with Kenya, but now came to denote peaceful game viewing as the new, conscious form of luxury consumption in the mushrooming lodges in and around national parks. Safari operators jumped on the opportunity of photo safaris; others exported their experience, capital, and a number of satisfied hunting clients to other Southern African states that were less accessible and spectacular for game viewing, but functioned as sanctuaries for the threatened species of the big-game hunter. With East Africa closed, Botswana, for example, gained popularity, while West German big-game hunters flocked to the German-run hunting farms in the former colony of Namibia in greater numbers than before.[107]

The fact that hunting safaris were banned in their original country created the misleading impression that preservation was the end of wildlife history and that trophy hunting had become a thing of an imperial past. The loss of moral acceptability in Western societies meant that the public display of the hunter elicited outrage rather than admiration. Because it accrued only negative social capital, trophy hunters withdrew into invisibility and the private satisfaction derived from trophies. Its comparative inconspicuousness for about a decade made it easier to dissociate trophy hunting from its imperialist implications and reinvent it as a form of conscious consumption of wildlife under the discursive regime of sustainable development. The return of trophy hunting in contemporary conservationist discourse shows that it did by no means vanish as a luxury practice. Rather it has been transformed and is now traded in a different discursive package.

Have we really witnessed a transformation of conspicuous consumption into conscious consumption, as the hunting lobby and parts of the academic literature on conservation, ecotourism, and wildlife management suggest? Recent research into the motives of international trophy hunters visiting South Africa casts some doubt that trophy hunting as a pro-poor activity is anything more than discursive window dressing. A questionnaire returned by six hundred trophy hunters who had visited the Eastern Cape between 1999 and 2003 reveals the spiritual being in nature, the thrilling experience of the chase, the collection of trophies,

---

[107] On the popularity of Namibia as a hunting destination among Germans from the Federal Republic see Rolf Hennig, "Die Entwicklung der Wild- und Jagdwirtschaft in Südwestafrika/Namibia," *Zeitschrift für Jagdwissenschaft* 33 (1987): 248–67.

and the challenge to the self as the main motivations for hunting. Only a tiny fraction of hunters was actuated by motives of conservation, and one searches in vain for pro-poor development among an otherwise extensive list of motivations.[108] Also a quick google of "safari hunting" or a flick through a current issue of any special-interest hunting magazine, like the German *Jagen weltweit*, reveals that the new discourse of pro-poor hunting has hardly made inroads into the marketing of trophy hunting: magazines and websites still relish in the heroism of imperial big-game hunters and outfitters exploit the century-old discourse of masculinity, privilege, wilderness, primeval backwardness, and unique adventure, all paired with the guaranteed customer satisfaction of quality trophies and a once-in-a-lifetime experience.[109] It may be the case that trophy hunting yields tangible benefits for community development, enables capital flows that would not exist otherwise, and constitutes the ecologically most reasonable form of utilizing and thereby conserving wildlife populations in regions where they would otherwise vanish. But encouraging "communities" to preserve their wildlife for the consumption of outside hunters represents only the latest attempt of attaching capitalist value to Africa's wildlife, while encouraging the trophy hunter includes the mobilization of imaginaries that are essentially colonial in origin. Apart from the awkward constellation of performing affluence in an environment of often abject poverty, it is these continuities that make trophy hunting such a contested and questionable form of sustainable development.

[108] Laetitia Radder, "Motives of International Trophy Hunters," *Annals of Tourism Research* 32, no. 4 (2005): 1141–4.

[109] See, e.g., the adverts in issue 6/2010 of *Jagen weltweit*, which includes extensive passages and pictures from James Sutherland's "The Adventures of an Elephant Hunter," released in 1912 (pp. 76–83).

Luxury as a global phenomenon:
Concluding remarks

Bernd-Stefan Grewe and Karin Hofmeester

We started this book by stating that luxury is a global phenomenon and that we wanted to demonstrate how a global history approach can give a deeper insight in luxury than the European or Northern Atlantic perspective. One of the questions this volume tried to answer is whether the concept of luxury could be used as a global analytical tool, and, if so, how a global approach to luxury commodities could be developed. These concluding remarks should summarize what the final benefits of this approach are – both for global history and the study of luxury. Until now, there has been very little historiography on this issue. Of course, historians have studied many aspects of luxury in Europe, and there is a wide range of literature on luxury commodities since Mesopotamian times and on the debates about luxury and consumption. For other areas, the historiography on luxury is of much more recent origin because, especially in former colonies, other historical questions were of more importance when the discipline released its imperial ties and reorganized itself during and after decolonization. Albeit there is some excellent research on global commodities such as sugar, coffee, tea, tobacco, or cocoa, few historians have tried to study luxury in a global perspective or to make comparisons between luxuries in different cultures. Our approach here is not comparative although the studies offer some interesting parallels. In our understanding, global history is primarily the history of connections between different areas of the world. Still, most historical research on luxury is designed in a local or national framework and rarely follows the traces of the objects across national borders.

The studies on luxury presented in this collection are different. They cover and link many of the areas of the early modern and modern world from Qing China and Mughal India to Venice and the Northern Atlantic, from eighteenth-century Japan through East Africa to Germany, Britain, and the United States, and finally from Java through the Netherlands to Ghana and from modern India to Kenya and Tanzania. Choosing these areas and periods, we were well aware that other regions would not appear in our collection.[1] Much more research is necessary to write a history of luxury in Central Asia, Northern Africa, and the Near and Middle East (which, of course, is another Eurocentric geographical naming of regions). Global history has offered many insights, especially into the economic links between different areas, and several major debates about the rise of the West, world systems, or the dependency of the Global South have taken place in the last decades. As valuable as these debates were, when the asymmetry of global political and economic connections is substantiated, the assumed asymmetry of these power relations will be part of the research design. We wanted to avoid this, expecting that our research could help to change the perspective on the so-called peripheries. Therefore, we brought together those luxury researchers who studied the agency of people in the Global South and who asked for the people's patterns of consumption and production looking for luxury practices in regions such as Africa, China, Japan, and India that are rarely studied as a consuming part of global economy.[2]

If we want to use the concept of luxury as a global analytical tool, the first question to answer is how do we conceptualize luxury not only in a European, but also in a global perspective? In some chapters, for example the one on the circulation of jewelry in the Mughal Empire, the question arose regarding whether we can classify a social practice to be a luxury if the people who practice it do not even have a word to designate it as luxury. This was a question we discussed intensively. The outcome was to make a difference between the two different levels of language we

---

[1] As the articles in Topik et al.'s *From Silver to Cocaine* cover various global commodities produced in Latin America, we decided to focus on other regions and their linkages. Steven Topik, Carlos Marichal, and Zephyr Frank, eds., *From Silver to Cocaine: Latin American Commodity Chains and the Building of the World Economy, 1500–2000* (Durham, NC: Duke University Press, 2006).

[2] The recent *Oxford Handbook of the History of Consumption*, ed. Frank Trentmann (Oxford: Oxford University Press, 2012) with articles by Craig Clunas on China and Jeremy Prestholdt on Africa is a welcome exception to the rule. Also *Towards a History of Consumption in South Asia*, ed. Douglas Haynes, Abigail McGowan, Tirthankar Roy, and Haruka Yanagisawa (Delhi: Oxford University Press, 2010) is useful though focusing very much on the late nineteenth and twentieth centuries.

use. The first level is the language of the sources, the second of the analysis. The sources give us much information about the specific regime of value that needs to be understood. If a language does not have a word for luxury this does not necessarily mean that the corresponding society does not know luxury, but simply that its members did not label it as such, often because they framed it a different way. But social status that is marked by the exclusive use of materials or an exclusive social practice is something universal as it could be observed in all societies studied in this volume (whether they had a word for class distinction or not). Even if we used a term coined in Europe, in order to prevent us from a projection of Eurocentric assumptions on contexts that are quite different, we tried to define our understanding of luxury in a more open form and be aware of a possible narrowness of the concept. This is the second level of using the term *luxury*. *Luxury* is used as an analytical term that first had to be defined in a way that is not limited to European thinking, but that is open enough to encompass similar attitudes in other cultures.

In *The Social Life of Things*, edited by Arjun Appadurai, the consumption of a number of commodities in prehistoric and medieval Europe, modern-day Madhya Pradesh (India), and Northeast Africa are analyzed. In his introduction Appadurai defines luxuries as those goods "whose principal use is rhetorical and social," their symbolic value being more important than their intrinsic value.[3] His characteristics of a luxury good largely resemble the six features we summed up in the introduction to this volume to give a preliminary definition of *luxury*: they are not mass goods; are exclusive, which often but not always means that they are expensive or exotic; move beyond the realm of everyday practicality; and should have special material qualities such as durability or extreme fragility – and are often made with extraordinary craftsmanship. They should be aesthetically pleasing, and last but certainly not least, they should be symbols of social status. These six features proved to be valid in many different areas and through quite distinctive social and cultural settings.

All luxury objects and practices (such as big-game hunting) studied in this collection have been rare and exclusive so they could be used to mark social status by practices of distinction, such as the "Real Dutch Wax" print textiles in Ghana or the gold necklaces given to brides in

---

[3] Arjun Appadurai, ed., *The Social Life of Things: Commodities in Cultural Perspective* (Cambridge: Cambridge University Press, 2008), 38.

modern India. Most of them were expensive according to the local money
system, such as glass beads in East Africa or Blue China in Britain, and
they were exclusive, as they were exotic. Like most of the other luxury
objects, golden jewelry and diamonds were not made for practical purposes although they could become economically very important to their
owners. The ivory keyboard of pianos and objects made of tortoiseshell
became luxuries also because of their material qualities and aesthetic
pleasing, especially their sense of touch – the tortoiseshell dildo being the
quintessential example of this feature.

The spectrum of luxury objects presented in the articles comprises
objects of different material consistence and origin: some luxury objects
are considered to be precious because of their indestructibility, such as
diamonds or gold, which has to be mined and refined; others were of animal origin such as hunting trophies, tortoiseshell, or ivory; a third group
was made with highly specialized technical skills that in this period could
not be imitated by others, such as Chinese porcelain, glass beads from
Venice, cotton textiles from India, and Real Dutch Wax prints in Ghana.
A final feature we discerned was the symbol of social status. Many examples of this can be found in this volume. Jewelry ownership was a basic
aspect of the Indian–Islamic concept of rule: by the ownership but also by
the traditions of gift giving, the Mughal emperor displayed his power and
marked the status of his subjects. The possession of certain types of glass
beads expressed royal power in Africa; women with gold jewelry in India
or a dress made from a Real Dutch Wax print in Ghana could show their
social status. One of the side effects of this social status characteristic can
be found in the imitations that were made of luxury commodities. We
have met a whole range of "fakes": diamonds made by Strass, imitation
gold jewelry in India, European imitation chintz, Chinese instead of Real
Dutch Wax prints, bone instead of real tortoiseshell, and Chinese porcelain made in Delft.

With these six features of luxury being represented in various parts of
the world in different moments in time, we felt safe in using our concept
of luxury as a global analytical tool. All classes and social strata consumed luxury or knew of exclusive luxury practices, but they all did so in
different ways, thus distinguishing themselves from other social groups
and ensuring their social cohesion. The different studies in this volume
thus make it possible to compare the different varieties in which luxury
was used and practiced. Turning to another important aspect, we should
now address the approach we chose in order to give those regional histories a global perspective: to write the global histories of luxuries.

Most articles in this volume focus on the circulation of luxury commodities and use (either implicitly or explicitly) the global commodity chain approach to follow their itineraries from their origin to the consumer and to reconstruct the linkages and interconnectivity between societies around the world. For example, following the various trajectories of the diamond from mine to ring finger shows a relatively simple linkage from the "hunger" for diamonds developed by the Europeans when they encountered them first in and around the mines and the courts in India, to the discovery of rough diamonds in the Portuguese colony of Brazil and the subsequent large-scale "importation" of slaves from Africa to work the mines in Brazil. Another straightforward connection can be found between the global demand for Chinese porcelain and the tremendous production increase in Jingdezhen. More multidimensional were the connections between the Indian printed cotton fabrics whose manufacturing was shifted to Europe (mainly to Britain), reshaped there, and subsequently exported to Africa. The industrial growth in Britain, partially a consequence of this globalization of cotton, led to a partial deindustrialization of the Indian cotton industry at the same time. Another example of a global commodity connecting at least three continents are the Real Dutch Wax prints, based on techniques and designs from Java (Indonesia) and reshaped by the Dutch, who relocated the production to Helmond and subsequently exported the products to various African countries.

As the global commodity chain approach helps us to see the connections between the different segments in the chain, the "social biography" approach shows us how people in different societies, or even within one society in different social contexts, attributed different meanings to the same objects. Take, for instance, the changing function of glass beads, which in the eyes of a visitor at the manufacture in Venice represented useless and mediocre items, but which in the East African hinterland became a luxury and were used as a substitute for money. An even wider variety of meanings can be found if we look at the meaning of the elephant. The native population in Africa for ages disregarded the tusk and hunted the elephant for its meat as well as for it symbolic value as a trophy, proving the courage of the hunter who protected his people and harvest by killing the big animal. In this context the tail was considered a much better trophy than the tusk. The Europeans with their hunger for ivory changed this meaning, leading to large-scale elephant hunting and a voluminous ivory trade, making the tusk the most precious part of the elephant. Typical nineteenth-century European bourgeois luxury commodities such as pianos and billiards were not complete without ivory keys or balls. Again later, the shooting of the elephant, either with a gun or a camera, became the quintessential luxury pastime for men with a nostalgic longing for colonialism and seemingly uncomplicated "country life" in the wilderness. When the killing part of the safari became too unethical for a number of Europeans, the elephant changed meaning again: now becoming a sweet creature in cartoons and films such as *Babar* and *Dumbo*.

The meaning people attributed to luxury commodities changed not only from one cultural context to another, but also from one situation to another. As the articles in this volume show, not only could glass beads and gold shift from luxury to currency, this could also apply to diamonds and tortoiseshell, all depending on the situation. In his *Social Life of Things*, Appadurai introduced the term "luxury register" to refer to the consumption of specific commodities that could turn into luxuries in certain contexts.[4] Maybe, this luxury register concept can also be used the other way around: in certain contexts, luxury commodities could turn into objects only valuated for their intrinsic worth though they still had all the "signs" of a luxury commodity.

Gender seems to be very important in defining the meaning of a luxury object. The gold given to a woman during an Indian wedding was meant to show her marital status for the rest of her life, whereas the gold given to a man could be traded for currency the day after the wedding. Not only gold in India could stress the marital status of a woman, a specific type of dress made from Real Dutch Wax with a particular print did so too. The gendered consumption of golden jewelry in India but also of tortoiseshell hair ornaments in Japan is closely linked to women's property and inheriting rights. For South Indian women, until very recently the personal gifts (money, clothing, and jewelry) directly given to them by their relatives were the only personal possessions a woman was supposed to own. For seventeenth-century Japanese, the ownership of personal luxury goods was one of the few ways women could legally hold property. For men, jewelry possession had less meaning as privately kept capital, and much more with publicly displayed power. As mentioned previously, jewelry ownership played a vital role in the Indian–Islamic male concept of rule: by displaying big-seize diamonds, pearls, emeralds, and rubies the rulers displayed their powerful position. For the less powerful, effeminate nineteenth- and twentieth-century European and North American city dwellers, going on a safari could mean a transformation – albeit

---

4 Ibid., 38–41.

temporarily – into real men. Here, the possession of hunting trophies not only symbolized the wealth of the globe-trotters, but also their power. This shows how gender and class could be linked up, as was also the case for the women wearing Real Dutch Wax: this cloth was meant for established, married women, not for young unmarried girls. Likewise, Venetian glass beads in various African countries could express the distinguished position of a woman.

Class and social status are crucial to understanding the significance of objects and practices in different societies. Practicing luxury or exposing luxury objects was a social code that could be understood by everyone and social distinction was marked through this. However, luxury was not only motivated by the desire of distinction, but it was also important for the social cohesion of a group, for example, if luxury commodities were used in ceremonies like the cotton textiles in South East Asia or if pieces of jewelry were given during the weighing ceremony in Mughal India. During ceremonies the group could even be enlarged – this is what Giorgio Riello (Chapter 5) calls the vertical ties in the social functioning of luxury: the gold donated in India to the temple was meant to serve the community, a larger group than just the caste one belonged to, and in Ghana women have to go to a funeral in real cloth of dark colors, not doing so would ruin the ceremony and upset the community. The horizontal class cohesion became manifest and visible when its members showed similar practices that followed unwritten rules of taste. Those who were not able to observe this convention showed that they were outsiders. A Japanese maid was not supposed to wear a tortoiseshell hair comb as this was considered to be too luxurious for her, thus showing her inclination to tempt men with sex in order to support her taste for luxury. This has been revealed in many other studies on luxury. But the global perspective on luxury stresses another aspect of class: the global biography of luxuries shows how the consumption of luxury mainly by wealthy or powerful people in one area of the world was linked to its production in another, and different classes from various regions were linked through economic ties (e.g., from English-style brilliants polished in present-day Surat to English cotton fabrics, which were inspired by Indian originals exported on a large scale to Africa and other continents, to the glass beads produced by women in Venetian workshops to be sold in Africa in return for slaves and ivory, which found their way in various other commodity chains).

The fact that various links included slaves means that the global perspective on luxury commodities can also give us new insights in global labor history. American cotton production, which boomed after the globalization of cotton fabrics; the digging for diamonds in Brazil; and the Venetian glass bead production and trade had a strong relation with the increase of the number of slaves being sold, though the exact connection in the latter case has yet to be established. For some luxury practices such as the safari, the connection between the various classes did not span long distances: in Tanzania and Kenya rich white men from Europe and the United States used and took over the land that was needed by the black native population for their subsistence farming. This shows how global connections could have their effects locally, and at the same time it shows that, next to gender and class, ethnicity also plays an important role in how luxury was perceived.

The analysis of global luxury commodities also teaches us how important patronage was for the production and therefore also the working lives of the most talented artisans working in the imperial porcelain workshops in China or the royal diamond polishing workshops in Mughal India. Strict divisions of labor and the prohibition to work for other employers were part and parcel of this patronage. This made the royal artisans almost a class in itself; in Mughal India the artisan class was even supplemented by a large class of treasurers and accountants who kept the administration of all luxury items in order. For the glass bead producers in Venice, being part of a special group of artisans with specific knowledge and skills meant that they were not allowed to leave the town and share their knowledge. In producing for a global market the distinction between various qualities of one commodity was vital as the chapters on Chinese porcelain, Indian cotton, and Venetian beads have shown. Local skills were needed but they had to be combined with knowledge on global consumption, including various tastes and attributions of meaning.

What are the benefits of global biographies of luxuries for global history? The study of the global itineraries of luxuries has some significance beyond the history of these special commodities and of the social practices linked to them. First, studying luxury in a global perspective combines economic connections with the social and cultural contexts in which they are produced, transported, manufactured, traded, and consumed. Thus the relevance of cultural factors for the functioning of global trade becomes evident not only in a period in which luxury trade was synonymous with global trade, a period that Bayly named "archaic globalization." We claim that even in modern times, the relevance of culture for the functioning of global interconnections should not be underestimated.

Second, the studies in this volume show that both approaches – the biography of objects and the global commodity chain approach – offer a decentered view on global economic relations. The initial decision of choosing those luxuries that are not consumed and practiced in the Northern Atlantic sphere help us to see quite clearly to what extent the definitions used by historians derive from a Eurocentric or North Atlantic–centric point of view. Various cultures in the world classify other objects and practices to be more luxurious than the "West." At the same time, the analysis of production, consumption, and valuation of luxury goods in countries of the Global South seriously questions the periphery label so often applied to these parts of the world.

Third, the contributions of this collection combine micro- and macroperspectives. The biographic approach on objects can integrate the valuation of objects, thinking, representations, and action of individuals while placing them into their local sociocultural context as well as showing their global connectiveness. Thus the connection between the local and the global sphere of historic processes can be described without narrowing the complexity of the situation. The global life of things offers fascinating narratives to better understand how and why global connections functioned across cultural and political borders.

Finally, what is the benefit of the global perspective when we look at luxury commodities and practices? First of all, there is the awareness of the global linkages and connections mentioned previously, which could be very important for the development of the global economy if we only think of all the luxury commodities produced in one part of the world that were consumed in another.

The notion of luxury items having different meanings in various social contexts has been much overlooked in historiography and raises the question regarding whether the often-used method of discourse analysis in cultural history is an adequate method to study the history of luxury. All chapters in this volume show that the social practices that were linked to the commodities and objects showed a much wider scope of varieties even within a social group or a cultural context than we had expected. This new insight could be of high relevance for the study of luxury in European context. Conceptions and practices of luxury differed a great deal through time and space, but the phenomenon was global.

The focus on the biographies of objects, following their circulation through different social contexts, makes it possible to add something new and very important to the concept of luxury. Almost all studies on luxury use a concept that is based on the material or social qualities of such objects and some studies that are more based on reflections about the categories they use even analyze the social practices linked to luxury. But very few historians discuss the temporal dimension of luxury. By using definitions of *luxury* deriving from sociology, economics, or cultural anthropology, the temporality of luxuries and of its practices are often ignored. What is to be learned from the studies in this volume is that the same object that usually is classified to be a luxury can be considered profane and lacking all attributes to make it a marker of high social status in some situations. Thus our collection can add a new dimension to the concept of luxury that is of utmost importance: the historicity of luxury. To differentiate between various historical and social situations and to put not only texts but also objects and practices into their specific context is the strength of historical science.

Index